Patent Inventions—Intellectual Property
and the Victorian Novel

Frontispiece. Illustration for Charles Dickens's 'A Poor Man's Tale of a Patent' by Fred Walker (1858). Reprinted from Charles Dickens, *Reprinted Pieces: The Lamplighter, To Be Read at Dusk, Sunday Under Three Heads* (Centennial Edition of the Complete Works, Heron Books 1969), 114. (By permission of the Syndics of Cambridge University Library.)

Patent Inventions—
Intellectual Property
and the
Victorian Novel

CLARE PETTITT

OXFORD
UNIVERSITY PRESS

OXFORD
UNIVERSITY PRESS

Great Clarendon Street, Oxford OX2 6DP

Oxford University Press is a department of the University of Oxford.
It furthers the University's objective of excellence in research, scholarship,
and education by publishing worldwide in

Oxford New York

Auckland Bangkok Buenos Aires Cape Town Chennai
Dar es Salaam Delhi Hong Kong Istanbul Karachi Kolkata
Kuala Lumpur Madrid Melbourne Mexico City Mumbai Nairobi
São Paulo Shanghai Taipei Tokyo Toronto

Oxford is a registered trade mark of Oxford University Press
in the UK and in certain other countries

Published in the United States
by Oxford University Press Inc., New York

British Library Cataloguing in Publication Data
Data available

Library of Congress Cataloging in Publication Data
Data available

ISBN 0–19–925320–X

1 3 5 7 9 10 8 6 4 2

Typeset by SNP Best-set Typesetter Ltd., Hong Kong
Printed in Great Britain
on acid-free paper by
Biddles Ltd.,
King's Lynn, Norfolk

In Memoriam

JANE PETTITT

1939–1986

Preface and Acknowledgements

It is impossible to think about intellectual property for as long as this book has taken to write, and not to become acutely aware of one's own roster of intellectual debts, while also realizing the impossibility of enumerating each one. But there are some people whose help has been so extraordinarily generous that I would like to record my special thanks to them. Kate Flint was the inspirational supervisor of my Oxford D.Phil. thesis who uncomplainingly read numerous subsequent drafts as it transmuted into this book, and whose continued friendship, now beamed from the other side of the Atlantic, has been a constant source of support. Joe Childers, David Inwald, and Vivien Jones were all early and excellent readers of the first chapters. Martin Daunton brought his historical expertise to bear on Chs. 2 and 3, and Helen Small and Francis O'Gorman both read the whole book in manuscript and made numerous invaluable and well-judged comments that reflected both their generosity as scholars and their own compendious knowledge of the period. Other friends and colleagues provided ideas and encouragement—notable among them were (in alphabetical order): Isobel Armstrong, Mary Beard, Gillian Beer, Lucy Bending, Becky Conekin, Kirsten Denker, Charles Feinstein, Stephen Gill, Heather Glen, Susan Manning, Adrian Poole, Louise Purbrick, Leigh Shaw-Taylor, Sally Shuttleworth, Jacqueline Tasioulas, and Barry Windeatt. The readers appointed by Oxford University Press also offered immensely valuable comments, and I hope that I have taken most of them on board. I am also grateful to everyone who participated in the Dickens Universe and Conference on 'Exhibitions' at the University of California at Santa Cruz in the summer of 2001: their enthusiasm provided just the fillip I needed to finish the book.

I would like wholeheartedly to thank the staff of the libraries I have used in researching this project. Latterly, the University Library, Cambridge has been my most frequent haunt and I want to record my particular gratitude to the staff of the Rare Books Room there for their friendliness and efficiency. Similarly at Newnham College Library and the English Faculty Library, Cambridge University, I have encountered only helpfulness. I was greeted with courtesy when I consulted George Eliot's books at Dr Williams' Library in Bloomsbury, and also when I used the Brotherton Library, Leeds, the Bodleian Library, Oxford, the British Library, and the Witt Picture Library, London. Money has come from the AHRB, which awarded me the luxury of a term's paid research leave in the autumn of 2001, and the British Academy, which made me a grant from its Overseas Conference Fund to help me give a paper at the Santa Cruz conference. This book started its gestation at Linacre College, Oxford, and after that continued its slow development at Pembroke College, Oxford, and Leeds University. My current academic home, Newnham College, Cambridge, has been extremely generous in providing research grants to cover conference expenses and two terms of leave from teaching. I would like also to thank the fellowship and students of Newnham, and the individuals that make up the Faculty of English in Cambridge, for many helpful and galvanizing conversations that made the writing of the book a less lonely and painful process than it would otherwise have been.

My editors at OUP, Sophie Goldsworthy, Frances Whistler, Elizabeth Prochaska, and Sylvie Jaffrey have been unfailingly helpful. The finishing of this book coincided with the birth of my second daughter, and Sophie and her team were wonderfully understanding and patient throughout.

My family, in the UK and Italy, has helped in less academic ways which often seemed even more vital. My sister is the reason I wanted a second child: I cannot imagine my life without her constant and reassuring presence. My father, Charles Pettitt, has helped me immensely by indexing the book, despite its being far from his own field of zoology, and the Ristuccias in Italy have been unfailingly generous in their support of both my career and my marriage since they first welcomed me into their family in 1994.

To thank Cristiano Ristuccia for his help with this book would seem woefully inadequate. I would first need to thank him for everything else: for our daughters, Kitty and Marina, for our life together, and for his refusal to let me ever give up trying. This book has been immensely important to me, but not—thankfully—as important as the 'everything else'.

Some of the discussion of images of Shakespeare in Ch. 3 has already appeared in 'Shakespeare at the Great Exhibition of 1851', in G. Marshall and A. Poole (eds.), *Victorian Shakespeare* (London:

Palgrave, 2003), ii. The section of Ch. 5 in which I discuss Elizabeth Gaskell's novella, *Cousin Phillis*, appeared, in a slightly different shape, in *Nineteenth-Century Literature*.

Naturally, all the errors and inaccuracies in the text are mine.

In Books lies the *soul* of the whole Past Time; the articulate audible voice of the Past, when the body and material substance of it has altogether vanished like a dream.

Thomas Carlyle

Contents

List of Figures

Abbreviations

CB   Charlotte Brontë

CD   Charles Dickens

ECG   Elizabeth Gaskell

FLG   *Further Letters of Mrs Gaskell*, ed. John Chapple and Alan Shelston (Manchester and New York: Manchester University Press, 2000)

GE   George Eliot

GEL   *The George Eliot Letters*, ed. G. S. Haight, 9 vols. (London: Oxford University Press; New Haven, Conn.: Yale University Press, 1954–78)

LCD i   *The Letters of Charles Dickens 1820–1839*, i, ed. Madeline House and Graham Storey (Oxford: Clarendon Press, 1965)

LCD vi *The Letters of Charles Dickens 1850–1852*, vi, ed. Graham Storey, Kathleen Tillotson, and Nina Burgis (Oxford: Clarendon Press, 1988)

LG   *The Letters of Mrs Gaskell*, ed. J. A. V. Chapple and Arthur Pollard (Manchester and New York: Manchester University Press, 1996)

LWMT *The Letters and Private Papers of William Makepeace Thackeray*, ed. Gordon N. Ray, 4 vols. (London: Oxford University Press, 1945–6)

TH   Thomas Hardy

WMT   William Makepeace Thackeray

Introductory
Heroes and Hero-Worship:
Inventors and Writers from
1818 to 1900

BUT UNFORTUNATELY BY SOME MEANS OR OTHER THE 'INGENIOUS AND MODEST INVENTOR' AS HE WAS STYLED BY DR. BIRKBECK, NEVER RECEIVED THE SLIGHTEST REMUNERATION. *SOME MEN LABOUR AND OTHER MEN ENTER INTO THEIR LABOURS*

THE inscription on the tombstone of John Swan, Engineer (1787–1869), at Abney Park Cemetery in Dalston, North East London, reminds us that in the nineteenth century, as now, intellectual property was a curious and slippery kind of property. Swan was the inventor of the 'screw propeller' and the 'self-acting chain messenger' and both inventions were taken up by the Royal Navy, but he received no payment for his ingenuity. Intellectual property was difficult to lay claim to, or to 'own', and sustaining any kind of proprietorial or remunerative relationship with one's ideas and inventions often proved problematic.

The nineteenth century represents a critical period in the history of the debate about mental labour. How far do men and women 'enter into' their labours? How far should that trace of their identity or corporeality be rewarded financially? And how long before that trace fades away and allows the invention—be it literary or mechanical—to revert to the possession of the general culture? Some took the extreme position that 'invention' only ever represented the rediscovery of something already extant. Ralph Waldo Emerson, for example, declared in his 1844 essay, 'The Poet', that 'poetry was all written before time was, and whenever we are so finely organized that we can penetrate into that region where the air is music, we hear those

primal warblings'.[1] Others, such as William Wordsworth and
Charles Dickens, went to considerable and well-documented efforts
to extend protection to intellectual property. In Parliament, intellectual property legislation was exhaustively debated and redrafted
from the 1820s onwards in an attempt to accommodate the fast pace
of technological change. Surprisingly, the mental labour of mechanical inventors such as John Swan, and of literary writers such as
Charles Dickens, was constructed and discussed in very similar terms
throughout the first half of the nineteenth century. Indeed, Dickens
himself, and many of his contemporaries, did not see—or chose not
to see—a sharp divide between the categories of literary and mechanical invention. The debate was ultimately less about the finer
points of copyright or patent law, than about how labour, and in
particular mental labour, was to be conceptualized in an emergent
democracy. And as a corollary to the questions about intellectual
property, was another question even more dizzying—what constituted an 'individual' in a democracy, and how might s/he be
identified?

This book takes the current critical discussion of copyright law
and the construction of the artist in the Victorian period out of its
literary-critical isolation and restores it to the wider debate in the
period about labour and value. This allows for a more complex and
resonant reading of Victorian novels in the context of intellectual
ownership than has been possible before. It helps us to discern the
political and social importance of the recasting of the artist as hero
from the Romantic period onwards, and to contextualize the artist-
hero in a wider political debate. The formation of a literary canon
and the promulgation of an idea of literature as an elevated and 'special' form of writing did not happen in a vacuum, as so much of the
recent criticism treating of the history of copyright law implies, but,
in fact, took place as part of a much wider reconceptualization of
labour, and particularly of mental labour. In this context, the culture
of 'posterity', which Andrew Bennett has recently ascribed to the
Romantic poets, was as much a part of a political attempt to
professionalize literary writing and other forms of intellectual
labour, as it was a 'poetic' or aesthetic projection.[2] Practitioners were

---

[1] Ralph Waldo Emerson, 'The Poet' (1844) in *Selected Essays* (1985), 259–84,
262–3.
[2] Andrew Bennett, *Romantic Poets and the Culture of Posterity* (1999).

pressing for increased representation and property rights in the law. Putting the argument for perpetual copyright to Thomas Noon Talfourd for example, William Wordsworth complains of:

> the statute law as it now stands, which is a composition or compromise between two opinions; the extreme point of one being, that, by giving his thoughts to the world, an author abandons all right to consider the vehicle as private property; and of the other, that he has the right in perpetuity, that descends to his heirs, and is transferable to those to whom he or they may assign it.[3]

Wordsworth himself passionately supported the latter 'extreme point', explaining elsewhere that 'I have gained much more from my long-published writings within the last five or six years than in the thirty preceding.' Copyright protection, he argued, should cover those works, such as his own, that do not immediately find their audience.[4] As Strathern has put it, 'Potential becomes an asset.'[5] For writers and inventors in the early nineteenth century, it was crucial that the law held out a promise of future value for their inventions, as only such an investment in futurity could mark them out as different from 'common labourers' who sold their work on a daily basis. ' "All my estate real and personal, consists in the hopes of the sale of books publish'd or unpublish'd," ' wrote Keats, describing quite literally his property in his own potential 'hopes' as a writer.[6] As early as 1825, an article in the *Mechanics' Magazine* entitled 'Encouragement of Inventions' lamented that such hopes on the part of inventors were often blighted, '[i]nstead of genius being cherished and rewarded as it deserves, it is matter of notoriety [*sic*] that it but rarely reaps the harvest of its own sowing.'[7] Considered together, the debates over intellectual property rights in the nineteenth century form an important commentary on the movement towards a modern

[3] William Wordsworth to Serjeant Talfourd, MP [18 April 1838] Letter 1255. Ernest de Selincourt (ed.), *The Letters of William and Dorothy Wordsworth: The Later Years*, ii. *1831–40* (1939), 924–6, 925.

[4] Wordsworth to Sir Robert Peel [3 May 1838] Letter 1260, 934–6, *Letters*, ii. 936. He adds that 'nor till very lately were the works of Shakespeare himself justly appreciated even within his own country' (936).

[5] Marilyn Strathern, *Property, Substance and Effect: Anthropological Essays on Persons and Things* (1999), 162.

[6] John Keats to John Taylor, 14 August 1820, Letter 282, *The Letters of John Keats 1814–1821*, ed. Hyder Edward Rollins, ii. *1819–1821* (1958), 318–19, 319.

[7] Anon., 'Encouragement of Inventions', *Mechanics' Magazine* (18 June 1825), 171–3, 172.

democracy, with its increasing emphasis on contractual models of citizenship, and thus on futurity and future value. Copyrights and patents allowed writers and inventors to gamble on future returns for their work. Intellectual property was thus a peculiarly modern form of 'stake-holding property'; its significance becoming more and more widespread with the application of new technologies such as the telegraph, which, as James Carey has argued, 'shift[ed] specula-tion from space to time, from arbitrage to futures'.[8] In fighting for intellectual property, both poets and inventors were fighting for the ownership of their own 'professional' future.

In a letter to William Wordsworth in 1838 in reply to the poet's re-quest for support for the new copyright bill, Sir Robert Peel asked, ' "If the right to such extended [copyright] protection be admitted, can we refuse it in the case of Patents? and of every discovery mainly owing to the ingenuity or skill of the discoverers." ' Peel's ready identification of patent and copyright protection suggests the rising currency in the 1830s of the analogy upon which this book turns.[9] Percy Shelley had drawn a parallel between poets and inventors in his 'Defence of Poetry', posthumously published in 1840, in which he declared that 'All the authors of revolutions in opinion are . . . necessarily poets as they are inventors.'[10] And Thomas Carlyle spoke of poets and inventors in the same breath in his 1840 lecture on 'The Hero as a Man of Letters', 'An inventor was needed to do that, *a poet*; he has articulated the dim struggling that dwelt in his own and many hearts.'[11] Throughout Carlyle's lecture, and, indeed, through-out the nineteenth century, rhetoric shuttles between technology and art in ways that show how much they had come to affect each other. Writing, claims Carlyle, is one of the 'things which man can do or make', alongside others, right down to the very bricks of London,

---

[8] James W. Carey, 'Technology and Ideology: The Case of the Telegraph', in *Communication as Culture: Essays on Media and Society* (1989), 217–18.

[9] William Wordsworth quoting Sir Robert Peel to Thomas Noon Talfourd [3 May 1838] Letter 1259, *Letters*, ii. 932–4, 933.

[10] P. B. Shelley, 'A Defence of Poetry', in *The Complete Works of Percy Bysshe Shelley*, ed. Roger Ingpen and Walter E. Peck (1930), vii. 109–40, 115. Shelley is discussing the work of Bacon here. The analogy of the poet and the inventor appears several times in Shelley's essay.

[11] Thomas Carlyle, 'The Hero as a Man-of-Letters. Johnson, Rousseau, Burns', in *Heroes, Hero-Worship and the Heroic in History* (1851), 249–315, 292. 'The Hero as a Man-of-Letters' was delivered on Tuesday, 19 May 1840.

'some man had to *think* of the making of that brick'.[12] He had made similar connections in 1829, in 'Signs of the Times', placing 'the Fausts and the Watts' alongside 'Homer and Shakespeare' as examples of 'gifted spirit[s]'.[13] In fact, by the end of the 1830s, analogies between mechanical inventors and literary inventors were commonplace, particularly in the debates that raged throughout the century about the ownership of all kinds of invention—both literary and technological. The rhetorical braiding together of the inventor and poet in these debates was partly symptomatic of a need to rewrite 'culture' in a way that could perform the difficult task of both acknowledging and resisting the effects of technological change. Marilyn Strathern has suggested that:

Ownership re-embeds ideas and products in an organism (whether a corporation, culture or individual author). Ownership gathers things momentarily to a point by locating them in the owner, halting endless dissemination, effecting an identity. We might even say that emergent forms of property signify new possibilities for corporeality or bodily integration in lives that observers constantly tell themselves are dispersed.[14]

The conflict between 'fixed identity' and 'dispersal' nestles at the core of any discussion of intellectual property, making it a fraught and unstable concept, particularly in a century that witnessed so many 'new possibilities' for 'endless dissemination'.

Carlyle was remarkable in seeing so early the necessary and irreversible links between technological advancement and a literate democracy. Yet he furiously and famously rejected the 'Mechanical Age', attempting to 'write over' technological change even in so directly applied a form as printing. In 'The Hero as a Man of Letters' he elided the processes of writing and printing by creating a significant neologism for the latter, 'Ready-writing', which, he claimed, was 'a simple, an inevitable and comparatively insignificant corollary' of 'the wondrous art of *Writing*'.[15] At the same time, he understood better than many at this juncture the vast social potential of print technology:

[12] Ibid. 266–7.
[13] Thomas Carlyle, 'Signs of the Times', *Thomas Carlyle: Selected Writings*, ed. Alan Shelston (1971), 73. Published anonymously.
[14] Marilyn Strathern, *Property, Substance and Effect* (1999), 177.
[15] Carlyle, 'The Hero as a Man-of-Letters', 249, 260, 249.

Literature is our parliament too. Printing, which comes necessarily out of writing, I say often, is equivalent to democracy: invent writing, democracy is inevitable. Writing brings printing; brings universal every-day extempore printing, as we see at present. Whoever can speak, speaking now to the whole nation, becomes a power, a branch of government, with inalienable weight in law-making, in all acts of authority. It matters not what rank he has, what revenues or garnitures: the requisite thing is, that he have a tongue which others will listen to; this and nothing more is requisite.[16]

In this passage, writing becomes a form of representation that is both liberating and threatening. His own situation as a writer of humble background made Carlyle particularly sensitive to the difficulty of creating an elevated public role, or a 'priesthood', for modern literary writing in a culture of 'every-day extempore printing'.[17] Back in 1795, Isaac D'Israeli, essayist and father of Benjamin Disraeli, had already identified the same 'problem': 'volumes have been multiplied, and their prices rendered them accessible to the lowest artisans, the Literary Character has gradually fallen into disrepute'.[18] As critics such as Siskin, Woodmansee, and Rose have shown, the response of self-consciously 'literary' authors was to develop an increasingly narrow and specialized definition of 'literature'. Clifford Siskin summarizes this shift: 'By the early nineteenth century, the work of the artist was reclassified within Romantic discourse as essentially psychological and was thus conceptually estranged from the materiality of worldly labor.'[19] Central to this Romantic construction of the artist's work was the idea of the investment of the artist within it, and the challenging of a traditional binary division between the 'artist' and the 'work'. This idea of the mingling of the author with the work was used to argue for the inalienable property right of the author in the first half of the nineteenth century. But, ironically, it was to the example of those same 'lowest artisans' who were getting their grubby hands on literary texts and thereby 'cheapening' them, that authors were then to turn in their early nineteenth-century campaign to win copyright protection. Campaigns for extended and accessible patent and copy-

[16] Carlyle, 'The Hero as a Man-of-Letters', 265.
[17] Ibid. See Jonathan Arac, *Commissioned Spirits: the Shaping of Social Motion in Dickens, Carlyle, Melville, and Hawthorne* (1979), 151–2.
[18] Isaac D'Israeli, *An Essay on the Manners and Genius of the Literary Character* (1795), p. xv.
[19] Clifford Siskin, *The Work of Writing: Literature and Social Change in Britain, 1700–1830* (1998), 153.

right protection ran alongside each other throughout this period, and borrowed from each other. Both came to revolve around the much-disputed terms 'originality' and 'utility': terms that were gaining currency in British intellectual and political debate from the mideighteenth century onwards, as the argument about the social value of mental labour gathered momentum.

Carlyle places a premium upon 'originality' in his lecture, in which the hero is '[a]n original man;—not a secondhand, borrowing or begging man,' and thus echoes one of the crucial terms in the parliamentary debates about intellectual property in the 1830s and 1840s.[20] The emphasis upon originality is hardly surprising when we consider that Carlyle was one of the chief popularizers of German aesthetic ideas in Britain in this period, and that he championed Thomas Talfourd's proposals for copyright reform.[21] Indeed, only the year before he delivered this lecture, he had personally petitioned Parliament in support of the Copyright Bill, stressing his own originality as a writer who 'wrote [books] by effort *of his own*'.[22] He suggests that, in order to rise above the babbling mass, the hero must display this elusive quality of 'originality', and then 'It matters not what rank he has.' Carlyle is discussing men-of-letters here, but in the 'democracy of writing', which he announces in his lecture, artisan-mechanics and inventors of the lowest rank were already applying their 'inalienable weight in law-making' through petitions to Parliament, pamphlets, and other campaigning literature demanding a cheaper and fairer patent law. As Carlyle reminded his audience in his lecture, inventors, like poets, were to be valued for their original thinking—they, too, found 'the beginning of a path', and the utility of their inventions was clear.[23] The campaigners for copyright reform imitated

---

[20] Carlyle, 'The Hero as a Man-of-Letters', 290, of Dr Johnson.

[21] Thomas McFarland has pointed out the complex cross-fertilization of ideas of originality in the eighteenth century. He suggests that from 1700 German scholars read English and Scottish writers with enthusiasm, but around 1800 'the stream of influence almost completely reversed its direction of flow'. Thomas McFarland, *Originality and Imagination* (1985), 47.

[22] Carlyle sent off his petition to Thomas Talfourd on 28? February 1839, *Letters*, xi. 36. He started planning his lectures in January 1840. Thomas Carlyle to the House of Commons [7 April 1839], *The Collected Letters of Thomas and Jane Welsh Carlyle*, ed. Clyde de L. Ryals and Kenneth J. Fielding, xi. *1839* (1985), 66–8, 67 (emphasis added). Carlyle's notion of originality was based on the idea of the transmission of eternal and unchanging truths.

[23] In 1843, a reviewer of Carlyle's lectures, *On Heroes and Hero-Worship*, reminds us of the important precedent of George Lillie Craik's *Pursuit of Knowledge under*

both their campaigning strategies and their arguments, particularly the argument for greater recognition as a profession. In 1818, Isaac D'Israeli was asking, 'Wherefore should not the literary character be associated in utility or glory with the other professional classes of society?'[24] By the 1830s, campaigners for copyright reform and the professionalization of writing were borrowing their claim for the utility of their work from the inventors and engineers, who could make a far clearer case for the use-value of their ideas. Later in the century, some novelists were also to find the analogy of engineering and mechanical creativity useful as a means of masculinizing the image of the profession of letters.[25] As this book shows, however, originality and utility proved difficult terms to balance in a debate that veered between the extremes of a Romantic rhetoric of individuality and a Utilitarian language of public usefulness and wealth generation.

THE LEGACY OF THE EIGHTEENTH CENTURY

Much has been obscured in the study of the development of the modern concept of 'intellectual property' by the persistence of rigid periodizations of 'English Literature'. This introductory chapter, although necessarily brief, attempts to reconnect the philosophical discussion of the mid-eighteenth century about the neglect of genius with the more pragmatic legal debate over ownership and intellectual property in the Victorian period.[26] In fact, many eighteenth-century terms and referents survived intact in discussions both of patent reform and of copyright extension throughout the first half

---

Difficulties—one of the foundational texts of 'invention literature'. [William Thomson], *Christian Remembrancer*, 6 (August 1843), 121–43. Reprinted in Jules Paul Seigel (ed.), *Thomas Carlyle: The Critical Heritage* (1971), 171–92, 172.

[24] [Isaac D'Israeli], *The Literary Character, Illustrated by the History of Men of Genius, Drawn from their Own Feelings and Confessions* (1818), 346.

[25] For the process of the masculinization of the novel form in the Victorian period, see Gaye Tuchman and Nina E. Fortin, *Edging Women Out: Victorian Novelists, Publishers, and Social Change* (1989); and Catherine Judd, 'Male Pseudonyms and Female Authority in Victorian England', in John O. Jordan and Robert L. Patten (eds.), *Literature in the Marketplace: Nineteenth-Century British Publishing and Reading Practices* (1995), 250–68.

[26] Paulina Kewes, among others, has made a persuasive case for the origins of the modern construction of the 'author' in the seventeenth century. See Paulina Kewes, *Authorship and Appropriation: Writing for the Stage in England 1660–1710* (1998).

of the nineteenth century. The heroes of Carlyle's lecture were all eighteenth-century men-of-letters. And it was the inventors of the eighteenth century who made up the canon of neglected genius for the patent law campaigners, as much as it was the Chattertons, Savages, and Otways who appeared again and again in nineteenth-century arguments for the extension of copyright protection for authors. Thus, in 1839, Arago recommended to posterity, 'our Papins and Vaucansons, our Watts and Arkwrights, and . . . other mechanists, unknown, perhaps, in a certain circle, but whose renown will go on augmenting from age to age with the progress of knowledge'.[27] The inventor-heroes commemorated in the pages of the penny magazines in the early nineteenth century—Arkwright, Watt, Boyle, and so on—were all names from a previous generation.[28] Bulwer Lytton set the play that he wrote to raise money for a Guild of Literature and Art, *Not So Bad As We Seem*, in the eighteenth century, but the play is clearly concerned with the commodification of literature in the nineteenth century, and fears that market-led production would operate against the notion of 'true' art, leading to genuinely high-quality work being driven out by cheap pulp. Tickets issued for admission (see Fig. 1) pictured the penurious Daniel Defoe and the painter, Richard Wilson—both of whom died in the eighteenth century.[29] And, despite his protest against Bulwer's 'historical' play that, 'The times are altered, [and] the people don't exist,' Thackeray also returned to the eighteenth century in his lectures on humourists of that period, and in the novel that grew out of

[27] M. Arago, *Life of James Watt with Memoir on Machinery Considered in Relation to the prosperity of the Working Classes. To which are subjoined, Historical Account of the Discovery of the Composition of Water by Lord Brougham and Eulogium of James Watt by Lord Jeffrey* (1839), 149.

[28] Anon., 'The Late Mr. Arkwright', *Chambers' Edinburgh Journal* (1 July 1843), 192. Anon., 'Memoir of James Watt, the Great Improver of the Steam Engine', *Mechanics' Magazine* (30 August 1823), 1–5. Anon., 'James Watt from Arago's *Life of Watt*', *Saturday Magazine* (4 February 1843), 46. Anon., 'Biographic Sketches: James Watt', *Chambers' Edinburgh Journal* (24 March 1832), 61–2. Anon., 'Arago's Life of Watt', *Chambers' Edinburgh Journal* (26 October 1839), 317–18. Anon., 'Robert Boyle', *Saturday Magazine* (9 March 1833), 91. 'The Eddystone Lighthouse', *Penny Magazine* (28 July 1832), 163. Anon., 'Smeaton', *Saturday Magazine* (17 October 1835), 148. Anon., 'Biographic Sketches: Thomas Telford', *Chambers' Edinburgh Journal* (21 February 1835), 29–30. Anon., 'Samuel Crompton, Inventor of the Spinning Mule', *Mechanics' Magazine* (14 July 1827), 446. Anon., 'Sir Humphry Davy', *Mechanics' Magazine* (13 June 1828), 279. Anon., 'The Independent Potter', *Mechanics' Magazine* (30 August 1823), 12. Anon., 'Disappointments of the Authors of Important Inventions', *Penny Magazine* (14 April 1832), 19.

[29] Defoe in 1731 and Wilson in 1782.

FIG. 1. Design for an admission ticket to performances in aid of the Guild of Literature and Art, from a drawing by E. M. Ward, ARA.

these lectures, *The History of Henry Esmond*.[30] The results were not only highly influential upon the process of literary canonization, but also—in the lectures' insistence on the identity of the artist with the work—helped to popularize the principle of writers' extended property rights in their books.

In order to control the kinds of modernization that might compromise their ownership of the processes of production, both groups actively created a sense of professional community by looking back to create a genealogy, or a pedigree for their respective occupations. As Peter Mandler has argued elsewhere, 'It was a natural instinct for advocates (*not* opponents) of change in a highly stable and hierarchical society to seek a pedigree, a tradition for their programme.'[31] Writers and inventors were quick to see that in order to promote their professional status, while protecting their intellectual property rights, it would be expedient to construct their trades as themselves a valuable heritage in need of protection. This accounts not only for an enthusiastic hagiography of eighteenth-century writers and inventors martyred to their genius, but also for the curious and increasing hero-worship of Newton and Shakespeare during the period. But in constructing themselves as part of the national heritage, writers and inventors ran the risk of suggesting that they and their works were part of the common patrimony. Balancing a claim for individual property in their labour against a claim for their labour as the 'natural' property of the people proved a perilous business.

As I argue in more detail in the following chapters, the eighteenth century continued to supply the vocabulary for discussions of intellectual property in the nineteenth century. It was in the eighteenth century and not the nineteenth, that a 'public' realm of print was first established.[32] The new technologies of the nineteenth century undoubtedly widened the sphere of 'publicity', but in this book I attempt to resist an unreflective technological determinism. New

---

[30] William Makepeace Thackeray, Speech at the Royal Literary Fund, 14 May 1851. The speech coincided with the first night of Dickens's *Not So Bad As We Seem*, and Thackeray used it to deprecate the Guild's project. See Lewis Melville, *The Life of William Makepeace Thackeray*, 2 vols. (1910), ii. 72–4.

[31] Peter Mandler, 'The Victorian Idea of Heritage', in *The Fall and Rise of the Stately Home* (1997), 21–69, 29.

[32] See Michael Warner, 'The Mass Public and the Mass Subject', in Bruce Robbins (ed.), *The Phantom Public Sphere* (1993), 234–56, 237. Warner discusses how, in the eighteenth century, 'a rhetoric of print consumption became authoritative, as a way of understanding the publicness of publication'.

technologies did not wipe out existing cultures, but rather imitated and interacted with them. Indeed, this book argues that the history of intellectual property offers a particularly resonant example of the affective power of strong and pre-established cultures over the challenge offered by new 'discourse networks'.[33] In fact, both the artisan mechanics and the literary writers were reasonably successful in protecting the 'mysteries' of their trades from the incursions of mechanization and mass-production.

T. W. Heyck in *The Transformation of Intellectual Life in Victorian England* has argued that it was the abandonment of the idea of Romantic genius that gave Victorian writers access to market power. Victorian writers, he says, 'stress[ed] self-discipline, hard work, methodical habits and temperate living. Such middle-class values implicitly rejected the romantics' notion of the artist as a genius seized by uncontrollable inspiration.'[34] I argue that, in fact, both stereotypes—the Romantic creator and the middle-class professional—maintained currency throughout the nineteenth century, and it was the irreconcilable tensions between the two that created the problems for the definition of intellectual property that are examined here.

In 1759, Edward Young's *Conjectures on Original Composition* had appeared anonymously. Young was the celebrated author of *The Complaint, or Night Thoughts* (1742–6), and his *Conjectures* are often cited as marking the beginning of the British debate over genius, although Young's pamphlet, in fact, had a very limited initial impact in Britain.[35] More immediately influential were William Duff's 1767 *Essay on Original Genius*, Alexander Gerard's *Essay on Genius* (1774), and Isaac D'Israeli's well-known 1795 *Essay on the Manners and Genius of the Literary Character*, which he followed

---

[33] Friedrich A. Kittler, *Discourse Networks 1800/1900*, trans. Michael Metteer with Chris Cullens (1990). Originally published in Germany as *Aufschreibesysteme* in 1985.

[34] T. W. Heyck, *The Transformation of Intellectual Life in Victorian England* (1982), 30. Later, though, he contradicts such a simple formulation by remarking that the nineteenth-century 'concept of the utility of art . . . was shared even by the Romantic poets', 191.

[35] M. H. Abrams, *The Mirror and the Lamp: Romantic Theory and Critical Tradition* (1953), 201. Young's work had more immediate influence in Germany. The influence of Young's *Conjectures* on the development of a British Romantic aesthetic, despite its limited initial impact, is also discussed by Clifford Siskin in *The Historicity of Romantic Discourse* (1988), and Jerome J. McGann, *The Romantic Ideology: A Critical Investigation* (1983).

with *The Literary Character, Illustrated by the History of Men of Genius*, in 1818. The work of both Duff and Gerard compares literary and mechanical creativity in ways that were to persist well into the nineteenth century. Both these Scottish Enlightenment thinkers describe inventive activity in terms of political economy and mechanics, in language different from the Coleridgean, or German organicist, descriptions of creativity, which would reject analogies of assemblage, or closed economies, in favour of transformative images of growth, exchange, and new currencies. Edward Young was, in fact, remarkably early in making a clear distinction between the two, and in privileging the organic as the more 'original': 'An *Original* may be said to be of a *vegetable* nature; it rises spontaneously from the vital root of genius; it *grows*, it is not *made*: *Imitations* are often a sort of *manufacture* wrought up by those *mechanics*, *art*, and *labour*, out of pre-existent materials not their own.'[36] We can see here how 'originality' is evolving as a euphemism for 'property'—made incontrovertible by 'growing' out of the artist himself (the artist in these discussions is invariably male) and remaining contiguous with him. And the term 'labour' is already gathering a patina of contempt, and would become even more corroded in the early nineteenth century, when Percy Shelley would argue aggressively for the separation of poetry from labour, and art from mechanical production, in order to secure a claim to posterity and the artist's right to property in his creations. Yet, significantly, Young does not exclude actual mechanics from his hall of fame: his list of geniuses includes both artists and scientists: '*Bacon, Boyle, Newton, Shakespeare, Milton.*'[37] Although it is unarguable that disciplinary boundaries were inscribed more and more forcefully in the period between the mid-eighteenth and mid-nineteenth centuries, inventors and writers continued to share a common language in which they theorized creativity and property in creativity. Indeed, 'art' at this time denoted both artistic and technological virtuosity.[38] This is a point well illustrated by Mary Shelley's 1818 novel, *Frankenstein; or The Modern Prometheus*, in which Victor Frankenstein, working in his laboratory, describes himself as an 'artist'.[39] Shelley's description

[36] Edward Young, *Conjectures on Original Composition*, ed. Edith J. Morley (1918), 7.
[37] Ibid. 34.
[38] 'Artist' in the *Oxford English Dictionary* at http://dictionary.oed.com.
[39] Mary W. Shelley, *Frankenstein or The Modern Prometheus*, ed. M. K. Joseph (1969), 55. All subsequent references appear in parentheses in the text.

of his work appears deliberately to muddle the mechanic and organic inspirational theories of creative process, and offers a useful example of the complexity of the issues at stake in this debate over the status and ownership of mental labour.

FRANKENSTEIN, OR THE MODERN PROMETHEUS: ART AS UNALIENATED LABOUR

'It is the fashion of the present day to raise up dazzling theories of genius,' wrote D'Israeli in 1818, the same year that *Frankenstein: Or the Modern Prometheus* was first published anonymously.[40] The novel offers a compelling fictional and symbolic articulation of the complex debate over those 'theories of genius' and the nature of originality itself, and is informed, both directly and indirectly, by the body of philosophical and Romantic works with which Mary Shelley was familiar.[41] It depicts the struggle over the disputed limits of intellectual ownership in a way that suggests Mary Shelley's own early misgivings about a Romantic project that many critics have since characterized as 'male'.[42] The nightmarishness of the

[40] [Isaac D'Israeli], *The Literary Character* (1818), p. vi.

[41] See Rosemary Ashton, 'Introduction', in *The German Idea: Four English Writers and the Reception of German Thought 1800–1860* (1980), 1–26. Also 'The Shelleys' Reading List', in *The Journals of Mary Shelley, 1814–1844*, ed. Paula R. Feldman and Diana Scott-Kilvert (1987), ii. 631–84. Mary Shelley read many of the European Romantic classics before 1818. For example, she read Schiller's *The Arminian, or, The Ghost Seer* (1789) in translation in 1816; and his *Don Carlos* (1787) in 1815 (p. 671). In 1815 she read Goethe's *The Sorrows of Werther* (1774), trans. Richard Graves 1779 (p. 650). She read Rousseau's *Julie, ou la Nouvelle Héloïse* (1761) in 1815 and again in 1817, and his *Émile; ou l'Éducation* in 1815 (p. 670). Lessing's *Emilia Galotti* (1772), she read in 1814 (p. 658). On Monday, 6 March 1816, Mary Shelley is reading *Despotism; or the Fall of the Jesuits*, by Isaac D'Israeli (1811). *The Journals of Mary Shelley, 1814–1844*, i. 68. D'Israeli recalls in the Preface to his *Literary Character* of 1818, that a copy of his first *Essay* of 1795 'has accidentally fallen [into] my hands [and which] formerly belonged to the great poetical genius of our times; and . . . it was twice read by him in two subsequent years, at Athens, in 1810 and 1811'. I assume that D'Israeli is here referring to Byron, which means that Mary Shelley may have heard Byron and Shelley discussing D'Israeli's ideas, even if she did not read the essay herself. [I. D'Israeli], 'Preface', *Literary Character*, p. iv.

[42] See Elsie B. Michie, *Outside the Pale. Cultural Exclusion, Gender Difference, and the Victorian Woman Writer* (1993); Anne K. Mellor, *Romanticism and Gender* (1993); Mary Jacobus, *Romanticism, Writing and Sexual Difference: Essays on The Prelude* (1989); Mary Poovey, *The Proper Lady and the Woman Writer. Ideology as Style in the Works of Mary Wollstonecraft, Mary Shelley and Jane Austen* (1984);

contiguity of the work and the author in *Frankenstein* raises the same questions about the desirability of the work–author identification as a letter that she wrote in April 1829, in response to Edward Trelawny's proposal to publish a life of Percy Shelley: 'There is nothing I shrink from more fearfully than publicity . . . to be in print—the subject of *men's* observations—of the bitter hard world's commentaries, to be attacked or defended! . . . I only seek to be forgotten.'[43] Only two years before she republished *Frankenstein* under her own name in Colburn and Bentley's Standard Novel series in 1831, Mary Shelley seems to suggest that 'to be in print' is to have a public literary identity largely independent of one's choosing and which is less a blessing for posterity than a public and visible curse. Yet Mary Shelley was in no position to surrender her own intellectual property at this time, and *Frankenstein* was republished under her—by then famous—name expressly in order to increase its sales, 'I have too much [publicity] & what is worse I am forced by my hard situation to meet it in a thousand ways.'[44]

'Remember, that I am thy creature' (100) the Creature tells Victor Frankenstein: like Mary Shelley, the miserable Victor seeks only to have his authorship forgotten, but is reminded constantly that his creation *belongs* to him. Elsie B. Michie has argued that, in *Frankenstein*, Shelley represents 'a process of production during which the producer inevitably becomes alienated from what he has made'.[45] I would argue that the novel rather chronicles Frankenstein's failure to alienate himself from his labour. In fact, the Creature remains so emphatically Frankenstein's intellectual property that there is no escape from their bond for either of them. Throughout the novel, the Creature insists on his shared identity with Frankenstein, 'my form is a filthy type of yours, more horrid even from the very resemblance' (130). Michie argues that Mary Shelley reverses Percy Shelley's ideal

Margaret Homans, 'Bearing Demons: *Frankenstein's* Circumvention of the Maternal', in *Bearing the Word: Language and Female Experience in Nineteenth-Century Women's Writing* (1986), 100–19; Ellen Moers, 'Female Gothic', in George Levine and U. C. Knoepflmacher (eds.), *The Endurance of Frankenstein: Essays on Mary Shelley's Novel* (1974), 77–87; Sandra M. Gilbert and Susan Gubar, 'Horror's Twin: Mary Shelley's Monstrous Eve', *The Madwoman in the Attic: The Woman Writer and the Nineteenth-Century Literary Imagination* (1979), 213–47.

[43] Mary Shelley to Edward John Trelawny, April [1829], *The Letters of Mary Wollstonecraft Shelley*, ed. Betty T. Bennett (1983), ii. 71–3, 72.
[44] Ibid.
[45] Elsie B. Michie, *Outside the Pale. Cultural Exclusion, Gender Difference, and the Victorian Woman Writer* (1993), 26.

of poetry as non-alienated labour, in order to demonstrate that artistic activity is, after all, production, not creation. But Shelley is closer to her husband than this reading allows, albeit with a difference in attitude. Rather than representing the Creature as a product, she literalizes the Romantic ideal of non-alienation, turning it into a nightmare in which the Creature and Frankenstein are symbolically trapped together in one representation.[46] The mistake so often made by schoolchildren, who call the Creature 'Frankenstein', is encouraged by the text itself. The identity between the two is shown to be at once threatening and obstinately enduring, and the Creature fails to achieve any useful, independent existence in the public world.

Mary Shelley insists upon the thematic centrality of the creative act in the novel, and the scene in which Frankenstein first invents the Creature, written in 1818, combines ideas of creativity as a disciplined and mechanical assemblage, and as psychologized inspiration. This bifurcated account seems to reflect the political struggle taking place both in literature and science at the time over the ownership of creative activity: is innovation the result of institutionalized processes, which make it a public or national property? Or does it rather happen as a 'special' and private process, which is the property of the artist alone? The fact that Victor Frankenstein moves from laboratory to garret room in the course of his work implies that the text comes to privilege the latter theory. But the private space of the 'workshop of filthy creation' (55) is also the site at which the project becomes monstrous and uncontainable. Shelley seems to be suggesting that the Romantic premium upon 'originality' and 'posterity' threatens to overwhelm and extinguish the individual artist. Insisting on his exclusive ownership of the work, the Romantic artist is stalked, and ultimately annihilated, by the creature he originally invented as security for his own posterity. Mary Shelley's novel appears to raise some uncomfortable questions about the relationship of fame to death.

---

[46] In choosing to leave no trace of the secret of the Creature's mechanism, both Frankenstein and the Creature himself transform him from a scientifically reproducible product, to an 'original', unrepeatable work of art. Frankenstein refuses to pass the 'recipe' to Walton, the journal that describes the 'series of disgusting circumstances', p. 130, is destroyed, and even the Creature himself intends to burn his 'miserable frame entirely' so that 'its remains may afford no light to any curious and unhallowed wretch, who would create such another as I have been', p. 222. I would argue, however, that the Creature figures throughout as *both* work of art and scientific experiment.

Victor Frankenstein early establishes his credentials as a mechanical inventor—'I made some discoveries in the improvement of some chemical instruments' (51), and it initially seems that the creation of life will be by a similarly mechanical process, through the assemblage of parts. But abruptly the narrative turns from a quasi-scientific discussion of 'causation', to something entirely different: 'from the midst of this darkness a sudden light broke in upon me—a light so brilliant and wondrous, yet so simple, that while *I became dizzy with the immensity of the prospect which it illustrated*, I was surprised, that among so many men of genius . . . I alone should be reserved to discover so astonishing a secret' (52).[47] The 'sudden light' shone on what has been secret signals inspiration, an effect that Percy Shelley chose to enhance when he added the sentence printed in italics. 'I became dizzy' reinforces the new psychologized idea of genius and inspiration, located in the very body of the author himself, over the old ideas of invention as the combination of extant material 'not their own' as Edward Young had put it. Almost immediately comes a reversal back into rule-based method, 'Some miracle might have produced it, yet the stages of discovery were distinct and probable' (52). But the 'inspiration' narrative is supported elsewhere in the account by references to Frankenstein's 'almost supernatural enthusiasm' (51), and his compulsive pursuit of scientific objects. In his 'solitary chamber', which is, of course, 'at the top of the house', like the Romantic artist's garret room, Frankenstein becomes the victim of his 'passion' (55) and imagination, but, like Percy Shelley's 'evanescent visitations', 'It was indeed but a passing trance' (54). D'Israeli, in his *The Literary Character*, had described the physical symptoms attendant upon Romantic creation as 'now an intermittent fever, now a silent delirium, an hysterical affection, and now a horrid hypochondriasm', and Frankenstein exhibits a similar pathology, 'Every night I was oppressed by a slow fever, and I became nervous to a most painful degree' (56).[48] All the referents of Romantic inspiration are here: the solitariness of the artist, the unconscious

[47] Emphasis added.
[48] [D'Israeli], *Literary Character*, 219. Shelley emphasized Frankenstein's illness in the 1831 text, adding, 'the fall of a leaf startled me, and I shunned my fellow-creatures as if I had been guilty of a crime. Sometimes I grew alarmed at the wreck I perceived that I had become; the energy of my purpose alone sustained me . . . and I believed that exercise and amusement would then drive away incipient disease', 56. I believe that Shelley strengthened her representation of the Romantic artist in the 1831 version of the text.

nature or 'trance' of the creative act, and the bodily suffering and martyrdom entailed by it. Dickens's *Household Words* would publish a very similar representation as late as 1850, when the reader is told that in order to be a successful poet, 'a man should live in a garret aloof, | And have few friends, and be poorly clad.'[49]

Yet Mary Shelley also offers that concurrent but contradictory narrative, in which Frankenstein appears as a methodical and rule-bound scientist, consulting books, inventing improvements to chemical instruments, gaining a professional reputation in the scientific establishment, respectful of his teachers and of the hierarchy of the institution.[50] He is no crazed maverick, but a fully enrolled student, who commands 'great esteem and admiration at the university', studying physiology in an insistently reasonable fashion, with 'no supernatural horrors' (51). This counter-narrative insists on the explicability of the 'distinct and probable' (52) steps towards the discovery, and on 'the improvement which every day takes place in science and mechanics' (53). Frankenstein's decision to build a 'gigantic' being, because 'the minuteness of the parts' (53) make the human scale too intricate, further corroborates this mechanical account. Yet the account once more shifts into the 'genius narrative', with Frankenstein's wild prognostications: 'a resistless, and almost frantic, impulse, urged me forward . . . with unrelaxed and breathless eagerness, I pursued nature to her hiding places . . . [and] disturbed, with profane fingers, the tremendous secrets of the human frame' (53–5). Shelley turns from an account of disciplined and patient scientific effort to a blatant dramatization of desire, representing the creative urge as uncontrollably libidinous, overspilling the disciplinary boundary between work and pleasure. The work that becomes pleasure in this period was, as Mary Shelley well knew, the work of writing—the work done 'for itself', that issued directly from the body and mind of the artist and remained morally his property in perpetuity, ensuring his reputation after death.[51]

Yet, once created, the Creature appears to be merely an assemblage of somewhat ill-fitting parts: 'yellow skin scarcely covered the work of muscles and arteries beneath', and his eyes are almost 'dun-white' (57). Percy Shelley inserted a sentence into his wife's

---

[49] 'The Flight of the Goddess', *Household Words*, 5/3 (13 April 1850), 49.
[50] Ingolstadt was well known for the high quality of its science teaching. See Samuel Holmes Vasbinder, *Scientific Attitudes in Mary Shelley's Frankenstein* (1984), 69.
[51] See Siskin, *The Work of Writing*.

manuscript explaining that Frankenstein is inspired to take up science by M. Waldman's assurance that 'The labours of men of genius, however erroneously directed, scarcely ever fail in ultimately turning to the solid advantage of mankind' (49). This may be the husband's creed—but the wife's text suggests otherwise. *Frankenstein* seems rather an uncompromising critique of the Romantic construction of originality, emphasizing its asocial irresponsibility, particularly through Mary Shelley's Godwinian critique of Victor's failure to 'own' his 'child'.[52] Ultimately, the 'solid advantage of mankind' is rather threatened than furthered by Victor's efforts, and the novel obliquely throws doubt on the social utility of the artwork.

Later, in volume ii, when he recounts the 'progress of my intellect', the Creature is newly represented as pure mind. While in one account he is the result of a failed experiment, in this version he is a creation of the Imagination. It is in this guise that he haunts Victor as if he were his ghost. 'I considered the being . . . nearly in the light of my own vampire, *my own spirit let loose from the grave*' (77, emphasis added), says Frankenstein, seeing the creature as the embodiment of his own posthumous self—or his reputation. The wished-for afterlife proleptically haunts the writer—the imagined future turning upon him. Shelley seems to suggest that an ambition for posterity and reputation is finally an ambition for self-annihilation, in the sense that truly enduring fame—and literary survival—necessitates the death of the author. Despite the ambiguities of the creative process as depicted in the novel, the story represents an unalienable property in the created object, but only in order to turn this into a nightmarish vision of reverse possession.[53]

In the Introduction that she wrote for the new edition of 1831, Mary Shelley modestly rejected any comparison of her own literary work with that of the male Romantic poets. She mentions both Byron, who was engaged in writing 'the third canto of Childe Harold' (6) while *Frankenstein* was being created, and her husband, whom she describes as 'more apt to embody ideas and sentiments in the radiance of brilliant imagery, and in the music of the most melodious verse that adorns our language, than to invent the machinery

[52] Fred Botting comprehensively reviews the many critical interpretations of *Frankenstein* in *Making Monstrous: Frankenstein, Criticism, Theory* (1991).

[53] William Godwin insisted on the importance of nurture to the development of the child. See William Godwin, 'Of the Sources of Genius', *The Enquirer. Reflections on Education, Manners and Literature. In a Series of Essays* (1797), 12–28.

of a story' (7). Casting herself, significantly, in the role of a mechanical inventor, rather than that of the Romantic creator who 'embodies' his visions, she implies a distinction between poetry and fiction, 'the machinery of a story', which allows her to distance herself from the very perils of posterity that she has delineated inside her text through a nightmarish vision of literal 'corporeality' and embodiment.[54] Yet by mid-century, after the considerable success of inventors in lobbying for their intellectual property rights, the analogy of mechanical invention was taken up by novelists who were deliberately trying to reinstate Romantic ideas of posterity and intellectual property through their 'embodiment' in the work.

INTELLECTUAL PROPERTY AND THE NOVEL

It is both in and through the Victorian novel that we can most clearly observe the pressures of the debate over intellectual property, the status of writers, and the instrumentality of literature in the nineteenth century.[55] Through the novel the links between technological progress and constructions of creativity become distinctly visible. We can witness the renegotiation of public and private property taking place both within the texts themselves, and in the self-presentation of their authors. In choosing the image of mechanical invention to describe her own creative process, Mary Shelley chose to emphasize the utility of her literary work over its 'originality'; and in this she anticipates the novelists of the mid-nineteenth century, some of whom used tropes of mechanical invention to develop an analogous rhetoric of literature and culture as an economically valuable public resource. The novel perhaps more than any other genre in the Victorian period was perceived both as the property of the public and as that of the author.

[54] Although elsewhere in the Introduction, she describes the story as coming to her in a 'waking dream' (10), aligning herself more closely with the psychologized construction of genius favoured by Percy Shelley.

[55] Many accounts of intellectual property law in this period say little about the novel form. Martha Woodmansee, for example, in her *The Author, Art, and the Market: Re-reading the History of Aesthetics* (1994) says little about fiction and prose in her discussion. Many nineteenth-century poems also mention inventors. For example, Elizabeth Barrett Browning's *An Essay on Mind* (1826); Caroline Norton's *The Child of the Islands* (1846); Augusta Webster's 'An Inventor', in *Portraits and Other Poems* (1870).

The increase in serial publication of novels as the century progressed perhaps contributed to this perception, as the reading public were encouraged to engage in the experience of assembling the 'story' themselves, part by part. As the boundary between the artwork and its consumers became less distinct, the form became increasingly resistant to traditional notions of 'art'. Part issue made it impossible to ignore the temporality and topicality that exposes the notion of the autotelic art-object and makes fiction a particularly problematic genre in relation to the copyright debate. Its conspicuous state of incompletion as each number appeared exposed traditional arguments about the perfection of artistic form. Its dissemination to a demographically wide readership, its implied investment in new print technologies, its frequent juxtaposition to journalistic discussion, and its capacity to react fast to public debate, make the serial an eloquently modern and interactive form of writing in the nineteenth century. Some writers, among them George Eliot, actively resisted the serial publication of their work in an attempt to strengthen both their reputations as 'serious' writers and their claims to intellectual property. But serial publication had irrevocably changed the form, and although George Eliot published *Adam Bede* as a three-volume novel, in its interest and engagement with topical and contemporary issues, and its style of address to the reader, it reflects those changes. Thus, the novel was able both to pose questions about the social value of art and to attempt to suggest some possible solutions by characterizing itself as a form that was capable of intervening in the public sphere.

Despite much of the rhetoric supporting its inception and extension, then as now intellectual property was peculiarly fungible, a long way from the Burkean ideal of perpetual property 'locked fast . . . forever':

The people of England well know, that the idea of inheritance furnishes a sure principle of conservation, and a sure principle of improvement. Whatever advantages are obtained by a state proceeding on these maxims, are locked fast in a kind of mortmain for ever. By a constitutional policy working after the pattern of nature, we receive, we hold, we transmit our government and our privileges, in the same manner we enjoy and transmit our property and our lives.[56]

---

[56] Edmund Burke, *Reflections on the Revolution in France*, ed. Conor Cruise O'Brien (1968), 120.

This high Tory view, which developed as a recoil against the French Revolution, characterized property as inalienable—'locked fast'— and corporally identified with the person—'our property and our lives'. But such a view clashed with the pragmatic reality of intellectual property rights. Copyrights and patents could be leased, sold outright, or split half-and-half with publishers or manufacturers.[57] In fact, the vast majority of jobbing writers in the nineteenth century were too poor to gamble on the possibility of a long-term return on their copyrights, and were obliged to sell off all their rights to the publishers immediately.[58] Most inventors laboured under the same necessities. The publisher George Routledge confirmed that it was only '[m]en like Lord Lytton and Dickens, and others, [who] did keep their own copyrights; but they did not keep them at first; they sold them and then repurchased them'.[59] Much of the anxiety about the division between the private and the public that we witness at mid-century originates in what has been termed the 'paradox at the heart of liberal property ideology'.[60] To consider him/herself free and autonomous, a person must be free to sell his/her property, but property is necessarily identified with the person, so that alienation breaks the link between the property and the person, which breakage threatens to transform 'freedom' into 'estrangement'.[61] The Victorian novelists discussed in this book tried to hold on to the ideal of the bond between the person and the property for their work, while also needing the flexibility, and ultimately, the freedom of contract that allowed them not merely to own, but also to sell and disperse, their books.

In the 1850s, Charles Dickens, Elizabeth Gaskell, and George Eliot participated in debates over the value and ownership of labour, such as those over copyright and patent reform and the controversy over married women's property. While these issues are clearly

[57] Peter Shillingsburg makes this point in his discussion of Thackeray's relationship to the literary marketplace. See Peter L. Shillingsburg, *Pegasus in Harness: Victorian Publishing and W. M. Thackeray* (1992), 112.

[58] See Nigel Cross, *The Common Writer: Life in Nineteenth-Century Grub Street* (1985).

[59] George Routledge examined by Mr Daldy, *Minutes of the Evidence taken Before the Royal Commission on Copyright together with an Appendix preceded by Tables of the Witnesses and of the Contents of the Appendix* (1878), *Reports from Commissioners, Inspectors, and Others*, Vol. 6, Session 17 January–16 August 1878, Vol. XXIV, p. 246 (504).

[60] Margaret Jane Radin, *Reinterpreting Property* (1993), 197.

[61] See ibid.

reflected in their novels, the publication of those novels and the celebrity of their authors also had a substantial effect on the subsequent direction of these debates. For example, George Eliot's novels were frequently cited on both sides of the discussion of copyright law in 1878 as examples of the kind of high-quality, best-selling fiction that should be both affordable and protected from foreign piracy.[62] Once they became celebrities, these Victorian novelists had considerable public influence, and they saw it as a duty to enter the debate about the social value of art. They used the novel form not just to reflect, but also to challenge received notions of intellectual ownership and responsibility.

This book owes much to Marxist theories of literature and culture, but my object in writing was not so much to intervene at a theoretical level, as to situate a discussion of creativity specifically and carefully at certain moments in the nineteenth century.[63] Rather than accepting assumptions about the links between material culture and literature, I have attempted to re-establish them through the accumulation of specific evidence from the period. It is, I think, both possible and fruitful to think about—for example—Elkington's electroplate vase displayed at the Great Exhibition and Dickens's *Bleak House* together, as long as the important distinctions between the two are maintained. Throughout, I seek to avoid flattening the literary text into just another category of historical document. The aesthetic is necessarily more than an ideological category, which is precisely why the Victorian novel lends itself so well to an examination of Victorian ideas of intellectual property. In its self-conscious creation of an imaginary, the Victorian novel not only reflects social relationships as they are conventionally articulated through the institutions of the law, education, and so on, but also posits new ways of structuring and thinking about such relationships. The imaginary space of the realist novel does not substitute so much as supplement any given account of the social contract. In reading Victorian novels in the context of the debate over Victorian property, then, I am not looking merely for references to the legal and public debates, but also for ways in which the novelists use their writing to work at imagining how far it is ever possible to own a creative act. An example

[62] George Eliot, *Adam Bede, Middlemarch*, and *Daniel Deronda* are mentioned on *Royal Commission on Copyright* 1878, pp. 44, 41, and 279 respectively.
[63] For a full bibliography of Marxist thinking on creativity, see Janet Wolff, *The Social Production of Art* (1993), 177–98.

might be the reading of Dickens's *Bleak House* in Ch. 4, in which I suggest that the famous double narrative of that novel imaginatively enacts Dickens's own difficulty in finding a model of ownership for his work. Esther's intense and embodied personal identity is pitted against the other dispersed, disembodied, and apparently sourceless narration. Dickens's deep possessiveness and self-identification with everything he produced, exacerbated by his bitter experience of piracy and unauthorized copying, competes in *Bleak House* with both his genuine generosity and need to be instrumental in his writing, and his lurking suspicion that all creativity is, ultimately, unownable. The double-text of *Bleak House*, therefore, raises questions about the origin of art, and the ownership of the art object. Many mid-Victorian novels reflect both explicitly and silently upon such questions at a time when the Romantic notion of the single author was coming under unprecedented pressure.

The book starts by showing that mechanical inventors and literary writers continued to inhabit the same discursive space into the late 1830s. It suggests that Carlyle's conflation of Faust with Watt and Shakespeare bespeaks a widespread unease in the early Victorian period about the social value of technology, the authorship of change, and the usurpation of traditional notions of culture. Carlyle's 'neglected genius' as man-of-letters is caught, as I will show, in precisely the same ideological double-bind as the neglected genius-inventor of the same period. If the nineteenth-century man-of-letters is to consolidate his social position, he has no choice but to embrace the emerging technologies of mass communication, but if he is to remain a spiritual hero, he must live beyond and outside them, trusting to posterity for his rewards: 'He, with his copy-rights and copy-wrongs, in his squalid garret, in his rusty coat; ruling (for this is what he does), from his grave, after death, whole nations and generations who would, or would not, give him bread while living,—is a rather curious spectacle! Few shapes of heroism can be more unexpected.'[64] In 1830 Charles Babbage had lamented the similar lack of appreciation for mechanical genius, commenting ruefully on the posthumous appreciation of 'the immortal Watt, who was neither acknowledged by his sovereign, nor honoured by his ministers, nor embalmed among the heroes and sages of his country'.[65] Men of letters may be

---

[64] Thomas Carlyle, 'The Hero as a Man-of-Letters', 250.
[65] [David Brewster], 'Review of Babbage, *Reflexions on the Decline of Science in England, and on Some of its Causes*', *Quarterly Review*, 43 (October 1830), 305–42,

unexpected heroes, but what is perhaps even more unexpected is their representational kinship with mechanical inventors into the 1830s.

Chapter 2 explores the striking proximity of representations of inventors and authors in the context of wider contemporary debates about class mobility and the ownership of intellectual labour and 'property in skill' in the turbulent decades of the 1830s and 1840s. By examining the uneasy alliance between the radical working class and the reform middle class in this period, the chapter shows how the lobbying activities of authors and inventors revealed the inadequacy of traditional ideas of labour for the analysis of new working practices. If the Reform Act of 1832 did little to enfranchise the population, it did at least raise public expectations, and the 1830s witnessed both the emergence of a peculiarly modern and recognizable system of political lobbying, and the widening power of the press.

'Democracy', as Carlyle pointed out, was increasingly invested in writing. Clifford Siskin has claimed that '[a] combination of technological and economic change points to the third decade of the nineteenth century as a kind of watershed: beyond that point lies the modern . . . fully "naturalized"—world of print.'[66] Although I am wary of making any such universal claim about a time when regional variation and uneven distribution of printed material across Britain made the situation by no means so simple, tracing out the patent and copyright debates through parliamentary papers and the periodical press is as good a way as any of showing up the strain that the new technologies were placing upon traditional forms and conceptions of labour and distribution in the 1830s and 1840s. It was through print, after all, that the inventor and the writer were connected—printing was the technology that allowed the two groups to borrow from one another, drawing the discussions of scientific and literary invention much closer than they had been in an earlier, less literate culture. And reading these debates, which bristle with contradictions and confusions, gives us a strong sense of an enforced adaptation to a new and uncharted territory that often seems to bewilder everybody.

---

315. Christine MacLeod has written that 'it was not until the third quarter of the nineteenth century that the commemoration of inventors became widespread', but I argue that a hagiography of invention was already established in the 1830s. Christine MacLeod, 'James Watt, Heroic Invention and the Idea of the Industrial Revolution', in Maxine Berg and Kristine Bruland (eds.), *Technological Revolutions in Europe: Historical Perspectives* (1998), 96–116, 98.

[66] Clifford Siskin, *The Work of Writing*, 11.

In Chs. 3 and 4 I explore the 1850s as the critical decade for understanding the confrontation between a traditional artisanal culture and the emergence of a consumer-based, rather than producer-based, model of labour. Between 1850 and 1860, what we have come to call commodity culture creeps into being, although my chapters take issue with much that has been written about this phenomenon. Chapters 3 and 4 form a pair: Ch. 3 discusses the Great Exhibition of 1851, and considers the nascent anxieties about copying and mass reproduction that this event both displayed and provoked. It also examines the 1852 Patent Reform Act, which grew out of the Exhibition, and adduces the possible reasons for the remarkable survival of the figure of the solitary and autonomous inventor in the parliamentary debate, now that a liberal economics of free trade was in the political ascendant. Although theoretically there is no opposition between free-trade policy and patent or copyright law, this was not the opinion of many MPs and lobbyists at the time. Macaulay, for example, anathematized copyright as 'monopoly' in his famous parliamentary speech of 1841.[67] At Westminster by the mid-century, there was a similarly powerful feeling from the free traders for the total abolition of the patent system, which they saw as outdated protectionism, obstructive to progress. Yet free-trade, anti-monopolist arguments were never to win out in any debate over intellectual property in the nineteenth century. Chapter 3 suggests that one reason for this in 1852 was the powerful influence of a literary lobby, which included Charles Dickens, upon the reform of the patent laws.

At the Exhibition of 1851, art and technology had been made to appear homologous, and writers and artists had been genuinely optimistic about a mechanized future. There still seemed much to be gained from the analogy between artistic and technological creativity, particularly as the 1852 Patent Amendment Act strengthened international protection for inventors and the literary lobby hoped such protection would soon be extended to writers. In their efforts to create a professional space for literature, writers fell upon the argument for utility that had dominated the patent debate, claiming literary creativity as morally and socially useful. Robert Patten has drawn attention to the characters of Daniel Doyce and Henry

[67] Thomas Babington Macaulay, 'Literary Copyright' [5 February 1841], *Speeches, Parliamentary and Miscellaneous* (1853), i. 285–300.

Gowan in Charles Dickens's *Little Dorrit*, suggesting that '[i]t may be to such characters and such passages that we should turn for an image of the artist working in and for society in Victorian literature.'[68] In Chapter 4, I take up his suggestion and show how the anxieties about authorship and ownership that were raised by the Exhibition also manifested themselves, albeit with varying degrees of transparency, in the literary writing of the 1850s. *Little Dorrit* is discussed in detail, as is Dickens's 'anti-Exhibition' novel *Bleak House*. I read both works in the context of the debate over intellectual property and authorial propriety precipitated by events at the Crystal Palace, and by the contemporaneous 'Dignity of Literature' dispute.

At the centre of the debate about the dignity of literature were anxieties about public display and performance, and the preservation of privacy and propriety—anxieties that I suggest were exacerbated by the prominence of the Exhibition, both in prospect, and in retrospect, throughout these years. According to one line of historical analysis, the 'complex discourse of property and propriety' in the nineteenth century is indicative of the 'mercurial instabilities of literary property in an era marked by the shift of the author's role as gentleman and scholar to that of professional trader in a new form of commodity'.[69] Both Dickens and Thackeray enjoyed the transformative potential of the marketplace, but both were also anxious about its ephemerality and sought a supplementary value for their literary work that supported a claim to its endurance and its greater public importance. It is no coincidence that the renegotiation of public and private spaces is central to the texts that both produced in the 1850s. It can be seen in Dickens's anxious inscription of domesticity and privacy in the novels, and Thackeray's privatization of public history, particularly in *The History of Henry Esmond*. Both writers create an alternative private domain in order to deflect from the other vital privatized economic space that the novels themselves occupy in the marketplace. All intellectual property legislation performs a balancing act between the interest of the public and the private interest of the author, as Charles Trevelyan pointed out in the Royal Commission on Copyright of 1878, 'the problem is to reconcile [the author's]

---

[68] Robert L. Patten, ' "The people have set Literature free": The Professionalization of Letters in Nineteenth-Century England', *Review*, 9 (1987), 1–34, 29.
[69] Rosemary J. Coombe, 'Challenging Paternity: Histories of Copyright', Review Article, *Yale Journal of Law and the Humanities*, 6 (1994), 397–422, 405.

just reward with the interests of the public'.[70] This chapter shows both Dickens and Thackeray engaging in very similar balancing acts within their own texts. If Dickens had recourse to the idea of the inventor as representative of the public interest in private acts of creativity, it also provided him with a reassuringly masculine image of invention with which to counter the perception of the writing of fiction as a feminine activity.

The fifth chapter, which focuses on the work of George Eliot and Elizabeth Gaskell in the 1860s, starts with a discussion of the campaign for married women's property rights, which both novelists supported. Creative women in this period had a very different relationship with their intellectual property to that of their male colleagues. While it was difficult for women to appropriate androcentric Romantic models of creativity, ironically the legal category of *coverture*, by which married women were 'covered' under the law by their husbands, made some women writers less anxious about participation in the marketplace than their male counterparts.[71] Gaskell and Eliot both contrived to retreat from the stereotype of 'the lady novelist' in different ways, but, unlike Dickens and Thackeray, they did not feel the need to masculinize the activity of writing.

This chapter argues that women writers took a very different view of their intellectual property. They tended to construct themselves as part of the community of consumers rather than producers. Female consumption was becoming increasingly visible in the 1860s and middle-class women in particular were being targeted both as readers and as shoppers in this decade.[72] Gaskell's and Eliot's work reflects more anxiety than Dickens's or Thackeray's about the effects of the growing global economy on consumers, and about the authenticity and quality of the product that they themselves were offering.

---

[70] Sir Charles Trevelyan, *Royal Commission on Copyright* (1878), 2.

[71] Margot Finn has argued that women perhaps exerted more economic power than is suggested by 'monolithic' readings of the property laws, such as those presented in Catherine Hall, *White, Male, and Middle-Class: Explorations in Feminism and History* (1992) and Leonore Davidoff and Catherine Hall, *Family Fortunes: Men and Women of the English Middle Class 1780–1850* (1987). Margot Finn, 'Women, Consumption and Coverture in England, c.1760–1860', *The Historical Journal*, 39/3 (1996), 703–22.

[72] For more on the moral panic about the female readership of sensation fiction in the 1860s, see Kate Flint, *The Woman Reader 1837–1914* (1993), 274–93. For more on the new patterns of shopping in the Victorian period, see Rachel Bowlby, 'Commerce and Femininity', in *Just Looking, Consumer Culture in Dreiser, Gissing and Zola* (1985), 18–34. Rachel Bowlby writes that 'women, at the time when [Marx] wrote and increasingly over the next fifty years, were the principal consumers', ibid. 27.

While she includes inventors in her work, Gaskell does not identify herself with them as Dickens did, nor is she involved in campaigning for copyright reform. If Dickens had used the analogy of the inventor to bring the writer closer to a public, masculine world, then Gaskell rather uses inventors to represent a technological expertise that is dangerously exclusive. It is the intellectually disenfranchised Phillis in Gaskell's novella *Cousin Phillis* who has to straddle the widening gap between an increasingly illegible technological culture and the search for an independent future for herself. Like Emerson, Gaskell quickly recognized the dangers of treating 'technology' as a category distinct from everyday life: she saw it instead as the 'organized nature' in which modern lives were embedded.[73] Her anxieties about intellectual ownership are less about her own property in her work, than about the importance of a fuller public ownership of the modern industrial culture which, in her view, needed to include and accommodate both women and the working classes.

Even early in her fiction-writing career, George Eliot was deeply concerned with the consumption of her work. In the case of both copyright and patent law, the limited time-span of private ownership before the invention or literary work enters the public domain effectively prioritizes the claim of the public over that of the author. Trevor Ross, writing about the history of copyright, takes issue with Martha Woodmansee and Mark Rose, and suggests that, in their haste to see copyright as constructing the 'original author', they have failed to see the importance of its other term: the 'public domain'.[74] I suggest that, in constructing her persona as a famous writer, Eliot chose to delimit this public domain rather than to attempt the far more perilous project of reinserting herself into the Romantic model of artistic production. Against the uncomfortable exposure of the Liggins affair of 1859, Eliot chose to draw attention away from her own dubious status as producer of the novels, by characterizing her books themselves as the agents of enlightenment amongst her

---

[73] R. W. Emerson, 'The Uses of Great Men', *Essays, Lectures and Orations* (1851), 327. George Eliot owned this edition. 'We have never come at the true and best benefit of any genius, so long as we believe him an original force. In the moment when he ceases to help us as a cause, he begins to help us more as an effect. Then he appears as an exponent of a vaster mind and skill . . . The destiny of organized nature is amelioration, and who can tell its limits?', 327.

[74] Trevor Ross, 'Copyright and the Invention of Tradition', *Eighteenth-Century Studies*, 26/1 (Fall 1992), 1–27, and Trevor Ross, *The Making of the English Literary Canon: From the Middle Ages to the Late Eighteenth Century* (1998).

readership. In what amounts to a rejection of the embodiment theory of Romantic writing, Eliot deliberately reinscribed the divide between the work and the artist, and this inevitably complicated her relationship to her work as property.

Eliot's reticence about her own degree of involvement with her work, and her ownership of it, is clear through the early fiction. In the curious novella, *The Lifted Veil*, for example, Eliot worries at the limits of her own intellectual property, and finally at the limits of her own selfhood, when she creates the 'torment' of Latimer's 'diseased participation in other people's consciousnesses'.[75] More generally, her tale is preoccupied by the difficulty of defining a line between mental privacy and public intellectuality. In *Brother Jacob* she shows through a kind of wish fulfilment how the 'growing heritage' should be protected from the chanciness and disruption of commercial competition.[76] A Burkean ideal of inheritance supplants a flexible and contractual model of property in the tale. And *Silas Marner* offers a full, if oblique, commentary on Eliot's fears about publicity and the circulation of her work at this time.

Clearly, much more than just copyright law was implicated in the formation of a 'national culture', but, with the growth in currency of the idea of 'the people' approaching the second Reform Act in 1867, the idea of a 'public domain' achieves an urgent political significance. In 1869, Eliot wrote that '[o]ne trembles to think how easily that moral wealth may be lost which it has been the work of ages to produce', condemning Byron's immorality as potentially degenerative of the culture.[77] Even at an early stage in her career as a novelist, it is possible to see the beginnings of Eliot's construction of an ideal of 'the culture' that posits a public space not defined by the market, but represented instead by 'moral wealth'—a phrase that sidesteps from economic to cultural capital. '[O]ur civilization . . . is helplessly in peril without the spiritual police of sentiments or ideal feelings. And it is this invisible police which we had need, as a community, strive to maintain in efficient force,' she wrote.[78] This uncomfortable personification of 'sentiments' as policemen mimics Eliot's own fantasy of

---

[75] George Eliot, *The Lifted Veil*, in Helen Small (ed.), *The Lifted Veil, Brother Jacob* (1999), 17.

[76] Eliot used this phrase in the epigraph to *The Lifted Veil* that she added in 1873, and appeared in print for the first time in the Cabinet Edition of 1878.

[77] George Eliot to Sara Hennell (21 September 1869), *GEL*, v. 56.

[78] George Eliot, 'Debasing the Moral Currency', *The Impressions of Theophrastus Such* (1995), 80.

the moral agency of her books. For Eliot, cultural patrimony is no longer guarded by civilization, but rather guards it: a reversal that allows her to fantasize her books as outliving not only their author, but also their critics and their readers. She deflected the difficulties surrounding her own relationship with her labour by personifying her books themselves as the agents of the social contract.

Chapter 6 moves into the last two decades of the nineteenth century. The final chapter shows that Thomas Hardy's later fiction both reflects and signals an important shift in thinking about creativity and ownership towards the end of the century. Although the hero-worship of the inventors of the industrial revolution continues, and, indeed, proliferates, in the popular literature of the 1860s and 1870s, the tone has modulated into that of fabular nostalgia, and many of these texts are explicitly targeted at children and young people.[79] As technological systems and networks spread into everyday life, the fiction of the single authorship of machines was demonstrably discredited. Technology became both more familiar and less visible, and the heroic inventor faded from view. Throughout the first three quarters of the century, the intellectual property debate had been a largely domestic one, which was often linked explicitly to notions of British supremacy and the making of the nation state. Towards the end of the century, with the increasing globalization of markets, and technological advances in printing and communications techniques, it became clear that the protection of intellectual property within island borders was ever more drastically inadequate. The corporatization of what were becoming engineering multinationals absorbed the heroic inventor into the R&D department, and the company's name effaced that of the inventor, both on patent applications and in the public perception of products.

[79] [Robert Cochrane], *Heroes of Invention and Discovery: Lives of Eminent Inventors and Pioneers of Science* (1879); Samuel Smiles, *Self-Help; with Illustrations of Character, Conduct, and Perseverance* (1866); Frederick C. Bakewell, *Great Facts: A Popular History and Description of the Most Remarkable Inventions During the Present Century* ([1859]); [Elias Taylor], *Great Inventors: The Sources of Their Usefulness and the Results of Their Efforts, Profusely Illustrated* ([1865]); *The Young Mechanic: A Book for Boys* (1871). The book starts: 'THERE never was a time when a taste for practical mechanics was so general among boys as it is now, in this year of grace 1870', 1; James Burnley, *The Romance of Invention: Vignettes from the Annals of Industry and Science* (1886); John Timbs, FSA, *Stories of Inventors and Discoverers in Science and the Useful Arts. A Book for Old and Young* (1860); J. Hamilton Fyfe, *The Triumphs of Invention and Discovery* (1861). Christine MacLeod focuses much of her discussion on this material on inventors that appears towards the end of the century.

Thus, the analogy on which this book has been based so far, between the inventor and the writer, was losing currency by the end of the century. This was partly because of the corporatization of invention, and partly because increased scientific specialization made it less easy for the two groups to share a language. But there were still some interesting links. Just as improvements in the technology of printing in the early nineteenth century had had a galvanizing effect upon the debate about intellectual property in the 1830s, so rapid improvements in electric technologies were to have a similarly drastic effect on ideas of intellectual ownership in the 1880s.

Since the Great Exhibition at mid-century, there had been profound changes in notions of origin. The exhibits in the Crystal Palace had silently posed questions about the feasibility of maintaining one stable point of origin for products in a technological age. Dickens had explored the possibility of originless narrative in *Bleak House*. Charles Darwin's work, published later in the decade, famously challenged the idea of the single origin of mankind, and posited instead a far more complex model of fusion and species-interdependence. Further work on genetics revealed the transmission of inherited characteristics through families, emphasizing the composite nature of the individual. By the end of the century, theories of the origin of ideas were also shifting, as a new interest in the workings of the unconscious mind, telepathy, and thought transference challenged the hitherto assumed boundaries of the rational individual. During the closing decades of the century a theory gained in currency that creative ideas were less the property of one individual consciousness, and more the unconscious product of the General Mind or *zeitgeist*, born out of the ether. The 'ether' became a powerful symbol in the late period for the shared unconscious, but the word was also used to refer to the 'raw' medium of electricity. Literary writers used electrical power to represent the power of telepathy or unconscious transmission, and Chapter 6 opens with a discussion of some of this popular fiction of the late century. While the idea of the ether fascinated writers, it also posed a new threat to theories of originality and individuality that they met by insisting on their property in ideas with redoubled vigour. In the debate over International Copyright in the 1870s and 1880s, writers were particularly anxious to ensure the continued control of their property overseas and after death.

The key patent issue in the 1880s and 1890s was electricity. Electricity is not an invention as such, it occurs naturally, so the debate

was not over the ownership of the power itself, but over the ownership of its applications. While patent law had traditionally put the
emphasis on the initial stages of invention, now the time-span of
patent protection became increasingly contentious, as rival electrical
companies competed to exploit new applications. The debate over
the point at which an invention should become freely public was
reignited by the municipal ownership of British electrical supply
systems in the 1880s, and the vicious patent wars over electrical
amenities and services in the 1880s and 1890s were fought out in
an international marketplace.

The debate over literary property shifted its focus in a similar way.
The International Copyright debate was less concerned with new
publication than with what happened to the notion of intellectual
property years, or even decades, after a new work had appeared. Not
only that, but it was also concerned with the ways in which publication could be controlled in a global marketplace, and most particularly, in North America.[80] Correspondingly, establishing 'originality'
became less important, particularly as new ideas about the congruity
of research and the intellectual ether challenged theories of solitary
inspiration and genius. 'Originality' in strict legal terms had always
been understood to refer to the mode in which an artwork was executed, rather than the raw ideas contained therein: at the end of the
nineteenth century that legal assumption became culturally 'true' for
the first time. In the 1880s and 1890s, originality was increasingly
perceived as subsisting in style rather than in matter, and from this
point on, writers worked harder at becoming self-conscious stylists
in order to innovate, and thereby to create property from the
common ether.

What has shifted in the debate about intellectual property, then,
since the mid-century, is not the construction of 'the original author',
which remains firmly entrenched as in all the previous debates, but
the emphasis on the role of legislation to *preserve*, rather than to establish, property. International Copyright was necessary to protect
literary property through long-distance transmissions and into an
ever more spatially dispersed future. The focus of the Parliamentary

---

[80] See N. N. Feltes, 'International Copyright: Structuring "the Condition of
Modernity" in British Publishing', in Martha Woodmansee and Peter Jaszi (eds.), *The
Construction of Authorship: Textual Appropriation in Law and Literature* (1994),
271–80, and Stephen Kern, *The Culture of Time and Space 1880–1918* (1983), 1.

Committee discussion of 1878 was no longer so much on the right to intellectual property, as on the means of its control.

The ever-growing global marketplace at the end of the nineteenth century made it difficult to imagine a public space that was not commercial.[81] As foreign markets opened up, it became more and more difficult for any writer to imagine that he or she was addressing a known constituency of readers. The open market often seemed just that: dangerously open and unknown. I argue that this was one of the reasons why international copyright protection was so important to British writers in the late century, and I take as an example Thomas Hardy, who made strong efforts to control the dissemination of his work not only over space, but also through time, even going so far as to ghost-write a biography of himself and arrange for it to appear after his death. And this preoccupation also makes itself visible in some of Hardy's novels of the late 1880s and early 1890s, discussed in Ch. 6, in which he ponders the present and future role of the artist in a decade that saw as much innovation in communications technologies as had the 1830s half a century before.

Finally, I argue that the preservation of the rights of the author in the international copyright laws at the end of the century does nothing to prove the inevitability of the Romantic model of creativity. Instead it was necessary to create and support a notion of individual identity at a time when the speed of dissemination and the increasing anonymity of consumption seemed to threaten the very notion of the free agency of the creative individual. As the division of labour and increased mechanization over the century made it more and more difficult to distinguish one originary source for any artwork, it became ever more important to insist upon the possibility of there being one. Through the six chapters of this book there runs a larger narrative about the determinants for the emergence of a modern definition of identity in a world increasingly contingent upon technology.

Structured as a series of close examinations of particular moments in the nineteenth century, starting with the 1830s, this book demonstrates how new constructions of identity emerged from a changing economy, and how perceptions of who might be in control of rapid social change also shifted during the period. According to Heidegger,

---

[81] See Miriam Hansen, 'Unstable Mixtures, Dilated Spheres: Negt and Kluge's *The Public Sphere and Experience*, Twenty Years Later', *Public Culture*, 5/2 (Winter, 1993), 179–212, 200.

the nineteenth and 'most ambiguous' century can 'never be understood by means of a description of the chronological succession of its periods. It must be demarcated and approached simultaneously from two sides.'[82] Although the organization of my chapters is broadly chronological, I am mindful of this caveat, and my intention is to show how ideas shifted back and forth during the period, rather than to trace any steady or continuous development. Intellectual property law was crucial throughout the nineteenth century to supporting a construction of the subject as a free, rational individual against the incursions of technology and global capital. My book asks what was invested in such an account of individual agency and how and why it was sustained against all the odds.

[82] Martin Heidegger, *Nietzsche*, vol i. *The Will to Power as Art*, trans. David Farrell Krell (1981), p. 85.

2

Property in Labour: Inventors and Writers in the 1830s and 1840s

Rise, Sons of Science and Invention, rise!
Make some new inroad on the starry skies;
Draw from the main some truths unknown before,
Rummage the strata, every nook explore.[1]

THE first Reform Bill passed on to the statute books in the summer of 1832. The working-class radical, and publisher of the *Weekly Free Press*, John Cleave, immediately responded by declaring at a meeting of the National Union of the Working Classes that, 'In every law which had been enacted for the last fifty years, property was the great object regarded . . . a war between labour and property had commenced.'[2] Indeed, the very issue of the franchise hinged on property ownership, and throughout the 1830s, many categories of property were coming under serious scrutiny.[3] In 1829 radical journalist Thomas Hodgskin had attributed the political turbulence of the time directly to the issue of property rights: 'the contest now going on in society, the preternatural throes and heavings which fitfully convulse it from one end to the other, arise exclusively and altogether from the right of property'.[4] What was crucially at stake from 1832 onwards

[1] Charles Tennyson, 'Phrenology', in Charles and Alfred Tennyson, *Poems by Two Brothers* (1827), 200–3, 202, lines 41–4.
[2] John Cleave, quoted in an account of a meeting on 18 June 1832 of the National Union of the Working Classes at the Mechanics' Institution on Theobald's Road, London. *Poor Man's Guardian* (23 June 1832), 435.
[3] Under the Reform Act of 1832, the qualification for Borough Franchise was the occupation, as either owner or tenant, of premises of the clear annual value of £10. This led to the phrase 'ten-pound householders'.
[4] [Thomas Hodgskin], *The Natural and Artificial Right of Property Contrasted. A Series of Letters, Addressed without Permission, to H. Brougham, Esq. MP, F.RS &c.*

was the question of how property representation could or should be defined. Was 'property' to be defined only as the ownership or occupation of real property, or land, or was there also a property in skill? Could a property in skill be individually owned, or was it a collective possession?[5] Throughout the nineteenth century, issues of property and ownership dominated legal and Parliamentary debates which were fundamental in laying down the foundations of the modern construction of democratic citizenship, and indeed, of nationhood.

In different ways, the definition of property underpinned some of the most important political debates that marked the 'upsurge of reform activity at the end of the 1820s'.[6] The 1830s saw extensive reform of the real property laws. In the same decade the anti-slavery campaigners were arguing for the limits of property—and that no man should own another.[7] And the strenuous debate over native title in South Australia, for example, at the Colonial Office, revolved around the question of whether the Aborigine people had a right to ownership of the land because they had laboured on it for generations. Thomas Fowell Buxton MP moved from campaigning for the abolition of slavery to campaigning for the rights of indigenous peoples, and, particularly, for aboriginal landrights, protesting that, 'It might be presumed that the native inhabitants of any land have an incontrovertible right to their own soil: a plain and sacred right, however, which seems not to have been understood.'[8] This debate raised important domestic questions about how far the British working classes could be considered to 'own' their nation if they were to be denied the property rights that were vital to a sense of citizenship in a democracy.

The two debates with which this chapter is most concerned, the patent and the copyright debates, both centred on the conflict

(Now the Lord Chancellor) by the Author of 'Labour Defended Against the Claims of Capital' (1832), p. i.

[5] John Rule has argued that '[i]t is fundamental that the property of skill was not viewed as an individual property right, but as a collective one.' John Rule, 'The Property of Skill in the Period of Manufacture', in *The Historical Meanings of Work*, ed. Patrick Joyce (1987), 99–118, 111.

[6] See I. J. Prothero, *Artisans and Politics in Early Nineteenth-Century London: John Gast and his Times* (1979), 272.

[7] Miles Taylor points out that the tactic of direct petitioning of Parliament used by the anti-slavery campaigners influenced the tactics of later radicals. Miles Taylor, *The Decline of British Radicalism, 1847–1860* (1995), 9.

[8] Thomas Fowell Buxton, *British Parliamentary Papers* (1837), 5. Quoted in Henry Reynolds, *The Law of the Land* (1992), 85.

between a perceived 'natural' and 'incontrovertible' right of property on the part of inventors and writers in their own productions, and the economic imperative of the marketplace and the national economy, which demanded that such 'unalienable' property be made alienable and ceded to public use. The challenge, in the case both of copyright and patent protection, was to forge an acceptable compromise between these two terms. In both debates, pro-protection campaigners placed high values upon 'originality' and 'national utility': but when a Romantic construction of the individual was pulled into stark confrontation with the exigencies of an emerging modern state, too often 'utility' and 'originality' seemed to be stubbornly incommensurate terms. Campaigners invested the debate with ideological and political meanings that necessarily obstructed any straightforward economic analysis or solution.

These two debates, over the rights of authors and the rights of inventors, shadowed each other throughout the first half of the nineteenth century, as I shall show. Sergeant Talfourd's repeated failure from 1837 to get a copyright bill through the Commons that protected the property of the author rather than that of the publisher, ran alongside similarly failed attempts to reform the patent law to offer affordable and accessible protection for the intellectual property of mechanical inventors. Although these two campaigns were motivated by completely different constituencies, and represented different and often opposed class interests, when a particular rhetorical strategy appeared successful for one group, the other lost no time in borrowing it. The two interest groups, of mechanics and of writers, frequently made rhetorical appeals to each other, often in terms of the perceived superiority of the legal title of the other to ownership of intellectual labour. This chapter shows that the debates were, in fact, far more influential upon one another than has previously been acknowledged. The confused and contradictory rhetoric generated by the two campaigns, for copyright and patent protection, bespeaks the fluid and unfixed relationship of 'new' forms of labour to property and social status. Ultimately, the work of redefining 'creativity' in a technological and increasingly democratic age led both backwards and forwards to perhaps the most fundamental and contentious question of the period: the question that J. S. Mill was to pose famously in his 1859 essay, 'On Liberty': what exactly were 'the nature and limits of the power which can be legitimately exercised by society over the individual?'[9] To whom did the new invention or the new book belong? And, if ownership was to be divided, what portion was the property of the inventor or the author, and what portion was the property of the British public?

This chapter explores the discursive relationship between writers and inventors in the 1830s and 1840s, and suggests reasons for the endurance and—indeed—the strengthening of the myth of genius and exceptionality as machine culture began in earnest to remake the ways in which people worked, lived, produced, and consumed. It explores the ways in which certain kinds of work, inventing and writing among them, were reconstructed as unalienated: how work was made to become pleasure. New technologies just coming into use guaranteed a proliferation of both machines and texts, which made questions of ownership and regulation appear peculiarly urgent at this time, and controls were considered necessary, not only to protect the originator, but also to ensure and enable growth for both the engineering and the literary sectors, both of which were struggling to assume 'professional' identities. Clifford Siskin traces to the turn of the nineteenth century, 'the purchase of writing on professionalization—its increased use both in particular occupations and in representing the value of those occupations to society'.[10] And it is to writing and texts that I now turn: the debates over intellectual property charted in this chapter are symptomatic of this process of professionalization that depended—in both cases—upon increased accessibility to the technology of printing, and upon increasing expectations of literacy. The results were more readers and critics for 'literature', and newly codified vocational education systems, which relied more and more on 'paper' qualifications in engineering.

My discussion attempts to reconstruct from this largely lost debate some of the contemporary anxieties about what kind of people were to be permitted to hold intellectual property in an avowedly democratic age. The next chapter takes the discussion on to mid-century, and to the 1851 Great Exhibition, where the conflict between

[9] J. S. Mill, 'On Liberty', in *Utilitarianism, on Liberty, Considerations of Representative Government* (1993), 69.
[10] Siskin, *The Work of Writing*, 130. Percy Shelley had argued that '[t]he production and assurance of pleasure in [the] highest sense is true utility', claiming that it would be 'an error to assert that the finest passages of poetry are produced by labour and study'. P. B. Shelley, 'A Defence of Poetry', in *Complete Works* (1930), vii. 109–40, 135–6.

individual creativity and mass manufacture was put on public display, and began to be publicly and widely debated. But to understand
more precisely how the complexities of such issues were already accruing throughout the early Victorian period, we need to turn to the
popular periodical press, and particularly to the debate in the 1830s
over patent protection for inventors.

INVENTORS IN THE PENNY PRESS OF THE 1830S

The Inventors of Britain—these are the true nobles of the land, the best
benefactors of their own country. 'Nelson and the Nile'—'Wellington and
Waterloo'—may be sounds agreeable enough to martial ears; but to those
who delight to cultivate the arts of social life, who rejoice in the contemplation of whatever adds to our store of pure and peaceful enjoyments, 'Watt
and the Steam-Engine'—'Arkwright and the Spinning-Machine'—are associations that will ever recur to their minds with much deeper and livelier feelings of gratitude and veneration. The engineers and mechanics are the true
bones and sinews of the nation.[11]

[T]he poor but ingenious artizan, the main agent of that [British] superiority,
[who] should of all classes be the most unfriended and unprotected . . . ineffectually struggling to display [his] talents, and doomed to poverty and misery by [his] efforts to render them available . . . [D]awning genius, shackled
by the oppressive bonds of poverty . . . But this is no child of the imagination—this is no overdrawn role, dressed out in mimic misery, to work upon
the feelings—but alas! the feeble outline only of but too truly existing
reality.[12]

These quotations, which come from cheap and popular periodicals
published in 1836 and 1825 respectively, are typical of the two
extremes of representation which persist throughout nineteenth-
century writing, both fictional and non-fictional, about the inventor.
On the one hand he is heroic, replacing Nelson and Wellington as the
embodiment of national agency and glory. And, in their turn, the inventors of periodical and popular science texts are powerful social
agents too, capable of inducing major social transformations: 'the

---

[11] Anon., 'The Mechanics' Almanac for 1837', *Mechanics' Magazine* (3 December
1836), 170–1, 170.
[12] Anon., 'On the Necessity and the Means of Protecting Needy Genius', *The
London Journal of Arts and Sciences*, 9 (1825), 308–19, 308–12.

few master-spirits thrown at distant intervals by God among mankind' (1842);[13] 'the greatest benefactors of the human race' (1894);[14] and 'the apostles of human progress' (1897).[15] Yet at the same time, and often in the very same texts, the inventor is a poor 'visionary' and a 'lunatic' and also a 'victim'. '[T]he miserable victim of his own powerful genius' (1825);[16] '[t]he poor, honest, industrious, and hard-working mechanic', and 'the poor, honest, unprotected genius' (1827);[17] 'a martyrology of modern inventors' (1847);[18] '[m]eritorious but unfortunate' (1859);[19] 'Martyrs of Science' (1860)[20] who have 'sad, simple histories' (1861);[21] 'alone, unfriended, solitary, slow' (1861);[22] 'martyr-inventors' (1886);[23] 'poor clever inventor[s]' (1897);[24] 'suffering neglect and persecution' (1897).[25] Inventors are defined by their class position, although also by their solitariness, and seen as unable to effect change of any sort. In fact, they are 'very nearly lunatics . . . the poor inventor has always been regarded as a visionary and a madman, rather than a benefactor to his country' (1879).[26] All these quotations are taken from cheap texts and periodicals published between 1827 and 1897. For at least seventy years, the popular representation of the inventor does not materially change: he remains both hero and victim. Looking back to the decade of the first Reform Bill, I suggest that this stereotype of the inventor emerges in the 1830s in response to a par-

---

[13] [Archibald Alison], 'The Copyright Question', *Blackwoods Edinburgh Magazine*, 51 (January 1842), 107–21, 109. Although the article is about literary copyright, examples of 'master-spirits' significantly include Newton and Watt.

[14] H. D. Fitzpatrick, *Patents for Inventions* ([1894]), 3.

[15] W. H. Baraclough, *Profit by Patents* (1897), 14.

[16] Anon., 'On Protecting Needy Genius', *The London Journal of Arts and Sciences*, 9 (1825), 308–19, 316. This refers to the inventor, James Cross, 'an humble mechanic' who died in penury (313).

[17] A.B., A Member of the Ennis Mechanics' Institute, Letter to the Editor, 'The Patent Laws', *Mechanics' Magazine* (26 May 1827), 324–7, both quotations at 324.

[18] Gardissal, 'Inventors and Inventions' [trans. from *La Presse*], *Mechanics' Magazine* (27 February 1847), 200–3, 201.

[19] Gilbert J. French, *The Life and Times of Samuel Crompton, Inventor of the Spinning Machine called the Mule. Being the Substance of Two Papers read to Members of the Bolton Mechanics' Institution* (1859), 106.

[20] John Timbs, FSA, *Stories of Inventors and Discoverers* (1860), p. viii. Timbs was helped in compiling this book by Bennett Woodcroft.

[21] J. Hamilton Fyfe, 'Preface', *The Triumphs of Invention and Discovery* (1861), p. v.

[22] Ibid.   [23] James Burnley, *The Romance of Invention* (1886), 44.

[24] Ibid. 11.   [25] Ibid. 14.

[26] Anon., 'Report of a speech by Admiral Selwyn to the Inventors' Institute', *Inventor's Record and Industrial Guardian*, 1/1 (15 March 1879), p. 1.

ticular and very specific historical and political moment, and not, as has too often been previously assumed, as the effluvia of a vague Victorian discourse of 'progress'.

Economic historians and historians of science writing about inventors have tended to pay scant attention to the 1830s. Both Robert Fox and Christine MacLeod, for example, focus on the period following the Patent Amendment Act of 1852, missing the importance of the four Parliamentary attempts to reformulate patent legislation between 1820 and 1835.[27] And William Cornish does not even mention the 1830s in his review of the historical development of the patent system.[28] In purely legislative terms, it is true that little happened. But that was partly the result of the complex tangle of conflicting interests that failed to find any balanced agreement through the debates on the bills that fell. If we look only at successful legislation, perhaps particularly in the case of intellectual property law, we are in danger of seeing only pragmatic political solutions and missing the powerful debates that preceded them. This is where periodicals become invaluable in helping to reconstruct the 'lost' debate of the late 1820s and 1830s.[29]

The representation of the inventor in the Victorian press in and after the 1830s was crucially entangled in other debates about intellectual property—dramatic copyright, lectures, and also the controversial six Literary Copyright Bills that were introduced between 1837 and 1842. The analogies between different forms of intellectual property were contentious and the close proximity of the patent discussion to the first Reform Act of 1832 made the discussion particularly tense in class terms, placing the rhetorical focus very clearly on the working man and the ownership of his labour. It is striking that, in this period, the inventor is almost always represented as working class and male. The 1820s and 1830s were very unsettled years. The vast drain on the national income of the Napoleonic Wars had left Britain, for all her much-vaunted supremacy, in poor eco-

---

[27] Christine MacLeod, 'James Watt, Heroic Invention and the Idea of the Industrial Revolution', in Maxine Berg and Kristine Bruland (eds.), *Technological Revolutions in Europe: Historical Perspectives* (1998), 96–116. In this useful article, MacLeod claims James Watt was the first example of the popular 'heroic' inventor, but in this chapter I hope to show that the 'heroism' of nineteenth-century inventors deserves a more sustained analysis than she offers. Robert Fox, 'Introduction', *Technological Change: Methods and Themes in the History of Technology* (1998), 1–15, 15.

[28] W. R. Cornish, 'The British Patent System: Historical Development', *Intellectual Property: Patents, Trade Marks and Allied Rights* (1999), 110–17.

[29] For further discussion of the figure of the inventor in the 1850s, see Ch. 3.

nomic shape. Working-class living standards began to stagnate in the early part of the nineteenth century because sluggish productivity—itself due to the incomplete and slow shift to industrial mechanization—failed adequately to meet the needs of an increasing population.[30] A policy of consumption-linked taxation contributed to the depression of both domestic and export markets. Only after 1850 did the industrial revolution and a raft of legal reforms genuinely begin to raise the living standards of the working people. In fact, in 1826 a sharp economic depression put severe pressure on working men, further diminishing opportunities for self-education. Proposals to extend the franchise bitterly divided Westminster and, consequently, any representation of the working-class man was vulnerable to political appropriation and manipulation.

The inventor seems to have offered a site upon which the class fantasies of different, and often opposed, interest groups could be projected. He could represent either working-class obedience or working-class resistance. He could also be used to allay fears about mechanization and the consequent deskilling of the elite artisan class. As the introduction of machines began to threaten the skilled workforce, a representation that could be turned around to dramatize working-class ownership of labour lent itself well to middle-class commentaries upon industrialization that looked for ways of palliating working-class discontent.

The *Penny Magazine* tells us that 'inventions were all, or nearly all, originated by working men', and *Chambers's Edinburgh Magazine* even goes so far as to suggest that being poor is a prerequisite to becoming an inventor, '[s]ince it appears . . . that so large a proportion of distinguished men were poor at the beginning, a question may naturally arise, are not men just the more apt, on that account, to become eminent?'[31] Inventors are represented as poor even when

---

[30] Charles Feinstein, 'Pessimism Perpetuated: Real Wages and the Standard of Living in Britain during and after the Industrial Revolution', in *Journal of Economic History*, 58/3 (September 1998), 625–58. See also R. C. O. Matthews, C. H. Feinstein, and J. C. Odling-Smee (eds.), *British Economic Growth, 1856–1973* (1982).

[31] Anon., 'Necessity the Mother of Invention', *Penny Magazine* (23 June 1832), 114–15, 115. This quotation refers particularly to the invention of lace machinery in Nottingham, but the point is also a general one. It was, significantly, only men that were included in this discussion. Michael Hancher has speculated that 'there is not much evidence that the *Penny Magazine* appealed to female readers', suggesting that it was the cheap periodicals set up in the mid-1840s, such as the *London Journal*, *Reynolds Magazine*, and *Reynolds Miscellany* which targeted a female readership. Michael Hancher, 'From Street Ballad to Penny Magazine: March of Intellect in the

they were not—James Watt's father, for example, ran a prosperous mathematical instruments business. In the 1830s, inventors were most often figured as 'mechanics'. Mechanics were already perceived by the middle-class press as a problematic subgroup of the working-class 'mass'. As G. W. Roderick and M. D. Stephens put it:

among the labouring masses there emerged a distinctive class of its own to form an aristocracy among the industrial workers. This was the 'artisan' or 'mechanic'. These were set apart from the others by their skills and expertise. They were not only the natural leaders in a technical sense but also in a political sense—the natural forms of radical dissent and political organisation.[32]

Even in the early 1820s, the artisan-mechanics were developing into this elite and skilled group. In 1824, Alexander Galloway, an engineer, remarked upon the 'strong desire [that] is now felt, among the working mechanics, for the acquirement of scientific knowledge to forward them in their labour'.[33] Artisans and mechanics, then, represented a particular problem for the middle-class commentator. On the one hand they were the 'virtuous' working-class, hungry for knowledge and 'rational' pursuits, on the other, the growing literacy and politicization of this group made its very rationality potentially threatening to the status quo.[34] But industrialization was also demonstrating how important mechanical ingenuity was to Britain's

Butchering Line', in Laurel Brake, Bill Bell, and David Finkelstein (eds.), *Nineteenth-Century Media and the Construction of Identities* (2000), 93–103, 98. Anon., 'Advancement in Life', *Chambers's Edinburgh Journal* (27 October 1832), 317.

[32] G. W. Roderick and M. D. Stephens, 'Mechanics' Institutes and the State', in Ian Inkster (ed.), *The Steam Intellect Societies—Essays on Culture, Education and Industry circa 1820–1914* (1985), 60–72, 61. See also Maxine Berg, *The Machinery Question and the Making of Political Economy 1815–1848* (1980); J. F. C. Harrison, *Learning and Living, 1790–1960; A Study in the History of the English Adult Education Movement* (1961); David Vincent, *Literacy and Popular Culture: England 1750–1914* (1989); Mabel Tylecote, *The Mechanics Institutes of Yorkshire and Lancashire before 1851* (1957); J. W. Hudson, *The History of Adult Education* (1851/1969). John Rule defines the term 'artisan' in Britain as describing 'those who through apprenticeship or its equivalent had come to possess a skill in a particular craft and the right to exercise it'. Rule, 'The Property of Skill', 102.

[33] Anon., 'Evidence of Alexander Galloway', Abstracted Report of the Select Committee of the House of Commons, on the Exportation of Machinery and Artizans, *London Journal of Arts and Sciences*, 9 (1825), 101–6, 104.

[34] This is a very general view. Ian Inkster has made the valuable point that there is such regional diversity in adult education and the status of mechanics in the nineteenth century, that it is dangerous to attempt to draw too many generalized conclusions, or to attempt to view this as a 'movement'. Ian Inkster, 'Introduction: The Context of Steam Intellect in Britain (to 1851)', in *The Steam Intellect Societies* (1985), 3–19.

national prestige and wealth, and it was not easy to ignore the contribution of the skilled labouring class. 'The prosperity of nations depends on nothing more than the encouragement of the inventive powers of individuals' as the *Saturday Magazine* put it.[35] As a representative of the elite of the working class, the inventor in popular texts is a remarkably rich contemporary example of the difficulties of representing an industrialized working-class subject in the early nineteenth century. But in this chapter, I am more interested in the ways in which a model of disenfranchised creativity emerged from this particular debate. For it was just this model that was to exert a significant influence upon the debate about literary property in the 1840s and through the 1850s.

In the pages of the Reform penny periodicals of the early 1830s, '[b]iographies of Men who have had a permanent influence on the condition of the world' and tales of artisan-inventors recast as heroes, afforded a pleasing liberal fantasy of working-class perseverance and self-control, alongside the insistent reinscription of social impotence.[36] These dichotomous representations of inventors reveal the ambivalence of the periodicals towards their readership. Reform penny periodicals were published by middle-class publishers, such as William Chambers, whose *Chambers's Edinburgh Journal* was established, in his own words as 'food of the best kind' to supply the 'universal appetite for instruction', or the radical Whig, Lord Brougham's, Society for the Diffusion of Useful Knowledge (SDUK), which set up the *Penny Magazine* in 1832 with a similar aim, to 'curtail [. . .] the circulation of a class of cheap publications offensive to morals, and even to common decency' by 'introducing, and stimulating the introduction by others, into quarters where books had hardly penetrated, of both literature and art'.[37] But how far into

[35] Anon., 'Encouragement of Inventions', *Saturday Magazine* (18 June 1825), 171–3, 172.

[36] Anon., 'Preface to Volume 1', *Penny Magazine of the Society for the Diffusion of Useful Knowledge* (18 December 1832), pp. iii–iv, iii (unpaginated).

[37] Lord Brougham is described by the *Dictionary of National Biography* as an energetic and ambitious man, somewhat given to self-aggrandisement, who campaigned fiercely for popular education and Parliamentary Reform: 'Since 1820 the subject of education had occupied much of his attention. In conjunction with Dr. Birkbeck, he helped to set on foot various mechanics' institutes. In 1825 he published his "Observations on the Education of the People", which before the end of the year had reached its twentieth edition. In this pamphlet . . . he proposed a plan for the publication of cheap and useful works, which he carried out by the formation of the Society for the Diffusion of Useful Knowledge.' Brougham was made Lord Chancellor in 1830. Leslie Stephen and Sidney Lee (eds.), *The Dictionary of National Biography*, ii.

these quarters did the publications of the Reform penny press finally penetrate? The *Penny Magazine*'s claim to a working-class readership was singled out for particular scepticism.[38] William Chambers suggested that the 'treatises of the Society . . . were purchased and read chiefly by persons considerably removed from the obligation of toiling with their hands for their daily bread'.[39]

The radical penny press had more credible claims to a working-class readership in this period. Thomas Hodgskin, founding editor of the *Mechanics' Magazine* in 1823, disparaged the interventionist agenda of the SDUK. Hodgskin was a Radical with considerable influence, the driving force behind the foundation of the London Mechanics' Institute, and editor of *Hansard's Parliamentary Reports*

Beal-Browell (n.d.), 1361. The Society for the Diffusion of Useful Knowledge was established in 1826 and dissolved in 1846. Alongside its *Library of Useful Knowledge* and the companion *Library of Entertaining Knowledge*, the Society published the *Cyclopaedias, or Atlas of General Maps*, the *Penny Cyclopaedia*, *A Manual for Mechanics' Institutes*, and the *Penny Magazine*. The disastrously low sales of the first volumes of the *Biographical Dictionary* dealt a death blow to the Society. [William Chambers], 'The Editor's Address to his Readers', *Chambers's Edinburgh Journal* (11 February 1832), 1–2, 1 (unpaginated). Chambers also produced best-selling encyclopaedias, almanacs, manuals of etiquette and self-improvement, and the like. See Patrick Brantlinger, *Spirit of Reform: British Literature and Politics, 1832–1867* (1977), 19–21. Anon., *Address of the Committee of the Society for the Diffusion of Useful Knowledge* (1846), 15. Price one penny, published every Saturday, the *Penny Magazine* had an average of eight printed pages and approximately four small engravings per issue. This debate resembles the earlier *Lesedebatte* in Germany which Martha Woodmansee discusses in ch. 4 of her *The Author, Art, and the Market*.

[38] The SDUK reports that its books have been read, 'from the cottage to the mansion. As many individuals as there are in the country who can read, so many are there who have seen and used some of the works which the Society has put forth.' Anon., *Address of the Committee*, 17. There is some evidence that working men did find the time and the concentration to read the SDUK's publications: Charles Knight, the publisher for the Society, quotes Christopher Thomson's *Autobiography of an Artisan* of 1847 as one example: 'Knight had unfurled his paper banners of free trade in letters. The "Penny Magazine" was published—I borrowed the first volume . . . [in order to afford the second volume] I determined to discontinue the use of sugar in my tea . . . and I looked as anxiously for the issue of the monthly part as I did for the means of getting a living.' Christopher Thomson, *The Autobiography of an Artisan* (1847), 319, quoted in Charles Knight, *Passages of a Working Life During Half a Century: The Second Epoch*, ii (1864), 183. How far Thomson's experience is typical is doubtful, however.

[39] William Chambers, *Memoir of Robert Chambers with Autobiographic Reminiscences of William Chambers* (1872), 229–30. But Chambers is also sceptical about the general success of '[t]he scheme of diffusing knowledge': 'the great end has not yet been gained', he admits in 1832. [William Chambers], 'The Editor's Address to his Readers', *Chambers's Edinburgh Magazine* (11 February 1832), 1–2, 1 (unpaginated).

from 1834 to 1837.[40] He complained that the Society's Committee was politically 'all so much of *one side*' (emphasis original) and warned of its monopolizing potential as a '[j]oint-stock association [. . .] for the supply of knowledge'.[41] The unstamped penny press was, predictably enough, even fiercer in its criticism. Henry Hetherington's *Poor Man's Guardian* of 1832, for example, viciously attacked the *Penny Magazine*:

week after week, the work is published containing a pack of nonsensical tittle tattle about forks and spoons, and smock frocks, bridges, waterfalls, and a thousand other things, no doubt entertaining enough, but to the poor and ignorant utterly useless. . . . Do we ever find these gentlemen penny writers say a word against the injustice suffered by the labouring poor? No.[42]

---

[40] Thomas Hodgskin (1787–1869) was, in fact, closely involved in Brougham's earlier project of the foundation of a Mechanics' Institute in London. He wrote the initial manifesto for the London Mechanics' Institute, declaring that, 'Men had better be without education . . . than be educated by their rulers; for then education is the mere breaking of the steer to the yoke.' Unreferenced quotation in Thomas Kelly, *A History of Adult Education in Great Britain from the Middle Ages to the Twentieth Century* (1992), 121. Hodgskin's writings are said to have influenced Karl Marx.

[41] Anon., 'Diffusion of Useful Knowledge', *Mechanics' Magazine* (Saturday, 5 May 1827), 194–200, 195 and 197. It was true that government sanctioned these publications: 'the "Penny" and "Saturday" magazines' and, indeed, the 'Mechanics' Magazine', were cited by name in the report of a House of Commons Select Committee of 1836 appointed to look into extending skills in the useful arts and design among British people '(especially the manufacturing population)'. The Committee clearly felt that they were effective organs of technological education: 'Such instruments may be said to form the paper-circulation of knowledge.' Anon., 'Report of the Select Committee Appointed to Inquire into the Best Means of Extending a Knowledge of the Arts and of the Principles of Design Among the People (especially the manufacturing population) of the Country; also to Inquire into the Constitution, Management, and Effects of Institutions Connected with the Arts', *Mechanics' Magazine* (19 November 1836), 120–44, all quotations at 123 (Special Supplement, price 6d.).

[42] Anon., 'Penny Magazine', *The Poor Man's Guardian. A Weekly Newspaper for the People* (4 August 1832), 486. Henry Hetherington was imprisoned three times for issuing this weekly newspaper in 1831 in contravention of the 'news tax'. Hetherington was not alone in his dislike of the educational aims of the liberal middle class: the *Poor Man's Advocate and People's Library* agrees that, 'These teachers seem to imagine, that it is of much more consequence to the working man to understand the "theory of the winds," which it is impossible he can control, than the theory of government, which can render him either happy or miserable.' Anon., 'Mechanics' Hall of Science', *Poor Man's Advocate and People's Library*, 6, Manchester (25 February 1832) [price 1d.], 43–5, 43. And a leader writer in the *Chartist Circular* in 1841 protests: 'These wiseacres would have no objection to our becoming members of Mechanics' Institutions. They would freely permit us to enter the portals of science, providing they could be assured that we would not appropriate to ourselves any of the benefits a knowledge of those sciences are calculated to confer.' Anon., 'Power and Advantages of Knowledge', *Chartist Circular*, Glasgow (23 October 1841), 453.

This makes it all the more surprising that the representations of inventors seem so similar in Radical and Reform journals alike. The *Chartist Circular*'s cry for 'a Radical Literary Reform' because '[h]istory does not condescend to extol the virtuous poor: it only venerates kings, priests, and generals,' seems to echo *Chambers's*, in 1832: 'No mistake could perhaps be greater than to suppose that we only can take an interest in the sorrows of very lofty and distinguished characters. Yet . . . how exclusively, for many ages, have poets confined their efforts to the tragedies of high historic life!'[43] The meeting at which a national monument to James Watt was planned was reported in detail both in the *Mechanics' Magazine* and the SDUK's *Penny Magazine*, and both promoted Watt as a national icon.[44] And as early as 1823, the *Mechanics' Magazine* was trying to elevate inventors to the status of biography, recognizing that the mechanical arts, 'still bear, even when their importance is acknowledged, part of the stigma attached to the vices and debased state of their first professors'.[45] With '[e]xamples like this of James Watt, combining great moral dignity with great skill and great attachment to the mechanic arts', the editors hoped to illustrate the moral worth of the engineers.[46] And this comment on the life of the mechanic, James Sandy, in the *Mechanics' Magazine* could equally have come from the pages of the *Penny Magazine*: 'From this brief history of James Sandy we may learn this very instructive lesson, that no difficulties are too great to be overcome by industry and perseverance, and that genius . . . will seldom fail to secure, unless by its own fault, competence and respectability.'[47] Yet biography performs very different ideological work in these journals. The Reform press is always careful to articulate limits. Even while assuring its readers that '[w]e believe there is hardly a condition, however low, from which a young man of good principles and unceasing industry may not elevate himself', it is also 'of course, not to be expected that *many* poor men should become rich; nor ought any man to set his heart on being so,' because 'if any

[43] Anon., 'Literary Reform', *Chartist Circular* (30 January 1841), 299. Anon., 'Annals of the Poor', *Chambers's Edinburgh Journal* (12 May 1832), 115–16, 115.
[44] Anon., 'Report of Meeting held to discuss Monument to the Late James Watt', *Mechanics' Magazine* (26 June 1824), 242–9. Anon., 'James Watt', *Penny Magazine* (31 August 1832), 209 (unpaginated).
[45] Anon., 'Memoir of James Watt, the Great Improver of the Steam-Engine', *Mechanics' Magazine* (30 August 1823), 1–5, 2.
[46] Ibid.
[47] Anon., 'Extraordinary Bed-ridden Mechanic', *Mechanics' Magazine* (5 June 1824), 167.

considerable number of such persons were to arise, their utility and their distinction would be diminished'.[48] The Reform press mystifies the difference between alienated and unalienated labour, by insisting both on the inventor's natural right to his inventions, *and* on the benefits of a machine culture in which the artisan's labour is the property of his employer. The representation of the artisan is, thus, involved in a fantasy of non-alienated labour (invention) while he is simultaneously up to his neck in alienated labour (in the 'shop' or factory).

In contrast, by fighting for property rights for the mechanic in the 1820s and 1830s, the Radical press and the technical journals were fighting for a more inclusive democracy, while also pointing to the contradictions inherent in the middle-class image of the working man. For these writers, the 'artisan republic', which traditionally sustained the move from apprentice to master, controlled competition, and protected craft and creative independence was threatened by an emerging economic orthodoxy that was intent upon the profit-maximizing pursuit of the best technique, at the expense of deskilling. In these journals, the inventor comes to represent the radical potential of the working class, and the importance of winning better property rights and status for that class. British artisan-radicals were early to use Lockean rhetoric in claiming ownership of their labour and 'knowledge'. In 1802, for example, shipwright artisan John Gast declared that, 'The produce of his labor [*sic*], to the mechanic, is surely as much an estate of inheritance to him, as the right of ownership over a large tract of land, is to its lordly proprietor.'[49] The evidence suggests that very few of the mechanics of the 1830s and 1840s were, in fact, the authors of what economists term 'macro-inventions'.[50] Although Charles Knight's 1831 *Results of Machinery*, published under the superintendence of the SDUK, devotes itself entirely to celebrating the 'inventions that constitute the power of civilization', David Vincent states categorically that in the early 1830s, the incidence of working-class invention was 'at a

---

[48] Anon., 'The Value of a Penny', *Penny Magazine of the Society for the Diffusion of Useful Knowledge* (21 April 1832), 62. Anon., 'Rich and Poor', *Saturday Magazine* (19 January 1833), 21. Anon., 'Advancement in Life', *Chambers's Edinburgh Journal* (27 October 1832), 317.

[49] John Gast, *Calumny Defeated: Or, A Compleat Vindication of the Conduct of the Working Shipwrights, during the Late Disputes with their Employers* (Deptford 1802), p. 9. Quoted in I. J. Prothero, *Artisans and Politics* (1979), 87.

[50] See Clare Pettitt, 'Working-Class Heroes: Inventors in the Penny Press, 1820–1840', forthcoming.

nadir'.[51] The names that recur throughout the pages of these magazines are, like Watt, all names from previous generations: Galileo;[52]
Newton;[53] Arkwright;[54] Watt;[55] Boyle;[56] Smeaton;[57] Telford;[58]
Crompton;[59] Davy;[60] Palissy;[61] Fulton.[62] Readers in the early 1830s
might have felt that most of these subjects, if not contemporary, were
at least within living memory, but by mid-century, the Watts,
Stephensons, Arkwrights, and Cromptons were already representa-

[51] Charles Knight, *The Working-Man's Companion. The Results of Machinery,
Namely, Cheap Production and Increased Employment, Exhibited: Being an Address
to the Working-Men of the United Kingdom* (1831), 25. Richard D. Altick records
that Knight's book sold 50,000 copies. Richard D. Altick, *The English Common
Reader: A Social History of the Mass Reading Public 1800–1900* (1967), 390. See also
Anon., 'Sir George Head's Home-Tour in the Manufacturing Districts', *Mechanics'
Magazine* (1 April 1831), 505–9. David Vincent, *Bread, Knowledge and Freedom: A
Study of Nineteenth-Century Working-Class Autobiography* (1981), 148. Evidence
given in the Select Committee on Patent Law in 1829 supports this view. Walter Henry
Wyatt, editor of the *Repertory*, which published copies of patent specifications, when
asked, 'Has the number of patents increased of late years?' replied, 'They increased
during that period when everything was alive, but at the present moment they have decreased very much.' 'Patents for Inventions; Report from Select Committee on the
Law Relative to Patents for Inventions. Ordered by House of Commons to be Printed
12 June 1829', *Reports from Committees 1829*, i. 415–676, 518. Sidney Pollard
agrees that '[t]he number of genuinely self-taught geniuses was remarkably small, in
spite of the large space they occupy in the literature'. Sidney Pollard, *The Genesis of
Modern Management: A Study of the Industrial Revolution in Great Britain* (1965),
104.
[52] Anon., 'Galileo', *Saturday Magazine* (16 February 1833), 59.
[53] Anon., 'Sir Isaac Newton', *Mechanics' Magazine* (28 October 1826), 411–13,
413. Anon., 'Sir Isaac Newton', *Saturday Magazine* (14 July 1832), 14. 'M.',
'National Statues. No. VII. Sir Isaac Newton', *Saturday Magazine* (26 December
1835), 241–3. Anon., 'The Week—Anniversary of Death of Isaac Newton', *Penny
Magazine* (22 December 1832), 375.
[54] Anon., 'The Late Mr. Arkwright', *Chambers's Edinburgh Journal* (1 July 1843),
192.
[55] Anon., 'Memoir of James Watt, the Great Improver of the Steam Engine',
Mechanics' Magazine (30 August, 1823), 1–5. Anon., 'James Watt from Arago's
Life of Watt', *Saturday Magazine* (4 February 1843), 46. Anon., 'Biographic Sketches:
James Watt', *Chambers's Edinburgh Journal* (24 March 1832), 61–2. Anon., 'Arago's
Life of Watt', *Chambers's Edinburgh Journal* (26 October 1839), 317–18.
[56] Anon., 'Robert Boyle', *Saturday Magazine* (9 March 1833), 91.
[57] Anon., 'The Eddystone Lighthouse', *Penny Magazine* (28 July 1832), 163.
Anon., 'Smeaton', *Saturday Magazine* (17 October 1835), 148.
[58] Anon., 'Biographic Sketches: Thomas Telford', *Chambers's Edinburgh Journal*
(21 February 1835), 29–30.
[59] Anon., 'Samuel Crompton, Inventor of the Spinning Mule', *Mechanics'
Magazine* (14 July 1827), 446.
[60] Anon., 'Sir Humphry Davy', *Mechanics' Magazine* (13 June 1828), 279.
[61] Anon., 'The Independent Potter', *Mechanics' Magazine* (30 August 1823), 12.
[62] Anon., 'Disappointments of the Authors of Important Inventions', *Penny
Magazine* (14 April 1832), 19.

tives of another age. In fact, from the mid-1820s, mechanics were feeling the pressure of an unregulated competitive market and the resultant job insecurity as never before. In towns, factory workers were increasingly regimented in unprecedented ways, and skilled labour was divided into disarticulated tasks, which, despite the best efforts of the middle-class commentators to persuade them otherwise, were clearly detrimental to any sense of ownership of the manufacturing process. Under these precarious conditions, it is not greatly surprising that the mechanics of the 1830s and 1840s did not introduce innovations and improvements with the same facility as their fathers' generation had done before them.[63] Yet the terms 'artisan', 'mechanic', and 'inventor' are very confused in this period in both the Reform and the Radical press. The foundational myths of the great inventors seem to have been as popular with the artisans themselves as they were with the Reform press, because they afforded ready examples both of original working-class genius and of the ungainsayable national utility of mechanical engineering.

Joel Mokyr, writing about the industrial revolution, points out that 'In general, much of the popular literature is concerned with the great breakthroughs (macro-inventions), whereas economists seem widely agreed that most productivity gains are generated by the smaller improvements (micro-inventions).'[64] If identification of a single inventor for the 'macro-inventions' is so difficult, and if it is the small improvements that really make a difference, why do the popular publications of the 1830s and 1840s insist on telling and retelling the narratives of macro-inventions? Paul Theerman has argued that this literary trend was born out of 'times of intense political, social, and economic dislocation in Britain and the United States. A simple and direct response was to turn to the heroism of the past to help secure the future and define the present.'[65] I would argue that, rather

---

[63] See Thomas Kelly, *A History of Adult Education in Great Britain* (1992). Kelly draws attention to the shift in the meaning of 'mechanic' from the 1820s onwards, reminding us that originally, 'the name "mechanic" did not mean primarily a machine operative . . . it meant, on the contrary, a craftsman, a "tradesman" in the northern sense', 117.

[64] Joel Mokyr, 'Technological Change, 1700–1830', in Roderick Floud and Donald McCloskey (eds.), *The Economic History of Britain Since 1700*, i. *1700–1860* (1994), 12–43, 15.

[65] Paul Theerman, 'National Images of Science: British and American Views of Scientific Heroes in the Early Nineteenth Century', in Joseph W. Slade and Judith Yaross Lee (eds.), *Beyond Two Cultures: Essays on Science, Technology, and Literature* (1990), 259–74, 270.

than 'turning to the heroism of the past', these publications actively create the heroes. The more technology endangered the political status quo, the more Reform commentators sought to author technology itself in an attempt to assimilate it into a narrative of exceptional human achievement. It is, in fact, common in the popular literature to find machines and inventions described as 'beautiful' and 'poetic'; the *Penny Magazine* in the explosive year of 1832, for example, becomes almost breathless over 'the wonders of mechanical invention . . . those beautiful and most effective contrivances', as if aestheticizing new inventions will make them indistinguishable from the latest pictures or sculptures.[66]

The radical working-class press claimed these heroes as its own, but refused the aestheticization, playing more on the disenfranchisement of its venerable mechanic-ancestors, and using the myths enthusiastically in campaigning for patent reform. The 1821 Bill for Encouragement of Philosophical and Mechanical Experiment had been thrown out, and further attempts to get patent law back onto the Parliamentary agenda had failed, so in 1827, as hopes of imminent legal reform receded, and the recession began to bite, the *Mechanics' Magazine* took up the cause, probably on the initiative of one of its editors, Joseph Clinton Robertson, who was also a practising patent agent. The editors declare that they 'see . . . now no other prospect of the emancipation of mechanical genius, except through the immediate agency of the press'.[67] Given the erstwhile low literacy levels of the mechanical trades, it is perhaps ironic that it was through the medium of writing, in more ways than one, that the campaign for fairer patent laws was to be fought and, finally, won. In 1829, a House of Commons Committee was appointed to examine and report on the problem, and the *Mechanics' Magazine* reported its proceedings from issue to issue, while making its own line clear, 'a reduction in the expense is the only *one thing needful*'.[68] Because accessible patents offered a means of articulating the perceived need for

---

[66] Anon., 'Machinery and Manufactures: Review of Charles Babbage's *The Economy of Machinery and Manufactures*', *Penny Magazine* (30 June 1832), 131–2, 130. Francis Klingender has shown that machines and inventions were regularly described as 'poetic' and 'beautiful' in the late eighteenth century, too. I would argue that the maintenance of this trope into a period of more intense mechanization in the nineteenth century is not only a continuation, but a deliberate strategy. Francis D. Klingender, *Art and the Industrial Revolution* (1968).

[67] Anon., 'The Patent Laws', *Mechanics' Magazine* (10 March 1827), 149–50, 150. Editorial comment.

[68] Anon., 'The Patent Laws', *Mechanics' Magazine* (18 April 1829), 154–6, 156.

a greater stake in their specialized labour, property in knowledge remained fundamental to the artisan-radicals' political demands through to the 1850s.[69]

PATENTS: INTELLECTUAL PROPERTY FOR THE WORKING CLASSES?

The gulf between the workshop and the printed page, between the apprenticed artisan and literate professional, yawned particularly wide in the early part of the nineteenth century. It is perhaps then ironic that, by the early 1840s, the figure of the inventor had become symbolically entangled with that of the literary man. In fact, patent and copyright privileges had always been intimately connected, as Mark Rose reminds us in his discussion of copyright in the eighteenth century:

> when printing privileges first appeared, printing patents and grants for mechanical inventions were not different in kind. Now, a hundred and fifty years later, traces of this original undifferentiation were inscribed in the statute . . . In order to argue that they had property in the copies they had bought, the booksellers would have to demonstrate why authors should be treated differently from inventors. Was a literary invention different from a mechanical invention? This was to become one of the most heated questions in the debate.[70]

Yet the borrowing worked both ways. In the nineteenth century, the fast-growing momentum of the campaign for copyright reform led to the appropriation of terms from the parallel debate about the patent system and its inadequacies, and, correspondingly, the patent reform lobby also used the example of literary intellectual property rights in their protests at the injustices suffered by mechanical inventors. The entanglement of the two campaigns in the 1830s and 1840s produced new and curious class alignments centred upon the issue of intellectual property. Both debates were concerned with issues of class and labour and, more particularly, of property in labour. This early convergence of the working-class inventor and the middle-class man-of-letters took place in the wider context of the development of

---

[69] Although it is, of course, important to remember that the artisan-radicals were never a homogeneous or monolithic group. Both I. J. Prothero and Miles Taylor have written on the diversity of British radicalism in this period.

[70] Mark Rose, *Authors and Owners: The Invention of Copyright* (1993), 45.

an unprecedented valuation of potentiality and futurity, as much as on the past and established tradition. At this particular historical moment, we can witness the beginnings of a new 'democratic' order, in which the categories of property and knowledge were re-examined and the value of labour and its relationship to social value was refigured. The whole debate was extremely revealing of what one writer called 'the fluctuations of rank' at this time.[71] It was, indeed, partly as an accident of the patent debate, and its concurrence with the copyright campaign, that the inventor came to be represented in a consistently dichotomous way, as both hero and victim.

Artisans and writers were also united in a concern about the ever-expanding global marketplace. In 1834, John Gast saw the expansion of the export markets, which Britain's colonial activities were opening up, as threatening to deskill British workers:

Since the Peace trade and Commerce have fallen off, and additional population have been thrown into the market of Labour; foreigners meet Englishmen in the field of competition, and heavy taxation forces down the price of Labour, to enable the Tradesman and the manufacturer to meet the foreign markets, all sorts of schemes is had recourse to, to cheapen the Articles for exportation, and the working man has been the greatest sufferer.[72]

And the reform of domestic copyright was soon threatened by these same foreign markets, which devoured cheap pirated editions to the detriment of their authors. Protection under patent and copyright law was presented by its supporters as vital to nation-building, and to protecting the quality of British workmanship. By 1852, the patent laws offered international protection to British inventions, but British literature did not receive full legal protection in foreign markets until 1891. As subsequent chapters discuss, the ascendancy of free-trade thinking and the simultaneous expansion of markets well beyond Britain were to put particular pressure on intellectual property rights up to the end of the century.

Briefly, the history of patent reform in this period is as follows. In 1820 and 1821 respectively, two patent bills were introduced in Parliament. Neither made it past a second reading and neither proposed to lower the cost of patents, although the 1821 bill emphasized

[71] Anon., 'Fluctuations of Rank Among Men', *Chambers's Edinburgh Journal* (18 January 1834), 401.
[72] Manuscript letter from Gast to Place [3 July 1834]. Quoted in Prothero, *Artisans and Politics*, 66.

the national need for 'men of genius' and suggested that a panel of expert Commissioners be appointed to examine patent applications, which should include 'practical mechanics'.[73] By 1825, trading conditions were deteriorating, and in 1828, the government appointed a Select Committee to look again at patent law. The *Mechanics' Magazine* was suspicious, warning that 'the interests of the poor man and the humble, are of no moment' to this committee.[74] Indeed, nothing came of its findings, so what Dutton calls 'the poorly defined and uncertain nature of the law [on patents]' continued into the 1830s.[75]

In 1833, in the turbulent wake of the first Reform Bill, Godson's Patent Bill was introduced.[76] This session also saw a reformed Law of Real Property, Bulwer's Dramatic Copyright Act, and furious debates over unstamped publications, all of which were reflected in the discussion of patents and intellectual property. An attempt to split Godson's bill into two—one dealing with administrative reform, and the other with expense of patents—came too late in the session and the original bill was held over for the next, with promises of a speedy

[73] 'A Bill for the Encouragement of Philosophical and Mechanical Experiment, and for the Protection of Patentees in their Rights. 8 February 1821', *Bills Public: Session 23 January–11 July 1821* [manuscript pagination: 21–6], i. 22. Throughout the debate the question of the expertise of the officials who examined patents and conducted trials was constantly under discussion. Until the reform of 1852, the jury on patent cases was composed of bureaucrats with little or no scientific background. Mark Isambard Brunel remarked that 'very frequently they can know nothing about what they so try'. Mark Isambard Brunel, 'Patents for Inventions', *Reports from Committees 1829*, i. 415–676, 460.

[74] Anon., 'Patent Laws', *Mechanics' Magazine* (18 April 1829), 156. Dutton remarks that this Select Committee does not seem to have been particularly 'stage-managed'. It was, however, unsystematic in its collection of evidence. H. I. Dutton, *The Patent System and Inventive Activity During the Industrial Revolution 1750–1852* (1984), 44. Broadly, its witnesses agreed that the patent system was necessary as a spur to inventiveness. There was little talk of abolition at this stage. It found that the inventor needed protection from the moment of his initial application for a patent, and that the caveat system was ineffective. Likewise, the problem of the invalidation of an entire patent on account of one unoriginal element was discussed. It was also told that the Board of Commissioners should include more scientific men. Mark Isambard Brunel felt that patents should remain expensive as a disincentive against the accrual of too many trivial patents, which could block innovation. An Appendix collated by John Farey included discussion of the difficulties of defining words such as 'manufacture' for legislative processes. 'Patents for Inventions', *Reports from Committees 1829*, i. 415–676, *passim*.

[75] Dutton, *The Patent System*, 204.

[76] 1833 was also, as J. S. Mill reminds us, the year that the right to 'property in human beings' was finally repealed. J. S. Mill, 'Of Slavery', book II, ch. V, *Principles of Political Economy* (1848), in *Collected Works of John Stuart Mill*, ed. Jean O'Grady and John M. Robson (1965), ii. 245–51.

return. In fact, the issue was not revisited until 1835, when Brougham introduced his successful bill, enacted in September of that year.[77] In the same year, intellectual property in other fields was under discussion. The Lectures Copyright Act was passed, and a Select Committee sat on 'Arts and Principles of Design and their Connection with Manufactures'. Talfourd was granted leave to introduce his first Copyright Bill in May 1837. W. A. McKinnon introduced two further patent bills in 1836 and 1837, both of which were wide-ranging, and proposed a radical reduction in the cost of patents. Despite much support from the invention interest, both failed.[78] Minor amendments to patent law were incorporated in 1839 and 1844, and the Designs Act, which protected property in industrial design, went through in the same year as the Copyright Act, in 1842, with a further amendment in 1843.[79] But it was not until 1851 that the issue of patents made it back into Parliament.

At issue in the patent and copyright debates was the redefinition of intellectual property. As Jeremy Bentham had seen early in the century, if Lockean arguments of 'natural law' are dispensed with, the concept of property becomes elusive and unstable, 'There is no image, no painting, no visible trait, which can express the relation that constitutes property. It is not material, it is metaphysical; it is a mere conception of the mind.'[80] The Chancellor of the Exchequer echoed this utilitarian definition in the 1838 debate over copyright protection, 'all property was the creation of the law . . . Property of every kind was the creation of the law justified by the principle of usefulness.'[81] The 1820s through to the early 1840s represented a critical moment for this 'mere conception of the mind' as the concept of property came under particularly fierce interrogation. Bentham, Mill, and Marx were all writing about property in very different ways in the 1830s and 1840s, and the formations that came out of

[77] Another Select Committee met behind closed doors in 1835 and did not publish a report.

[78] See *Mechanics' Magazine*, 35 (1837), 487–91.

[79] In 1839, a technical amendment was made to Brougham's Act to tighten legislation on the granting of extensions, and in 1844 the Judicial Committee of the Privy Council was empowered to extend patents up to a period of fourteen years. See Dutton, *The Patent System*, 57.

[80] Jeremy Bentham, *Principles of the Civil Code* (first published in French, 1802; published in English, 1830). This extract reprinted in C. B. Macpherson (ed.), *Property: Mainstream and Critical Positions* (1978), 39–58, 51.

[81] Chancellor of the Exchequer, Second Reading of the Copyright Bill (25 April 1838), *Hansard*, Parl. Debs. (series 3), vol. 42, col. 581.

this time were to underpin the theorizing of intellectual property for the rest of the nineteenth century, and, indeed, much of the twentieth and beyond. Jeremy Bentham upheld the concept of private property as the foundation of civilization, which is presumably why he is quoted so frequently in the middle-class Reform press. *Chambers's*, for instance, quotes him in 1834, ' "It is the security of property", says Bentham, "that has over-come the natural aversion of man from labour, that has given him the empire of the earth." '[82] And the *Saturday Magazine* frequently returns to this Benthamite view, 'in any country in which property is secure, and the people industrious, the wealth of that country will increase'.[83] Bentham and Mill agreed with Adam Smith that patents, although contrary to the free-trade spirit of strict utility, were necessary 'monopolies'. Bentham saw patents as 'proportionately and essentially just' as 'a recompense for industry and genius and ingenuity', and Mill concurred, although for Bentham's 'justice', he characteristically substitutes 'morality', 'it would be a gross immorality in the law to set everybody free to use a person's work without his consent and without giving him an equivalent'.[84] Broadly, though, Mill and Bentham both offer economic arguments of social utility in support of patent protection.

Christine MacLeod has claimed that 'Discussion of inventiveness was absent from debates surrounding the reform of the patent system in the 1820s and 1830s.'[85] But to ignore the debate over patents in the 1820s and 1830s is to miss the point at which the figure of the inventor is most clearly implicated in Reform thinking. Even a discussion seemingly so technical as that of patent law engaged with the wider Reform movement. The patent debate was about reform in a

[82] Anon., 'The Rights of Property' (From Mr. Wade's 'History of the Middle and Working Classes'), *Chambers's Edinburgh Journal* (11 January 1834), 396–7, 397.

[83] Anon., 'Rich and Poor', *Saturday Magazine* (19 January 1833), 21–2, 21. See also Anon., 'Society: Division of Labour—Division of Property' (Extracted from Bishop Sumner's 'The Records of Creation'), *Saturday Magazine* (11 January 1834), 14–15, 15.

[84] *Jeremy Bentham's Economic Writings. Critical Edition Based on his Printed Works and Unprinted Manuscripts*, W. Stark (ed.) (1952), i. 263. Bentham, while maintaining that 'monopolies in general are pernicious institutions' makes an exception for patents. Ibid. 264. J. S. Mill, *Principles of Political Economy with some of their Applications to Social Philosophy*, ed. W. J. Ashley (1909), 933. See also J. S. Mill, 'Labour of Invention and Discovery', in Jean O'Grady and John M. Robson (eds.), *Collected Works of John Stuart Mill* (1965), ii. 41–3.

[85] Christine MacLeod, 'Concepts of Invention and the Patent Controversy', in Robert Fox (ed.), *Technological Change Methods and Themes in the History of Technology* (1998), 137–53, 141 n. 12.

much wider sense than Dutton would have it when he claims that the lobbyists were 'all concerned with administrative change, not with the basic economic principles justifying patents'.[86] The reform of the patent system and the administrative changes discussed at this time were themselves reflective of basic principles of political representation and access to property rights. This was a time when, to some, at least, it seemed possible that the boundaries of class and property could be redrawn to create a more democratic model of society. Politically, the central conflict in the patent debate of the 1830s was between the Whig Reformers and the Radicals. After 1832, Radical Members were very vocal on behalf of their industrialized constituencies and highly suspicious of what they saw as the half-hearted reformism of the Whigs. Thomas Hodgskin, for example, bitterly complained that the Whigs were forever 'tinkering up of some of the defects of the Law' while 'throw[ing] no light on its principles'.[87]

The progress of intellectual property legislation drew the patent and copyright debates together time and time again. Bulwer's Dramatic Copyright Act was going through the House of Commons at the same time as Godson's bill. The third reading of Brougham's Patent Bill took place alongside the second reading of the Lectures Publication Bill.[88] Brougham brought in a Copyright Bill late in the 1838 session, modelled almost entirely on his Patent Bill.[89] The analogies between copyright and patent rights were complicated, though, by Radical opposition to Talfourd's 1837 Copyright Bill, which, against the background of Reform and the unstamped publications controversy, seemed, to the very same Radical MPs who were enthusiastically recommending patent protection, to represent another 'tax upon knowledge'.[90] Ironically, the Radicals found them-

[86] Dutton, *The Patent System*, 34.

[87] [Thomas Hodgskin], *The Natural and Artificial Right of Property Contrasted* (1832), 6.

[88] The Lord Advocate claimed that 'the principle of the Bill was this, that every man had as much right to claim security for his lectures, as for his book, or any other fruit of his labours or ingenuity' (24 August 1835), *Hansard*, Parl. Debs. (series 3), vol. 30, col. 954. The radicals, Wakley and Warburton, spoke against the bill, Warburton claiming he 'knew of no abstract right of property in those cases the public good was the only test by which they could decide', col. 954. The Radicals used the utilitarian argument to oppose copyright provision, and the Lockean one to support patent reform.

[89] The bill was introduced too late in the session and did not proceed. See Catherine Seville, *Literary Copyright Reform in Early Victorian England: The Framing of the 1842 Copyright Act* (1999), 58.

[90] This was similar to the line Macaulay took in his famous 1841 Speech against the Copyright Bill, 'it is a tax on readers for the purpose of giving a bounty to writers'.

selves aligned with Brougham against the Copyright Bill, despite a dislike, which they shared with Talfourd, of Brougham's Benthamite principles. The Radicals saw Talfourd's bill as privileging and protecting the property rights of the middle class, whereas Brougham and his followers saw it as an offence to utilitarian policy and a threat to the publishing interest, of which Brougham, with his SDUK, was, of course, a member.[91] The Radical MP, Warburton, described the 1838 Copyright Bill as 'a most pernicious Bill', a middle-class piece of legislation, 'which would sacrifice the best interest of the public to the profit of a few rich men',[92] whereas patent law reform would primarily benefit the working classes. Swynfen Jervis, a Radical who had been involved in drafting Godson's Patent Bill, spoke against Talfourd's Copyright Bill of 1838, 'The House would not sanction a law to be adopted with regard to literary property which was different from the law relating to any other property.'[93] The implication is clear: if Parliament would not make intellectual property a category open to all classes, and reform the patent legislation accordingly, then he would oppose the Copyright Bill. Similarly, the Radical MP Joseph Hume argued against copyright on public interest grounds using the patent analogy, 'if the extension of protection were granted to bookmakers, it must be granted to other men of talent, the authors of ingenious inventions . . . Many persons were of the opinion that the inventions of the one class were quite as conducive to the comfort

'Literary Copyright', Thomas Babington Macaulay, *Speeches* (1853), i. 285–300, 292.

[91] Catherine Seville has also speculated that Brougham's opposition to the bill was tied up with personal enmities and with his increasingly embattled position in Parliament in the late 1830s. See Catherine Seville, *Literary Copyright Reform* (1999), 57–9.

[92] Petition from the 'inhabitants of Shoreditch', 2,188, presented by Hume, 27 February 1840, with thirty-seven signatures. Quoted Seville, *Literary Copyright Reform*, 95–6. Seville discusses the role of petitions from the public during the copyright controversy. For example, George Birkbeck organized a petition against the bill which was presented by Hume, 9 May 1838 (Seville, 91–2). Another petition came from 'Mechanics and others, especially Engineers' (Seville, 95). Petitions were also presented to Parliament throughout the 1820s and 1830s on the subject of patent reform.

[93] 'Letters Patent Bill. Clauses proposed to be Added by Mr Jervis', *Bills 1833*. Jervis's amendments were described as 'unintelligible verbiage' by Lloyd (1833), *Hansard*, Parl. Debs. (series 3), vol. 19, col. 382. Swynfen Jervis, Speech on Second Reading of Copyright Bill (1838), *Hansard*, Parl. Debs. (series 3), vol. 42, col. 589. Jervis was described by Carlyle as 'a dirty little atheistic radical', Thomas Carlyle to John A. Carlyle (3 June 1840), *The Collected Letters of Thomas and Jane Welsh Carlyle*, xii. *1840*, ed. Clyde de L. Ryals and Kenneth J. Fielding (1985), 157–60, 159.

and happiness of the world as effusions of literary genius'.[94] The reverse rhetoric is telling—authors are described as 'bookmakers' with an implication of manufacturing, while inventors have become 'authors'. Another Radical, Dr Thomas Wakley, used a similar tactic, and asked 'why [was] a distinction . . . made between the mere bookwright and the producer of other inventions?'[95]

PROPERTY IN BRAINS: THE ANALOGY OF COPYRIGHT

The Copyright Bill was first introduced by Talfourd in 1837, and versions of it were presented every year until 1842. The bills divided powerful interest groups and caused a long controversy that was keenly reported in the periodical press, which was itself of course implicated in the proposed legislation. Much has been written about the complicated history of British copyright law, and this is not my direct concern here.[96] It is important, though, to understand the wide public interest in the copyright debate in order to map the ways in which its terms leaked into the quieter and less widely reported patent debate. From the first, Talfourd's Copyright Bill differed from Brougham's in that it sought to put the emphasis on the intellectual property of the author rather than on that of the publisher, thus constructing the author as the moral owner of his labour in a way that Godson had already attempted for the inventor when presenting his failed Patent Bill of 1833.[97] Rhetorically, the supporters of the copyright bills relied heavily on ideas of genius and originality to justify the proposed 'monopoly' for the author. It was the charge of monopolizing that derailed the bill again and again: a charge made most famously by Macaulay in a speech of 1841.[98] Monopoly became a

[94] Joseph Hume, Speech on Second Reading of Copyright Bill (1838), *Hansard*, Parl. Debs. (series 3), vol. 42, cols. 568–9.

[95] Wakley (April 1842), *Hansard*, Parl. Debs. (series 3), vol. 41, col. 1378.

[96] See, in particular, John Feather, *Publishing, Piracy and Politics: An Historical Study of Copyright in Britain* (1994); Mark Rose, *Authors and Owners* (1993); David Saunders, *Authorship and Copyright* (1992); Martha Woodmansee, *The Author, Art, and the Market* (1994); and, for the 1842 Copyright Act, Catherine Seville, *Literary Copyright Reform* (1999).

[97] Talfourd himself was reasonably well known as a playwright in the nineteenth century. His literary reputation has faded today.

[98] 'Copyright is monopoly, and produces all the effects which the general voice of mankind attributes to monopoly', Thomas Babington Macaulay, 'Literary Copyright', *Speeches* (1853), i. 285–300, 289. Macaulay gave the speech on 5 February 1841.

central concern in political rhetoric between 1830 and 1860, along-side the rise of free-trade policy, and both patents and copyrights came under attack as monopolies at various points. Thus, despite the fundamental differences between the issues, broad analogies could be drawn between copyright and patent reform—the rhetoric of the anti-monopolists is similar, and those who pleaded for extended pro-tection for writers or inventors often used the same representation of the deserving genius working thanklessly for the good of his country.[99]

Early in the 1820s, while it was already acknowledged that the lit-erary man's creative efforts were, to a certain extent, his property, and he was able to protect them from imitation and to sell them on the open market, the case was less clear for inventors.[100] At the establishment of the London Mechanics' Institute in 1823, Mr Sher-rif Laurie made this point by opposing the cases of inventors and writers: 'If there was one class of men which deserved to be enlight-ened more than another, it was that of the Mechanics of England [applause]. They had done more for their country than all the poets and imaginative writers that ever lived.'[101] From the mid-1820s on-wards, it became more and more common for the similarity of the claims between writers and inventors to be stressed. In 1827, the *Me-chanics' Magazine* explicitly made the comparison that was to be-come a very familiar one over the next two decades:

Literary property, from the historical Folio to the diminutive Essay, is securely guarded by the copyright acts . . . But in the mechanical world it is widely different . . . And where, I would enquire, exists the great difference between the produce of the application of the man of letters and the me-chanical student, which affords grounds for such opposite legislation? It is not the employment of the pen or pencil, it is not the mental energies re-quired; these are common to both; it is not the distinction of rank, for high or low alike suffer from it.[102]

---

[99] As in the patent debate, the writer or author in the copyright debate was always referred to as male.

[100] The 1814 Copyright Act had provided for a twenty-eight-year term or the author's lifetime if it were longer, so the author was already legally established as, to some degree, the owner of his literary property.

[101] Anon., 'Public Meeting for the Establishment of the London Mechanics' Insti-tute: Report of Mr. Sheriff Laurie's Speech', *Mechanics' Magazine* (15 November 1823), 182.

[102] G.S.E., 'The Patent Laws', *Mechanics' Magazine* (10 March 1827), 149–50, 149. Letter from G.S.E. to the Editor.

And the periodical went on to appeal to the authorities to 'put the ingenious mechanics, with regard to the securing their inventions [*sic*], on the same footing with authors of literary productions'.[103] The analogy is most commonly, but not exclusively, used by Radical commentators in an attempt to elevate the status of artisans by placing them alongside men-of-letters, who were already showing signs of organizing themselves into a profession in the 1830s and 1840s. It can also be found, however, in Reform publications, such as *Chambers's* that echoed the analogy in a discussion of the rights of the mechanical inventor: 'his [the inventor's] drawing or pattern is a kind of creation, analogous to that of literary composition'.[104] The scientist, David Brewster, pointed out in 1830 that the inventor was at a disadvantage because '[h]e who has invented a new steam-engine cannot, like the author of a new romance, dispose of it forthwith'.[105] But the rhetoric was reversible, and it was sometimes the copyright lobby that used the example of patents to protest—particularly over the lack of adequate international copyright agreements. Thus, David Brewster, again, this time writing on International Copyright in 1838, used the analogy of the 'mechanist' who 'invent[s] an improvement' and 'will reap the fruits of his industry abroad' to protest that 'the rights of labour, the security of property, are grossly invaded in the persons of authors'.[106] After the 1852 Patent Amendment Act, the campaign for International Copyright drew much of its fire from the international protection of mechanical invention.

In fact, the analogy was so pervasive by the late 1830s that Talfourd himself was forced to take on the 'supposed analogy between the works of an author and the discoveries of an inventor'. Although he was careful to concede that 'there are points of similarity between the cases', he also thought that 'there are grounds of essential and obvious distinction'.[107] The great distinction hinged, he argued, on genius. Any mechanical invention: 'if it were not hit on this

---

[103] Anon., 'The Patent Laws', *Mechanics' Magazine* (5 May 1827), 277–8, 277.

[104] Anon., 'Popular Information on Political Economy: Patents', *Chambers's Edinburgh Journal* (13 March 1841), 59–60, 60. Unlike the *Mechanics' Magazine*, *Chambers's* does not support a long period of copyright/patent protection.

[105] [David Brewster] Review of Babbage, *Reflexions on the Decline of Science in England, and on Some of its Causes*, *Quarterly Review*, 43 (October 1830), 305–42, 331.

[106] [David Brewster] 'International Law of Copyright', *Monthly Chronicle* (April 1838), 163–8, 164 and 167.

[107] Sergeant Talfourd, Speech on Second Reading of Copyright Bill (1838), *Hansard*, Parl. Debs. (series 3), vol. 42, cols. 565–6.

year by one, would probably be discovered the next by another; but who will suggest that if Shakspeare [*sic*] had not written "Lear", or Richardson "Clarissa", other poets and novelists would have invented them? . . . Who can improve the masterpieces of genius?'[108] Nevertheless, he continued with the analogy, and claimed that literature could not, in fact, command as much protection as mechanical invention, as '[t]he fact discovered, the truth ascertained [in a literary work], becomes at once the property of mankind.'[109] Similarly, the Chancellor of the Exchequer spoke out against the patent/copyright analogy, which, he claimed, perniciously attempts 'to raise the pretensions of genius in its application to mere mechanical inventions over the powers of intellect as applied to literature'.[110] The distinction between the 'mere' mechanical inventor and the intellectual writer can be read as a class difference. Even in 1829, the *Mechanics' Magazine* had seen a disparity in the perceived rank of writers and engineers, 'And in what respect is the writer of a book more deserving of being lightly taxed than the inventor of a new machine? . . . Is the right of a poor man to the fruits of his skill and industry, so different from that of a rich man . . . ?'[111] Writers were perceived to be 'rich' and belonging to a higher class than inventors. Although Arago confidently declared in his *Life of Watt* in 1839 that '[t]he author, the artist, and the engineer, are recognised and appreciated throughout the world by all that is most noble and elevated in man—by judgment, mind and intelligence,' his book itself represents an attempt to elevate the status of engineers at a time when their social position was still at best ambiguous.[112] *Blackwood's*, angry in 1842 with what it saw as the inadequacy of the new copyright law, seemed to support the analogy when it protested on behalf of inventors in all fields: 'science, medicine, mechanism or literature': 'The intellect of man is his highest property . . . why is the labour of the philosopher to be less valued and protected than the labour of the peasant?'[113]

---

[108] Ibid.   [109] Ibid. col. 566.

[110] Chancellor of the Exchequer, Speech on Second Reading of Copyright Bill (1838), *Hansard*, Parl. Debs. (series 3), vol. 42, cols. 583–4. He contends that all inventions proceed from 'the impulse given to the general mind by the works of those of loftier genius', col. 584.

[111] Anon., 'The Patent Laws: A few Questions for the Consideration of those who think that Patents should be expensive', *Mechanics' Magazine* (25 April 1829), 166–7, 167.

[112] M. Arago, *Life of James Watt* (1839), 151.

[113] Anon., 'Things of the Day: Copyright', *Blackwood's Edinburgh Magazine*, 4 (May 1842), 634–6, 635. This article supports the extension of both copyright and

At the crux of the argument around both the copyright and the patent laws was the problematic relationship between the labourer and his labour. In 1825, the *Saturday Magazine* drew attention to the productiveness and creativity of inventors, while neatly sidestepping the complex issue of ownership: 'Every other species of property is something gained by individuals, from the common stock; but the productions of invention are positive additions to that stock made by individuals.'[114] The House of Commons Select Committee of 1829 heard that knowledge was becoming more and more a form of marketable property. Arthur Howe Holdsworth, a member of the Committee, argued that there could never be 'too many patents':

One man has a property in the funds, another in land, a third in the powers of his head, evidenced by his inventions; and I conceive that if you were to attempt to limit the number, you would at once cramp men's ingenuity, and not give those who are clever their fair value in the market, because their brains are the only property which they possess.[115]

Other witnesses to this Committee strongly disagreed: Mark Isambard Brunel, for example, felt that more open access to patents would lead to unlimited patenting 'like lottery offices . . . if they [patents] were cheap, there would be still more obstacles in the way of good ones.'[116] This disagreement illustrates very clearly the clash of interests that results in the overall incoherence of the 1829 report. Holdsworth argues from a position of principle: his impulse is to give the poor, working-class inventor 'the fruits of his labour', in the phrase that echoes through the patent and copyright debates right up to the 1850s.[117] Brunel is arguing from a more pragmatic standpoint,

patent protection, and argues that the new Act does not go far enough. 'The whole law relating to invention, whether in science, mechanism, medicine, or literature, is founded on a principle totally contradictory to justice' (634–5). The writer uses the analogy of real property (land) to substantiate this point. The term 'philosopher' here is used in its old sense, as a natural philosopher, or scientist.

[114] Anon., 'Encouragement of Inventions', *Saturday Magazine* (18 June 1825), 171–3, 172.

[115] Evidence of Arthur Howe Holdsworth, 'Patents for Inventions', *Reports from Committees 1829*, i. 415–676, 533. The proceedings of this Committee were closely reported in the *Mechanics' Magazine*. See Anon., 'Minutes of Evidence on the Patent Laws', *Mechanics' Magazine* (10 March 1827), 390–7, 393.

[116] Evidence of Mark Isambard Brunel, 'Patents for Inventions', *Reports from Committees 1829*, i. 415–676, 452.

[117] The phrase was first popularized by Locke. Seville claims that it had strong Chartist connotations by the 1830s and 1840s, and it is certainly used by the Radicals in both the patent and the copyright debates, but, as I show, it is also frequently used by other interest groups. See Seville, *Literary Copyright Reform*, 26.

in terms of social utility, as a working engineer and patentee. Later in the same year, in refuting the argument most commonly used against affording or extending protection for intellectual property in mechanical invention—that of 'the public interest'—a correspondent to the *Mechanics' Magazine* alleges an underlying class prejudice against mechanics:

It is therefore clear, that it is the interest of the *poor* mechanic only, that must be sacrificed for the public advantage. The publisher does not lower the exorbitant price of his volumes for the benefit of society; yet his copyright is not laid open, his property is considered sacred: can these contraries be reconciled? . . . Will the mechanic suffer calmly the curtailment of his rights . . . He is one of a body of men rising daily into increased importance.[118]

The *Mechanics' Magazine*'s view, that the artisanal class is 'rising daily in increased importance' at this time, is to be expected from a publication that campaigned for the professionalization of engineering. Yet it is true that the changing social status of both the profession of writing and that of mechanical engineering hinged on the issue of intellectual ownership. As an index of identity, and particularly of middle-class professional identity in this period, the ownership of intellectual property was vital.

The need to establish ownership beyond the current limited term in order to establish social and professional status was made very clear by those who supported the copyright bills. Sergeant Talfourd, in an important speech he gave in Parliament on the second reading of the 1838 Copyright Bill, characterizes writers as 'the silent toilers after fame, who in this country, have no ascertained rank, no civil distinction in their hours of weakness and anxiety.'[119] And Wordsworth, an active campaigner for copyright extension, wrote, 'say what you will, the possession of Property tends to make any body of men more respectable, however high might be their claims to respect upon other considerations'.[120] The writing profession was already achieving a class-status leap by the 1830s, and *Chambers's* was able to declare by 1842 that '[i]ndeed, the literary has been scarcely behind the legal profession during the last age, in respect of

---

[118] Anon., 'The Patent Laws', *Mechanics' Magazine* (10 March 1827), 149–50, 150. Letter from G.S.E. to the Editor.

[119] Sergeant Talfourd, Speech on Second Reading of Copyright Bill (1838), *Hansard*, Parl. Debs. (series 3), vol. 42, col. 556.

[120] William Wordsworth to Thomas Noon Talfourd (25 October 1838), *The Letters of William and Dorothy Wordsworth*, vi. *1835–1839*, ed. Alan G. Hill (1982), 634–7, 636.

the cases of advancement from one grade of society to another which
have been achieved by it.'[121] Charles Dickens is given as 'an extraordinary example . . . He walks the world more in the manner of a
Roman conqueror than any man since the days of Rome.'[122] In fact,
as we shall see in Ch. 3, Dickens had his own problems with finding
his place as a successful man-of-letters.

The representation of writing as labour in the copyright debate
also brought it rhetorically closer to invention. *Chambers's* declared
in 1833 that: 'It was an ignorant fashion amongst the mental labourers of other days to despise your class, the physical labourers. They
have learnt to know your value, and you should learn to know theirs.
Both classes are working-classes. No one can say that the mental
labourers are not workers.'[123] The drawing together of the working
class and the literate middle class as 'both . . . working classes' is
highly significant as indicative of a new formulation of labour and of
identity.[124] Although this example is taken from a journal hostile to
the extension of the copyright term, which deliberately characterizes
writing as 'labour' in order to show that it deserves no more special
protection than any other work, the same argument was also used by
pro-copyright campaigners to show how deserving authors were of
extended protection.[125] Richard Monckton Milnes, for example,
himself an upper-class writer and MP, argued passionately for the extension of copyright using the same rhetoric of 'useful labour': 'in
order to render that property more valuable to those who laboured
so usefully to promote the instruction of the people and the happiness and prosperity of all classes of the community'.[126] In fact, it was
true that by the 1830s and 1840s writers were likely to be working in

[121] Anon., 'The Literary Profession', *Chambers's Edinburgh Journal* (6 August
1842), 225–6, 225.

[122] Ibid.

[123] Anon., 'Science and Labour' (Taken from 'Rights of Industry, forming a
volume of The Working Man's Companion'), *Chambers's Edinburgh Magazine* (21
December 1833), 376.

[124] In the case of *Chambers's*, this is also an anti-revolutionary fantasy of class
unification.

[125] William and Robert Chambers even published a pamphlet attacking Talfourd's
proposals, *Brief Objections to Mr. Talfourd's New Copyright Bill* (1838).

[126] Richard Monckton Milnes, Speech on Second Reading of Copyright Bill (1838),
Hansard, Parl. Debs. (series 3), vol. 42, cols. 580–1. Milnes may here have been trying
to appease radical opposition to the bill by characterizing authors as labourers and
stressing their utility for 'all classes'. Milnes was the first Baron Houghton, and a
friend of Charles Dickens.

exchange for money in a vastly increased literary marketplace: writing had, indeed, become a form of alienated labour.[127]

Curious alignments thus emerge from the rhetoric of the intellectual property debates and the emphasis on labour is taken up by Reform and Radical writers alike. Reform writers used it to stress the imitability of success, as we have seen. Samuel Smiles in his *Autobiography* emphasized the unexceptionalness of the literary man of the nineteenth century:

in the last century, [. . .] the literary man was a *rara avis*, a world's wonder, who was fêted and lionised until he became irretrievably spoilt; but now, when all men are readers, and a host of men have become writers, the literary man is no longer a novelty; he drags quietly along in the social team, engages in business, economises and succeeds, just as other men do.[128]

In 1832, *Chambers's* was making a similar point: 'In recent times, and in the present day, we find the greater proportion of authors free of the peculiarities which were fashionable among their predecessors; occupying half their time with some ordinary pursuit, and taking up the pen in most cases in the intervals of business.'[129] The *Saturday Magazine* in 1837 invoked the similarity between manual and mental labour in an attempt to dissipate Radical ideas about the strength of the labouring class, disparaging the:

notion that has crept into the minds of our mechanics, and is gradually pervading, that manual labour is the only source of wealth; that it is at present very inadequately rewarded, owing to the combinations of the rich against the poor; that mere mental labour is comparatively worthless; that property or wealth ought not to be accumulated or transmitted . . . James Watt and Robert Fulton were worth more to society than five hundred thousand ordinary men.[130]

---

[127] See Mary Poovey, 'The Man-of-Letters Hero: *David Copperfield* and the Professional Writer', in *Uneven Developments: The Ideological Work of Gender in Mid-Victorian England* (1988); Patrick Parrinder, *Authors and Authority: English and American Criticism 1750–1990* (1991); N. N. Feltes, *Modes of Production of Victorian Novels* (1986); Martha Woodmansee and Peter Jaszi (eds.), *The Construction of Authorship: Textual Appropriation in Law and Literature* (1994); John Gross, *The Rise and Fall of the Man of Letters: Aspects of English Literary Life since 1800* (1991); Clifford Siskin, *The Work of Writing* (1998).

[128] Samuel Smiles, *Autobiography*, ed. Thomas Mackay (1905), 153.

[129] Anon., 'Peculiarities of Authors', *Chambers's Edinburgh Journal* (12 May 1832), 117.

[130] Anon., 'Capital and Labour', *Saturday Magazine* (8 April 1837), 133. It is notable that the article claims Watt and Fulton for the side of 'mental labour'.

In contrast, the *Chartist Circular* in 1841 used the same conflation of working and middle-class interests to emphasize the radical political agency of authors, and to stress their solidarity with the labouring classes, or 'people':

> The advance of the people and the lowering of the aristocracy have been effected through the medium of the press. The position of authors has been much altered . . . Authors are not to be so easily purchased as formerly . . . Authors in England have little to expect from the Government and the Aristocracy. Pensions have been given, but they have been given for the support of political opinions, not as a reward of talent.[131]

The *Chartist Circular* is, predictably enough, categorical about the ownership of labour: 'When any one by his own labour enhances the value of the raw material, the value thus gained being the produce of his labour, is manifestly and peculiarly *his own*.'[132] *Chambers's* in 1833 also assured the working man of his property in his own knowledge, although in slightly different terms: 'Your [the labouring man's] counter-control to the absorbing power of capital is the equally absorbing power of skill—for that also is capital. Knowledge is power, because knowledge is property.'[133] The *Saturday Magazine* in 1835 served up much the same argument: 'The knowledge which an individual may acquire, is as much a species of capital as the sums of money which another individual may have in his iron chest, or at his banker's. Those who possess money may hire the talents of the well-informed, and thus make an exchange of capital.'[134] An 'exchange' of capital gives the impression of a transaction between equals. But the *Chartist Circular* took a different view ' "Knowledge", says Lord Bacon, "is power". It is of your knowledge and power they are afraid, not of your ignorance.'[135] 'Knowledge is Power' was also the motto of the *Poor Man's Guardian*, which, in an article entitled 'On the Evils of Individual Property', repined 'unfor-

---

[131] Anon., 'The Fourth Estate', article extracted from the *New Monthly*, *Chartist Circular* (10 July 1841), 396.

[132] Anon., 'The Wisdom of Our Ancestors, or What is Property?' *Chartist Circular* (8 February 1840), 77.

[133] Anon., 'Science and Labour' (Taken from the 'Working Man's Companion'), *Chambers's Edinburgh Journal* (21 December 1833), 375–6, 376. This article also recommends the work of Isaac D'Israeli.

[134] Anon., 'Labour and Capital' (Abridged from the Economical Library), *Saturday Magazine* (26 December 1835), 246–7, 246.

[135] Anon., 'The Useful Education of the Unenfranchised Working Man', *Chartist Circular* (9 May 1840), 135.

tunately, it is as true that property is power as that knowledge is'.[136] Whatever the *Saturday Magazine* was suggesting, the Radical press saw clearly that knowledge would only become a power analogous to capital if the working man was permitted to hold some unalienable property in his knowledge, and was not forced continually to 'spend' it for his immediate subsistence.

The *Poor Man's Guardian* also attacks Brougham and the Whigs for their attitude to the property rights of the labouring classes: 'The object of the *"Society for Diffusing Useful Knowledge"* is to cause the few to take from the millions the whole produce of their labour,'[137] and as evidence the writer quotes a poem printed in the *Penny Magazine* of 1832, entitled 'The Weaver's Song': 'Weave, brothers, weave!—*Toil is ours*;| But toil is the lot of men.'[138] The comment is scathing: 'Supposing, for instance, Mr. Procter [aka Barry Cornwall, the poet and friend of Dickens] were to write a poem to save him from starvation, and he received a few shillings for it, and at the same time the bookseller made a fortune by the sale, he would not be very much disposed to thank any one for consoling him in the way he here attempts to satisfy the weavers.'[139] The use of copyright here as an analogy makes the perceived class distinction between writers and skilled artisans particularly visible. And as a riposte, the magazine published its own version of the poem, 'The Weaver's Song: *Not by Barry Cornwall*': 'Why should I toil from morn till night,|Producing wealth I can't enjoy?|Why should base robbers thus unite| The honest to destroy!'[140] Thomas Hodgskin also attacks the SDUK for its propagandist literature for the working classes, and its mystification of labour:

---

[136] Anon., 'On the Evils of Individual Property', *Poor Man's Guardian* (20 August 1831), 53–4, 54.

[137] Anon., 'Dissertation on First Principles of Government', *Poor Man's Guardian* (7 January 1831), 236–7, 237.

[138] Anon., 'Penny Magazine', *The Poor Man's Guardian. A Weekly Newspaper for the People* (4 August 1832), 486 (emphasis original). 'The Weaver's Song' first appeared in the *Penny Magazine* (7 July 1832). Barry Cornwall was a friend of Dickens.

[139] Ibid. 487.

[140] Anon., 'The Weaver's Song: *Not by Barry Cornwall*', *The Poor Man's Guardian. A Weekly Newspaper for the People* (3 November 1832), 587. The *Penny Magazine* was not the only outlet for this kind of verse, the *Saturday Magazine*'s 'The Hymn of the Lancashire Cotton Spinner' also celebrated resignation in the face of suffering, 'Teach me to feel my thread of life| By hands Divine is spun,| And still in sorrow, want, and strife,|To say—"GOD'S WILL BE DONE!"' Anon., 'The Hymn of the Lancashire Cotton Spinner', *Saturday Magazine* (28 July 1832), 30.

In its Companion to the Almanack for 1828, it is written 'Capital, money, and property (land), are no more than the savings made from the produce of labour beyond the portion which was required for the preservation of the individuals who have worked to raise it' . . . The statement being in a book intended for the people is quite unpardonable.[141]

Already, by the mid-1820s, labour is clearly a highly politicized and contested term, and rights of property in labour in a surplus economy continued to exercise theorists and politicians throughout the 1830s.

'THE FRUITS OF THEIR LABOUR': MORAL ARGUMENTS FOR INTELLECTUAL PROPERTY

The moral argument that authors should be entitled to 'the fruits of their labour' was frequently used by supporters of the copyright bills. But Catherine Seville, comparing copyright to patent law, claims in her recent book on literary copyright that there was no need to resort to such moral arguments for patents: 'a patent grant is firmly based in a system of economic reward, a system which is regarded as of benefit both to patentee and state. There is therefore no particular need to argue that the basis for protection is a moral one, as the practical and economic arguments are sufficiently convincing.'[142] This may be the case in terms of pure theory—but it clearly remained necessary in the 1830s to argue for patent protection from a moral basis, as even a cursory examination of the Parliamentary papers reveals. For, as Frank Trentmann has pointed out, 'How groups understand economic concepts may be complex, ambiguous, indeed contradictory compared to high theory.'[143] Asking leave to introduce the bill in February 1833, Godson argued *both* from a moral position and from

---

[141] [Thomas Hodgskin], *The Natural and Artificial Right of Property Contrasted*, 162–3. In 1825, the *Mechanics' Magazine* had already pointed to the productiveness of the workman in a technological economy that has radically changed its productivity levels from subsistence to surplus, '[l]abour, to be productive of abundance, must be skillfully directed . . . wealth is that additional product which the labourer, by the assistance of mechanical invention, is capable of creating.' Anon., 'Preface to Fourth Volume', *Mechanics' Magazine* (1825), p. iii (unpaginated).

[142] Seville, *Literary Copyright Reform*, 12.

[143] Frank Trentmann, 'Political Culture and Political Economy: Interest, Ideology and Free Trade', *Review of International Political Economy*, 5/2 (Summer 1998), 217–51, 238.

a more orthodox Benthamite one of innovation incentive, stressing the utility of patents to 'the wealth and the trade of England'.[144] But there is no denying the high moral tone of his speech, in which he calls upon the House to 'giv[e] inventors the fruits of their labour' and continues:

the rule of law ought to be, that the man who had matured an invention for the use of the public—who had spent years of toil and study in the attainment of the object, who had thought much and laboured long, who endured many privations, and incurred considerable expense, and had, at last, presented the public with some useful or convenient article, ought to have every doubt given in his favour.[145]

In fact, in the discussion of 1833, the moral arguments are as strong, if not stronger, than the trade arguments. In this period the basic principle of patent protection was generally left uncontested, whereas later the high liberalism of the mid-century produced a strong abolitionist campaign. Back in the 1830s it was less important for those arguing for extending patent protection to produce counter-arguments in economic or commercial terms, and the recent Reform debate, and growing threat of Chartism, drew political attention to the moral and democratic reasons for amending the law. The focus of Godson's bill, rhetorically at least, was on 'the complaints made by poor persons' about the inadequate accessibility and protection of the current law, which left 'poor inventors' vulnerable to exploitation.[146] Godson frames his Bill as a response to the public, reporting that he has 'received letters from almost every county in England . . . but more specifically from Manchester, Birmingham, and Leeds, at which places, as well as at London, public meetings had been held'.[147]

Like Seville, Dutton claims that moral arguments for patents from 'natural law' had been 'widely discredited' by the late 1820s.[148] He quotes J. R. McCulloch: 'If anything can be called a man's exclusive property, it is surely that which owes its birth entirely to

---

[144] Richard Godson, 'Leave to Introduce a Bill to amend laws respecting Letters-Patent for Inventions' (1833) *Hansard*, Parl. Debs. (series 3), vol. 15, cols. 974–88, 976.

[145] Richard Godson, ibid. col. 977.

[146] Richard Godson, ibid. col. 975. Godson's answer to the problem of the expense of patents was to leave the cost of a fourteen-year term unchanged, and to offer in addition a much cheaper seven-year option.

[147] Richard Godson (1833) *Hansard*, Parl. Debs. (series 3), vol. 19, col. 383.

[148] H. I. Dutton, *The Patent System* (1984), 18.

combinations formed in his own mind, and which, but for his ingenuity, would not have existed,' but he concurs with the *Westminster
Review*'s dismissal of the natural law argument, 'to talk of the natural rights of an inventor is to talk nonsense'.[149] Dutton concludes that
'no worthwhile commentator took [the natural law argument] seriously'.[150] But this is not, in fact, the case, particularly if we are
prepared to allow Radical commentators' voices as 'worthwhile'.
Thomas Hodgskin, for one, published a pamphlet entitled *The Natural and Artificial Right of Property Contrasted* in 1832 in which he
attacked Bentham and Mill 'and their arrogant disciples', his
particular target being Lord Brougham.[151] Hodgskin quotes Locke
*'the labour being the unquestionable property of the labourer, no
man but he can have a right to that it is joined to'* and contrasts this
to the legal right of property, pointing out that 'the law has always
been, and is at present made, by men who are not labourers'.[152] Finally, he puts his faith in '[t]he multiplication of trades, manufacturers, and artizans, and generally of all the inhabitants of towns,' who
'unit[e] in their own persons the character both of labourers and capitalists'.[153] In his view, the rise of a professional middle class of
'labouring capitalists' will transform 'the whole of society to equal
and free men'.[154] Marx was impressed by Hodgskin's work in political economy, and it would be wrong to discount the Radical position
in the debate, which was influential in its use of the natural law argument not just in the periodical press, but also in Parliament itself.

It is true that in introducing his 1835 Patent Bill, Brougham entirely ignored natural law arguments, presenting his legislation as a
practical compromise, claiming that it would be difficult to secure
'the concurrence of all the interests involved in the matter' for a more
thorough measure.[155] Nor does he make any mention of public pressure for reform. Predictably, the Radical MPs, and some less Radical,
were dismayed by a Bill which was, in truth, much less ambitious

---

[149] J. R. McCulloch, *Scotsman* (26 May 1826). Quoted in Dutton, *Patent System*,
18. *Westminster Review*, 26 (1829), 329. Quoted Dutton, *Patent System*, 18.

[150] Dutton, *Patent System*, 18. Dutton adds that arguments from natural law were
used more commonly in continental Europe.

[151] [Thomas Hodgskin], *The Natural and Artificial Right of Property Contrasted*,
22. The pamphlet was written in 1829.

[152] Ibid. 25 and 47.   [153] Ibid. 95 and 101.   [154] Ibid. 101.

[155] Henry Brougham, 'Introduction to a Bill on the Subject of Patent Laws' (3 June
1835), *Hansard*, Parl. Debs. (series 3), vol. 28, cols. 472–7, 472. Although he clearly
believed in reform, and had said of Godson's Bill that it was 'a measure of great importance'. Lord Chancellor (Henry Brougham) (8 August 1833), *Hansard*, Parl. Debs.
(series 3), vol. 20, col. 440.

than Godson's 'more extensive and useful' one of 1833.[156] Brougham's Bill did not attempt to lower the cost of patents at all. MacKinnon called it a 'miserable bungling piece of legislation', and Lennard felt that '[a]s a measure of reform the Bill [Brougham's] was one of the most scanty he had ever seen'.[157] MacKinnon believed the law should be entirely rewritten, objecting that the main injustice of the law as it stood was 'the expense incurred by those gifted individuals who were obliged to apply for a patent to secure to themselves the fruits of their labours'.[158] In fact, far from abandoning the natural law argument, the Radicals used it enthusiastically in 1835 as the foundation of their main objection to Brougham's Bill.[159]

William Cornish reminds us that 'the rights [of intellectual property] . . . are all dealt with by broad analogy to property rights in tangible movables', and the broadness of this analogy lies at the root of the problems of definition.[160] Analogy is always open to rhetorical manipulation, and so Arthur Howe Holdsworth could analogize property in patents with money and land: 'One man has a property in the funds, another in land, a third in the powers of his head,' and Robert Southey could draw a powerful rhetorical comparison between land and literary property:

a law which should allow you the use of the trees upon your estate for eight-and-twenty years, and after that term make them over to the Carpenter's Company, would not be more unjust than that which takes from me and my heirs the property of my literary labours, and gives it to the Company of Booksellers.[161]

Both are using the analogy to argue for increased protection of intellectual property, which allows them to evade the complex problems

---

[156] Lennard (13 August 1835), *Hansard*, Parl. Debs. (series 3), vol. 30, cols. 466–9, 468.

[157] Mackinnon (13 August 1835), ibid. Lennard (13 August 1835), ibid. cols. 466–9, 468 (both quotations).

[158] Mackinnon (13 August 1835), ibid. col. 466.

[159] Perhaps the most useful dispensation made by the 1835 Bill was the option to extend the patent term on the rationale that the inventor 'if not protected in the enjoyment of their property, will either cease to exercise their skill, or will conceal their inventions, which will be lost, as has frequently happened, to the great detriment of society' (4 September 1835, *Journal of the House of Commons*, 90 (1835), 646.) The great example here was Watt, who would not have benefited financially by his patent but for an extension granted upon it. (Appendix (B) to Report from Select Committee on Law Relating to Letters Patent (1829), 605.)

[160] W. R. Cornish, 'Starting Points', *Intellectual Property* (1999), 3–24, 3.

[161] Robert Southey, Letter to C. W. Williams Wynn Esq., MP (23 May 1813), *Selections from the Letters of Robert Southey*, ed. John W. Warter (1856), ii. 323–5, 323.

of specific definition of terms. In fact, it was proving difficult to
define what exactly *did* constitute patentable property in the 1830s.
The speed of technological change challenged the old model of
macro-invention, and, as the Lord Advocate remarked, the problem
of the definition of a patent was now beyond 'the ingenuity of the
most acute lawyer'.[162] The almost desperate attempts of the three
lawyers who drafted the 1833 bill to define the possible subjects of a
patent show this to be, indeed, the case.[163] Without analogy to fall
back upon, Godson and his colleagues admitted that 'it is impossible
to enumerate every kind of Manufacture which ought to be protected by Letters Patent'.[164] In this, as in much else in this debate,
Watt was taken as an example. Watt did not invent the steam engine,
but rather invented an important improvement to the steam
engine—a condenser. 'Micro-inventions' or improvements were not
strictly patentable: all the elements of a specification had to be previously unpatented for the application to proceed.[165] While this situation clearly needed reassessing, the division of innovation into
component parts was bound to complicate any straightforward definition of originality. And one of the recurrent problems throughout
this period of intense legislation was the definition of originality.
Chambers's, hostile to copyright reform in 1838, blatantly fuses the
'author' and the 'inventor' in a discussion of originality that shows

[162] The Lord Advocate (13 August 1835), *Hansard*, Parl. Debs. (series 3), vol. 30,
col. 470.

[163] 'Bill to Explain and Amend Laws Respecting Letters Patent for Inventions', 27
February 1833. *Bills 1833*, p.170. The bill was drafted by three solicitors: Richard
Godson, Benjamin Rotch, and Archibald Rosser. Their formulation of the subjects of
patents was as follows: 'AND whereas Doubts have arisen respecting the new Manufactures or Subjects for which Patents ought legally to be granted; AND whereas
Doubts have also arisen as to the extent of the Use of a Manufacture, which may prevent its being the lawful subject of Letters Patent; AND whereas it is impossible to enumerate every kind of Manufacture which ought to be protected by Letters Patent; BE
it further Enacted, That all new Substances or Things made; that all new Machines;
that all new combinations or arrangements of Machinery or Things, either already
known or newly discovered; that all Principles newly discovered, and all new Applications, which, when reduced into practice, produce some new Article fit for sale; that
all Chemical Discoveries, Methods or Process, which result in or produce an Article of
Commerce, shall be the subjects for which Letters Patent shall be granted.' The phras-
ing of the bill was generally criticized for being too loose and vulnerable to abuse. See
Dutton, *Patent System*, 46–7.

[164] See note above.

[165] Witnesses to the Select Committee of 1829 had often adverted to this problem.
Brougham also acknowledged it to be a problem in his speech of June 1835 (see Henry
Brougham, 'Introduction to a Bill on the Subject of Patent Laws' (3 June 1835),
Hansard, Parl. Debs. (series 3), vol. 28, cols. 472–7, 474).

clearly just how closely the two debates were running alongside one another at this time:

the notion that each author is the creator of the ideas he promulgates . . . is obviously absurd . . . Ideas are truths existing in nature . . . We, for example, call James Watt the inventor of the steam-engine; but this is wrong. The principle of the steam-engine was coeval with the creation of matter and natural forces . . . what was to hinder other men from hitting upon it too?[166]

Ideas of genius and exceptionality were also highly flexible in this debate. Tracking the different rhetorical deployments of ideas of genius on both sides can be confusing. Sometimes, genius was played down in favour of a representation of the creator as labourer. *Chambers's* dismisses the 'sentimental wailings over the hard fate of genius', and protests that:

Authors stand here in precisely the condition of labourers: they do a piece of work, and receive their wages. Although the mental faculties are the instruments, and the labour is a most honourable one, the materials used are common property, and the workman has no better grounds for any subsequent claim on the result of his exertions, than a mason has on the house which he helped to rear, or a coachmaker on the vehicle he constructed.[167]

The intent is to put the emphasis on the *technology* of writing, rather than its mystique. Yet, in the same article, the opposite argument is mobilized when *Chambers's* argues that tightening up the copyright laws will not adversely affect the production of '[o]riginal works of genius' because they 'are never written in the main with a view to pecuniary remuneration, but come forth in obedience to totally different motives'.[168]

It was, of course, rhetorically effective when arguing for fairer protection of intellectual property rights, to insist upon the immense value of the inventions of the engineer and the writer in terms so hyperbolic as to create him anew in the image of a hero. Talfourd's

---

[166] Anon., 'The New Copyright Bill', *Chambers's Edinburgh Journal* (28 April 1838), 112. A similar argument is used in *Chambers's* in 1841, 'There can be no claim of creation, but only of finding out what has all along existed in the great laboratory of nature.' Anon., 'Popular Information on Political Economy: Patents', *Chambers's Edinburgh Journal* (13 March 1841), 59–60, 60.

[167] Anon., 'The Literary Profession', *Chambers's Edinburgh Journal* (6 August 1842), 225 (unpaginated)–226, 226. Anon., 'Proposed New Copyright Law', *Chambers's Edinburgh Journal* (21 April 1838), 104.

[168] Anon., 'Proposed New Copyright Law', *Chambers's Edinburgh Journal* (21 April 1838), 104.

1838 speech in the House of Commons exploited the stereotype of the heroic genius to the full:

Let any man contemplate that heroic struggle, of which the affecting record has just been completed; and turn from the sad spectacle of one who had once rejoiced in the rapid creation of a thousand characters glowing from his brain, and stamped with individuality forever, straining the fibres of the mind, till the exercise which was delight became torture . . . The pen falls from his hand on the unmarked paper, and the silent tears of half-conscious imbecility fall upon it.[169]

Like the inventor at the beginning of this chapter, 'unfriended and unprotected . . . [and] ineffectually struggling', this writer also heroically struggles. Dickens had dedicated his *Pickwick Papers* to Talfourd the year before, in gratitude for his work to reform the copyright law and to 'secur[e] to [authors] and their descendants a permanent interest in the copyright of their works'. Talfourd's speech echoes the terms of Dickens's dedication, which suggested that the proposed reforms would transform the profession of letters: 'Many a fevered head and palsied hand will gather new vigour in the hour of sickness and distress . . . many a widowed mother and orphan child, who would otherwise reap nothing from the fame of departed genius but its too frequent legacy of poverty and suffering.'[170] The writer/inventor is, at one and the same time, a waged labourer, and a self-sacrificing genius, or as the *Chambers's* article goes on to characterize him, 'a man of genius starving over the production of a work which is to delight all his fellow creatures for all time'.[171]

The use of genius as an explanation for creativity has been explained by David Vincent as a reaction against industrialism:

[Genius] was a useful critical weapon for assaulting Locke's empiricist psychology, and as such was incorporated into the Romantic tradition as an integral part of the commitment to natural spontaneity which was developed as a defence against the increasingly mechanical ethos of the industrializing society of the early nineteenth century.[172]

[169] Sergeant Talfourd, Speech on Second Reading of Copyright Bill (1838), *Hansard*, Parl. Debs. (series 3), vol. 42, col. 560.
[170] CD, *The Posthumous Papers of the Pickwick Club* (1986), 39. Anon., 'On the Necessity and the Means of Protecting Needy Genius', *The London Journal of Arts and Sciences*, 9 (1825), 308–19, 308–9.
[171] Anon., 'Literary Remuneration', *Chambers's Edinburgh Journal* (27 June 1835), 169 (unpaginated)–170, 170.
[172] David Vincent, *Bread, Knowledge and Freedom* (1981), 33.

This may well have been the case, but ideas of genius when applied to the inventor, are also curiously supportive of that very mechanized and industrial culture, in that they encourage a divisive and anti-democratic notion of exceptionality.[173] This was recognized by the *Mechanics' Magazine* in 1827:

the mechanics or working classes, had . . . been looked upon as mere machines by which the capitalist expected to make his money, and the manufacturer to extract his wealth. It is true, that here and there would spring from among them bright examples of native genius; but so few were they in comparison to the mighty mass, that they were looked upon as wonders, and regarded with surprise and admiration.[174]

Ideas of genius, which may have originally been used by radicals to oppose the forces of mechanization and industrialization, later fall into the hands of the industrialists themselves, and are turned to work as a powerful way of controlling, through the conservative popular press, the social aspirations of the masses. If the self-made man remains a 'wonder', the threat to the status quo is limited.

The muddling of technician and genius is significant, too, in the representation of the mechanical inventor. The *Mechanics' Magazine* draws attention to the similarities between inventors and other creators: 'all who, by the exercise of their *genius*, make any new addition to the knowledge, wealth, and resources of the country, are equally entitled to encouragement and protection'.[175] Arago, in his 1839 *Life of Watt*, discusses the ongoing row over patent duties, and rehearses the arguments against the remuneration of inventors, 'men of genius, and the manufacturers of ideas':

Ideas! They exclaim, surely they cost no labour and no trouble. Who besides, they add, can prove that in a very short time they would not have occurred to all the world? . . . Men of genius, and the *manufacturers of ideas*, it seemed, ought to remain strangers to anything like material enjoyments; and their history, forsooth, should continue to resemble the legends of the martyrs.[176]

---

[173] Mark Rose has recently used a similar argument, suggesting the intimate connections between Romantic aesthetic theory and the formulation of copyright legislation. See *Authors and Owners* (1993).

[174] Anon., 'London Mechanics' Institution', *Mechanics' Magazine* (27 January 1827), 60–2, 61.

[175] Anon., 'The Patent Laws', *Mechanics' Magazine* (18 August 1827), 74–9, 78 (emphasis added).

[176] M. Arago, *Life of James Watt* (1839), 94.

For those arguing against extending copyright or patent protection, it was, indeed, a common line to emphasize that the author/inventor was a technician, and not a creator *ab initio*. In this platonist view, every invention is waiting to be discovered, and, as Talfourd had put it, 'if it were not hit on this year by one, would probably be discovered the next by another'.[177] Yet the inventor was also seen, like the writer, as in possession of an unaccountable power of creativity. As Arago remarked, in his *Life of Watt*, when discussing Watt's lack of interest in capitalizing upon his inventions, 'It is not without reason that society stamps with its reprobation those who withdraw from circulation the gold hoarded in their coffers': a metaphor that places a very high social value on Watt's ideas, and suggests that they are not, in fact, readily reproducible.[178] The tension between the two views is clear—between the inventor as a genius in the Kantian sense, whose productions are inimitable, and the inventor as a common labourer.[179]

Although Radical campaigners for patent reform saw writers as 'rich men', this was not the common stereotype. In his celebrated essay, *An Essay on the Manners and Genius of the Literary Character*, Isaac D'Israeli had written in 1795:

A NUMEROUS and an important body of men, diffused over enlightened Europe, and classed under no particular profession, are, during the most arduous period of their life, unassisted and unregarded; and while often devoting themselves to national purposes, are exposed not only to poverty, the fate of the many; to calumny, the portion of the great; but to an ugly family of particular misfortunes. These are men of letters.[180]

---

[177] Sergeant Talfourd, Speech on Second Reading of Copyright Bill (1838), *Hansard*, Parl Debs. (series 3), vol. 42, cols. 565–6. There is some truth, of course, in this view of invention, and the patent system is partly intended to provide an incentive for accelerating the speed of innovation.

[178] Anon., 'Arago's Life of Watt', *Chambers's Edinburgh Journal* (26 October 1839), 317–18, 317. This review of Arago's book is largely unfavourable, '[a]s a piece of biography, it has little or no merit', 317.

[179] Kant said of genius that '[i]t cannot indicate scientifically how it brings about its product, but rather gives the rule as *nature*. Hence, where an author owes a product to his genius, he does not himself know how the *ideas* for it have entered into his head, nor has he it in his power to invent the like at pleasure, or methodically, and communicate the same to others in such precepts as would put them in a position to produce similar products.' Immanuel Kant, *Kant's Critique of Aesthetic Judgment*, ed. James Creed Meredith (1911), 169.

[180] Isaac D'Israeli, *An Essay on the Manners and Genius of the Literary Character* (1795), 1 [unpaginated].

Isaac D'Israeli's son, and man-of-letters, the young Benjamin Disraeli, speaking in the Parliamentary copyright debate, picked up where his father had left off in the defence of the literary profession, but rejected notions of the author as poor and withdrawn from society, rather rewriting him as socially powerful: 'The poet and the scholar of the present days was not to be confounded with the monk of feudal times. Literary men exercised great power, often an irresistible power; and he would ask, whether it was wise or right for that House to debar from the right of property in their works the creators of opinion?'[181] By 1847, G. H. Lewes felt able to declare in an article in *Fraser's*, 'Literature has become a profession. It is a means of subsistence almost as certain as the bar or the church,' although he goes on to reveal just how persistent the stereotype of the author is proving, even at mid-century: 'The real cause is the want of respect which John Bull feels for the profession—the inability he feels to conceive the author otherwise than as lazy, impracticable and poor.'[182]

So, in the cases both of mechanical engineering and of writing, three or four contradictory characterizations appear. Inventors and writers can be respectable middle-class professionals; or improvident and lazy; or starveling geniuses; or mere vehicles. The stereotypes were appropriated for both sides of each debate in the 1830s. The inventor-writer is a genius, so it can be argued that he needs protection to help him fulfil his creative destiny, or equally, it can be argued that he needs no such protection as his destiny will be fulfilled anyway through the sheer force of his vocation. The inventor-writer is a labourer like any other and therefore needs protection because he ought to benefit by his labour, as other labourers do, or does *not* need protection because he should sell his goods in the open market like any other labourer. The rhetoric is unstable, as we have seen, and the recourse to analogy by so many of the participants in this debate licenses a philosophic irresponsibility that sustains such mystifications. Nevertheless, the two campaigns, for copyright and patent protection, were historically important, in drawing together and

---

[181] Benjamin Disraeli, Speech on Second Reading of Copyright Bill, 1838, *Hansard*, Parl. Debs. (series 3), vol. 42, col. 580. Disraeli's father, Isaac D'Israeli, was the author of the immensely popular *An Essay on the Manners and Genius of the Literary Character* (1795) and *The Literary Character* (1818) which were often quoted in the popular periodical press during the 1820s and 1830s. See notes 24, 41, and 48 in Ch. 1.

[182] [G. H. Lewes], 'The Condition of Authors in England, Germany, and France', *Fraser's Magazine* (March 1847), 285–95, 285 and 294.

defining the professions of writing and engineering at a time when the ownership and social status of such 'new' forms of labour was—indeed—uncertain and fluid.

CONCLUSION

Writing about the copyright debate in 1837, Thomas Hood said, 'the legislature . . . will have *indirectly* to determine whether literary men belong to the privileged class,—the higher, lower or middle class,—to the working class,—productive or unproductive class,—or, in short, to any class at all'.[183] The rhetorical similarities between the copyright and the patent debates, both in Parliament and in the periodicals, which have hitherto passed largely unnoticed, make it clear how unsettled were ideas of intellectual property in the 1830s. At this moment of Reform, trades such as writing and engineering were, to some degree at least, organizing themselves around this central issue, as professional status always depends upon the trading not of labour, but of knowledge. The patent reform of 1835 did little to help working-class inventors, and the Copyright Act of 1842, although in many ways significant, represented a compromise that was a far cry from Talfourd's original, ambitious plan of copyright protection for an author's life and then sixty years after death. No international copyright agreement was yet in view, either, leaving successful British authors vulnerable to piracy overseas.[184] Neither battle was won outright: but the fights were significant in showing the complexity of the issues about social identity that were perceived to be at stake.

The fables of working-class inventors published in the Reform periodicals offer a fantasy of working-class intellectual property that was useful in diverting attention away from the contemporary controversy over the ownership of labour. As we have seen, labour was a highly contentious term in the 1820s and 1830s. Marx makes the distinction between two versions of property in labour clearly in *Das Kapital*: 'Political economy confuses on principle two very different kinds of private property, of which one rests on the producer's own labour, the other on the employment of the labour of others. It for-

---

[183] Thomas Hood, 'Copyright and Copywrong', *Athenaeum* (1837), 264.

[184] Talfourd originally wanted to cover media other than books, and to include international copyright. Eleven versions of the Copyright Bill were presented to Parliament in five years. See Seville, *Literary Copyright Reform*, 16–19.

gets that the latter not only is the direct antithesis of the former, but absolutely grows on its tomb only.'[185] In the 1830s, the inventor comes to stand for these two 'antithetical' models of labour at the same time—he represents the obedient employee: patient, industrious, and content with his place in society; as well as the dynamic agent of progress, the owner of his own labour, and the personification of the possibilities of social betterment promised by a democratic and meritocratic society.

Throughout the nineteenth century, concepts of the 'self' came under increasingly aggressive negotiation. A growing capitalist economy encouraged, and indeed created, a rhetoric of possessive individualism that conflicted with more organic, mutually supportive models of community. The Victorian inventor can be read as a manifestation of this struggle over the contested concept of selfhood, and this may be one reason for the resilience of the stereotype throughout the century. The inventor is both individual and servant of the state, and by standing for both self *and* society, he offers one representational solution to the conflict of selfhood, and more particularly, of working-class selfhood, in the nineteenth century. In the 1830s, the inventor first became the focus of a complex debate about class, labour, and property that proved extremely important in the second Parliamentary discussion of patent law in the early 1850s.

Charles Dickens was at the start of his career in the early 1830s, working hard as a Parliamentary reporter. He was already involved in campaigning to extend copyright protection for authors, and a close friend of Talfourd's.[186] Talfourd was, in fact, on the Committee appointed to manage the conference between the Lords and the Commons on Brougham's 1835 Patent Bill, so it is possible that the friends discussed the issues of intellectual property in more than purely literary terms. Dickens was certainly reporting in the House

---

[185] Karl Marx, 'The Modern Theory of Colonisation', *Capital*, i. ch. 33.

[186] Even at this early stage of his writing career, Dickens was already having trouble with his own intellectual property: his sketch 'The Bloomsbury Christening' had been pirated for an unauthorized stage production in 1834. Dickens writes, 'it is very little consolation to me to know, when my handkerchief is gone, that I may see it flaunting with renovated beauty in Field-lane' (*LCD* i. 42). His story 'Dinner at Poplar Walk' was also pirated in a magazine appropriately named the *Thief* (*LCD* i. 33). The year 1837 finds him holding out for a new copyright agreement with his publisher, Bentley (*LCD* i. 312). Dickens dedicated his *Pickwick Papers*, when it came out in volume form in 1837, to Talfourd, in appreciation of 'the inestimable services you are rendering to the literature of your country' by his work for copyright reform. Charles Dickens to T. N. Talfourd (27 September 1837), *LCD* i. 312–13, 313.

on 27 February 1833, when Godson's bill had its first reading.[187] It is also likely that he reported Brougham's introduction to the second reading of the 1835 Patent Amendment Bill for the *Morning Chronicle*.[188] It was the renewed discussion of patents in the 1850s that provoked Dickens's response in writing his *Poor man's Tale of Patent* (1850) and *Little Dorrit* (1855–7): texts that are generally read as specifically concerned with the patent debate of the early 1850s, but it is, in fact, to the broader debate about intellectual property of the 1830s that these texts return, with their Reform emphasis on working-class inventors, and their fluid movement between models of mechanical and literary originality and inventiveness.[189] In 1830 David Brewster wrote that

our *literary and scientific* men [should be] allowed, like other ranks in society, to aspire to the honours of the State . . . the possessor of the highest endowments of the mind,—he [to] whom the Almighty has chosen to make known the laws and mysteries of his works,—he who has devoted his life, and sacrificed his health and the interests of his family, in the most profound and ennobling pursuits,—is allowed to live in poverty and obscurity.[190]

---

[187] Dickens reported Stanley's speech in the Commons on the Irish Disturbances Bill for the *Mirror of Parliament* on 27 February 1833 (*LCD* i. 30 n. 4 and 126–7). On the same day, Henry Lytton Bulwer 'Presented a Bill to explain and amend the Laws respecting Letters Patent for Inventions: And the same was read for the first time'. *Journal of the House of Commons*, 88 (27 February 1833), 130. Dickens may well also have reported Godson's introductory speech the week before on 19 February. A full transcript certainly appears in the *Mirror of Parliament*, i. 325–9. As Parliamentary reporters sat in the House for 45-minute sessions and then returned to the office to write up what they had 'taken' in shorthand, it is not certain that Dickens would have been in the House for the first reading of this bill, but as he was in the House that day, he would certainly have known that it was coming up. For more information on Dickens's career as a Parliamentary reporter, see Kathryn Chittick, '1828–1833 The Parliamentary Reporter', in *Dickens and the 1830s* (Cambridge: Cambridge University Press, 1990), 1–17. For more on Parliamentary reporting at the time, see Anon., 'Newspaper Reporting', in the *Metropolitan*, 5 (November 1832), 278; and Charles Ross, Evidence to the Select Committee on Newspaper Reporting (*Parliamentary Papers*, 17 (1878), 36).

[188] The bill was introduced by Brougham on 3 June 1835. His speech was reported in full in the *Morning Chronicle* of 4 June 1835, under the title 'Patents', 2 (unpaginated), col. 1. Dickens was certainly in London and reporting daily at this time. He writes frequently to his fiancée, Catherine Hogarth, to tell her how exhausted he is by his reporting work during June. See *LCD*, i. 63–4.

[189] See Ch. 4 for further discussion of Dickens's response to the intellectual property debate in his fiction.

[190] [David Brewster] 'Review of Babbage', *Quarterly Review*, 43 (October 1830), 305–42, 331 (emphasis added).

It is only by looking back to the ways in which the interests of 'literary and scientific men' were braided together in the earlier part of the century, in their joint bids for intellectual property and professional status, that we can come close to restoring the contemporary resonance of Dickens's use of mechanical invention as analogous for artistic creativity.

The rhetorical similarities of the copyright and the patent debates of the 1830s also remind us of the permeability of the boundaries between the arts and industry in this period. The full influence of the one sphere upon the other is yet to be fully appreciated. From the late eighteenth century onwards, the term 'culture' had been gaining in both currency and elasticity as a means of embracing both technologies and texts, and texts as technologies. Carlyle, in his curious, gloomy celebration of the explosion of print culture in 'The Hero as a Man-of-Letters' could take in the whole of the situation in 1840 much better than it will ever be possible for us to do today. But, by looking closely at the documents still available, we can discern the borrowings (perhaps ironic in a debate that revolved around ideas of originality), by one lobby from the other during the turbulent 1830s and 1840s, and we can discern, despite the complexities, that what was at stake was a reformulation of certain kinds of labour. And at mid-century, the Great Exhibition of the Works of Industry of All Nations provides us with another brief but sharp glimpse of the effects of the onrush of technology upon received ideas of high culture. As the next chapter shows, an increasingly mechanized market only continued to inflate the concepts of originality and single authorship as the fulcrum of value.

3

The Art of Inventing and the Inventor as Artist: Intellectual Property at the Great Exhibition

IN May 1851, Charlotte Brontë took the train from Haworth on a rare foray to London. Along with more than six million others that summer, she visited the Great Exhibition of the Works of Industry of All Nations at Hyde Park.[1] She wrote a description of her experience in a letter to her father:

It is a wonderful place—vast—strange new and impossible to describe. Its grandeur does not consist in *one* thing but in the unique assemblage of *all* things—Whatever human industry has created—you find there—from the great compartments filled with Railway Engines and boilers, with Mill-machinery in full work—with splendid carriages of all kinds—with harness of every description—the glass-covered and velvet spread stands loaded with the most gorgeous work of the goldsmith and silversmith—and the carefully guarded caskets full of real diamonds and pearls worth hundreds of thousands of pounds. It may be called a Bazaar or a Fair—but it is such a Bazaar or Fair as eastern Genii might have created. It seems as if magic only could have gathered this mass of wealth from all the ends of the Earth—as if none but supernatural hands could have arranged it thus—with such a blaze and contrast of colours and marvellous power of effect.[2]

In fact, she went five times. Her response is typical of most recorded reactions to the Exhibition which 'bewildered and yet delighted the mind'—even Queen Victoria went home 'dead beat and my head

---

[1] In fact, the turnstiles recorded six million visits, rather than visitors. Many, like Charlotte Brontë, went to the Exhibition more than once.

[2] Charlotte Brontë to the Revd Patrick Brontë, 7 June [1851], *The Letters of Charlotte Brontë, with a Selection of Letters by Family and Friends 1848–1851*, ed. Margaret Smith, ii (2000), 630–1.

really bewildered by the myriads of beautiful things'.[3] Out of
Brontë's bewilderment and confusion loom the 'Railway engines'
and the 'Mill machinery in full work', alongside the precious work of
the gold- and silversmiths. While she dignifies the description with
the generalized language of the supernatural and the marvellous, it is
nevertheless imbued with a strong sense of private ownership: property at the Exhibition is 'carefully guarded', for example, and this is
a commercial 'Bazaar', after all. Indeed, the Queen treated the Exhibition as a grand department store, confessing to 'a wish to buy all
one saw!'[4]

Brontë seems to need to remind herself that the diamonds and
pearls exhibited as part of this 'splendid' and 'most gorgeous' spectacle are 'real'. There was so much in this Exhibition that was not
'real': that was copied, imitated, die-cast, lithographed, electro-
plated, stereotyped, daguerreotyped, galvano-plastic, and so on, that
the Exhibition itself posed questions about the relationship of mon-
etary to aesthetic value and the status of the 'real' and 'original' in an
emerging economy of reproduction and imitation.[5] These were questions that most mid-Victorian writers and artists could only dimly
formulate—as we see Brontë doing here in her letter home. The Exhibition was, as she says, 'strange new and impossible to describe'
because it represented a moment of crisis in the history of representation, although the full implications of this were far from clear in
1851. In Ch. 5, I argue that it is only in the literature of the 1860s that
we begin to see such issues deliberately discussed. In 1851 the questions were, quite simply, 'bewildering'. At this time, many writers
and artists were welcoming new technologies, while only dimly perceiving the fact that the rapid growth of mass communications and
manufacturing techniques guaranteed a constantly renewable threat
to embattled conceptions of genius and uniqueness in art. Many saw
a problematic future for the protection of patent and copyright
property, but still could not help but applaud the expansion in

---

[3] Samuel Leigh Sotheby, *A Few Words by Way of a Letter Addressed to the Directors of the Crystal Palace Company from Samuel Leigh Sotheby* (1855), 28. Queen
Victoria's Exhibition Journal, 29 April, quoted in C. R. Fay, *Palace of Industry, 1851:
A Study of the Great Exhibition and its Exhibits* (1951), 45. Charlotte Brontë
describes the Exhibition as 'bewildering', *The Letters of Charlotte Brontë*, ii. 625.
[4] Queen Victoria's Exhibition Journal, 17 May 1851, quoted in Fay, *Palace of
Industry*, 53. On 8 August 1851 she records, 'We went up to the Gallery to choose
some dresses,' ibid. 66.
[5] Nikolaus Pevsner, *High Victorian Design: A Study of the Exhibits of 1851* (1951).

cultural consumption which seemed to be creating opportunities for both artisans and artists. In the 1840s and early 1850s, the notion of the autonomous artist was suffering a perilous near-dissolution. As we shall see, the skilled artisan and the artist become almost indistinguishable at the Exhibition. In 1846 Prince Albert had become President of the Society of Arts, the body that administered the Exhibition, with Dickens as its Vice-President and Henry Cole as its Chair. Albert's Presidential Address underlined the importance of measures 'to wed high art with mechanical skill', and Henry Cole's coinage of the term 'Art Manufactures' represents a deliberate attempt to meld the two by insisting on skill, rather than genius, as the primary source of aesthetic value.[6]

The Great Exhibition of 1851 also offered a challenge to the traditional idea of the mechanical inventor by its celebration of manufacturing efficiency through the division of labour. Prince Albert, in a speech promoting the Exhibition to London businessmen at the Mansion House, reminded his audience that 'the great principle of division of labour . . . is being extended to all branches of science, industry, and art'.[7] The Exhibition put patent law back on the Parliamentary agenda, but it is curious that the resulting Patent Act of 1852 continued to insist on a model of the inventor as autonomous creator. The free-trade victories of the 1846 repeal of the Corn Laws, the repeal of the Navigation Acts, and the reductions in Imperial Preferences in 1849 paved the way for the opening up of export trade. Although, in purely theoretical terms, there is clearly no conflict between a free-trade economy and patent protection, this was not the way that many MPs saw it at the time.[8] And artisans traditionally feared export markets, believing that they would cheapen

[6] Prince Albert, Presidential Address; Henry Cole, *Fifty Years of Public Work of Sir Henry Cole, K.C.B.* (1884), i. 103. Cole was a Commissioner for the Exhibition and the Chairman of the Council of the Royal Society of Arts in 1851. He was one of the main forces behind the Great Exhibition. Prince Albert was the sponsor of the Exhibition and had become President of the Society of Arts in 1845. Maxine Berg has pointed out that in the eighteenth century the Society of Arts encouraged craft and imitation, 'Imitation came to pervade the language of invention during the eighteenth century. The institutions which most clearly convey this are the Society of Arts, Manufactures and Commerce, and patent applications and specifications.' Maxine Berg, 'From Imitation to Invention: Creating Commodities in Eighteenth-Century Britain', *Economic History Review*, 55/1 (2002), 1–30, 17.

[7] Prince Albert's Speech at the Mansion House 1849, quoted Cole, *Fifty Years of Public Work*, ii. 213.

[8] The election of 1847 returned a record number of Radical MPs to Westminster, a result that was never to be matched again.

goods and threaten their autonomy as workers, as we saw in Ch. 2.[9] In addition, many of the free traders themselves saw patents as 'monopolies' and advocated their total abolition, just as Macaulay had used 'copyright' and 'monopoly' as synonymous terms in his 1841 Parliamentary speech against Talfourd's copyright bill. He argued, from free-trade principles, that 'the effect of monopoly generally is to make articles scarce, to make them dear, and to make them bad'.[10] As Frank Trentmann has pointed out, 'In popular knowledge . . . different perceptions have structured and read the economy in different ways. Free trade was no exception, though its ideological power in legitimating itself as common sense and a scientific fact as indisputable as gravity has helped to dehistoricize it.'[11] Because free trade later became an axiom of Gladstonian liberal economics, it is easy to assume it was always accepted as such. In fact, as the patent debate of 1851–2 shows, it was a highly elastic and unstable term in the early 1850s.

This makes it all the more remarkable that the model of mechanical invention as the solitary, autonomous, even unalienated labour of one individual survived at all. The Select Committee Reports make it perfectly clear that this stereotype was outmoded, if it had ever existed. This chapter argues that the reform of the patent law at mid-century was profoundly affected by a literary lobby, including Charles Dickens and other members of the Society of Arts, which maintained the analogies with copyright law despite the evidence that industrial innovation had now become a largely corporate, and not an individual, endeavour. Talfourd's 1842 Copyright Act was a hard-won victory: in 1851 there was still no agreement on international copyright, and writing was yet to be fully recognized as a profession. Robert Patten has argued that 'authors were instrumental, especially through their social contacts with M.P.s, in obtaining the passage of the 1842 Copyright Act', and to Dickens and others, it might have seemed that to surrender the construction of the autonomous inventor in patent law at a time when the boundaries between technology and modern art seemed to be so slippery, would

---

[9] Working-class radical John Gast argued in 1834 that 'all sorts of schemes is had recourse to, to cheapen the Articles for exportation, and the working man has been the greatest sufferer'. See Ch. 2 n. 72.

[10] Thomas Babington Macaulay, 'Literary Copyright', *Speeches* (1853), i. 285–300, 289.

[11] Frank Trentmann, 'Political Culture and Political Economy: Interest, Ideology and Free Trade', 226.

have been to risk laying open to dangerous attack the principle of copyright protection for writers.[12]

It is clear from the literature of this particular summer that the difficulty of attributing intellectual property rights, and the effect of a fast-developing capitalist marketplace on concepts of creativity, originality, authenticity, and genius were much in everyone's mind. Legal discussions about patents, international copyright, and piracy in 1851 were not taking place in a vacuum—their currency is the currency of the Exhibition exhibits, the currency of the letters that Dickens, Thackeray, Brontë, and Gaskell wrote over that summer, and the currency of all the writing on the Exhibition from Hunt's illustrated guide books, to Ruskin's passionate warning in his 'The Opening of the Crystal Palace'.[13] In 1851, the future of art seemed uncertain. It was difficult to discern exactly what an artist was, or to predict what he or she would become in the future.

MACHINERY IN MOTION

This chapter shows the crucial importance of the close juxtaposition of artworks and machines at the Exhibition of 1851 to the subsequent discussion of the status and intellectual property of the artist and the inventor. I suggest that it is important that Charlotte Brontë did not notice only machinery at the Exhibition, but 'machinery *in full work*'. The emphasis on technologies of production in the machinery courts extended into the displays of fine and decorative arts, too, and I suggest that this created anxieties that led in turn to an enduring reinscription of ideas of autonomous authorship. The first section of this chapter starts in the Machinery in Motion section of the Exhibition, and then moves into the Fine Arts Court. Starting at F. & C. Osler's Crystal Fountain in the centre of the ground floor, and walking up the Main Avenue West, a visitor walked through the Fine Arts Court (sculpture, modelling, mosaics, enamels, etc.) straight into the hydraulic press, steam hammer, fire engines, marine engines, locomotives and railway apparatus, carriages, etc. and on into Machinery in Motion, in four divisions, which comprised 'the largest

---

[12] Robert L. Patten, ' "The people have set Literature Free" ', 15.
[13] Ruskin's pamphlet was published on the reopening of the Crystal Palace on the new site at Sydenham in 1854.

compartment in the building'.[14] Statues and machines vied for the visitor's attention. William Whewell asked at the time, 'may not we expect that . . . the very language of Art and Industry, and the mode of regarding the relations of their products, shall bear for ever the impress of the Great Exhibition of 1851?'[15] This chapter argues that this was, in fact, the case, although perhaps not in quite the ways that Whewell optimistically predicted.

Before the Exhibition opened its glass doors, the *Daily News* speculated that '[m]achinery, we fear, will not form the most popular, however it may be the most extensive department of the Exhibition.'[16] That prediction was proved very wrong. By general consensus, the most popular attraction by far was the impressive display of working machinery.[17] Henry Mayhew noted that 'the machinery . . . has been from the first the grand focus of attraction'.[18] Certain exhibits were much discussed, such as 'the extraordinary instrument called Appold's centrifugal pump', 'which poured forth a voluminous cascade, to the great delight of a constant throng of spectators'.[19] Henry Mayhew gives a detailed, if idealized, account of the Machinery section of the Exhibition:

But the chief centres of curiosity are the power-looms, and in front of these are gathered small groups of artisans, and labourers, and young men whose red coarse hands tell you they do something for their living, all eagerly listening to the attendant, as he explains the operations, after stopping the

---

[14] *By Authority of the Royal Commission: Official Catalogue of the Great Exhibition of the Works of Industry of All Nations* [Third Corrected and Improved Edition] (1851), 3. (Hereafter referred to as *One Vol. Exhibition Catalogue.*) *The Art Journal Illustrated Catalogue The Industry of All Nations, 1851* (1851), p. xxxv.

[15] Revd W. Whewell, 'The General Bearing of the Great Exhibition on the Progress of Art and Science', *Lectures on the Results of the Great Exhibition of 1851, Delivered Before the Society of Arts, Manufactures, and Commerce, at the Suggestion of H.R.H. Prince Albert, President of the Society* (1852), 1–34, 27–8.

[16] Unreferenced quotation, Fay, *Palace of Industry*, 82.

[17] Machines for Direct Use (Class V): 400 from UK, 7 from UK Dependencies and 91 from 'foreign' countries. Manufacturing Machines and Tools (Class VI): 241 UK machines to 125 'foreign'. Civil Engineering (Class VII): 192 from UK and Dependencies to 30 from 'foreign' states. *First Report of the Commissioners for the Exhibition of 1851 to the Secretary of State for the Home Department* (1852), 173.

[18] Henry Mayhew and George Cruikshank, *1851: or, the Adventures of Mr and Mrs Sandboys and Family who came up to London to 'enjoy themselves' and to see the Great Exhibition* (London: David Bogue, n.d.), 160.

[19] Anon., *The Industry of Nations, Part II: A Survey of the Existing State of Arts, Machines, and Manufactures* [Published under the Direction of the Committee of General Literature and Education, Appointed by the Society for Promoting Christian Knowledge] (1855), 255 and 260.

loom. . . . Round the electroplating and the model diving bell are crowds jostling one another for a foremost place. At the steam brewery, crowds of men and women are constantly ascending and descending the stairs; youths are watching the model carriages moving along the new pneumatic railway; young girls are waiting to see the hemispherical lampshades made out of a flat sheet of paper; indeed, whether it be a noisy flax-crushing machine, or the splashing centrifugal pump, or the clatter of the Jacquard lace machine, or the bewildering whirling of the cylindrical steam-press,—round each and all these are anxious, intelligent, and simple-minded artisans, and farmers, and servants, and youths, and children clustered, endeavouring to solve the mystery of its complex operations.[20]

Oddly, in an otherwise compelling account of the Exhibition, Thomas Richards has written that 'no one could possibly mistake the Crystal Palace for a factory. Nothing happened at the Great Exhibition but the sight of things just sitting there, mute and solid.'[21] But evidence from Mayhew and others, including Brontë, of the 'thousand iron monsters snorting and clattering', tells us instead that the entire north-western corner of the building vibrated all day with 'Machinery in Motion', and must, in fact, have sounded far more like a factory than an art gallery.[22] Indeed, the Commissioners were anxious to represent the whole process of manufacture as expressively as possible, and to avoid leaving the machines 'mute and solid'.[23] In an attempt to represent *process*, rather than merely exhibit 'things just sitting there', several entire manufacturing processes were demonstrated from start to finish. 'Messrs. Hibbert and Platt, who are the most extensive manufacturers of cotton machinery in this country, have produced a series of engines for the treatment of cotton from its raw state upwards,' and also on display was the 'wonderful automaton' of a French paper-making machine, which 'is a complete system, for the raw material enters at one extremity, and the finished product emerges from the opposite end'.[24] The popular periodical, the *Illus-*

---

[20] Mayhew and Cruikshank, *1851*, 160–1.

[21] Thomas Richards, *The Commodity Culture of Victorian England: Advertising and Spectacle* (1990), 30.

[22] Mayhew and Cruikshank, *1851*, 137.

[23] The Commissioners recommended to exhibitors that, 'the Producing Mechanism . . . should always be accompanied with sufficient specimens of the Raw Material, in its several stages of manufacture, and of the finished product, to make the operation of the Machinery intelligible', *First Report of the Commissioners* (1852), 23.

[24] Anon., *Industry of Nations*, II, 122. The cotton machines proved extremely popular with visitors: 'The crowded state of the building in that part testified to the interest it excited.' Henry Hensman, 'On Civil Engineering and Machinery Generally',

trated Exhibitor was enthusiastic: 'Would we study the processes of manufacture? . . . here, then, we may pursue the varied manipulations, from the first rude idea to the finished accomplishment in the articles themselves.'[25] As we shall see, mechanized production processes were not solely confined to displays of industrial machinery—they extended into the Fine Arts court too. But it was the Machines in Motion that attracted the largest crowds, and established the process of making, including the display of the incomplete and only half-finished, as central to the epistemology of the Exhibition.

What attracted such crowds to this part of the building? Was it, as Charlotte Brontë would have it, the pure spectacle, whose 'wonders appeal too exclusively to the eye and rarely touch the heart or head?'[26] Predictably enough, the Commission insisted it was a public desire for education which brought the punters in: 'The great attention paid by the Public to the department of the Exhibition devoted to Machinery indicated how eagerly such facilities for acquiring knowledge were used.'[27] Yet it is worth pausing to consider just what it was possible to learn from these displays, and who was visiting them. Mayhew's crowds are, after all, reported to be 'endeavouring' to understand how the machines work. Many middle-class commentators fantasized about the educational effects of the Exhibition, hoping that working-class men 'may see and innoculate their fellow-workmen', and even Ruskin, although not generally a supporter of the project, felt it might rouse dormant intellects into activity. But there is evidence that this was not, in fact, the case. For a start, the Exhibition never did attract many of the labouring poor because it was expensive to visit, even on the famous 'shilling days': 'The Crystal Palace is not for the masses who *cannot* pay, but for those above the mass who *can* pay,' as one commentator put it, adding that it was more likely to attract 'the well-dressed mechanic, and smaller tradesmen, and clerks, &c.'.[28] Indeed, Dickens's brief official in-

Lectures on the Results of the Great Exhibition of 1851 (1852), 403–40, 422. Anon., *Industry of Nations*, II, 190.

[25] Anon., 'Introduction', *Illustrated Exhibitor* (7 June 1851), 1–3, 3.

[26] Brontë, *The Letters of Charlotte Brontë*, ii. 666.

[27] *Second Report of The Commissioners for the Exhibition of 1851 to the Right Hon. Spencer Horatio Walpole* (1852), 29.

[28] William Felkin, *The Exhibition in 1851 of the Products and Industry of All Nations. Its Possible Influence upon Labour and Commerce* (1851), 9 (emphasis original). John Ruskin, *The Opening of the Crystal Palace Considered in Some of its Relations to the Prospects of Art* (1854), 4. Anon., *A Letter to the Right Honourable*

volvement with the 'Working Classes Committee' ended precipitately when he and others decided that the Committee did not enjoy the full confidence and support of the Exhibition's Commissioners.[29] Nevertheless, there is evidence that many of those who were then termed the 'respectable poor' did both subscribe to the Exhibition fund and make it to the Exhibition itself, often through local co-operative schemes and friendly societies set up for the purpose, and that there was considerable enthusiasm for the Exhibition from these quarters.[30] But it remains difficult to speculate about how individual visitors viewed the event: whether as pure spectacle, or as an educational excursion, or as both. Indeed, the categories of education and entertainment were not necessarily perceived to be mutually distinct at mid-century.

The Earl of Derby, on the Proposed Opening of the Crystal Place on the Lord's Day (1853), 12. This pamphlet concerns the proposal to open the New Crystal Palace at Sydenham on Sundays, but the comment seems equally valid for the Exhibition itself as a leisure attraction. Although it was the 'Shilling Days' that ultimately secured the financial success of the Exhibition, the first Shilling Day came and went without attracting the crowds expected. The Executive Committee excused itself from the embarrassment of having billeted 'hundreds of extra police' to deal with the non-existent crowds by pointing to the self-denial of the working classes, and Henry Cole claims they were '*kept away by the apprehension that the crowds would be enormous*', Cole, *Fifty Years of Public Work*, i. 195 and 196 (emphasis original). Henry Mayhew attributed it instead to apathy, adding that 'this tendency to put high and heroic motives on everyday conduct is the besetting sin of the age'. Mayhew and Cruikshank, *1851*, 154.

[29] The Working Classes Central Committee grew out of the fears expressed by Commissioners about social discipline at the Exhibition. Dickens served alongside Thackeray, Forster, Bentham, Robert Chambers, Charles Knight, W. J. Fox, and others on this short-lived Committee. Its principal objects were to inform the 'working classes throughout the United Kingdom of the nature and objects of the Exhibition', 'to assist in promoting the visits of the working classes to the Exhibition', and to publish information about accommodation for the working classes in London. However, the Royal Commission refused to appoint them as an Official Committee. Cole reports the reason as being Colonel Reid's fear that 'the Prince should put himself at the head of a democratic movement'. He recalls that 'Dickens was very strongly in favour of the necessity of dissolving and he moved, and then Charles Knight drafted, a resolution, which Vincent seconded' to that effect. The Committee was duly dissolved at the end of June 1850. See Cole, 'Fears of the Working Classes', *Fifty Years of Public Work*, i. 188–93, *passim*.

[30] See Jeffrey Auerbach, 'Integration and Segregation', in *The Great Exhibition of 1851: A Nation on Display* (1999), 128–58. Although Auerbach approaches the question of working-class participation largely through the official documents and rhetoric, and does not discuss working-class responses to the Exhibition in any detail. See also Peter Gurney, 'An Appropriated Space: The Great Exhibition, the Crystal Palace and the Working Class', in Louise Purbrick (ed.), *The Great Exhibition of 1851. New Interdisciplinary Essays* (2001), 114–45. See also Brian Maidment in the same collection, whose essay 'Entrepreneurship and the Artisans: John Cassell, the

And there was another problem, which would be acknowledged later in discussions about the setting up of the museums on the South Kensington site which grew out of the success of the Exhibition. Representing machinery and the modern age was difficult. As one commentator explained: 'In many cases, [manufacturing processes are] noisy, offensive, and dirty, or requiring conditions of heat or damp, which made it impossible to carry them on in the presence of spectators; and if not labouring under these disadvantages, at least requiring long explanations and experiments to make them intelligible.'[31] In 1851, Britain was on the verge of a machine age, and it would soon become impossible to represent technology without supplying a great deal of technical information beyond the evidence of the machines themselves. The Commissioners, in their anxiety to illustrate the whole process of cotton manufacture, and their provision for 'attendants' at exhibits to 'explain' them, were already acknowledging the ever-widening cognitive gap between seeing and knowing (and, ultimately, between skilled mechanics and unskilled labourers).[32] Crowds in the machine rooms 'with their noses almost touching the wheels, as they vainly endeavoured to make themselves acquainted with their bewildering details', could perhaps hope to make some headway, but the newest technologies on display in 1851 resembled nothing familiar at all.[33] Merely looking at the electric telegraph instruments at the Exhibition, for example, would tell the spectator little about what they did or how they worked, and explanations became essential. As *All the Year Round* commented in 1859, 'its working is secret and bewildering to the average mind', and the mysteries of telegraphic communication were unfolded in presentations given by the exhibitors, to the Queen, among many others, who 'had the electric telegraph show explained and demonstrated'.[34] While the crowds might be 'watching intently the operations of the moving

Great Exhibition and the Periodical Idea' (79–113) examines the popular periodical, *The Illustrated Exhibitor*, as an 'artisan journal'.

[31] Revd Robert Willis, 'On Machines and Tools for Working in Metal, Wood, and Other Materials', *Lectures on the Results of the Great Exhibition of 1851* (1852), i. 293–320, 294.

[32] Appendix II, 'Decisions of Her Majesty's Commissioners, and Regulations of the Executive Committee', *First Report of the Commissioners for the Exhibition of 1851* (1852), 8.

[33] Mayhew and Cruikshank, *1851*, 137.

[34] Anon., 'House-top Telegraphs', *All the Year Round* (26 November 1859), 106–9, 107. Queen Victoria, *Exhibition Journal* (9 July 1851), quoted in Fay, *Palace of Industry*, 63.

mechanism', this was no guarantee that, without any scientific education, they understood what they saw, or were learning anything from it.[35] Charlotte Brontë acknowledged this gap when she said that 'those who possess a large range of scientific knowledge' could take more from the Exhibition: 'Once I went with Sir David Brewster and perceived that he looked on objects with other eyes than mine.'[36] Dickens, too, felt overwhelmed by the spectacle and 'used up' by it: 'So many things bewildered me. I have a natural horror of sights, and the fusion of so many sights in one has not decreased it.'[37] He worried about 'the bewilderment of the public', predicting that the Exhibition would not deliver the educational entertainment it promised, and feeling that visitors 'will come out of it at last, with [a] feeling of boredom and lassitude'.[38]

The enthusiasm of the Exhibition Commissioners to make the exhibits intelligible tells us something about the control of knowledge at the Exhibition. Richards points to the way that the exhibits in the Crystal Palace 'promised, in a way which it is very hard to pin down, that each and every one of them would one day be democratically available to anyone and everyone'.[39] Certainly, there was an attempt to make the public, or at least the British part of it, feel a sense of ownership and identity with the machinery and other exhibits. But the incomprehensibility of many of these exhibits prohibited much sense of ownership. While visitors were invited to dip their handkerchiefs freely into a fountain of 'Rimmel's toilet vinegar', exhibits remained clearly private property.[40] The social impact of machinery had already complicated straightforwardly optimistic readings of machinery as democratizing. At the Great Exhibition of 1851, the situation was not quite as clear as Thomas Richards and other Foucauldian critics would have us believe. Undoubtedly, visitors were, to an extent, being 'disciplined' into the appreciation of objects as universally available commodities, but the Machinery in Motion exhibits made far more ambiguous demands upon them than this. The working machines pointed towards a new economy in which the

[35] Mayhew and Cruikshank, *1851*, 161.
[36] Brontë, *The Letters of Charlotte Brontë*, ii. 666.
[37] Charles Dickens to the Hon. Mrs Richard Watson (11 July 1851), *LCD* vi. 428.
[38] Dickens to Wills (27 July 1851), *LCD* vi. 449.
[39] Richards, *Commodity Culture*, 19.
[40] *The Bleak House Advertiser*, i. 20. Louise Purbrick has written interestingly on the tension between educational display and private property at the Exhibition. See Louise Purbrick, 'Knowledge is Property: Looking at Exhibits and Patents in 1851', *Oxford Art Journal*, 20/2 (1997), 53–60.

processes of production were growing increasingly difficult for non-experts to understand. This knowledge-gap was creating a society which was becoming rapidly less legible to ordinary people. As it slipped from their intellectual grasp, they owned their 'own' culture less and less.

The difficulty those nineteenth-century spectators encountered in understanding these machines has been described by Walter Benjamin as a kind of homesickness for those 'who have yet to learn to master, not this nature [technology] itself, but humanity's relationship to it'.[41] He points to the forms taken by the new technologies, which imitated the old forms they were destined to overcome, just as early photography supposedly mimicked painting.[42] Already in 1851, the analogies by which machines are described are under strain. As earlier in the century, there is still an attempt to aestheticize machines, both by physically ornamenting them in gothic or neoclassical styles to resemble pieces of contemporary furniture, and by describing them as 'beautiful'. The Catalogue describes, for example, the 'beautiful automaton card-setting engine', and Hibbert and Platt's machines 'have never been equalled in beauty'.[43] The *Illustrated London News* eulogized 'machines, so beautiful in their workmanship and so perfect in their finish as almost to take rank amongst works of art'.[44] The other dominant image is of the machine as man's 'iron substitute', and the catalogue points out that '[t]he machinery included . . . has this distinguishing feature, that it is representative of man himself engaged in industrial production.'[45] Because man has been substituted for by machine, the two are identified as analogous, 'the substitution of the iron arms and fingers of the machinery, for the bone and sinew and nerves of the cunning artificer', and descriptions of machines in terms of human consciousness and actions were common.[46] De la Rue's much admired envelope-folding machine 'with its magic "finger"', for example, 'closely followed several actual

---

[41] Susan Buck-Morss, *The Dialectics of Seeing: Walter Benjamin and the Arcades Project* (1989), 70.

[42] Ibid. 111.

[43] *By Authority of the Royal Commission: Official Descriptive and Illustrated Catalogue of the Great Exhibition 1851*, 3 vols. (plus one suppl. vol.) (1851) i. 262. (Hereafter referred to as 3 Vol. Exhibition Catalogue.) Anon., *Industry of Nations, II*, 122.

[44] *Illustrated London News* (19 April 1851), 311.

[45] John Wilson, 'Agricultural Products and Implements', *Lectures on the Results of the Great Exhibition of 1851* (1853), ii. 3–41, 39. 3 Vol. Exhibition Catalogue, i. 262.

[46] Lewis D. B. Gordon, 'The Machinery of the Exhibition, As Applied to Textile Manufactures', *The Art Journal Illustrated Catalogue* (1851), pp. I**–VIII**, I**.

movements of the human form divine', and machines were described as functioning 'as though conscious, and endowed with volition'.[47] Nevertheless, the Catalogue has to admit that '[s]ome of these machines present the most singular and anomalous forms,' and, like the electric telegraph, the very newest technologies were moving away from recognizable and anthropomorphic actions.[48] Although the potential of these new processes and new technologies was still largely hidden from view at the Exhibition, it was already clear that they were poised to change everything.

The desire to identify machines as substitute bodies masked a further desire, to write machines into a narrative of nature that made them seem less alien and less threatening to human social identities.[49] Yet the danger of such an identification is that it can achieve quite the opposite effect and threaten to make machines into strangely autonomous agents with the potential to intervene in and disrupt the human world. The Victorian fascination with automata of all kinds pivoted on the *frisson* of this double identification of machines as *unheimlich*: both familiar and strange. The doubleness of these representations was exacerbated by the uncomfortable obverse of the analogy, too. For if machines resemble men, men must also resemble machines, and Ruskin had said in 1849, in his influential *The Seven Lamps of Architecture*, that '[i]t is indeed possible, and even usual, for men to sink into machines themselves.'[50] Radical opposition to the deskilling of labour during the first phase of mechanization in the 1820s and 1830s had often made use of such an analogy. The language associated with machines in 1851 reveals an ambivalence about the impact of machine culture upon social relations, as even anthropomorphic figures of containment threaten to collapse into nightmarish images of machines as tyrannical masters, and men diminished into mere mechanism.

The disjunction between the 'beautiful' machinery and its 'moral effects' was masked but nevertheless discernible in the displays in the

---

[47] Mayhew and Cruikshank, *1851*, 134. Unreferenced quotation from *Illustrated London News*, given by Pevsner in *High Victorian Design*, 24. Samuel Warren, *The Lily and the Bee: An Apologue of the Crystal Palace* (1851), 62.

[48] 3 Vol. *Exhibition Catalogue*, i. 262.

[49] See Mark Seltzer, *Bodies and Machines* (1992).

[50] John Ruskin, *The Seven Lamps of Architecture* in *The Library Edition of the Works of John Ruskin on CD Rom* (1996), viii. 84. I do not wish to go further into this identification as Mark Seltzer has already discussed it at length. Charlotte Brontë herself used the analogy in her 1849 novel *Shirley: A Tale*.

Crystal Palace. It creeps quietly into some of the promotional literature, but is kept muted, 'Wonderful mechanical result! What are the
moral results?' is a question left hanging at the end of one 1851 essay,
for example.[51] In Mayhew's rosy view, the Exhibition offered a way
to correct some of these moral results, and 'to inculcate a pride of
art—to make the labourer find delight in his labour—to change him
from a muscular machine into an intellectual artist', although he acknowledges that, in a market dominated by cheap, mass-produced
products, 'workmen are beginning to feel that skill—the "art of industrial occupations"—is useless, seeing that want of skill is now
beating them out of the market'.[52] It is left eloquently unclear how
machinery will come to transform labourers into artists, rather than
the other way around. The rhetoric attaching to the machines in
1851 uses analogies to create a sense of a familiar identity for machines, but also to foreclose any further consideration of the possible
social impact of the rapidly developing machine culture. On the
whole, it is striking how little discussion there is about the conditions
of production in the literature surrounding the Exhibition.

Richards underplays the kinetic element of the spectacle at the
Great Exhibition, perhaps because it threatens to complicate his
view of the Exhibition as purely concerned with commodity display.
His view is of a seamless 'integration' of productive technology into
an Exhibition that was primarily concerned to create consumers:
'The Crystal Palace did not isolate production from consumption; to
the contrary, it successfully integrated the paraphernalia of production into the immediate phenomenal space of consumption.'[53] Tony
Bennett agrees that at the 1851 Exhibition, 'the stress was shifted
from the processes to the products of production'.[54] Yet, the emphasis in the vast and noisy Machinery in Motion section was evidently
squarely on production. Although Richards tells us that people
were prevented from touching exhibits, the work of disciplining the
British public into obedient consumers was far from complete.[55] The
Illustrated London News commented that working-class visitors
were 'more prone to touch, feel, and finger the goods than they ought

---

[51] Gordon, 'The Machinery of the Exhibition', pp. I**–VIII**, VIII**.
[52] Mayhew and Cruikshank, *1851*, 158.
[53] Thomas Richards, *Commodity Culture* (1990), 30.
[54] Tony Bennett, 'The Exhibitionary Complex', *New Formations*, 4 (Spring 1988),
73–102, 94.
[55] Richards, *Commodity Culture*, 32.

to have been', and Dickens's account of a school trip to the Exhibition records 'the greater part [of the group occupied themselves by] wetting their forefingers, and drawing a wavy pattern over every accessible object'.[56] Clearly, not every visitor was taken in by the Exhibition's attempt to make 'commodities appear autonomous and untouchable'.[57] Richards insists that '[b]y placing a spotlight, not on the means for producing the world (machines), but rather on the things produced (commodities), the Exhibition proposed that the ends of production, the things produced by all the burgeoning forms of industrial technology, become the ends of representation.'[58] On the contrary, visitors to the Machine Rooms were clearly asked to think about how things were put together, and how they worked. They were asked to witness 'the raw material enter[ing] at one extremity' and then 'the finished product emerg[ing] from the opposite end'.[59] In between were displayed the various stages of incompletion. While Richards's point that 'the exhibition made it extremely difficult to pinpoint the origins of individual objects' may have been true elsewhere in the building, in the Machinery section, the raw materials and the origins of products were openly displayed.[60]

The 1851 Exhibition can be viewed as a stark dramatization of an epistemological crisis, representing, as it did, the shift in expertise from the consumer, who handled the finished product with a knowledge of its provenance for evidence of its quality, to a professional expertise about production technologies that guaranteed consistent quality. The production process was becoming increasingly important as the new focus of expertise, '[with the end of the Guild monopolies] [u]ntil knowledge was rebuilt on the firm foundation of a production process it would be extremely difficult to categorise and evaluate goods in the absence of the old regulatory structure'.[61] It *was* extremely difficult to categorize or evaluate goods in the early 1850s, as we shall see, and knowledge was recentring on the production process in an attempt to create new standards of authenticity and to prevent fraud. But in 1851, none of this had quite coalesced,

[56] *Illustrated London News*, 31 May 1851, quoted in Richards, *Commodity Culture*, 37. Charles Dickens to the Hon. Mrs Richard Watson (11 July 1851), *LCD* vi. 429.

[57] Richards, *Commodity Culture*, 32.   [58] Ibid. 57.

[59] *The Industry of Nations*, II, 190.   [60] Richards, *Commodity Culture*, 60.

[61] William M. Reddy, 'The Structure of a Commodity Crisis: Thinking About Cloth in France Before and After the Revolution', in Arjun Appadurai (ed.), *The Social Life of Things: Commodities in Cultural Perspective* (1986), 261–84, 280.

and the categories were still oddly fluid, copies and originals, machines and art objects stood side by side in ways that inevitably threw the traditional indices of quality into disarray. Indeed, the principle of *caveat emptor* was often invoked by the liberal free-traders, throwing the burden of responsibility onto the consumer. Commercial fraud was a significant problem in the early 1850s. Samuel Smiles wrote in *Self-Help* that '[t]here are tradesmen who adulterate, contractors who "scamp", manufacturers who give us shoddy instead of wool, "dressing" instead of cotton, cast-iron tools instead of steel, needles without eyes, razors made only "to sell", and swindled fabrics in many shapes.'[62]

For the visitor, to move from the machinery section into the neighbouring Fine Arts Court, must have been to experience a noticeable hiatus between productive, dynamic, noisy process and these static, silent objects.[63] But the emphasis that the Commissioners insisted upon placing on materials and techniques in the Fine Art Court also drew attention to productive processes, and away from constructions of spontaneous genius. Paintings, for example, were admitted to the Exhibition 'not so much as examples of the skill of the artist, as of that of the preparer of colours'.[64] The powerful narrative thus created by the topography of the Exhibition served to underwrite the commodification and commercialization of art that was underway in mid-nineteenth-century Britain. Rather than exhibiting 'Culture' as compensatory to a brutalizing industrialism, in the Crystal Palace, the process by which industrialization creates a particular kind of cultural consumerism was acted out every day in front of the spectators. The Exhibition, with its working examples of line production and emphasis on the diversity of craftsmen employed in the manufacture even of art objects, explicitly celebrated the division of labour. Ironically, and perhaps unintentionally, the difficulties of representing machinery and the machine age led to a significant

---

[62] Samuel Smiles, *Self-Help: With Illustrations of Character and Perseverance* (1910), 337.

[63] The category of Fine Arts ('Sculpture, Models and Plastic Art, Mosaics, Enamels, etc.') was closely restricted at the Exhibition. Sculptures had to be by living artists, or artists who had died within three years of 1 January 1850. Pictures could only be admitted as demonstrating a new material or technique. Nikolaus Pevsner remarked that '[n]othing could be more characteristic of the uneasy position of the fine arts in the mid-Victorian milieu than the fact that they were excluded from the 1851 Exhibition,' *High Victorian Design*, 119.

[64] 3 Vol. *Exhibition Catalogue*, ii. 819. 'Paintings, as works of art, are excluded; but, as exhibiting any improvements in colours, they become admissible,' 819.

emphasis on art as commodity. Nevertheless, and perhaps less contradictorily than at first appears, there emerges in much of the surrounding literature a discernible anxiety to establish single authorship.

ORIGINALS, COPIES, AND IMITATIONS

John Ruskin was horrified by the Crystal Palace, which he described as a 'colossal receptacle for casts and copies of the art of other nations', but he was prescient enough not to dismiss it as unimportant.[65] More recent commentators have tried to do so, though. 'As for the importance of the Great Exhibition, it had none', Christopher Hobhouse claims, 'It did not bring international peace: it did not improve taste.' Paul Greenhalgh similarly describes the art exhibited in the Crystal Palace as 'on the whole, unimportant', because 'the vital rôle the fine arts were to play in most future exhibitions did not emerge in 1851'.[66] But, as Ruskin realised, 'Fine Art' was not awaiting the moment spontaneously to 'emerge': rather, the kind of 'art' that was selected for display in the Crystal Palace in 1851 tells us something crucial about the ambivalent status of aesthetic creativity in the mid-nineteenth century.

Ruskin was right—the Exhibition did contain an unconscionable number of casts and copies, both grand and trivial, from 'slabs of glass to imitate various kinds of marble'; 'specimens of wood painted in imitation of mahogany, maple and oak'; a '[s]uit of leather clothes, to imitate superfine black cloth'; to a 'casting from an antique statuette of Bacchus'; and Elkington's 'fine bronzes from the antique done by that reducing machine'.[67] Ruskin decried '[a]ll the stamped metals, and artificial stones, and imitation woods and bronzes, over the invention of which we hear daily exultation—all the short, and cheap, and easy ways of doing that whose difficulty is its honour'.[68]

[65] John Ruskin, 'The Opening of the Crystal Palace' (1854), 7.

[66] Christopher Hobhouse, *1851 and the Crystal Palace, being an account of the Great Exhibition and its contents; or Sir Joseph Paxton; and of the erection, the subsequent history and the destruction of his masterpiece* (1937), 149. Peter Greenhalgh, *Ephemeral Vistas. The Expositions Universelles, Great Exhibitions and World's Fairs, 1851–1939* (1988), 13.

[67] Quoted in Pevsner, *High Victorian Design*, 33 (Class 26, No. 2 and No. 109); *One Vol. Exhibition Catalogue*, 107 (Class 20, No. 177) and 150 (Class 30, No. 138). Queen Victoria's Exhibition Journal, quoted in Fay, *Palace of Industry*, 54.

[68] John Ruskin, 'The Lamp of Life', *The Seven Lamps of Architecture* (1849), in *The Library Edition of Works* (1996), viii. 219.

Much that was displayed as art at the Exhibition was machine-made, even if hand-finished. Elkington's electroplating process received high praise, specimens of Jordan's machine wood-carving were on display, and Queen Victoria remembered seeing 'medals made by machinery, which not more than 15 years ago were made by hand'.[69] Visitors were delighted by the zinc and bronze copy of Kiss's statue of the Amazon, which they took to be the original, but terribly disappointed by the authentic Koh-i-Noor diamond, which did not look real enough: 'nobody . . . could say that it was not a piece of glass' as the *North British Review* complained.[70]

The idea of the Exhibition also exposed wider and more general fears about mass publication that made provenance or origin difficult to establish. After all, it was not only copies that were on display—many of the machines exhibited were actually demonstrating this new facility of replication. Some of these 'Producing mechanisms' were manufacturing cultural artefacts on the premises, such as the vertical printing press 'invented by Mr Applegath' which was working at the Exhibition 'the whole time printing the "Illustrated [London] News" '.[71] It consumed '[s]heets of white paper, entering at one end of a machine, and duly delivered at the other in the form of a printed newspaper'.[72] These very new technologies of mass publishing seemed to some to threaten intellectual property: one witness to the Select Committee discussing the need for the protection of inventions at the Exhibition, worried that 'the publicity given by such means as the newspapers', could lay open ideas to theft, 'if a man chooses to do so, cannot he puff himself off as the inventor of an ingenious contrivance in the newspapers all over the country?'[73] Acquiring correct information about the provenance of objects and texts was becoming increasingly difficult.

[69] Queen Victoria's Exhibition Journal, quoted in Fay, *Palace of Industry*, 59–60.

[70] The casting of Kiss's statue in Berlin was by Geiss, with a commercial purpose, as the *Art Journal* realized: 'We have no doubt that the exhibition of these statues, so admirably calculated for gardens in England, will be followed by a large importation of similar works.' *Art Journal Illustrated Catalogue* (1851), 37. Anon., ' "The Exposition of 1851; or, Views of the Industry, the Science, and the Government of England" by Charles Babbage, Esq. (London 1851)', *North British Review* (August 1851), 529–68, 543.

[71] Henry Hensman, 'On Civil Engineering and Machinery Generally', *Lectures on the Results of the Great Exhibition of 1851* (1852), 431.

[72] Willis, 'On Machines and Tools for Working in Metal, Wood, and Other Materials', *Lectures*, 295.

[73] Evidence of A. P. Newton, Patent Agent, and of William Carpmael, Engineer and Patent Agent, Witnesses, *Minutes of Evidence, Taken Before the Select Committee of*

Ruskin was not the only contemporary commentator to disapprove of all this fakery. Matthew Digby Wyatt also deplored the results '[w]hen people paint and grain papier mâché to make it look like oak or other valuable woods'.[74] It was this issue of *value*, and the means of establishing value, that troubled both Ruskin and Wyatt when confronted with such imitations. The paradox of the new manufacturing techniques was that they seemed to destroy aesthetic value, while creating aesthetic objects, pictures, and books, with an unprecedented fecundity. Ruskin even coined the phrase 'Operative Deceit' to describe 'the substitution of cast or machine work for that of the hand', thus identifying value as moral and social rather than economic: 'For it is not the material, but the absence of the human labour which makes the thing worthless.'[75]

But there were those who were more optimistic about the future of machine copying. Ruskin's adversary, Henry Cole, for one.[76] The Department of Practical Art, set up after the Exhibition with Cole's participation, offered three collections of casts imitating well-known statues for art schools for sale at subsidized rates, with a genuine enthusiasm for their educational value.[77] Even Digby Wyatt applauded 'Mr. Cheverton's process' for the reproduction of classical sculpture 'microscopically, and almost magically . . . to bring down faultless models of the very best class of works of art to the level of the pockets of the great majority among us'.[78] The economic point was echoed by Charles Babbage, the 'author' of the calculating engine, who agreed with Ruskin both in his disgruntlement about the

the House of Lords Appointed to Consider the Bill Intituled, 'An Act to Extend the Provisions of the Designs Act, 1850, and to give protection from Piracy to Persons exhibiting New Inventions in the Exhibitions of the Works of Industry of all Nations in One thousand eight hundred and Fifty-one;' And to report thereon to the house., Brought from the Lords, 25 March 1851, 32.

[74] Matthew Digby Wyatt, 'An Attempt to Define the Principles which should Determine Form in the Decorative Arts', *Lectures on the Results of the Great Exhibition of 1851* (1853), ii. 215–51, 245.

[75] John Ruskin, 'The Lamp of Truth', *The Seven Lamps of Architecture* (1849), in *The Library Edition of Works* (1996), viii. 81 and 84.

[76] See Robert Hewison, *Ruskin and Oxford: The Art of Education* (1996).

[77] *First Report of the Department of Practical Art* (1853), 72–3.

[78] Matthew Digby Wyatt, *An Address Delivered in the Crystal Palace on November 3, 1855, At the Opening of an Exhibition of Works of Art belonging to the Arundel Society, and Consisting of Tracings and Drawings from Paintings by Giotto and other early Italian Artists, with some illustrations of Greek Sculpture and of Ancient Ivory-Carving* (1855), 22. It was originally hoped that Ruskin would deliver this address, although it is hard to imagine him enthusing quite so readily about these copies.

Exhibition, and about the 'definite line of demarcation' between art and manufacturing:

The characteristic of the fine arts is, that each example is an individual—the production of individual taste, and executed by individual hands; the produce of the fine arts is therefore necessarily costly. The characteristic of the industrial arts is, that each example is but one of a multitude,—generated according to the same law, by tools or machines, (in the largest sense of those terms,) and moved with unerring precision by the application of physical force. Their produce is consequently cheap.[79]

But for Babbage, mass production can only enhance the individual hand-work, enabling 'art to be appreciated and genius to be admired by millions whom its single productions would never reach; whilst the producer in return, elevated by the continual presence of the multiplied reproductions of the highest beauty, acquires a new source of pleasure, and feels his mechanical art raised in his estimation by such an alliance'. Although Babbage's enthusiasm for a new democracy of art is undoubtedly genuine, his description of the union of the fine with the industrial arts is as unconvincing as Cole's 'Art Manufactures' in that it evades the tangled questions of originality and authenticity.[80]

Many literary authors shared his optimism, while only dimly perceiving that the new technologies they welcomed as democratizing fine art also threatened its status. Thackeray, for example, in his 1840 *Paris Sketch Book* applauds lithography as 'the very best ally that art ever had; the best friend of the artist, allowing him to reproduce rapidly-multiplied and authentic copies of his own works (without trusting to the tedious and expensive assistance of the engraver); and the best friend to the people likewise, who have means of purchasing these cheap and beautiful productions'. He is aware that, in England, machine engraving is growing in popularity as 'commercial speculation . . . [w]e confess to a prejudice in favour of the honest work of *hand*, in matters of art, and prefer the rough workmanship of the painter to the smooth copies of his performances'.[81] So while he applauds 'authentic' copies lithographed by the artist himself, he dimly perceives the threat of commerce and the

[79] Charles Babbage, *The Exposition of 1851; or, Views of the Industry, the Science, and the Government of England* (1851), 48–9.
[80] Ibid. 49.
[81] William Thackeray, *The Paris Sketch Book by Mr Titmarsh* (1885; originally published in 1840), 193.

proliferation of the inauthentic 'smooth copies' which are machine-engraved. He fails, however, to comprehend the inexorable path from the one to the other. Indeed, by 1851, professional machine-engraving was the dominant technology for the reproduction of pictures. Wilkie Collins shared Thackeray's enthusiasm about new printing and copying technologies. In a letter he wrote during the run of the Exhibition, he excitedly speculates on the £20,000 profit made by the first two volumes of Macaulay's *History*, and he goes on to draw a parallel with the visual arts: 'Landseer's "Duke of Wellington re-visiting the field of Waterloo" . . . is to be engraved: and the sum of £3,000, has been given to the painter, for the mere right of . . . making a print of it . . . Truly, there is no want of encouragement among us, for good Literature and good Art!'[82] Collins speaks as if intellectual property is secure—in his account, the painter is in control of his property and his profits in the painting, as is Macaulay in his text. But others were more ambivalent. Tennyson, for example, who had invested heavily and disastrously in the 1840s in ' "The Patent decorative Carving and sculpture company" ', often refers in his letters to the 'wood scheme' alongside his other business of writing.[83] He wrote, '500 of my books are sold . . . I have made a sensation. I wish the wood-works would make a sensation!'[84] It would be tempting to speculate that Tennyson viewed both activities as equally commercial enterprises, but in fact he was very ambivalent about the commercial reproduction and copying of the more personal elements of his own work. He held back the publication of *In Memoriam A.H.H.* for years, for example, 'I have no wish to send [it] out yet,' and recoiled in horror from the idea of his portrait being hung at the Royal Academy Exhibition.[85] It was probably Dickens, though, with

[82] Wilkie Collins to R. H. Dana (17 June 1850), *The Letters of Wilkie Collins 1838–1865*, i, ed. William Baker and William M. Clarke (1999), 62.
[83] Alfred Tennyson to Thomas Harwicke Rawnsley (?17 March 1841), *The Letters of Alfred Lord Tennyson 1821–1850*, ed. Cecil Y. Lang and Edgar F. Shannon, Jr. (1982), i. 190–1. The company seems to have been mainly concerned with ecclesiastical carving, like Jordan's. Matthew Allen wrote, 'My friend Clissold has just ordered a screen. The Bishop of London's Brother two more chairs, and the Bishop of Chester has sent for two chairs—stalls etc. organ etc. two screens—finials—etc. etc.' Matthew Allen to Alfred Tennyson (?November 1841), *The Letters of Alfred Lord Tennyson*, i (1982), 197.
[84] Alfred Tennyson to Edmund Lushington (8 September 1842), *The Letters of Alfred Lord Tennyson*, i (1982), 209–10. I am indebted for this point to an anonymous reader of my work for Oxford University Press.
[85] Alfred Tennyson to Elizabeth Russell (30 November 1844), *The Letters of Alfred Lord Tennyson*, i (1982), 231. 'I would sooner sit a hundred times than be hung up

his strong business sense, who came closest to understanding even at mid-century the kind of pressures an ever-expanding mass market could exert on cultural production. In the Guild's play, *Not So Bad As We Seem*, Wilmot, played by Dickens, disguised as the publisher Curll, refuses the poet David Fallen's masterpiece saying, 'Can't expect such prices for poetry now-a-days, my dear Mr. Fallen. Nothing takes that is not sharp and spicy.'[86]

Tennyson's failed business venture of the 1840s was based on 'the late French invention of a new mode of carving wood', and at mid-century, wood-carving had been only recently mechanized.[87] Ralph Nicholson Wornum, in his prize-winning essay on the Exhibition, waxed lyrical about Jordan's machine-carving and its commercial potential: 'These specimens of machine-carving, the most delicate touches only being given by the hand, are quite equal to the general average of that executed wholly by hand; and where many examples of one design are required, as in church-carving, the saving of labour and expense must be enormous.'[88] His suggestion that machine and hand carving are 'quite equal' is anathema to Ruskin who insists upon the difference between the two in *The Seven Lamps of Architecture*, claiming that machine carving is easily identified by 'the look of equal trouble everywhere—the smooth, diffused tranquillity of heartless pains . . . [whereas] men cool and tire as they complete'.[89] For Ruskin, the value of hand carving is invested in the individual personality of the carpenter which transfers into his work: because 'the record of thoughts, and intents and trials . . . is the worth of the thing, just as much as the worth of anything else we call precious'.[90] It was the problematic issue of identity that underlay much of the

there, at least, by name, so don't put that into Laurence's head, please,' Alfred Tennyson to Stephen Spring Rice (early April 1845), ibid. 236.

[86] Sir Edward Bulwer Lytton, *Not So Bad As We Seem; or, Many Sides to a Character. A Comedy in Five Acts As First Performed at Devonshire House, in the Presence of Her Majesty and His Royal Highness The Prince Albert* (1851), 84.

[87] Charles Tennyson Turner to Charles Tennyson D'Eyncourt (October 24 1841), *The Letters of Alfred Lord Tennyson*, i. 196.

[88] Ralph Nicholson Wornum, 'The Exhibition as a Lesson in Taste: An Essay on Ornamental Art as Displayed in the Industrial Exhibition in Hyde Park, in which the Different Styles are Compared with a View to the Improvement of Taste in Home Manufactures', *Art Journal Illustrated Catalogue* (1851), pp. I***–XXII***, XIV***, illustrated, p. 132.

[89] John Ruskin, 'The Lamp of Life,' *The Seven Lamps of Architecture* (1849), in *The Library Edition of Works* (1996), viii. 214.

[90] John Ruskin, 'The Lamp of Truth', ibid. viii. 82.

discussion of both artistic value and intellectual property. Aesthetic value is predicated on authored artefacts with an established provenance, belonging to one building or place, and bearing the marks of the human hand. The cathedrals of Ruskin's *Seven Lamps* are, emphatically, irreplaceable, and take no part in an economy of exchange: ultimately, Ruskin refused to acknowledge the commodity value of art, and, indeed ironized the idea of commercial art in *'A Joy Forever' and its Price in the Market* (1857).

Writing about carpets rather than wood-carving, Brian Spooner has pointed to the historical moment when, 'authenticity (as we understand it now) became an issue . . . when with the appearance of mechanically produced clone-commodities we began to distinguish between the social meaning of handicraft and that of mechanical production, as well as between uniqueness and easy replaceability'.[91] The Exhibition provides us with an extraordinary close-up of the precise moment when the 'social meanings' of handicraft and machine manufacture were still unresolved, and anxieties about authenticity were surfacing. Despite all the rhetoric generated by the Exhibition about the annihilation of space and time by new technologies—'by annihilating the space which separates different nations, we produce a spectacle in which is also annihilated the time which separates one stage of the nation's progress from another'— many inventions seemed to create a novel sense of remote distance.[92] The experience of the new telegraph technology, for example, in a practical way brought communicants closer together, but also drove them further apart as the telegraph signal was devoid of personality, unlike handwriting or the human voice. Henry Cole saw this problem clearly: 'the products of machinery, which bear only very dully and remotely the mark of their original source in the hand and brain of man, have come to be contrasted with works of art which bear such marks vividly and directly', although he optimistically announced a 'reconciliation and alliance between the two'.[93] But, to some commentators in 1851, it looked less like a reconciliation and

[91] Brian Spooner, 'Weavers and Dealers: The Authenticity of an Oriental Carpet', in Arjun Appadurai (ed.) *The Social Life of Things: Commodities in Cultural Perspective* (1986), 195–235, 226.

[92] Whewell, 'The General Bearing of the Great Exhibition on the Progress of Art and Science', *Lectures*, i. 11. The phrase was fashionable in the spring of 1851. The *Illustrated London News*, for example, writes of 'the practical annihilation of space and time which we owe to the railway system'. *Illustrated London News*, 18 (3 May 1851), 343.

[93] Cole, *Fifty Years of Public Work*, i. 104–5.

alliance, and more like a frightening muddle. How was it possible to distinguish between Jordan's church screen and a painstakingly hand-carved version? Or, even more difficult and therefore more problematic, how to tell a Dickens novel from a pirated Dickens novel?

It is striking that these fears about discrimination and identity surface just at the time when a new apprehension of a 'mass' culture is emerging. The Crystal Palace had its part to play in this, too: some have characterized it as the first mass tourism event, and Dickens, overwhelmed by the 'fusion of so many sights', was so worried by the thought of the crowds converging on London in the summer of 1851 that he spent most of the season in Broadstairs in 'Expositional absence'.[94] Certainly many of the visitors who recorded their experience of the Exhibition were aware of the novel feeling of absorption into a mass. Samuel Warren, for example, wrote, 'A unit unperceived, I sink into the living stream again!—Nave, transept, aisles and galleries, pacing untired: insatiate! . . . spectacle now lost in the Spectators: then spectators, in the spectacle.'[95] Similarly, Douglas Jerrold, when he visited the Exhibition, 'felt of no more account in the multitudes than as one grain of sand to the million millions of grains that shone crystallised above and around me'.[96] The sense of being lost and bewildered in the mass seeps into descriptions of the aesthetics of the Exhibition too: Ralph Wornum, for example—troubled by the decorative confusion of the exhibits—fears the end of the 'distinct' and 'individual' identity in art:

The time has perhaps now gone by, at least in Europe, for the development of any particular or national style, and for this reason it is necessary to distinguish the various tastes that have prevailed throughout past ages, and preserve them as distinct expressions; or otherwise, by using indiscriminately all materials, we should lose all expression, and the very essence of ornament, the conveying of a distinct aesthetic expression, be utterly destroyed.[97]

The fear underlying this is of the annihilation of identity and history by a mass, and increasingly a cosmopolitan, culture. It is no accident that so much emphasis is placed upon taste in the literature

---

[94] Charles Dickens to W. H. Wills (7 April 1851), *LCD* vi. 349.

[95] Warren, *The Lily and the Bee*, 45. For mass tourism and the Exhibition see Auerbach, 'Integration and Segregation', 151–8.

[96] Douglas Jerrold, 'Christmas Thoughts of the Crystal Palace', *Illustrated London News* (20 December 1851), 738.

[97] Wornum, 'The Exhibition as a Lesson in Taste', *Art Journal Illustrated Catalogue*, p. xxii***.

surrounding the Exhibition. In a culture in which it is increasingly difficult to discern the difference between the copy and the original, the ability to discriminate is both paramount, and ideologically loaded.[98] Commentators frequently bemoan the public's lack of taste and need for education. William Thackeray, for example, laments 'the many, who have not yet certainly arrived at properly appreciating fine art'.[99] Ruskin admits that hand-work cannot always be distinguished from machine-work, if men 'reduce their labour to the machine level . . . the effect of the whole, as compared with the same design cut by a machine or a lifeless hand, will be like that of poetry well read and deeply felt to that of the same verses jangled by rote'.[100] '[M]any', he adds, cannot tell the difference. The literary analogy is telling, poetry 'well read' or recited 'by rote': the difference between the two is elusive and vague—a personal matter of feeling, inflection, and education. In the face of an encroaching machine culture, Ruskin seems to be trying to claw back some marker of aesthetic value. But if value is both so fragile and so extrinsic, available only to the perception and sensitivity of certain consumers, intrinsic aesthetic value becomes hard to evaluate.

During the Parliamentary discussion of what to do with Paxton's Exhibition building, a telling exchange occurred between the engineer, Sir William Cubitt, and the Director of the British Museum, Edward Hawkins, who were discussing the possible establishment of an art school in the building:

[Cubitt:] You think a modern work, exactly like the original, would do just as well for the purposes of artists? [Hawkins:] Not quite; but I would have there a cast of every well-known statue in Europe . . . [Cubitt:] My remark was *exactly* like them (if you can have casts exactly like any one of the antiques); if they were exactly like the originals they would be equally useful for the purposes of artists? [Hawkins:] Yes, supposing you could get them exactly like them; but there is the material and a great deal more comprised in perfect identity . . . [Cubitt:] Identity and similarity are different things? [Hawkins:] They may be similar, but not the same. There is the effect of time and age on the surface, and other differences.[101]

[98] As Pierre Bourdieu has pointed out, the cultivation of 'taste' also helps to stimulate economic activity. Bourdieu, *Distinction: A Social Critique of the Judgement of Taste*, trans. Richard Nice (1984).

[99] Thackeray, *Paris Sketch Book*, 194.

[100] John Ruskin, 'The Lamp of Life', *Complete Works*, viii. 214.

[101] *Report of the Commissioners Appointed to Inquire into the Cost and Applicability of the Exhibition Building in Hyde Park* (1852), 34 (emphases added).

Copies, unmarked by time, unanchored by their contexts, evade history to move out of their rightful places. They summon up a nightmare of endless repetition that also underlies Ralph Wornum's powerful disgust for the exhibits in the Crystal Palace, those 'endless specimens of the prevailing gorgeous taste of the present day, which gives the eye no resting-place, and presents no idea to the mind, from the want of individuality in its gorged designs'.[102] The haunting imagery of formlessness and excess again reverts to the underlying and frightening idea of the undifferentiated mass and its deleterious effect upon aesthetic values. The emotive force of Wornum's language alerts us to the latent power of the exhibits, so many of them excessive in their decorative detail. Merely to dismiss them as meaningless *kitsch* is inadequate. The exhibits of 1851 summoned up such powerful feelings for contemporary observers such as Wornum and Ruskin, because they seemed to encode an attack on history, identity, and English culture. Ruskin felt that promiscuous copying not only detracted from the original, but actually destroyed it: 'Many of these [shop ornaments] are in themselves thoroughly good copies of fine things, which things themselves we shall never, in consequence, enjoy any more.'[103] Even Henry Cole's Society of Arts acknowledged that '[m]uch of the *conventional* value of a picture depends upon its being *unique*.'[104] For Ruskin, whose writing about the new copy culture is never less than apocalyptic, the destruction of the original was tantamount to the destruction of history, and, therefore, the undermining of all possible referents of identity.

In fact, much of the celebratory rhetoric about the Exhibition focused on the collapsing of history in the Crystal Palace. The *Edinburgh Review* extravagantly suggested that the Exhibition 'unroll[ed] this before the eyes of men, the whole stream of history furnishing its contingent,—placing Archimedes, Arkwright, Davy, Jacquard, Watt, and Stephenson side by side'.[105] William Whewell

---

[102] Wornum, 'The Exhibition as a Lesson in Taste', *Art Journal Illustrated Catalogue*, p. v***.

[103] John Ruskin, 'The Lamp of Beauty', *The Seven Lamps of Architecture* (1849), in *The Library Edition of Works* (1996), viii. 157.

[104] Society for the Encouragement of Arts, Manufactures, and Commerce, *Report of the Artistic Committee to the Council* ([1858]), 8. The Committee was appointed in December 1857.

[105] 'Official Catalogue of the great Exhibition of the works of Industry of All nations, 1851 4th corrected edition, 15th September 1851', *Edinburgh Review*, 94 (October 1851), 557–98, 562.

saw '[t]he infancy of nations, their youth, their middle age, and their maturity, all appear, in their simultaneous aspect, like the most distant objects revealed at the same moment by a flash of lightning in a dusky night.'[106] But such positive readings of the collapse of history can flip all too easily into Ruskin's apocalyptic and terrifying vision of modernity as an exile from all origins. When *he* gazed into the Crystal Palace to read the future, Ruskin saw only a sad travesty of the past, and history lying in ruins: 'We shall wander through our palaces of crystal, gazing sadly on copies of pictures torn by cannon-shot, and on casts of sculptures dashed to pieces long ago. We shall gradually learn to distinguish originality and sincerity from the decrepitudes of imitation and palsies of repetition; but it will be only in hopelessness.'[107] Ruskin's dystopic vision of a world in which a debased commodity culture has prevailed powerfully expresses the anxiety which also surfaced at the Exhibition itself to reinscribe objects with versions of authorship and originality.

AUTHORSHIP AT THE EXHIBITION

At the close of the Great Exhibition, William Whewell, scientist and Master of Trinity College, Cambridge, was invited to give a lecture about its effects by the Royal Society of Arts. He spoke on the 'Progress of Art and Science', and his lecture started with an elaborate analogy between the 'literary art' and '*material* art':[108]

The *Poet*, as the Greeks called him, was the *Maker*, as our English fathers, also were wont to call him. And man's power of making may show itself not only in the beautiful *texture* of language, the grand *machinery* of the epic, the sublime display of poetical *imagery*: but in those material works which supply the originals from which are taken the derivative terms which I have just been compelled to use.[109]

[106] Whewell, 'The General Bearing of the Great Exhibition on the Progress of Art and Science', *Lectures*, i. 1–34, 13. The intrinsic racism of such interpretations was borne out by the layout of the Exhibition itself, which represented nations such as India as in their technological 'infancy', while Britain was represented as the technological 'parent', thus shamelessly discounting the important technology transfer that had taken place in the eighteenth and early nineteenth centuries from India to Britain, particularly in the textiles industries.

[107] Ruskin, 'The Opening of the Crystal Palace', 18.

[108] Whewell, 'The General Bearing of the Great Exhibition on the Progress of Art and Science', in *Lectures*, 1–34, 6.

[109] Ibid. 5.

Whewell was trying to link together the disparate elements of the Exhibition, which otherwise threatened to overwhelm him. Indeed, this Exhibition made little hierarchical distinction between art objects, machines, and scientific instruments, and the catalogue frequently lists several diverse objects under one entry: for example: 'No. 205. Mordan: Sampson & Co., City Road—Manufacturers. Bright steel fire-proof jewel box, decorated with ormolu ornaments. And complex self-acting rose engine and tracing machine.'[110] Like Charlotte Brontë, Whewell is bewildered by this extraordinary medley of exhibits, and devotes much of his lecture to discussing classification in such detail as to reveal a profound anxiety about the lack of order in the Crystal Palace. Similarly, his use of the literary analogy in his search for some cohesive descriptive model reveals an underlying preoccupation with both *legibility* and *provenance*. He fantasizes the Exhibition itself as a text that needs 'reading' and each exhibit as potentially legible, too, seeing 'a vast multitude of compositions—not of words, but of things'.[111]

The powerful but unspoken concept that informs Whewell's lecture is that of authorship: compositions necessarily presuppose composers. Yet, in reality, the Exhibition represented a challenge to the literary model that Whewell chose, and he is unable to develop his analogy too precisely according to the traditional notion of authorship. This is a difficulty everywhere apparent: in the Catalogue, 'Works in Precious Metals, Jewellery Etc.' are introduced thus, 'upon the reduction of the unshapen metal into its present forms, the artist and mechanic have both been occupied, and . . . the result is to indicate not less the talent of the one than the industrial skill of the other'.[112] The sentence is structured to level 'talent' and 'skill' into one concept so that it becomes difficult to decide who owns which part of the work. So much in the Exhibition was copied that it became difficult to attribute one author even to artworks. Matthew Digby Wyatt's sumptuous volumes of illustrations of the 'choicest specimens' of 1851 makes this multiple authorship clear.[113] Plate 77,

---

[110] 3 Vol. *Exhibition Catalogue*, i (Section II, Class 6: Manufacturing Machines and Tools), 291.

[111] Whewell, 'The General Bearing of the Great Exhibition on the Progress of Art and Science', in *Lectures*, i. 1–34, 6.

[112] 3 Vol. *Exhibition Catalogue*, ii. 671.

[113] Matthew Digby Wyatt, *The Industrial Arts of the Nineteenth Century. A Series of Illustrations of the Choicest Specimens Produced by Every Nation at the Great Exhibition of Works of Industry, 1851 Dedicated, by permission, to his Royal*

for example, of the statue of 'The Boy at the Stream' by J. H. Foley, is 'cast in Bronze by Hatfield of London'. He goes on to give biographies of both Foley and Hatfield, in which Hatfield's 'zeal for the attainment of perfection in his art' is taken as seriously as Foley's.[114] John Bell's popular 'Andromeda' was cast in bronze, and Wyatt writes, 'While, therefore, a high meed of praise must be awarded to Mr. Bell for the talent he has displayed in this composition, we must at the same time recognise the skill with which the processes of founding have been carried out by the Coalbrook Dale Company, and the dextrous manipulation of the chasers whom they employ.'[115] Again talent and skill are combined in the object so that it is difficult to decide who owns which part of the work. Thomas Richards mentions 'a little enclosure called the "Medieval Court," the handiwork of A. W. Pugin.' But this was not really handiwork at all, as Wyatt's description makes clear, 'Plate 82, Jewellery in the medieval style Hardman, Birmingham.' 'Designed by PUGIN' is added in much smaller letters underneath. As one journal noticed at the time, 'The most striking and serious difficulty felt by the committee, is that of determining to whom the merit of perfection in various branches of manufacture is to be attributed . . . Who is to decide whether to the designer or to the manufacturer the palm of merit is due?'[116]

Whewell's response to this challenge is to use language to create a sense of the closeness of mechanical and artistic labour. He speaks of 'an artificer, an artisan, an artist'—allowing the words to slide into one another as if they were interchangeable.[117] But Wyatt draws attention to the division of labour: 'clerks, artists, modellers, carvers, pattern-makers, moulders, furnace-men, casters, finishers, smiths, fitters, japanners, painters, gilders, bronzists, and decorators, all contribute to the elaboration of that extraordinary series of objects,'

Highness the Prince Albert, 2 vols. (1851–3). The volumes themselves represented 'the most important application of Chromo-Lithography to assist the connexion which should subsist between Art and Industry . . . [and] has been produced upon a scale of magnitude, and with a degree of rapidity, unexampled in this or in any other country', i. p. ix (unpaginated).

[114] Ibid. i. pl. 77.

[115] Ibid. i. pl. 53. 'Jewellery in the Medieval Style, Manufactured by Hardman of Birmingham. Designed by Pugin', ii. pl. 82.

[116] *The Journal of the Great Exhibition of 1851 its Origin, History and Progress*, 2 (23 November 1850), 33. This was an occasional publication produced by the office of *The Critic* and the *London Literary Journal*.

[117] Whewell, 'The General Bearing of the Great Exhibition on the Progress of Art and Science', in *Lectures*, i. 16.

he says.[118] Nevertheless, the Commissioners insisted upon maintaining a link between exhibitor and exhibit, and asked that every exhibitor should 'state in what capacity he appeared, [as] it is often difficult to define the precise degrees of merit belonging respectively to the capitalist who supplies the means and stimulates the production of an article, the manufacturer who actually executes the work, the designer who imparts beauty, and other persons who in various ways contribute to bring it before the world'.[119] The Official Catalogue, itself a 'work produced by many thousand authors', subsequently listed exhibits not under their own functions or names, but under an originary name of some kind.[120] It gives the following possibilities as modifications on the traditional role of author: 'Inv. Inventor; Des. Designer; Mod. Modeller; Sculp. Sculptor, Carver or Engraver; Exec. Executed by; Prod. Producer; Manu., Manufacturer; Imp. Importer; Prop. Proprietor; Pat. Patent Reg. Registered; Impr. Improver; Pro. Reg. Provisionally Registered.'[121] This was a continuation of the earlier policy of the Society of Arts, which had run competitions for 'Art Manufactures' in the 1840s in which '[i]t was a condition . . . that the manufacturer's name should be given, and attached to any object rewarded.'[122] Digby Wyatt comments on the Coalbrook Dale Company's wrought iron dome built to house Bell's sculpture 'The Eagle Slayer' that it 'do[es] credit alike to Mr. Bell, the sculptor, and to the Company'.[123] The addition of the 'Company' is significant as the role traditionally taken by the author or inventor is increasingly taken over in the Exhibition by corporate enterprise: this is the grey dawn of brand marketing. Elkington and Mason of Birmingham; Fox, Henderson & Co.; Hardman of

---

[118] Digby Wyatt, *The Industrial Arts*, i. pl. 19. ' "Bell's Eagle Slayer" and its Dome' (Coalbrook Dale Company).

[119] *First Report of the Commissioners*, p. xliii.

[120] Robert Ellis, 'Preface', *3. Vol. Exhibition Catalogue*, i. pp. v–viii, vi. See also non., 'The Catalogue's Account of Itself', *Household Words* (23 August 1851), 519–23.

[121] 'Abbreviations Used in the Work', *One Vol. Exhibition Catalogue*, 2 (unpaginated). An example from the full Exhibition Catalogue, from 'Class 6: Manufacturing Machines and Tools' is: 'Booth and Co., Preston, Lancashire—Manufacturers; Crabtree, Thomas, Godley, near Halifax—Manufacturer; Dalton, John, Mottram-in-Longendale—Inventor; Preston, Francis, Manchester—Manufacturer; Parr, Curtis, & Madeley, Manchester—Manufacturers and Patentees.' *3 Vol. Exhibition Catalogue*, i. 268.

[122] Cole, *Fifty Years of Public Work*, i. 105.

[123] Digby Wyatt, *The Industrial Arts of the Nineteenth Century*, i. pl. 19. ' "Bell's Eagle Slayer" and its Dome' (Coalbrook Dale Company).

Birmingham: these are names that appear again and again in accounts of the Exhibition, standing in the place where the author once stood. Fox, Henderson & Co., the company that had cast the iron girders for the Crystal Palace itself, exhibited a hydraulic press draped with an enormous banner with the company's name emblazoned across it.[124] Despite, or perhaps because of, the expansion of the division of labour, the conspicuous display of provenance was an important part of the Exhibition.

This bespeaks a still considerable desire on the part of the organizers and exhibitors to author objects, despite the evident difficulty of doing so in an increasingly technologically sophisticated world. On the one hand the Exhibition celebrated the impact of technology on traditional notions of art. Whewell spoke of the necessity for 'a common language' for 'the manufacturer, the man of science, the artisan, [and] the merchant', and it was already clear that this language could no longer be the heroic language of authorship: rather it would be a language 'in which they could speak of the objects *about which they are concerned*'.[125] On the other hand, the rhetoric of heroic invention in the arts and sciences persisted, as the Exhibition offered an unmissable opportunity for the rehearsal of the heroic-inventor version of industrial history, celebrating 'the toiling sons of genius and of labour', and much ephemeral verse was written in 1851 to the same purpose, 'No Newtons lost, to Heav'n and Earth, shall perish in this age | Unknown, uncrown'd, without a place, reserved in Fame's great page— | No Watts unprized, No Arkwrights scorn'd,—seek an untrophy'd grave, | Foster'd shall be each faculty, the Almightiest Ruler gave.'[126]

Many of the exhibits, too, represented such historical heroes. Elkington, Mason, & Co. exhibited an electroplate vase decorated with four statuettes representing Newton, Bacon, Shakespeare, and Watt, with a model of Prince Albert 'surmounting the composition' (see Fig. 2).[127] The whole was 'intended to represent the triumph of science and the industrial Arts in the Great Exhibition. The style is Elizabethan enriched.'[128] Elkington's was a Birmingham manufac-

---

[124] *The Industry of Nations*, II, 108.
[125] Whewell, 'The General Bearing of the Great Exhibition on the Progress of Art and Science', in *Lectures*, i. 25 (emphasis added).
[126] Thomas Bazeley, 'Cotton as an Element of Industry; its Confined Supply, and its Extending Consumption by Increasing and Improving Agencies', *Lectures on the Results of the Great Exhibition of 1851* (1853), ii. 107–46, 108. Lady Emmeline Stuart Wortley, *Honour to Labour. A Lay of 1851* (n.d.), 8.
[127] *Art Journal Illustrated Catalogue*, 195.   [128] Ibid. 195.

contribution of Messrs. Elkington,—a Vase, intended to represent the triumph of Science and the Industrial Arts in the Great Exhibition; the style is Elizabethan enriched. Four 'statuettes on the body of the vase represent Newton, Bacon, Shakspeare, and Watt, commemorating Astronomy, Philosophy, Poetry, and Mechanics respectively. On the four bas-reliefs, between these figures, the practical operations of Science and Art are displayed, and their influences typified by the figures on the base, indicating War,

Rebellion, Hatred, and Revenge, overthrown and chained. The recognition and the reward of peaceful industry are symbolised by the figure of Prince Albert surmounting the composition, who, as Patron of the Exhibition, is rewarding the successful contributors. The height of the vase is four feet; it was designed and modelled by Mr. W. Beattie. Among the other manufactures of this firm, is a group, in silver, representing "Queen Elizabeth entering Kenilworth Castle."

FIG. 2. Elkington's electroplate vase showing
Netwon, Bacon, Shakespeare, and Watt.

tory at the forefront of the new electroplating technology. The vase also offers material proof of how important it had become in 1851 to find an ancestry and provenance for modern inventive practices in order to defuse their threat to traditional notions of art. Henry Ellison confronted just such a threat in a sonnet entitled, 'To Artists who Look with Jealous Eyes on Artistical Processes, Such as Chromalithography [*sic*], etc. etc.'

> Fear not—the great, creative mind of Man
> Takes a far wider scope than sense can span;
> And all these rare inventions have but worth
> As means and instruments, whereby he can
> Mould more completely to his will this earth,
> And give his own divine conceptions birth![129]

Industrial production processes put pressure on traditional eighteenth-century ideas of the creative individual.

The portrayal of Shakespeare shoulder to shoulder with the inventor-industrialist Watt on this vase is evidence of how poets and inventors were memorialized in this period as jointly foundational to England's greatness. But the odd pair also demonstrate how slippery the boundaries between cultural production and commercial manufacturing seemed at the Great Exhibition. Representations of Shakespeare were very popular: 'Particularly admired was a round table of rosewood, finely inlaid with mother-of-pearl, metal and ivory, having in its centre a portrait of Shakespeare surrounded by scenes from [his plays],' and, according to the *Athenaeum*, 'one of the noblest works in the Exhibition' was a full-length statue of Shakespeare by J. Bell (see Fig. 3).[130] Visitors to the Exhibition could order copies from Henry Cole, aka Felix Summerly, whose catalogue also listed a 'Shakespeare Clock' modelled by Bell. Both items were manufactured in the new material designed to imitate marble cheaply, Parian, by Minton & Co., and there was also listed 'The Shakespeare Salver or Card Dish', featuring designs by D. Maclise of 'The Seven Ages of Shakespeare'. We are told that the [electroplate] dish 'will aim to be worthy of the best days of Benvenuto Cellini'.[131]

---

[129] Henry Ellison, 'To Artists Who Look with Jealous Eyes on Artistical Processes, Such as Chromalithography, Etc. Etc.', in *The Poetry of Real Life. Sonnets* (1844), 66.

[130] Yvonne ffrench, *The Great Exhibition: 1851* (n.d. [?1951]), 246, and Cole, *Fifty Years of Public Work*, ii. 183, quoted from the *Athenaeum*.

[131] Cole, *Fifty Years of Public Work*, ii. 182, 183, 188. The dish, if not original, is an early example of the limited edition, 'a limited number of copies will be made . . .

FIG. 3. 'Shakespeare' by John Bell.

Bell's statue, which was itself copied from the Janssen bust in the Holy Trinity Church, Stratford, spawned a new generation of copies in Felix Summerley's workshops.

It is not surprising that Shakespeare featured so prominently at the Exhibition, as the poet was coming increasingly to prominence at this time as an emblem and reminder that 'Britain's greatness rested on the ideas and successes of its heroes,' as Jeffrey Auerbach puts it.[132] The image of Shakespeare is able to perform complex ideological work: standing for autonomous authorship (despite the fact that much of his work was collaborative), and for the common patrimony of English culture, as distinct from the nobility of inherited class. This representation of Shakespeare as, in some ill-defined way, common property and democratically available was played upon by *Punch* in a cartoon published on 5 July 1851, entitled 'Dinner-Time at the Crystal Palace'.[133] The cartoon shows Bell's statue of Shakespeare, with its inscription clearly visible 'One touch of Nature makes the whole world kin,' presiding over a crowd of proletarian visitors who perch around its base to eat packed lunches and breastfeed their babies (see Fig. 4).[134] In fact, the popularity of Shakespeare at an Exhibition that managed to present a seeming cornucopia of democratically available products and knowledge, while also celebrating private property and ownership, can be explained by his capacity to look both ways at once: his work is the property of all England, but also representative of individual and unique genius. Standing for both the author and the people, Shakespeare becomes symbolic of the site at which the public and private ownership of

when the models will be destroyed', 182. There was also a stained glass window on display by E. Baillie, which depicted 'Shakspere at the Court of Queen Elizabeth'. See Anon., 'Sculpture and the Plastic Arts', in the *Illustrated Exhibitor* (18 October 1851), 383–4, illustration 383.

[132]   Auerbach, *The Great Exhibition of 1851*, 113.

[133]   The statue is pictured in the engraving of the 'British Nave' in *Dickinson's Comprehensive Pictures of the Great Exhibition of 1851. From the originals painted for HRH Prince Albert by Messrs. Nash, Haghe, and Roberts, R. A. Published under the Express Sanction of His Royal Highness Prince Albert, President of the Royal Commission, to whom the work is, by permission, dedicated* (1854), ii (unpaginated). An engraving of 'Bell's Statue of Shakspere' appears in the full catalogue of the Exhibition, *3 Vol. Exhibition Catalogue* (1851), ii. 847 (unpaginated). A more detailed engraving can be found in the *Illustrated Exhibitor* (5 July 1851), 86.

[134]   For a more detailed discussion of this cartoon, and of representations of Shakespeare at the 1851 Exhibition more generally, see my forthcoming article 'Shakespeare at the Great Exhibition of 1851', in *Victorian Shakespeare*, ii, ed. Gail Marshall and Adrian Poole (forthcoming 2003).

THE LAST DAYS OF SMITHFIELD.

SMITHFIELD is going, is going, is going,
Smithfield is going, and soon will be gone;
No more will the lowing, the lowing, the lowing
Of ring-droves in agony startle the dawn.

No longer the squeaking, the squeaking, the
   squeaking
Of pigs, with lambs' bleating, will tunefully blend;
Nor females with shrieking, with shrieking, with
   shrieking,
As they fly from the mad ox, our ear-drums will
   rend.

The drovers, by swearing, by swearing, by swearing,
No longer will heighten the sheep-dog's fierce bark,
While the torches are flaring, are flaring, are flaring,
On each market morning, so early, by dark.

Those cruel brutes' oak sticks, their oak sticks,
   their oak sticks,
No more on the horns of the oxen will ring;
They'll soon cease to poke sticks, to poke sticks,
   to poke sticks,
Armed with goads, in the flank the poor creatures
   to sting.

The Market's Committee, Committee, Committee,
Let us hope, will not make the Lords throw out
   the bill;
So, preserving the City, the City, the City
In its old vested rights, and its nastiness still.

TRIFLES (NOT SO) LIGHT AS AIR.

WE understand that the Commissioners of
Police are about to issue orders for the regulation of the now inconveniently crowded balloon
traffic of the Metropolis. So long as the intrepid
voyagers were likely to confine their collisions to
each other, it was not thought necessary for the
authorities to interfere, as the evil was likely to
correct itself to a certain extent, and so mitigate
the mischief. There was not so much objection
to the inconvenience falling upon the heads of
the aeronauts, but now that the aeronauts seem
likely to fall on to the heads of the public, something should be done to put a stop to the
nuisance. We believe it is in contemplation to
give directions, that no balloon be allowed to
set down, or tumble down, within a mile of the
Crystal Palace. Had that volatile daughter of
air, MRS. GRAHAM, let out her grappling-irons,
the other day, upon the Exhibition, they would
have proved the most serious difficulties it has
yet had to grapple with.

An Error Corrected.

AT the War Medal dinner, LORD SALTOUN,
the Chairman, said—
   "When he alluded to woman—he begged pardon, he
meant ladies."

Ergo, a lady is not a woman.

ONE TOUCH OF NATURE
MAKES THE WHOLE WORLD KIN.

DINNER-TIME AT THE CRYSTAL PALACE.

FIG. 4. 'Dinner Time at the Crystal Palace'.

cultural property confront one another not only in the Crystal Palace but also in the literature it generated, and in the copyright and patent debates at the time.

This conflict between public and private ownership of knowledge at the Exhibition is clear in the documentation surrounding it. Prince Albert had claimed in his 1849 speech at the Mansion House that, 'knowledge acquired becomes at once the property of the community at large. Whilst formerly discovery was wrapt in secrecy, the publicity of the present day causes that no sooner is a discovery or invention made, than it is already improved upon and surpassed by competing efforts.'[135] To the burghers of the City of London, Albert presented the 'transparent envelope' of the Crystal Palace as a temple to the victory of Free Trade and a new and open 'spirit of friendly competition'.[136] The Catalogue tells a different story, excusing the vagueness of some of its descriptions of exhibits as due to the inventor's desire 'to reveal as little as possible of the specific character of his articles', and the *Athenaeum* had reported on the eve of the Exhibition, that '[a] fear of piracy was the shadow here and there infesting the general cordiality with which the [Exhibition] was hailed'.[137] The official 'Rules for Visitors to the Exhibition' stated that '[n]o drawing of any article exhibited can be taken except upon a written authority from the proprietor, countersigned by an officer of the Executive Committee'.[138] Charlotte Brontë was right to notice the guards on her visit. Mr Douisthorpe, for example, showed his wool-combing machine for the first time at the Exhibition, and it was 'very jealously watched, and its working parts were generally, as far as possible, concealed from public inspection'.[139] The Exhibition staged a kind of democratic free-for-all, in which British visitors were encouraged to feel a pride of ownership in the exhibits, but the large majority of them were privately owned, and emphatically not 'the property of the community at large', as Albert would have had it.[140]

Indeed, the Exhibition itself was fraught with contested property rights from the beginning. There was even a minor dispute over who

---

[135] Prince Albert's Speech at the Mansion House in 1849, quoted in Cole, *Fifty Years of Public Work* (1884), ii. 212–13, 213.

[136] *First Report of the Commissioners*, p. liv.

[137] Henry Cole, 'Introduction', *Volume One: Index and Introductory. 3 Vol. Exhibition Catalogue*, i. 25. *Athenaeum* (22 December 1849), 1305.

[138] *First Report of the Commissioners*, 30.

[139] Anon., *The Industry of Nations*, II, 136–7.

[140] 'Most popular of all was J. M. Farina's fountain of *Eau-de-Cologne*, which played continually throughout the whole run of the Exhibition, and into which hand-

first thought up the idea: Henry Cole claimed he was the begetter, but 'Francis Fuller . . . another member [of the Society of Arts], declared in an aggrieved testamentary document that he himself was the originator'.[141] Then it was Paxton's turn to be challenged as inventor of the building, because several of the 240 entrants in the original competition had proposed glass and iron structures.[142] Among the displays, the electric telegraph, Parian ware, and electroplating were all contested inventions, and Henry Cole warned Lord Northcote that the manufacturer, Mr Osler, 'must not be brought into any contact with Mr. Minton, as they have had serious disputes, and gone to law with one another under circumstances which have left a strong impression'.[143] By examining issues of intellectual property at the Exhibition, it is perhaps easier to see how the construction of the autonomous author was attenuated to its extreme by the 1850s. The fuss over intellectual property rights revealed just how fragile such a reading of the heroic author/inventor had become by 1851, but also revealed the great cultural investment in such an idea, which, as Mark Rose has argued, 'is deeply rooted in our conception of ourselves as individuals with at least a modest grade of singularity, some degree of personality'.[144] Jeffrey Auerbach has described the Great Exhibition as a 'cultural battlefield'. But the battle spilled out well

kerchiefs were freely and repeatedly dipped. Of this and the fountain of Aqua d'Oro, 270 gallons were distributed among the public.' ffrench, *The Great Exhibition: 1851*, 247.

[141] Ibid. 12.

[142] 'Some doubts have been at various times raised respecting that gentleman's [Paxton's] claim to be regarded as the inventor of the most characteristic features of the great structure.' Anon., 'Official Catalogue of the Great Exhibition of the Works of Industry of All Nations, 1851: 4th corrected edition, 15th September 1851', *Edinburgh Review*, 94 (October 1851), 557–98, 572.

[143] Henry Cole to Lord Northcote quoted in Yvonne ffrench, *The Great Exhibition: 1851*, 56. The invention of the telegraph was claimed by both Wheatstone and Cooke. Wheatstone pointed to his scientific attainments as Professor of Natural Philosophy at King's College London as proof of his priority, while Cooke claimed that his role in projecting and managing the telegraph as a complete system were proof that his was the superior part of the inventive process. See Iwan Rhys Morris, *Frankenstein's Children: Electricity, Exhibition, and Experiment in Early-Nineteenth-Century London* (1998), 163. The invention of Parian ware was contested by Herbert Minton and Alderman Copeland (Pevsner, *High Victorian Design*, 123), and Matthew Digby Wyatt tells us that '[t]he original invention of the electrotyping process has been claimed by two persons,—by Mr. Thomas Spencer of Liverpool, and by Professor Jacobi of St. Petersburg, and their rival claims were laid before the Chemical Section of the British Association for the Promotion of Science, at a meeting of that body in Glasgow' ('Group of Objects Executed in Electrotype by Elkington and Mason of Birmingham', *The Industrial Arts*, ii. pl. 79).

[144] Mark Rose, *Authors and Owners* (1993), 142.

beyond the railings of Hyde Park that summer. By looking more closely at issues of intellectual property both at the Exhibition and at Westminster, we can start to unravel what, until now, has been the largely unexplored connection between the theorization of artistic and technological creativity. The triumph of the literary precedent in the case of patent law serves to remind us that in the mid-nineteenth century, technology was still being written into a conventional model of culture—even if, in half-hidden ways, it was already at work rewriting and transforming that culture.

PATENTS AND PROPERTY AT THE EXHIBITION AND THE 1852 PATENT ACT

What effect did a glass exhibition building have on ideas about property? It is tempting to speculate that the startlingly transparent nature of the Crystal Palace, with its 'prevalence of light . . . and an absence of all shadow', exacerbated worries about displaying, or, as the Victorians also put it, 'publishing' exhibits, and laying them open to piracy.[145] The ease with which it was now possible to replicate objects and texts led, inevitably, to anxieties about copying, too. The Preface to the Official Catalogue may have congratulated the British public on '[t]he friendly confidence reposed by other nations in our institutions; the perfect security for property; [and] the commercial freedom', but many felt that security for property and commercial freedom were in direct conflict in the Crystal Palace.[146]

Certainly, the preparation for the Exhibition brought the law on intellectual property into sharp focus. Piracy at the Exhibition seemed so easy: one commentator remarked that, 'by going round the Exhibition and examining the articles; I have no doubt that I could seal a great number of patents'.[147] Similar fears were expressed at the public meetings held around Britain to discuss regional contributions to the Exhibition, 'it was a constant question by artizans and others how, under the existing patent laws, they could exhibit their inventions without forfeiting protection to the fruit of their talent

---

[145] Anon.,'A Glance at the Exhibition', *Chambers's Edinburgh Journal*, 15–16 (31 May 1851), 337. Cole, *Fifty Years of Public Work*, ii. 182. 'The Inkstand also is published separately in Bronze in the ancient Florentine mode.'

[146] 'Extracts from the Preface to the Catalogue of the Exhibition', quoted in Cole, *Fifty Years of Public Work*, ii. 208.

[147] 'Sealing' was the technical term for achieving a successful patent.

and skill'.[148] The problem was a serious one. The patenting process as it stood was still costly, unwieldy, and often ineffective. The Manchester Local Committee decided 'to raise a fund to assist artisans and others who were unable to send articles to the Exhibition from want of pecuniary resources', but the scheme was not successful and '[t]he working men . . . generally refused to exhibit on finding that mechanical inventions had no security from piracy.'[149] The difficulty was compounded by the mismanagement that led to a promise of patent protection in the 1850 Prospectus for the Exhibition later being withdrawn when it became clear that it would be impossible to enforce it within the current terms of the law. At this point, in London alone, '75 Exhibitors had withdrawn their demands for space, and we then found we had not enough to fill up the space allotted to us'.[150] The Commissioners had intimated that a lucifer-match making machine would be a welcome exhibit, but not one lucifer-match making company in London would exhibit for fear of piracy. The London committee finally resorted to using some well-established and securely patented machinery, such as Nasmyth's steam-hammer, to fill empty spaces.

As a result of this dispute, the subject of patents was raised urgently in the House of Commons in April 1851, only a month before the Exhibition was due to open. Colonel Sibthorp was insistent that Parliament should use the opportunity offered by the Great Exhibition to return to the issue of patent legislation, 'he believed nothing would have been done but for the Exhibition of the Industry of all Nations . . . Since 1829, they had all been asleep respecting the good of the country, and the freedom of the country',[151] and he continued: 'Foreigners could come and pirate the inventions of our country-men,' and then 'undersell the ingenious and laborious mechanics of our own land'.[152] A temporary, last-minute measure, the Protection

---

[148] 'Report from Mr. Peter Le Neve Foster upon the Working of the "Protection of Inventions Act 1851"', Appendix XXIII, *First Report of the Commissioners*, 109.

[149] 'Statement of the Operations of the Manchester Local Committee', *First Report of the Commissioners*, 54–5.

[150] 'Statement of the Proceedings of the Metropolitan Committee', *First Report of the Commissioners*, 56.

[151] Colonel Sibthorp (1 April 1851), *Hansard*, Parl. Debs. (series 3), vol. 115, col. 891.

[152] Ibid. col. 892. Sibthorp was a notorious Parliamentary enemy of the Exhibition, and created a great stir about the proposed destruction of the elm trees on the Hyde Park site. Paxton subsequently designed his building around the trees, and the effect was generally agreed to be felicitous. See ffrench, *The Great Exhibition: 1851*, 76–84.

of Inventions Act 1851, was hastily passed to protect unpatented British inventions displayed at the Exhibition, but would expire in April 1852, so the subsequent debate about permanent reform was attended by a degree of urgency. After the Exhibition, the Patent Laws were still unreformed and temporary protection was fast running out. It was renewed until the end of October 1852, but the Commissioners spelt out the urgency of the situation in strong language in their First Report on the Exhibition: 'a great injustice is committed towards the applicants under this Act. They exhibited their inventions; they disclosed them to the public in the confident hope (I might almost say under a pledge) that before their protection expired, they would be enabled easily and cheaply to perfect their rights under a new and improved system of patent law'.[153]

'I hope the Patent Law will get through!' Prince Albert told Henry Cole in May during one of his frequent visits to the Exhibition.[154] It was only three years since Albert himself had been involved in litigation about his own intellectual property, when his amateur etchings had been pirated and offered for sale.[155] The Prince went to law in 1848 but the Engraving Copyright Acts left the prints without statutory protection, and the case was finally won as Lord Chancellor Cottenham was able to find ' "a clear and absolute property" in the Prince', a property that may not have been so clear or so absolute if the royal plaintiff had had to rely upon the copyright laws alone.[156] Perhaps this brush with intellectual property law had made the Prince firm in his support of patent reform, despite his rhetoric at the Mansion House about 'knowledge acquired becom[ing] at once the property of the community at large'.[157] Henry Cole himself claimed that the Exhibition would have been impossible without Peel's sup-

---

[153] 'Report from Mr. Peter Le Neve Foster upon the Working of the Protection of Inventions Act 1851', Appendix XXIII, *First Report of the Commissioners*, 168.

[154] Cole, *Fifty Years of Public Work*, i. 183. Henry Cole records showing the Prince the papers he was holding on Patents, possibly including his own, 'Jurisprudence Connected with Inventions', on 29 May 1851.

[155] Prince Albert made impressions of his and Victoria's drawings, and struck plates from them, in order to make copies in small numbers as gifts for their friends. He used a private printer for this work whose assistant had covertly accumulated copies of the prints. These copies were then sold on and a catalogue was issued by their new owner, advertising them for sale to the public. Information from Daniel F. Tritter, 'A Strange Case of Royalty: The Singular "Copyright" Case of Prince Albert v. Strange', *Journal of Media Law and Practice*, 4 (1983), 111–29.

[156] Ibid. 113.

[157] Prince Albert's 1849 Speech at the Mansion House quoted Cole, *Fifty Years of Public Work*, ii. 213.

port of free trade and the loosening of 'the fetters of our commercial tariff', but he is equally wedded to the idea of invention as the triumph of intellect rather than the business of commerce.[158] Although there is no necessary conflict between the two, free trade was often perceived at the time as opposed to any form of protectionist legislation, such as that applied to intellectual property. In its simplest terms, the impulse to dispersal and dissemination encoded in free-trade thinking seemed to be conceptually opposed in some way to the fixity of identity and control of exposure represented by copyright or patent ownership.

A letter to the Mayor of Birmingham about the Exhibition is typical in its muddling of the terms 'labour', 'workmanship', 'ingenuity', and 'genius' in a way that recalls Whewell's light skip from artist to artisan in his Exhibition lecture:

We shall all agree that, whatever gratification we may receive in the forthcoming Exhibition from the beautiful forms, the brilliant colours, or the exquisite workmanship of the countless products of human labour and ingenuity which will meet our eyes, such pleasure will be secondary in the reflective mind to our delight in contemplating the efforts of genius, as developed in the new and striking inventions which will, doubtless, enrich and adorn that high festival of nations.[159]

This confusion of terms continues in the Parliamentary debate about patent reform, although, as we shall see, 'labour' and 'workmanship' were more widely used terms in that debate than 'genius'. Nevertheless, the pro-free-trade and anti-monopolist opinions of many of the MPs concerned were to be drowned out by the popular attachment to ideas of autonomous authorship and private property in ideas, and I argue that a small and influential group of largely literary men were instrumental in maintaining such popular ideas. Leaving Hyde Park and the Crystal Palace, and making our way south-east across London to another newly built landmark, Charles Barry's Palace of Westminster, we will follow the Patent Debate, which Henry Cole

---

[158] Cole, 'The International Results of the Exhibition of 1851', *Lectures*, ii. 419–51, 421. Cole's lecture was given on 1 December 1852.

[159] Letter from the Recorder [D. Hill] to the Mayor of Birmingham, Appendix B, 'Report and Minutes of Evidence Taken Before the Select Committee of the House of Lords appointed to consider of the Bill intituled, "An Act further to amend the Law touching LETTERS PATENT FOR INVENTIONS;" and also of the Bill, intituled, "An Act for the further Amendment of the Law touching Letters Patent for Inventions," And to Report thereon to the House'. *Reports from Committees*, vol. 18, Session: 4 February–8 August 1851, 638 (MS pagination).

and the Society of Arts had been busily kindling throughout the 1840s, and which had finally flared up during the Exhibition.[160]

The debate that ensued in Parliament showed how pervasive and tenacious the stereotype of the 'poor artisan inventor' proved to be in the 1850s, despite all the evidence from the enquiries of the Select Committee on Patents and the Exhibition itself. In his speech at the opening ceremony on 1 May 1851, Prince Albert had spoken of 'the great readiness with which persons of all classes have come forward as Exhibitors', but Henry Hensman felt that 'there has been a great disappointment to all parties, in not finding more hidden mechanical talent brought to light from the working classes'.[161] As is also clear from the subsequent Parliamentary enquiries, the solitary working-class inventor is even more elusive in the 1850s than in the 1830s. For the public, the stereotype of the poor, struggling inventor had proved remarkably resilient, and indeed, it was public opinion that was to have a decisive effect in preventing the faction who argued for the total abolition of patent law from winning the day. The stereotype was fuelled by an ever-growing popular literature of inventors and invention, and the Exhibition itself had a significant influence, giving, as it did, an unprecedented prominence to the ideas of the previously unfashionable Society of Arts, with its stress on autonomous authorship and the natural property rights of inventors.[162] Through

---

[160] Cole had been working hard on the patent question since March 1849, when he called the attention of the Council of the Society of Arts to the 'legislative recognition of the rights of inventors'. In his diary, he records that he is pleased to have 'carried his resolution as to Tax on Invention against the Patent Agent feeling'. In August 1850, he talked to J. S. Mill on the subject of patents. Cole collected publications on patents and agreed with Mr Justice Stephen that '[t]here was no branch of law which contained so many and such interesting principles as the law of Patents.' Mr Justice Stephen at a meeting held at the Society of Arts on 2 December 1881, quoted in Cole, 'Reform of the Patent Laws. Part I 1848–1852', *Fifty Years of Public Work*, i. 272–8, 278. Cole was not alone in this. There were eleven patent law reform societies by 1851, according to Louise Purbrick, 'Knowledge is Property', 57.

[161] 'Ceremonial Observed at the State Opening of the Exhibition, Thursday 1 May 1851', Appendix xv, *First Report of the Commissioners*, 79. Hensman, 'On Civil Engineering and Machinery Generally', *Lectures*, i. 438. Under Class 6, though, there were only 6 applications under the Designs Act (a provisional year's protection) and 19 under Protection of Inventions—not a huge take-up. Overall, there were 224 UK applications for Designs Act and 453 for Protection of Inventions, but few in the department of machinery.

[162] In 1851 Charles Babbage remarked that the Society of Arts 'has for years been languishing in premature decay', *The Exposition of 1851*, 22. He added, 'They constitute no distinct combination of men into a powerful class, like the Bar, the Navy, or the Army: they are of no party, and finally, they are not fashionable,' 22.

the Exhibition, a small but vocal lobby pulled off an extraordinary publicity stunt, all the more extraordinary because, by the 1850s, the terms of the debate had shifted away from the concerns of the 1830s with Reform and class injustice, and towards a rhetoric of the market and *laissez-faire*, so that invention was now generally discussed more as a function than as a vocation. Nevertheless, the publicity the Exhibition gave to authored inventions, and the rhetoric of genius which it reanimated, made it difficult for parliamentarians to sustain a discussion that ran alongside and sprang from events at the Crystal Palace, purely in terms of political economy and social realities. Cole glossed the Patent Laws as 'laws for the recognition of the rights of intellectual labour', revealing his investment in the moral deserts of the inventor rather than in patents as innovation incentives or commercial contracts. And his friend and Society of Arts member Charles Dickens used the same argument in his 'A Poor Man's Tale of a Patent', as we shall see.

Walter Benjamin has commented on this period of the nineteenth century and its failure to meet the challenge of technology head-on, instead producing 'reactionary cultural forms'.[163] The idea of the inventor that the Society of Arts and the Exhibition helped to sustain was itself a reactionary one that, like so much else in the Exhibition, looked nostalgically backwards in a disavowal of the encroachments of modernity. The stereotype of the inventor was no longer propaganda in the hands of the Radicals, but newly appropriated by a liberal lobby, which found it impossible to relinquish its investment in a traditional model of autonomous authorship despite the immense challenges posed by technology. Henry Cole claimed that the Society of Arts was 'the principal author of the new Patent Law', and it certainly seems to have had an undue influence upon the Committee, and to have treated the subject as analogous to 'a general system of *International Copyright*, both in the *Arts* and in *Literature*'.[164] In fact, once again, the analogy between patent and copyright law which was urged by powerful commentators at the time, including Dickens, took the place of a debate that, had engineering already achieved fuller professional status, might have produced a very different kind of result. The Society consisted almost entirely of civil servants and writers with little or no experience of mechanical

---

[163] Buck-Morss, *The Dialectics of Seeing*, 124.
[164] Cole, 'On the International Results of the Exhibition of 1851', *Lectures*, ii. 419–51, 433 and 445.

engineering, science, or manufacturing.[165] Because it characterized these two intellectual property issues as similar, the largely literary Society was heavily invested in the retention of the inventor's rights as the central issue in the patent debate.

Indeed, Henry Cole was the only witness to the Select Committee of 1851 to return to the argument of natural law to justify intellectual property for inventors: 'To say that the labourer, beneficially working for the public, is not to enjoy the fruits of his exertions, seems to be contrary to the fundamental principles upon which society goes on.'[166] The Lockean argument, which, as we have seen, was frequently mobilized in the debate of the 1830s, had been largely eclipsed by ideas of social utility and innovation incentive in 1851. But Cole's Society of Arts persisted doggedly with the natural law argument: 'as long as the State recognises the existence of rights in any property, all the arguments which fortify such a recognition apply, in equal or greater force, to the rights of property in invention'.[167] The power of the Society of Arts at this time is evidenced by the inclusion of its *Report on the Rights of Inventors* in the Report of the Select Committee on Patents of 1851. Its Report uses a rhetoric that seems almost archaic in the context of the debate of the 1850s. After making patent law explicitly analogous to copyright ('[i]t would seem to be unnecessary to argue this point even at all, whilst the State

[165] With the exception of Bennet Woodcroft, Professor of Machinery at University College, London. Other members were Milner Gibson who had dinner with Charles Dickens in February 1849, and Owen Jones who illuminated an inscription for Gad's Hill on Falstaff's connection with the place. See John Forster, *Life of Charles Dickens* (1911), ii. 234.

[166] Henry Cole, Witness, 'Report and Minutes of Evidence Taken Before the Select Committee of the House of Lords appointed to consider of the Bill intituled, "An Act further to amend the Law touching LETTERS PATENT FOR INVENTIONS;" etc.', 498 (MS pagination). Henry Cole was a civil servant and in 1852 was appointed General Superintendent of the new Department of Practical Art, set up by the Board of Trade. Cole had invited Dickens to become a member of the 1851 Exhibition's Working Class Committee (*LCD* vi. 57 and n.). See n. 29 above. Dickens was always somewhat ambivalent about the utilitarian aims of the Department, which he satirized in his *Hard Times*, but he remained on cordial terms with Cole, writing to him in 1854 that, 'we shall meet at last at some halfway house where there are flowers on the carpets, and a little standing-room for Queen Mab's Chariot among the Steam Engines', Dickens to Cole (17 June 1854), *LCD* vii. 354.

[167] 'Society of Arts: Extracts from the First Report on the Rights of Inventors', Appendix C, 'Report and Minutes of Evidence Taken Before the Select Committee of the House of Lords appointed to consider of the Bill intituled, "An Act further to amend the Law touching LETTERS PATENT FOR INVENTIONS;" etc.', 640 (MS pagination).

recognises right of property in literature of all kinds'), the Society goes on to characterize invention as labour of a sacred kind:[168]

because his labour is highly intellectual, hardly to be hired in the labour-market,—is it less worthy of reward than the bodily labour of the lower class? On the contrary, every one must feel that inventive labour has its rights, which are not only entitled to equal recognition, but, being intellectual, are entitled, if possible, to a higher kind of recognition than other kinds of human labour. It may be called, for want of a more comprehensive phrase, a *natural* right, the exercise of which should be left perfectly free, and recognised as peculiarly sacred.[169]

The rhetoric of the 'sacred' and 'higher' status of intellectual labour is recognizably a classed one: intellectual labour is higher than 'the bodily labour of the lower class', and the Report also makes an appeal to ideas of genius otherwise barely mentioned in the Select Committee Report. This is a rhetoric in which Dickens was already fluent, on behalf of those other intellectual labourers—the men of letters. Looking at his 'A Poor Man's Tale of a Patent' alongside Cole's Parliamentary interventions, it becomes clear that Dickens and Cole were both using the patent debate of 1851 as a vehicle for their own ideas about intellectual property.

The Great Exhibition moved the patent debate in other new directions, too. In the 1850s, a fresh emphasis was placed on the linkage of intellectual labour with national prosperity, a link that the Exhibition was able to demonstrate: 'but though beneath the crystal roof were ranged all the choicest works of the whole world, there was nothing in any way comparable for skill, for mind, for work—nothing so plain, so solid, and yet so eminently handsome—nothing, indeed, so thoroughly English as that iron type of our indomitable energy to be found in the machinery'.[170] A glow of national pride suffused the proceedings. Cole reported that 'the *Industry*, and perhaps even the *Art* of the United Kingdom, took the first place in the race' and the *Edinburgh Review* agreed: 'To the inventive genius of her sons England owes the foundation of her commercial greatness.'[171] Thackeray also reported a patriotic reaction to 'the Christial [*sic*]

---

[168] Ibid. 641 (MS pagination).
[169] Ibid.   [170] Mayhew and Cruikshank, *1851*, 137.
[171] 'Art. II—1. *The Patent Journal*. Nos. 1.–100. London: 1846–7–8. 2. *The Mechanic's Magazine*. Vols XLVII. And XLVIII. London: 1846–7–8', *Edinburgh Review*, 89 (January 1849), 47–83, 81.

Palace . . . I think the English compartment do beat the rest entirely and that (let alone our Ingynes wh [*sic*] be incomparable) our painters artificers makers of busts and statuas [*sic*] do deserve to compare with the best foreign'.[172] His use of a deliberately archaic language of the 'olden times' for this comment reinforces a sense of an unchanging British identity and superiority. Britain's manufacturing prowess was also used to justify her imperialist ambitions. India's raw products, for example, were 'undiscovered and unused till our commerce and the wants of our manufacturers sought them out. Resting upon them, we strive to build on substantial and permanent foundations the structure of empire and government in India.'[173] The Select Committee of 1851, appointed to look into the question of patents once again, also used a rhetoric of national technological supremacy with more complacency than had been displayed in the discussion of the 1830s.[174] Sir David Brewster, for example, claimed that 'no country can be compared with ours in the state of the industrial arts'.[175] The focus of the Parliamentary discussions had shifted from the working man to the nation state.

After all, politics had moved on since the turbulent days of the 1830s, animated by Reform and fears of Chartist insurrection. At mid-century, class antagonisms were by no means resolved, but official rhetoric was more sophisticated in its evasion of them. There was another period of economic depression between 1848 and 1852, which contributed to the re-emergence of pressure for the reform of patent law, but generally, the living conditions of the working class were recovering at mid-century after the negative impact of mechanization earlier in the century. These changes are reflected in the debate, which was more about the management of innovation, and less concerned with the property rights of inventors. The poor artisan inventor, although still discernible in the Parliamentary rhetoric,

---

[172] W. M. Thackeray to Mrs Brookfield (29 April 1851), *LWMT* ii. 767. For a fascinating discussion of the Victorian construction of the 'Olden Time', see Peter Mandler, 'The Victorian Idea of Heritage', in *The Fall and Rise of the Stately Home* (1997), 21–69.

[173] Cole, 'International Results', *Lectures*, ii. 439. 'India and Indian Contributions to the Industrial Bazaar', *The Illustrated Exhibitor*, 317–19, 318. For a fuller discussion of imperialism at the Exhibition, see Auerbach, 'Nationalism and Internationalism', in *The Great Exhibition of 1851*, ch. 6, 159–89.

[174] Mayhew and Cruikshank, *1851*, 137.

[175] Sir David Brewster, Witness, 'Report and Minutes of Evidence Taken Before the Select Committee of the House of Lords appointed to consider of the Bill intituled, "An Act further to amend the Law touching LETTERS PATENT FOR INVENTIONS;" etc.', 557 (MS pagination).

was less prominent, and, both in the Houses of Parliament and in the Select Committee of 1851, there was much disagreement as to whether he actually existed or not. The hero-victim stereotype of the inventor persisted, but, at Westminster anyway, he was more often acknowledged as a stereotype.

The 1852 legislation started as two separate bills, one, a private bill prepared by Lord Brougham in response to a request from the Manchester Patent Reform Committee; and the other by Earl Granville for the government. Both were rejected by the Select Committee appointed in 1851, and 'an amalgamation of the provisions contained in them both' was proposed for discussion in the House of Lords in early July.[176] By August, this third bill had reached the House of Commons and the debate was tense, partly because it was dangerously close to the end of the session and the bill would fall if not passed quickly. Mr Labouchère, the Secretary of the Board of Trade, and a supporter of the bill, complained that it had been discussed 'endlessly'.[177] This was no doubt partly due to a strong faction who would have liked to abolish patent law altogether, and who attempted to derail the bill by prolonging the debate with persistent objections to the fundamental principle of patenting. In growing frustration at this 'disorderly proceeding', Viscount Palmerston pointed out that withdrawing the bill would not have the effect of abolishing patents, but the bill did, in fact, fall at the end of the 1851 session and the two bills had to be reintroduced in the spring of 1852, then again amalgamated into one, which ran through the same Parliamentary session as an International Copyright Bill.[178] On 1 July 1852 the Patent Law Amendment Bill received Royal Assent and the new law came into effect on 1 October 1852. It was generally acknowledged to be a useful reform, addressing all the major problems identified in Committee: lowering the cost of patents, abolishing the flawed caveat system, and overhauling the administrative procedures attendant upon patent applications. It also established a comprehensive index of specifications, and a patent agent and member of the Society of Arts, Bennet Woodcroft, was appointed the first Superintendent of Patent Specifications.

The broad battle lines had been drawn up in the 1830s, and the skirmishes were similar. Those hostile to extended access to patent legislation generally argued against ideas of exceptionality, while

---

[176] Earl Granville, 1 July 1851, *Hansard*, Parl. Debs (series 3), vol. 118, col. 5.
[177] Mr Labouchère, ibid. col. 1918.
[178] Viscount Palmerston, ibid. col. 1921.

eschewing analogies with other kinds of intellectual property, and suggesting that patents were not only unnecessary but positively counterproductive as incentives to innovation. Supporters of the bill stressed intellectual property rights and the value of patents for accelerating technological progress. What has changed is the degree of extremity of the hostility to patent protection. In 1830 those hostile to extension of patent protection did not recommend the abolition of the entire system. In 1851 John Ricardo, Chairman of the Electric Telegraph Company and the nephew of David Ricardo, spoke for John Lloyd, William Cubitt, Isambard Kingdom Brunel, and the Master of the Rolls, all abolitionists, in protesting that all really important inventions, such as paper, glass, and printing, had been made without the promise of a patent, and adding scornfully that it was 'only small inventions in the making of sealing-wax, great coats, or paletots, that seemed to require the protection of a patent'.[179] To this, MacGregor, a Radical, retorted, '[a] man had as perfect a right to ownership in the production of his own intellect as to any other property which he might be possessed of'. The Radicals continued with the familiar arguments of the 1830s about starving and neglected inventors and, indeed, Wakley, who had been so vocal in the debates of twenty years before, was still there:

What did the public do for inventors? They often treated them with scandalous neglect. What was done for Harvey or for Jenner, in his own profession? Jenner's family were absolutely in want; there were no monuments to his memory, and his name was almost unknown in this country. The inventor was entitled to a vested right in his invention.[180]

Familiar, too, from the 1830s, is his solution, 'the law of copyright and of patent ought to be the same'.[181] But the House was less frightened by Radical opinion in 1851 than it had been in the early 1830s, and the murmurings about public opinion are reflective of a broader public, not just the elite artisanal group of yesteryear. This more literate, better-informed public, both upper and lower middle-class, was more able to hold the government to account than in pre-

---

[179] J. L. Ricardo, 25 July 1851, ibid. col. 1541. A paletot is a 'loose outer garment, coat, or cloak, for men or women', *Oxford English Dictionary* at http://dictionary.oed.com/.

[180] Thomas Wakley, 25 July 1851, *Hansard*, Parl. Debs (series 3), vol. 118, col. 1548.

[181] Ibid. col. 1548. Wakley, in fact, supported the bill. He was not alone in using the copyright analogy.

Reform days. And this public was attached to the image of the poor, suffering, working-class inventor.

The 1852 Patent Act went through the same session of Parliament as an International Copyright Bill that fell, and the Society of Arts lobby identified the two closely, and applied ideas of 'genius' and 'authorship' to both. Henry Hensman, reviewing the situation in 1852 in his Society of Arts lecture, moves seamlessly from 'all the glaring abuses' of the patent laws to 'international arrangements as to copyright', and Henry Cole, unsurprisingly enough, does the same in his lecture, stressing the need for better information in both cases: 'ample means should exist for ascertaining in this country what inventions have been patented abroad', which should link with 'a general system of International Copyright'.[182] But in Parliament, the analogy with copyright law was used less frequently than in the 1830s. In 1851, there are occasional mentions of the links: the Solicitor-General, for example, declared patent law 'a very wide subject, which is connected with the question of copyright'; the Duke of Argyll 'held there was no distinction between the case of a man who invented a useful machine, and a man who published beautiful ideas'; and the Radicals agreed, as they had done in the 1830s.[183] In fact, elements of the 1842 Copyright Act were used in drawing up the new Patent Bill.[184] But, overall, the new emphasis in the 1851 debate on innovation incentive moved the focus off the inventor and on to the national economy, and thus away from a model of copyright law that was still predicated on ideas of individuality and authorship.

H. I. Dutton agrees with Colonel Sibthorp's claim that the patent question had lain dormant for a long time: 'For most of the 1840s patent reform attracted little attention. Free trade and the revival of

[182] Henry Hensman, 'On Civil Engineering and Machinery Generally', *Lectures*, i. 437–8. Cole, 'On the International Results', ibid. ii. 432–3.

[183] Solicitor-General, 'Report and Minutes of Evidence Taken Before the Select Committee of the House of Lords appointed to consider of the Bill intituled, "An Act further to amend the Law touching LETTERS PATENT FOR INVENTIONS;" etc.', 627 (MS pagination). Duke of Argyll, 1 July 1851, *Hansard*, Parl. Debs. (series 3), vol. 118, col. 19.

[184] Thomas Webster, the solicitor who was charged with amalgamating the two original bills into one, told the House that '[t]he 20th clause, for making a false entry a misdemeanour, and the 21st, for expunging entries, are on the analogy of the Copyright Acts.' Thomas Webster, 'Report and Minutes of Evidence Taken Before the Select Committee of the House of Lords appointed to consider of the Bill intituled, "An Act further to amend the Law touching LETTERS PATENT FOR INVENTIONS;" etc.', 612 (MS pagination).

working-class unrest in 1842 and 1848 were the dominant domestic issues.'[185] Yet free trade and working-class unrest were both issues that had already proved pertinent to the patent debate, as we have seen. And free-trade arguments became even more entangled with the patent question in the 1850s, as a powerful 'abolitionist' faction emerged, attacking patents as 'monopolies'. Earl Granville, introducing the Patent Bill, admitted his own abolitionist position, but added, 'Poll the country, and the mass would be found favourable to giving patent rights to inventors.'[186] The Master of the Rolls said baldly, 'I think it is a wrong principle to reward inventions by giving a monopoly.'[187] Almost a third of the witnesses examined by the Select Committee declared against the principle of patenting.[188] The abolitionists claimed that Britain had outgrown the need for such a system. Isambard Kingdom Brunel declared that 'in all branches, whether in manufactures or arts of any sort, we are in such an advanced state . . . that a good invention now is rarely a new idea, that is, suddenly propounded or occurs by inspiration, but it is simply some sensible improvement upon what was last done.'[189] William Cubitt and John Lloyd echoed this view.[190] Free-trade orthodoxy was represented on this committee by none more eloquently than John Ricardo, who argued that the market would reward invention by putting the inventor 'at his real value', although he had to concede that this would depend upon a 'fair and proper relation between master and servant', as, in his opinion, the master should privately reward a worker for an invention.[191] The abolitionists deliberately

[185] H. I. Dutton, *The Patent System* (1984), 57.

[186] Earl Granville, 1 July 1851, *Hansard*, Parl. Debs. (series 3), vol. 118, col. 5.

[187] Master of the Rolls, Witness, 'Report and Minutes of Evidence Taken Before the Select Committee of the House of Lords appointed to consider of the Bill intituled, "An Act further to amend the Law touching LETTERS PATENT FOR INVENTIONS;" etc.', 390 (MS pagination).

[188] Among thirty-three witnesses, there were eight who openly declared their hostility to the principle of patents.

[189] Isambard Kingdom Brunel, Witness, 'Report and Minutes of Evidence Taken Before the Select Committee of the House of Lords appointed to consider of the Bill intituled, "An Act further to amend the Law touching LETTERS PATENT FOR INVENTIONS;" etc.', 482–3 (MS pagination). Brunel's enthusiastic dislike of the patent system makes it unlikely that he was the model for Dickens's Daniel Doyce.

[190] William Cubitt, 'the very advanced state of scientific and practical knowledge', and John Horatio Lloyd, who held patents unnecessary '[i]n this country, and in the state of society in which we are now,' ibid. 598.

[191] John Lewis Ricardo, Appendix A, ibid. 634 and 397. J. L. Ricardo's evidence is attached as an appendix because, mistakenly, it was not taken under oath.

shifted the rhetorical focus away from the poor deserving inventor, or even from the more realistic working-class employee, and placed it instead on what they claimed to be the distributive justice of the invisible hand. They also focused their arguments on the national expediency of the free-market system: John Fairrie, for example, claimed that 'the progress of [national] improvement . . . would be as rapid, or even more rapid, if it were not obstructed at every turn by patents'.[192]

Nevertheless, the representation of the working-class inventor remained a controversial one in the debate of the 1850s, as some of those in favour of maintaining and reforming the patent system fell back on the popular stereotype. In April of 1851, calling for a new bill, Lennard was still claiming that '[i]t was well known that poor workmen were the chief inventors; but the heavy expense of a patent made it impossible for them to apply for one.'[193] It seems, indeed, to have been 'well known' but whether or not it was a just reflection of the state of the engineering profession in the 1850s is not clear. There was certainly dissension on the Select Committee. Thomas Webster, a barrister, was sure that 'many of those improvements in an established trade are made by workmen'.[194] William Fairbairn, a civil engineer, and head of the Manchester Patent Reform Committee, when asked what class of persons inventors belong to, at first seemed to agree, 'I think they are chiefly mechanics, and people connected with practical chemistry,'[195] but he went on to clarify this:

Generally, in large establishments, by the working partner, from the circumstance that there is always one of the partners who takes a laborious part in the manipulation of the whole of the process of manufacture; and very frequently it occurs that he becomes thoroughly acquainted with the whole of the process; and from his great experience, and a desire to expedite the work, he becomes an inventor.[196]

In fact, the precision of Fairbairn's answer is illuminating and suggests that the working-class inventor was not the poor, solitary artisan of the stereotype, but was more likely to be a partner in a firm,

---

[192] John Fairrie, Witness, ibid. 400.

[193] Lennard, 1 April 1851, *Hansard*, Parl. Debs. (series 3), vol. 115, col. 894.

[194] Thomas Webster, Witness, 'Report and Minutes of Evidence Taken Before the Select Committee of the House of Lords appointed to consider of the Bill intituled, "An Act further to amend the Law touching LETTERS PATENT FOR INVENTIONS;" etc.', 250 (MS pagination).

[195] William Fairbairn, Witness, ibid. 409.   [196] Ibid. 409.

with a vested interest in improving productivity levels, or reducing production costs. It is clear, too, from Fairbairn's description, that a knowledge of the manufacturing process as a whole was necessary for invention, so, as operatives became less skilled, it became less easy for them to originate inventions.[197] Finally, asked whether inventions often emanated from the 'mere workman', he replied, 'At times, that is so; but I do not think those cases are so numerous as many persons imagine.'[198] Fairbairn, although sceptical about the principle of patents, was a reformist, not an abolitionist.

Even on the reform side there was a clear shift from arguing from a moral basis for a reward for the inventor, to arguing for patents as an economic incentive for invention: a move from individual to collective interest, perhaps as a riposte to the economic challenge from the abolitionist side.[199] For example, Paul Rapsey Hodge, civil engineer and reformist, says 'if I had no hope of protection, and no hope of deriving benefit from my thoughts and my labour, all I should do would be to go on mechanically with my occupation, as I had been accustomed to do.'[200] Invention as a compelling act of genius is replaced by invention as a rational response to economic stimuli. And other, reformist witnesses, although they mentioned the prohibitive cost of patents as one problem, were less focused on the poor inventor than on enumerating all the various administrative obstacles to an effective patent system. Richard Prosser, for example, recommended cheap patents, which he claimed 'would give rise to a ... class of legitimate inventors, persons who would invent for

[197] 'Many of the large manufacturers in Lancashire and the West Riding find it worth their while to employ skilful mechanics at high salaries, for no other purpose than to suggest improvements in the machinery,' '*The Patent Journal*', *Edinburgh Review*, 89 (January 1849), 47–83, 81.

[198] William Fairbairn, Witness, 'Report and Minutes of Evidence Taken Before the Select Committee of the House of Lords appointed to consider of the Bill intituled, "An Act further to amend the Law touching LETTERS PATENT FOR INVENTIONS;" etc.', 415 (MS pagination).

[199] Here, my argument differs from Christine MacLeod's, who has claimed that what she terms 'the heroic ideology' of inventors was born with the patent debate of the early 1850s. I contest that it was already well established by mid-century, so much so that its pervasiveness made it difficult for the abolitionists to prevail, even though the reformists in 1851 and 1852 were not using the heroic inventor stereotype as freely as they had in the 1830s. MacLeod, 'Concepts of Invention'.

[200] Paul Rapsey Hodge, Witness, 'Report and Minutes of Evidence Taken Before the Select Committee of the House of Lords appointed to consider of the Bill intituled, "An Act further to amend the Law touching LETTERS PATENT FOR INVENTIONS;" etc.', 325. (MS pagination).

the sake of being paid for anything which they were employed to invent'.[201]

The more uncompromising abolitionists went so far as to deny that inventors were a significant group at all. William Cubitt, for example, President of the Institution of Civil Engineers, and hostile to the system, claimed 'there is less room for inventions than people imagine'.[202] John Horatio Lloyd, a barrister and abolitionist, agreed, 'the class of meritorious inventors is a much narrower one than people suppose'.[203] And, always extreme in his rhetoric, Brunel declared that it was, in fact, the patent system which was to blame for poor would-be inventors ending up in the workhouse, 'the poorer class of inventors ruin themselves by the attempt to work out some idea for the sake of getting a patent'.[204] But it was not only the abolitionists who dismissed the stereotype of the poor working-class inventor. William Carpmael, a patent agent and the only witness to defend the system as it stood, agreed, 'it has been supposed that there is a large number of poor inventors who cannot afford to take a patent . . . but I believe that there are few, if any, inventors in that position'.[205]

It is striking from these testimonies that the witnesses were conscious of denying a formed public opinion—the poor, struggling inventor was what 'people imagine' or 'people suppose'. The notion of the struggling inventor, which was, as we have seen, largely generated as a propagandist tool in the 1820s and 1830s, was firmly lodged in the public consciousness by the 1850s. The disappointing lack of take-up for the Protection of Inventions Act by working-class exhibitors called the existence of the poor inventor into question, and Charles May was perhaps more right than he realized when he said, 'I think the class of inventors are [sic] certainly the creation of the patent law.'[206] In fact, the popular periodical press perpetuated

[201] Richard Prosser, Witness, ibid. 549–50.
[202] William Cubitt, Witness, ibid. 451.
[203] John Horatio Lloyd, Witness, ibid. 598.
[204] Isambard Kingdom Brunel, Witness, ibid. 483.
[205] William Carpmael, Witness, 'Minutes of Evidence Taken Before the Select Committee of the House of Lords Appointed to Consider the Bill Intituled, An Act to extend the provisions of the Designs Act, 1850, and to give Protection from Piracy to Persons Exhibiting New Inventions in the Exhibition of the Works of Industry of all Nations in One thousand eight hundred and Fifty-one' (25 March 1851), 9. This view was contested by Thomas Webster and Charles May.
[206] Charles May, Witness, 'Report and Minutes of Evidence Taken Before the Select Committee of the House of Lords appointed to consider of the Bill intituled, "An Act

this public sympathy through its continued use of the stereotype of the inventor. The abolitionists in the 1851 debate are all aware of public opinion weighing heavily against them. Lloyd remarks that offering patent protection is 'like selling a prize in a lottery' but he knows that this is an 'unpopular opinion'.[207] Similarly, Colonel Reid, another abolitionist, knows that his 'opinion . . . [is] at variance with the prevailing opinion of the public, both here and in the United States'.[208] Both Earl Grey and Mr Labouchère, in the face of abolitionist protest, defended the bill as 'expedient', and both cited 'public opinion' as making more radical measures impossible.[209]

It is clear that, although the overwhelming majority of the witnesses to the Committee, both abolitionist and reformist, felt that the debate had, or should have, moved beyond the popular stereotype of the inventor into a broader discussion of free-trade principles and national interest, it was difficult to ignore public opinion. The parliamentarians did their best. Instead of 'artisan' or 'inventor', the term most frequently used by witnesses to describe the potential innovator is 'worker' or 'operative'.[210] The change in terminology is significant: in moving from an image of the autonomous inventor to the operative in a manufactory, the debate dramatizes a paradigmatic shift in the Parliamentary discussion of invention from unalienated to alienated labour. The image of the working-class inventor, and his right to his intellectual property, as discussed in the previous chapter, embodied a fantasy of non-alienation which had been enthusiastically taken up by the Reform press in the 1830s in mitigation of the encroaching machine culture that was progressively displacing the skilled artisanal class. That fantasy, perhaps less necessary in socially more stable times, was obscured from view in the 1851 discussion, which focused, instead, on the best

---

further to amend the Law touching LETTERS PATENT FOR INVENTIONS;" etc.', 607 (MS pagination). Charles May also judged that 'the bulk of the valuable improvements of the country originate from the manufactories', 607–8.

[207] John Horatio Lloyd, Witness, ibid. 598.

[208] Colonel Reid, Witness, ibid. 545.

[209] Earl Grey, 'in the present state of public opinion, it was not expedient to act upon those views, but that they should rather content themselves with improving the condition and state of the present law' (1 July 1851), *Hansard*, Parl. Debs. (series 3), vol. 118, col. 21. Mr Labouchère also felt that the Bill was 'expedient', and that Parliament could not afford to 'wait until public opinion was ripe for such a sweeping alteration [as abolition]' (25 July 1851), ibid. col. 1542.

[210] See evidence of Paul Rapsey Hodge, Isambard Kingdom Brunel, William Carpmael.

method of trading inventive property in a more explicitly capitalist marketplace.

Charles Dickens's name appears in the Report of the Select Committee on Patent Reform, in Appendix D, as a member of the Committee for Legislative Recognition of the Rights of Inventors, which had been set up by the Society of Arts.[211] Cole had befriended Dickens in the late 1840s, and was able to enlist his aid now that the Society of Arts, with Prince Albert's patronage, wielded considerable power. Dickens's contribution to Cole's campaign, 'A Poor Man's Tale of a Patent', had appeared in *Household Words* in October 1850, and, with a circulation nearly as high as that of *The Times*, Dickens's weekly was undeniably influential. In fact, Dickens was a Vice-President of the Society of Arts, 1850–1, during the period in which arrangements for the Exhibition were underway, and he served briefly on the Working Classes Central Committee of the Great Exhibition, although his letters at this time reveal that he was far more concerned with his own Guild of Art and Literature than with the success of the Exhibition. The Guild was intended '[t]o encourage Life Assurance and other Provident Habits among Authors and Artists to render such assistance to both as shall never compromise their independence; and to found a new Institution where honourable rest from arduous labour shall still be associated with the discharge of congenial duties'.[212] Dickens and Bulwer Lytton worked hard for a few years at the beginning of the 1850s, taking plays on tour to raise funds. Although the scheme finally collapsed, Forster claims of Dickens that 'there was no project of his life into which he flung himself with greater eagerness than the Guild'.[213] Dickens's aim

---

[211] Henry Cole sent Dickens his 'Jurisprudence Connected with Inventions' (30 September 1850), and Dickens used it as source material for his own 'A Poor Man'sTale of a Patent', writing to Cole that, '[y]our proof has greatly interested me. I shall be happy to "join the Union", and I am now at work on a paper for Household Words, which I hope may help the question in a taking manner.' Dickens to Cole (25 September 1850), *LCD* vi. 180. Cole's 'proof' was a treatise on the defects of current patent law—published as 'The Rights of Inventors' by the Society in December 1850. The union is The Patent Law Reform League. Their first public meeting, at which Dickens was not present, was held October 22 (*Daily News*, 23 and 26 October 1850; *Illustrated London News*, 2 November 1850), *LCD* vi. 180. Dickens had joined the Society of Arts, or 'The Royal Society for the Encouragement of Arts, Manufactures and Commerce', in 1849. See Jeremy Phillips, *Charles Dickens and 'A Poor Man's Tale of a Patent'* (1984).

[212] Play-bill for Guild Benefit Performance of *Used Up* (3 September 1852), reproduced in John Forster, *The Life of Charles Dickens*, (1911), ii. 282.

[213] Forster, ibid. ii. 423.

was to 'change the status of the literary man in England', which he still perceived to be less exalted than it should have been.[214] This passionate preoccupation coloured his involvement in Cole's patent campaign. Still unprotected by an international copyright agreement, Dickens felt that he and his fellow writers were vulnerable in just the same way as he imagined the inventors at the Exhibition to be, and his appeals for inventors were, like Cole's, founded on passionate moral arguments and constructions of autonomous authorship.

Despite the fact that his own brother was a civil engineer, Dickens unequivocally adopted the terms of the debate of the 1830s—the debate he perhaps remembered from his reporting days. Finally, he was partly responsible for re-establishing the myth of the poor artisan inventor in the public consciousness, which made the abolition of patents such a politically unpopular option. His own investment in a concept of autonomous authorship, his involvement with the Guild, and with the campaign for an International Copyright agreement, deeply influenced his construction of the inventor.[215] This investment becomes even clearer in the uses to which he puts mechanical invention in the novel that he started in 1855, *Little Dorrit*. Daniel Doyce appears as an 'unreconstructed' inventor of the 1830s, and many of Dickens's own anxieties about authorship and intellectual property are expressed through his situation. Dickens and Cole, and the Society of Arts, were able to exercise a surprising influence on the patent debate at mid-century, and they were keen to conserve the construction of the individual inventor despite all the evidence that invention was no longer a solitary or neglected pursuit.

The Great Exhibition may have been the reason that patent law was reformed, but it also had a large part to play in maintaining traditional ideas of authorship in the face of a technological culture, and, thus, in enshrining the myth of the 'poor, worthy inventor' in the law for many years to come. Nothing could be a neater example of the double face of an Exhibition that met the challenges of the future by creating a fictional past.

The Great Exhibition of 1851 provides a usefully focused lens through which to examine mid-nineteenth-century debates about

---

[214] Charles Dickens to Bulwer Lytton, c.1850, quoted Forster, ibid. ii. 423–4.
[215] See Alexander Welsh, *From Copyright to Copperfield: The Identity of Dickens* (1987), and Gerhard Joseph, 'Charles Dickens, International Copyright, and the Discretionary Silence of *Martin Chuzzlewit*', in Martha Woodmansee and Peter Jaszi (eds.), *The Construction of Authorship* (1994), 259–70.

aesthetic value, intellectual property, and the status of artists and inventors. But it is important to remember that this event also had its own effect on those debates. Henry Cole predicted before the opening of the Exhibition that '[t]here can be no doubt that the Exhibition will give rise to many new relations between men and things,' and I have argued that this was, indeed, the case. Much was contradictory and muddled at the Exhibition, but the display forced a temporary identification of art and technology, bringing the two more closely together than they had ever been before (or since).[216] The emphasis on division of labour and the promotion of commerce in the Crystal Palace threatened traditional constructions of authorship, identity and provenance, and aesthetic value. It is for this reason that the fiction of the inventor as autonomous creator prevails in the patent debate of the early 1850s. It is difficult to understand from today's perspective how the surrender of the 'rights' of the autonomous mechanical inventor in the mid-1850s could have threatened the recently established intellectual property rights of the author. But at the time, influential literary commentators such as Charles Dickens saw the issues of intellectual property for inventors and for authors as analogous, or even identical, and campaigned to protect the claims of professionalism which were vested in intellectual property for practitioners in both fields.

One Saturday in May 1851, three weeks after the Crystal Palace had opened its doors, the *Illustrated London News* ran a lead article on 'The Copyright Question' alongside an engraving of the opening night of Bulwer Lytton's play, *Not So Bad As We Seem*, and an article on 'The Guild of Literature and Art', which discussed literary pensions. The proximity of all these subjects on the page graphically illustrates the ways in which the Crystal Palace, Dickens's and Bulwer's Guild project, and the debate about authorship and intellectual property more generally, were pushing closely against each other during the summer that the 'Great Exhibition of Arts and Industry . . . brought men together'.[217] The temporary Act that had offered a 'protection to designers and inventors', and the internationalism of the display at the Crystal Palace, made the Exhibition into an opportunity to discuss other kinds of intellectual property, and an international copyright agreement with the United States

---

[216] Cole, *Fifty Years of Public Work*, i. 383.
[217] Anon., 'The Copyright Question', *Illustrated London News*, 18 (24 May 1851), 439–40, 440.

in particular, was optimistically expected.[218] In fact, no agreement would be reached until 1891, but in the early 1850s it seemed very close, and Thackeray is positively exultant in a letter of 1853, 'I hear the most cheering accounts of the International Copyright bill, wh upon my conscience will make me 5000 dollars a year the richer.'[219] Yet, even while the events at Hyde Park spawned such optimism, they also put on display as never before the problematic nature of authorship in an increasingly technologically sophisticated marketplace, and this bald exposure of the mechanics of cultural production produced ripples of reaction in literary circles for the next few years. Surprisingly, few of the literary texts of the early 1850s represent the Exhibition directly. Perhaps the spectacle at the Crystal Palace was too 'bewildering', 'vast—strange new and impossible to describe', in Charlotte Brontë's words, and its meanings still too obscure, for writers to know what to make of it. Or perhaps it was the very exposure of the anomalous condition of 'art' in a mass culture that made representing art and artists so fraught in the years directly following. Certainly, some of the 'new relations between men and things' that Ruskin and others had seen announced by the Exhibition do creep into the fiction of the 1850s, and it is with the discussion of one such narrative, a short story by Wilkie Collins, that this chapter ends.

WILKIE COLLINS, *MR. WRAY'S CASH-BOX* (1851/2)

In the autumn of 1851, as the Great Exhibition of the Works of Industry of All Nations closed its doors, a young Wilkie Collins wrote that '[o]n Friday morning last, an idea came into my head for a *Christmas Book*'.[220] He had first met Dickens in the spring of 1851, when the painter, Augustus Egg, suggested Collins for the part of Smart in the Guild play, *Not So Bad As We Seem*. He had been busy

---

[218] Anon., 'The Copyright Question', *Illustrated London News*, 439.

[219] William Makepeace Thackeray to Mrs Baxter (16 February 1853), *LWMT* iii. 204. See also W. H. Wills, in a postscript to a letter from Charles Dickens to Richard Henry Horne (2 March 1853), also expecting an imminent agreement, 'This will, we expect, very much increase the sale of *Household Words*.' Reprinted in [T. J. Wise], *An Account of the First Performance of Lytton's Comedy 'Not So Bad As We Seem' with Other Matters of Interest, by Charles Dickens* (1919), 13. Mr Edward Everett, then the American Secretary of State, brought the matter of International Copyright before Congress again in 1853. See S. S. Conant, 'International Copyright I. An American View', *Macmillan's Magazine*, 40 (May 1879–October 1879), 151–61.

[220] Wilkie Collins to Edward Pigott [Autumn 1851], *The Letters of Wilkie Collins*, i, ed. William Baker and William M. Clarke (1999), 74.

with performances ever since, promoted to the larger part of Shadowly Softhead when Douglas Jerrold dropped out early in 1852. The themes of Collins's Christmas book seem to have been suggested by the Guild's campaign for the protection of needy writers, and by the Great Exhibition's display of 'incessant copying without discrimination', as Matthew Digby Wyatt had put it.[221] The relentless emphasis on reproductive technologies in the Crystal Palace suggested a new 'democratic availability' for cultural artefacts, which it was now possible to copy and disseminate in larger numbers and more cheaply than ever before, and this democratization of culture lies at the heart of Collins's story. Indeed, Collins seems to draw particularly upon Henry Cole's 'Felix Summerley' manufactory which was selling copies of Bell's version of the Janssen bust of Shakespeare throughout the Exhibition.

'*King Public* is a good king for Literature and Art!' Collins declared at the beginning of 1852.[222] In this story, originally titled *The Mask of Shakspeare*, he seems less concerned with the protection of intellectual property than with its dissemination. The 'curious *fact*' that had suggested the story to Collins was that of a stonemason working in the Stratford-upon-Avon church, who had surreptitiously taken 'a mould from the Shakespeare bust. What he had done was found out, however; and he was forthwith threatened by the authorities having care of the bust, with the severest pains and penalties of the law—though for what special offence was not specified.'[223] But later he is exonerated and assured 'that he need fear no penalty whatever, and that if he thought he could dispose of them, he might make as many casts as he pleased, and offer them for sale anywhere'. So he sold 'great numbers' of them in England and North America.[224]

---

[221] Digby Wyatt, 'An Attempt to Define the Principles which should Determine Form in the Decorative Arts', *Lectures*, i. 215–51, 239. Digby Wyatt visited the Collins family in Rome, when Collins was a boy of 13. Catherine Peters, *The King of Inventors: A Life of Wilkie Collins* (1991), 42.

[222] Collins to Pigott (16 February 1852), *Letters of Wilkie Collins*, i. 82. Collins is speaking of his dramatic tour with Dickens in *Not So Bad As We Seem.*

[223] Collins to Bentley (23 October 1851), *Letters of Wilkie Collins*, i. 73. The bust by Gerard Johnson (or Geraert Janssen) in the parish church at Stratford was originally coloured, but had been whitewashed by Edmond Malone in 1793. Its colour was restored in the late 1860s. Information from *The Letters of Alfred Lord Tennyson 1821–1850*, ed. Cecil Y. Lang and Edgar F. Shannon, Jr. (1982), 182 n. 1.

[224] Wilkie Collins, Preface, *Mr. Wray's Cash-Box*, in Wilkie Collins, *The Frozen Deep and Mr Wray's Cash-Box* (1996), 75–141, 75. All subsequent references are to this edition and appear in parentheses in the text.

Collins takes Shakespeare, seen in the early nineteenth century as the property of the literate elite, and shows him as standing instead for a common and accessible culture, just as the Bard had done at the Exhibition. 'What is Shakespeare', asks the narrator, 'but a great sun that shines upon humanity—the large heads and the little, alike? Have not the rays of that mighty light penetrated into many poor and lowly places for good?' (86).

Reuban Wray is an actor 'of the lower degree' (83) and is 'a remnant of a bygone age, [trying] to keep up with a new age which has already got past him' (87–8). Wray, despite taking only 'spearbearer' parts on stage, knows every line of Shakespeare. One night he hides in the church in Stratford and secretly takes a cast from the bust of Shakespeare there, 'I felt as if I had robbed the bank, or the King's jewels, or had set fire to a train of gunpowder to blow up all London; it seemed such a thing to have done!' (99).[225] Terrified he may be arrested for his 'theft', he flees with his granddaughter and a loyal artisan friend, known as Julius Caesar, and the cast packed in the 'cash-box' of the title. When he is later robbed, and his cast smashed, Wray's own identity begins to fracture, and his sanity is saved only because his granddaughter and Julius Caesar make the journey back to Stratford to recast the bust. The family is adopted by a wealthy benefactor, perhaps significantly named Mr Colebatch, who suggests that Wray starts to produce the casts commercially, and the story ends with the success of the new business. Thus, with the help of Colebatch's benign patronage, Wray is able, after all, to 'keep up with the new age'. Wray's poverty and low class status allow the story to establish a crucial distinction between cultural and economic value: Wray is a poor man, but his bust of the Bard is 'the treasure which the greatest lord in this land doesn't possess' (102), and when he is persuaded to share his treasure with 'other lovers of Shakspeare', (137) surely Henry Cole (Colebatch) himself would have applauded the dissemination of cheap culture in 'batches'.

Wray insists that the Stratford bust is 'the only true likeness of Shakspeare! It's been done from a mask, taken from his own face after death—I know it, I don't care what people say, I know it' (96). Yet what Wray is happy to take as 'proof' (102) in fact raises questions about the closeness of his copy to the 'original'. Wray's precious

---

[225] Collins wrote to his friend Edward Piggott, 'I am nothing like so well acquainted with the process of . . . [taking a cast], as I ought to be. I want to know all about *moulds*, *plaster* of Paris, and so forth—and I must apply to some sculptor.' Collins to Piggott [autumn 1852], *Letters of Wilkie Collins*, i. 74.

cast is, in fact, at a considerable remove from Shakespeare's living face if it is a cast of the bust which was 'done from' another cast of Shakespeare's face after death. Indeed, on his visit to Stratford in 1840, Tennyson had felt rather differently about the bust, noting that 'I should not think it can be a very good likeness' (46). And Collins's story itself later demonstrates how copies can deceive by their very perfection. Wray's first cast, 'a beautiful cast! A perfect cast!' (100) is later substituted by another, taken by his granddaughter, and Wray's easy acceptance of the new cast as the old one stands as proof of the ability of copies to mask their true provenance. 'Shakespeare' is reproduced many times, and in various ways in the story, both on the stage and in plaster of Paris, but never so eloquently for the story's real theme as when his image is smashed to smithereens by robbers. Wray's pathetic attempts to restore the cast starkly reveal the fragility of the icon, and the nullity behind it. Rather than leading back to Shakespeare, the text moves away, replacing one copy with another until the original is entirely effaced. Although the narrative does not seem fully aware of the modernity of its themes, it offers a vertiginous sense of the loss of the original, such as has fascinated writers on modernity from Benjamin to Baudrillard ever since. Jean Baudrillard, for example, makes the phenomenon central to his theory of modernity: 'the original no longer even exists, since things are conceived from the beginning as a function of their unlimited reproduction'.[226] No such pessimism is available in Collins's story, though—to a young writer in 1851 the prospect of easier and easier facilities of reproduction seemed liberating rather than threatening.

Yet, despite the rhetoric of democratic availability, 'Shakspeare' is not freely available to all at the end of the story, only to those who are able and prepared to pay the substantial price of a guinea for him. Rhetorically, the story seems to claim that 'culture' both has and does not have a price. The Exhibition dramatized a similar paradox, presenting itself as neither a museum nor a department store. While the Commission had decided that the objects displayed at the Exhibition should not carry price tags, they all had prices.[227] Charles Babbage felt that this decision was a grave mistake: 'The price in money is the

---

[226] Jean Baudrillard, *Simulacra and Simulation*, trans. Sheila Faria Glaser (1994), 99. Originally published in French in 1981.

[227] Henry Cole wrote that '[a]fter much examination and inquiry, the Commissioners resolved that prices were not to be affixed to the articles exhibited,' Cole, 'Introduction', *3 vol. Exhibition Catalogue*, i. 15.

most important element in every bargain; to omit it, is not less absurd than to represent a tragedy without a hero, or to paint a portrait without a nose.'[228] Collins, with Babbage, seems to celebrate a free-trade consumerism that transports culture into private, domestic spaces, thus, paradoxically, enabling the construction of a 'public' culture. As Dickens also saw, it was only by allowing and encouraging the private ownership of culture, through 'the increase of commerce and the exchange of commodities' that 'culture' could construct itself as a public phenomenon.[229] It is the image of Shakespeare that wakes Tidbury-on-the-Marsh from the economic paralysis of the story's opening scene, in which the branch banker vainly awaits a customer from behind 'the brass rails of his commercial prison-house'. (77) At the end of *Mr. Wray's Cash-Box*, Shakespeare has been transmogrified into a 'pretty round sum of money'—cultural capital has been converted into commercial capital, and Shakespeare is newly 'owned' by the 'loads' of people who desire a stake in the national heritage, and are able to afford one (136).[230]

Wilkie Collins clearly shared none of Ruskin's distaste for the new technologies of cultural reproduction, and was generally optimistic about their results.[231] Indeed, like Dickens, he was quick to pick up on new ways of creating income out of them. In the 1840s and 1850s, engravings became cheaper as the process was mechanized, and Collins, as a journalist on the *Leader*, suggested including '[n]otices of new prints, for instance, [which] might bring print-selling adver-

[228] Babbage, *The Exposition of 1851*, 81.

[229] Babbage went on to argue that '[t]he essential principle of the Exposition being the increase of commerce and the exchange of commodities, it might even be contended that sales should be permitted on the premises,' ibid. 88.

[230] The commercialization of national heritage was, of course, well underway by the 1850s. For the debate over the origins and development of the 'heritage' industry in Britain, see Martin Wiener, *English Culture and the Decline of the Industrial Spirit, 1850–1980* (1981); Robert Hewison, *The Heritage Industry: Britain in a Climate of Decline* (1987); Raphael Samuel (ed.), *Patriotism: The Making and Unmaking of British National Identity*, i. *History and Politics* (1989); J. Corner and S. Harvey (eds.), *Enterprise and Heritage: Crosscurrents of National Culture* (1991); Linda Colley, *Britons: Forging the Nation 1707–1837* (1992); Georgina Boyes, *The Imagined Village: Culture, Ideology and the English Folk Revival* (1993); Peter Mandler, *The Fall and Rise of the Stately Home* (1997).

[231] Ruskin, in fact, accused Collins himself of plagiarizing, describing *Mr. Wray's Cashbox* as 'a gross imitation of Dickens—He cannot be a man of genius—or he would not have done such a thing—Every bit of the book is not merely imitated—but stolen.' Letter 225 (5 May 1852), *Ruskin's Letters from Venice 1851–1852*, ed. John Lewis Bradley (1955), 270–1.

tisements. What do you say to a circular, sent round to the print-sellers?'[232] By the mid-1850s, however, he had already grown more circumspect about the effect of new technologies on intellectual property, and American piracy of his work was to plague him throughout the 1860s and 1870s.[233] In March 1855, Collins responded to a report in the *Athenaeum* that a forgery of a picture by his friend Edward Ward had been sold as the original. He made an immediate connection between literature and the visual arts in his response, because he was preoccupied at the time by the Parliamentary debate over the future of the Stamp Act, which would be repealed in mid-June that year:

The whole question of protection of the interests of authors as well as artists in their own works, is coming before the public—in connection with the taking off of the Newspaper Stamp, which will enable any scoundrel who starts a low paper to steal articles from good papers—or *whole books* with perfect impunity, as the act now stands—just in fact as the scoundrel stole your name and sold his copy of your picture with it. If nothing else will do, the authors must have a *League* and the artists must join them. Parliament and hereditary legislators don't care a straw about us or our interests—we must somehow make them care.[234]

Oddly, Collins seems to discount the arguments of Radicals and Liberals alike, that the Newspaper Stamp represented a 'tax upon knowledge', and he views its repeal with alarm, imagining the newly enfranchised popular press to be founded by scoundrels and based upon piracy. This is a far cry from the celebration of copying and dissemination as the means of the cultural and financial enriching of the poor in *Mr. Wray's Cash-Box*. He promises to mention Ned's case to Dickens when he next sees him, and it is most likely to his deepening friendship with Dickens that he owes his new-found scepticism.

Appearing a few months after the Great Exhibition, in the year of the new Patent Bill, and in the midst of the activities of Dickens's

---

[232] Collins to Pigott (12 January 1852), *Letters of Wilkie Collins*, i. 80.

[233] See Collins to John Hollingshead (25 February 1873), *Letters of Wilkie Collins 1866–1889*, ii. 362–3, in which Collins speaks of 'the barbarous indifference of the House of Commons where the interests of literature and art are concerned', 362.

[234] Collins to E. M. Ward (20 March 1855), *Letters of Wilkie Collins*, i. 139. See also 139 n. Reports that one of the paintings of the brother of Charles James Ward, Edward Matthew Ward (Ned), was copied and sold as an original appeared in the *Athenaeum* (10 March 1855). Ward's solicitor, Henry Darvill, proposed in the same issue that the government should stamp all originals to prevent fraud. An Editorial in the *Athenaeum*, 17 March 1855, reviewed the matter further.

new Guild of Literature and Art, Collins's 1851 story seems to gain greatly in significance, and simply makes more sense, if we read it in the context of the cultural events happening around it. Shakespeare is transformed into *kitsch*, in a way that—albeit inadvertently—suggests the threat of debasement, even as it celebrates the democratizing force of free trade. A narrative that ends by suggesting that culture is both the free property of everybody, and costs a full guinea, enacts the bewilderment over the notion of value in this period with unselfconscious clarity. The next chapter examines Dickens's writing of the 1850s and suggests that similar themes preoccupy him, and that he attempts to solve some of these contradictions between the public and private ownership of cultural property through his literary writing.

4

'The spirit of craft and money-making': The Indignities of Literature in the 1850s

'THE more we see of Life and its brevity, and the World and its Vanities, the more we know that no exercise of our abilities in any Art, but the addressing of it to the great ocean of humanity in which we are drops, and not to bye-ponds (very stagnant) here and there, ever can or will lay the foundation of an endurable retrospect.'[1] 'The great ocean of humanity' that had swept through the Crystal Palace in the summer of 1851 also represented the new mass readership that Dickens identified as both his best market and his best hope for immortality: distinction, he suggests, can only be achieved by a surrender to the mass. In pitching themselves at an 'endurable retrospect', clearly the challenge for all writers at mid-century was to find the right balance between the ownership and the address of their work, so as to allow their literary property to circulate, without losing control of it. In thinking about Dickens's work at this time, then, it is less useful to see privacy and publicity as opposed terms, than as highly confused terms, which were ultimately inextricable.

Both Dickens and Thackeray supported Sir Henry Cole's aim to publicize the benefits to the consumer of free international trade through the Great Exhibition. Indeed, Thackeray had supplied the illustrations for Cole's own free-trade publication, *The Anti-Corn Law Circular* in 1839, and Dickens's *Household Words* enthusiastically espoused free-trade policies.[2] Dickens saw no contradiction between his pro-free-trade position and his emotive campaign for the rights of inventors and writers to better property rights. An article

[1] Charles Dickens to W. R. Macready (14 January 1853), *LCD* vii. 10.
[2] Peter L. Shillingsburg, *Pegasus in Harness* (1992), 40. See e.g. Anon., 'France and Free Trade', *All the Year Round* (10 March 1860), 466–72.

published in *Household Words* in August 1850 made this position explicit, declaring that 'our nominally protective laws [are] not unfrequently laws prohibitive of industry', and that while '[l]egitimate and wholesome protection preserves the property we wish to guard against our enemies; impolitic and unwholesome protection too securely preserves property to us which we are most anxious to get rid of—by sale or barter,—against our best friends, our customers.'[3] *Bleak House* and *Little Dorrit* provide ample evidence that Dickens was concerned to make all his work 'for circulation', like his *American Notes*, but equally that he was concerned to reserve his writing as his unalienable property, and preserve its 'propriety'—its wholeness and dignity. It has been suggested that Dickens disavowed his involvement in the capitalist marketplace.[4] But far from being ashamed of the 'trade' of writing, Dickens wilfully and deliberately drew the analogy between manual labour and writing, while at the same time looking for a value for his talent that was supplementary to its market rate.[5] As Victor Bonham-Carter reminds us, in 1850 'the book trade was still in the early stages of change', and Dickens was himself one of the agents in the process of the commodification of literature. His journal *Household Words*, launched in 1850, was innovative in its combination of quality of content with cheapness, and the publication of his novels in monthly instalments made them more readily affordable for the expanding reading public. Issued with each instalment of *Bleak House* was 'The Bleak House Advertiser': pages of advertisements for all kinds of commodities, including Pears soap; Mappin and Webb's electro-silver plate and cutlery; Coleman's Mustard; and Bryant and May's matches. The Rimmel cosmetic company featured an advertisement that reminded readers of the fountain of 'Rimmel's toilet vinegar' at the Exhibition.[6] Nevertheless, Dickens remained ambivalent about the popular

---

[3] Anon., 'Comic Leaves From the Statute Book', *Household Words* (17 August 1850), 502–4, 503.

[4] Mary Poovey and Jeff Nunokawa have written about the circumscription of the domestic from the economic in Victorian writing. See *Uneven Developments* (1988) and *The Afterlife of Property* (1994).

[5] Daniel Hack has discussed this issue of the supplementary value for writing in the period. See Daniel Hack, 'Literary Paupers and Professional Authors: The Guild of Literature and Art', *Studies in English Literature 1500–1900*, 39/4 (Autumn 1999), 691–713.

[6] Victor Bonham-Carter, *Authors by Profession* (1978), i. 72. *The Bleak House Advertiser*, i. 20.

market, and he was as aware of the riskiness of the emerging market structures, as he was of the opportunities they afforded.

Bruce Robbins has written that 'no sites are inherently or eternally public. The lines between public and private are perpetually shifting, as are the tactical advantages and disadvantages of finding oneself on one side or the other.'[7] In the 1850s, Dickens worked hard at representing and critiquing (and thus reinforcing) the notion of the public sphere, which in turn helped shore up his construction of the territory of the marketplace as private. The distinction was reinforced in Dickens's work by his intimacy of address to the reader. While some critics have suggested that this was the means by which Victorian writers rejected the impersonal terms of Romanticism, and attempted to win the trust of their readers, in fact this pseudo-intimacy becomes a strategy by which Dickens is able to homogenize, while appearing to individuate, a reading public in his bid to create a private marketplace for his fiction.[8]

The debate over intellectual property mimics that much wider negotiation in the period between private and public, which, as Jürgen Habermas and others have shown, were terms that depended upon one another for their currency. Habermas contests that '[t]he positive meaning of "private" emerged precisely in reference to the concept of free power of control over property that functioned in capitalist fashion.'[9] For the nineteenth-century writer or inventor, then, private property was necessarily staked on an open marketplace, and retaining a 'free power of control' could prove hazardous in such a competitive and unregulated environment. The extent to which display both underwrote and threatened the value of intellectual property became very clear at the Exhibition, revealing how closely the debates about patenting and copyright mirrored one another in their

---

[7] Bruce Robbins, 'Introduction: The Public as Phantom', in Bruce Robbins (ed.), *The Phantom Public Sphere* (1993), pp. vii–xxvi, xv.

[8] Janice Carlisle argues that the Victorian writer rejected the 'impersonal terms' of Romanticism: 'The poet had imagined his artistic function in impersonal terms such as the Aeolian harp or the fading coal, or in the figures of solitaries like Alastor or Kubla Khan, but such definitions could only exacerbate the Victorian distrust of the artist.' *The Sense of an Audience: Dickens, Thackeray, and George Eliot at Mid-Century* (1982), 27. Helen Small puts forward an argument much closer to my own in her article, 'A Pulse of 124: Charles Dickens and a Pathology of the Mid-Victorian Reading Public', in James Raven, Helen Small, and Naomi Tadmore (eds.), *The Practice and Representation of Reading in England* (1996), 263–90.

[9] Jürgen Habermas, *The Structural Transformation of the Public Sphere: An Inquiry into a Category of Bourgeois Society* (1962/1989), 74.

anxieties about privacy and utility. The cultivation of publicity and celebrity were necessary, in both cases, to establish a market value for the private intellectual property. It is no coincidence, for example, that the 'literary lion' was a phenomenon that emerged in the early Victorian period. Both Dickens and Thackeray literally performed to the public—Dickens through his public readings, Thackeray through his lectures, in an effort further to consolidate their authority and the property in their work.[10] But publicity and display also laid the same property open to misappropriation and theft. Dickens, of course, was entirely familiar with the vulnerability of intellectual property, as his novels were frequently pirated, and the furore he caused in the United States on his visit there in 1842 by publicly condemning the American piracy of British books is well known.[11] Thackeray's work, too, was freely appropriated from early in his career as a journalist. *The Yellowplush Papers, Jeames's Diary*, and *The History of Samuel Titmarsh* were all pirated, two of them in North America, although Thackeray characteristically reacted with less rancour than Dickens, treating the piracies as good publicity in themselves.[12] For both authors, serialization offered one way of extending the period of control over their intellectual property, as part issue impeded, or, at least, slowed piracies down. Despite Dickens's enthusiasm for free-trade policy, some 'customers' were emphatically not his best friends.

Trevor Ross has argued that the copyright debate actively created the public domain in the mid-eighteenth century, and that, until then, there was no sense of a national literature belonging to the people.[13]

[10] Harriet Martineau, 'Literary Lionism', *The London and Westminster Review*, 32/2 (1839), 261–81.

[11] See John Forster, *The Life of Charles Dickens* (1911), ii. 208 ff. See also Alexander Welsh, *From Copyright to Copperfield: The Identity of Dickens* (1987). For more on piracies of Dickens's early work, see Ch. 2 n. 186. On 25 March 1843, after his American problems, Dickens convened the first meeting of the Society of British Authors. But he dropped out soon afterwards 'as well convinced of its apparent hopelessness as if I saw it written by a Celestial Penman in the book of Fate'. Charles Dickens to Charles Babbage (27 April 1843), *LCD* iii. 477–8.

[12] *The Yellowplush Papers* ran in *Fraser's Magazine* from November 1837 to August 1838, and was promptly pirated by Cary and Hart. In 1846 *Jeames's Diary* was lifted from *Punch* by William Taylor & Co. of New York; and in November or December of 1848 a pirated American edition of *The History of Samuel Titmarsh* appeared.

[13] Trevor Ross, 'Copyright and the Invention of Tradition', *Eighteenth-Century Studies*, 26/1 (Fall 1992), 1–27, 15–16. See also Philip Connell, 'Bibliomania: Book Collecting, Cultural Politics, and the Rise of Literary Heritage in Romantic Britain', *Representations*, 71 (Summer 2000), 24–47.

I would argue that, while Ross's claim is an important one, the historical fluctuations between the two 'terms' of the copyright law were more nuanced than this account suggests. Certainly, in the mid-eighteenth century, with the first extension of readership, and the development of a modern literary marketplace, and at a time when copyright laws were still largely conceived as offering protection for publishers and booksellers, the emphasis may well have been upon consumption and reading. Towards the end of the eighteenth century though, the poets and writers, themselves concerned to establish the author's property in the text, deliberately placed a renewed emphasis on the scene of production. Around the Exhibition of 1851, such an emphasis on production was revived energetically by the copyright lobby, with a new accent on utility, in an attempt to 'cash in' on the success of patent law amendments. Yet we can also see emerging in the literature around the Exhibition an emphasis on the consumer and on consumer taste. In fact the two ideas—that of a culture belonging to the people, and that of knowledge as privately owned—were both in play at once. The challenge for writers working in the 1850s and 1860s was to find a workable balance between them.

One way of denying the powerful determinism of the evolving print technologies was to indulge in the kind of aesthetic nostalgia we have already seen operating at the Exhibition. In an attempt to find a locus of value for the author beyond the marketplace, Dickens looked back to the patent debate of the 1830s, and then even further back, to the period that generated the rhetoric of that debate: the eighteenth century.[14] Thackeray did the same, although he took a rather different view. This was ironic, perhaps, in that in returning to the eighteenth century, Dickens and Thackeray were only returning to the stereotypes generated by similar pressures in that first period of rapid market change. In a sense, this return to the previous age of letters worked less to emphasize the progress that literary men had made towards professionalization in the nineteenth century, than to expose the difficulties that they were still encountering in trying to make the trade of writing a dignified and independent one.

Pausing to consider the 1850 'Dignity of Literature' dispute that flared up between Forster and Thackeray over the issue of civil

[14] For a fascinating discussion of Dickens's eighteenth-century inheritance as a novelist, see Helen Small, 'The Debt to Society: Dickens, Fielding, and the Genealogy of Independence', in Francis O'Gorman and Katherine Turner (eds.), *The Victorians and the Eighteenth Century: Reassessing the Tradition* (2003).

pensions for writers, the first part of this chapter examines the pre-occupation of the literary profession with establishing the 'propriety' of writing in a decade in which, as we have seen, a mass market was developing with unprecedented rapidity. Dickens and Forster are generally characterized as the opponents of Thackeray in this dispute, but in fact all three writers were keen to establish the public utility and instrumentality of literary writing in order to establish a value for it beyond the ephemerality of the marketplace.[15] But its marketplace value remained important, as they needed to realize as much private property from their writing as possible. The chapter continues with a sustained discussion of two of Dickens's most complex works, *Bleak House* and *Little Dorrit*, showing the ways in which the displacements of authorship in these texts can only be properly understood in the context of the debates about the professionalization of authorship that had become newly urgent in the wake of the debate over intellectual property provoked by the Exhibition.

'THE DIGNITY OF LITERATURE': THACKERAY *VS.* DICKENS AND FORSTER?

As Ch. 3 showed, the question of the status of authorship had been contentious for many years. Throughout Talfourd's many attempted copyright bills and then into the 1840s, the pressure from literary groups, both informal and formalized, had been increasing for a recognition of the rights of authors to be considered as professionals and to be rewarded appropriately.[16] In the eighteenth century, writers had used the example of mechanical invention to campaign for copyright protection. After the Copyright Act of 1842, artisans had used improved copyright law to campaign for reforms in patent law, but ten years on, when the new Patent Act went through in 1852, writers again turned to the patent law to put pressure on the

---

[15] For previous accounts of the 'Dignity of Literature' dispute, see Mark Cronin, 'Henry Gowan, William Makepeace Thackeray, and "The Dignity of Literature" Controversy', *Dickens Quarterly*, 16/2 (June 1999), 104–45; Michael Lund, 'Novels, Writers and Readers in 1850', *Victorian Periodical Review*, 17 (1984), 15–28; Craig Howes, '*Pendennis* and the Controversy on "The Dignity of Literature"', *Nineteenth-Century Literature*, 41/3 (December 1986), 269–98, 296.

[16] See Victor Bonham Carter, *Authors by Profession*, i (1978); N. N. Feltes, *Modes of Production of Victorian Novels* (1986); John Sutherland, *Victorian Novelists and Publishers* (1976) and *Victorian Fiction: Writers, Publishers, Readers* (1995); Nigel Cross, *The Common Writer: Life in Nineteenth-Century Grub Street* (1985).

government to seek ratification of an international copyright agreement. The rhetoric shuttles back and forth between these two categories of intellectual property throughout the century, and the result is a legal and cultural construction of the author that owes much to that of the inventor, and *vice versa*, despite all the obvious differences between the two constituencies. Both groups were attempting to transcend their mixed class origins and to form themselves as professions, and both were seeking an all-important recognition from the state.[17] Both were also trying to establish themselves as nationally important occupations, appealing to the patriotism of the lawmakers to protect British inventions and literature from piracy abroad.

The rhetoric about patent law and international copyright generated by the Exhibition brought intellectual property back into sharp focus and the early 1850s, like the late 1830s, proved to be a critical moment in the struggle for the professionalization of both inventors and writers. At this point, more than at any other in the century, the two debates seem to have collapsed into one another. This can partly be explained by the prominence of the Patent Amendment Bill that seemed to augur so well for an International Copyright agreement. In fact, no agreement would be reached with the United States until 1891, but the *Illustrated London News* was cautiously optimistic in 1851: 'perhaps, it is not too much to hope, that, amid the other civilising and ennobling results for which we may have to thank the industrial gathering of 1851, an international copyright may be included'.[18] That it seemed natural that an 'industrial gathering' should produce an international literary *copyright* agreement demonstrates how closely the two debates about intellectual property were running alongside one another at this time.

It is striking that the debate in the periodicals over the status of writers at this time is never conducted solely in literary terms. Even the so-called 'Dignity of Literature' spat of 1850, in which Thackeray responded to charges made by the *Morning Chronicle* and by Forster in the *Examiner*, that scenes in his novel *Pendennis* had brought the literary profession into disrepute, was conducted

---

[17] See W. J. Reader, *Professional Men: The Rise of the Professional Classes in Nineteenth-Century England* (1966), 69–71.

[18] Anon., 'The Copyright Question', *Illustrated London News*, 18 (Saturday, 24 May 1851), 439–40, 440. Henry Cole mentioned international copyright as one of the probable results of the Exhibition in his lecture, 'On the International Results of the Exhibition of 1851', *Lectures*, 445.

in terms that were not exclusively literary. The original *Morning Chronicle* article objected to '[p]rotection to literature or science', and Forster wrote in the *Examiner*, arguing for '[t]he importance of encouraging literature (under which term is here included all intellectual effort in art and science)', yoking together the examples of Newton and Burns.[19] The reasons for this are complex. Certainly, the rhetoric generated by the impending Exhibition conflated art and science in a way that invested the term 'art' with its full contemporary ambiguity—describing as it did in the nineteenth century, both the literary, visual, and musical arts but also the art of the artisan. This ambiguity initially promised to be useful to the campaigners for the professionalization of authorship. David Brewster acknowledged this in 1851: 'Martyrs at the same stake, Art and Science have risen in allied resistance to their common foe [the government], and marching as they do under the Royal banner of the Exposition, they will not lay down their arms until they have achieved a joint and glorious triumph.'[20] Indeed, all the mainstream periodicals in the period running up to the Exhibition see the two claims as allied, and seem to be unable to discuss the one without reference to the other. In 1848 the *Edinburgh Review,* discussing literary property, complains of 'a country where, by the most unhappy of inversions, it is the invention which makes the fortune and the inventors who starve'.[21] And an article of 1849 about mechanical inventions lurches into the reverse comparison, '[i]n literature, as in manufactures [. . .] as among mechanical inventors and merchant adventurers,—the rewards of industry are divided into great prizes, and blanks,' going on to include Byron alongside Davy with 'all labourers in the field of intellect'.[22] Early in 1852, the *Edinburgh Review*, again, in an article about international copyright, discusses 'the case both of copyright and patent, under our slow and inadequate recognition of a property in ideas'.[23] Clearly, at mid-century, the two causes were seen, if not as synonymous, at least as directly comparable.

[19] *Morning Chronicle* (3 January 1850), 4, and [John Forster], 'The Dignity of Literature', *Examiner* (19 January 1850), 35.
[20] [David Brewster], 'Mr. Babbage on the Exposition of 1851', *North British Review*, 15 (August 1851), 529–68, 565.
[21] Anon., 'Walpole's Letters to the Countess of Ossory', *Edinburgh Review*, 88 (October 1848), 339–60, 346. This is a quotation from Mr Smythe (the Member for Canterbury) speaking at the Manchester Athenaeum in October 1843.
[22] Anon., 'The Patent Journal', *Edinburgh Review*, 89 (January 1849), 47–83, 48 and 50–1.
[23] Anon., 'A few Words on International Copyright—Assemblée Nationale Legislative. Projet de loi relatif à une Convention littéraire entre la France et la

In claiming professional status, the members of the Guild of Literature and Art, most prominently Dickens, Bulwer Lytton, and Forster all placed a strong emphasis on the *instrumentality* of literature, claiming that literary interventions in public life could have a direct, practical effect.[24] Wilkie Collins counted himself among 'those who follow Literature as a study and respect it as a Science', responding, like Dickens, to the need to distance himself from the stereotype of the man-of-letters as only sporadically occupied between long periods of lazy improvidence.[25] But the critic David Masson, writing about *Pendennis* and *David Copperfield*, was worried by a view of literature as instrumental. He complained that Dickens 'step[ped] beyond the province of the artist' in exercising 'the functions of the social and moral critic', seeing instrumentality as contradictory of a construction of aesthetic value that rests upon the autonomy of the artwork.[26] Crucially, Dickens refused to admit this conflict. Like Forster, he saw no contradiction in using mechanical invention as an analogue of artistic creativity. The analogy between copyright and patent law that he had heard rehearsed in the patent debate of the 1830s had caught his imagination, and the exclusion of both inventors and writers from the middle class made the similarities between them more compelling to him than the differences. If we read the character of Daniel Doyce in *Little Dorrit* as representing a literary, as well as a mechanical, inventor, it is clear that Dickens sees the arguments for the professional status and national utility of both groups as parallel. Dickens seems to suggest that literature, too, should be considered as one of the 'useful arts'.

One advantage to the authorship lobby of linking itself with invention, engineering, and the industrial arts, was clear. The Exhibition had boosted the public image of inventors and engineers, and

Grande-Bretagne, précédé de l'expose des motifs présenté par M.TURGOT, Ministre des Affaires Etrangère. 11 Nov., 1851', *Edinburgh Review*, 95 (January 1852), 145–52, 147.

[24] The Guild ran alongside the Royal Literary Fund that, despite its Radical origins, Dickens felt was mismanaged. He attempted to reform the RLF, with no success. To this end he was elected to its Council in May 1851. Thackeray remained faithful to the RLF.

[25] Letter of Dedication to the first edition of *Basil; A Story of Modern Life* (1852), i. p. xvii. Quoted in Catherine Peters, *The King of Inventors* (1991), 116. For a similar argument about the need to dismiss the Romantic stereotype of the artist as idle, see Michael Lund, 'Novels, Writers and Readers in 1850', *Victorian Periodical Review*, 17 (1984), 15–28.

[26] [David Masson], 'Thackeray and Dickens', *North British Review*, 15 (May–August 1851), 57–89, 65.

laid great stress on the national utility of their work, '[t]o the inventive genius of her sons England owes the foundation of her commercial greatness,' as one commentator had written.[27] The authorship lobby was particularly energetic in associating itself with such rhetoric in this period: Bulwer Lytton, for example, has his writer David Fallen in *Not So Bad As We Seem* describe his poem as 'my grand bequest to my country!' and John Forster, in his articles on the 'Dignity of Literature' is insistent on connecting the utility of science and art: 'Services done to the State by distinguished efforts in art, literature and science, are . . . unequivocal . . . The claims of literature and science are for a due recognition and recompense of such valuable service rendered to the State. They are advanced, not on behalf of individuals, but of the class.'[28] Making the 'class' include scientists, whose work was already recognized as unequivocally useful by the public and Prince Albert alike, perhaps helped to divert attention away from the thorny issue of the actual function of literature. Even so, when Forster announces that '[w]e would not remove [literature] from the duties it fulfils, but strengthen its power of discharging them, and making them more generally contribute to the welfare of society,' his airy vagueness about those duties, and his propping up the claims of literature on the more solid example of science, reveal a profound uncertainty at this time about the precise nature of the value of literature.[29] Ironically, in its eagerness to professionalize, the authorship lobby of the 1850s risked dismantling the construction of 'transcendent' literary value that the earlier debates over copyright law had produced. A return to a conflation of mechanical with literary creativity did present problems for those who campaigned for recognition for the profession of authorship. Although Dickens and the Guild tried to reinstate the Romantic image of the writer as inseparable from the work, and as lending the work a value supplementary to any exchange value, such a position proved difficult to maintain when they were also making use of the utility analogy of

[27] Anon., '*The Patent Journal*', 81.

[28] Sir Edward Bulwer Lytton, *Not So Bad As We Seem* (1851), Act 4, Scene 2, p. 83. [John Forster], 'Encouragement of Literatuer [*sic*] by the State', *The Examiner* (5 January 1850), 2.

[29] [John Forster], 'The Dignity of Literature', *The Examiner* (19 January 1850), 35. Nevertheless, the need of science at this time to establish itself more securely should also not be forgotten. Both Babbage and Brewster use the phrase 'the Dignity of Science', for example. Nevertheless, it remained easier to convince government of the utility of science than of literature.

mechanical science. Writing about Pre-Raphaelite painting, for example, Dickens warned that the Royal Academy would be led into trouble, 'by attaching greater weight to handicraft, than to any other consideration', but in his own representation of writing at mid-century, he himself often finds it difficult to represent art as simultaneously a mysterious process 'informed with mind and sentiment' and a rule-bound and 'useful' profession.[30]

Martha Woodmansee has suggested that 'it was not until the eighteenth century that [the arts] came to be thought of as constituting a distinct domain, the "*fines arts*," or simply "art," which is distinguished from the variety of other human activities'.[31] In fact, this process never reached completion—and will never do so—as the boundaries between certain activities remain constantly negotiable. The Great Exhibition, as we have seen, conspicuously entangled the arts and crafts, handwork and machine work, making identifications between the two both easy and powerful, however dangerous in terms of protecting Romantic constructions of originality and value. Romantic writers had been anxious to dispose of the model of craftsmanship for writing, and to insist instead on models of inspiration and genius. By conflating diverse categories of intellectual property in order to push through further protective legislation, authors risked unmasking Romantic ideas of autonomy and spontaneous creation, and exposing the more homely craft of the writer beneath.

'[W]riting, and specifically the representation of writing, became a contested site during this [mid-Victorian] period', according to Mary Poovey.[32] Certainly, it was over the question of how writing should be best 'represented', both politically and aesthetically, that Thackeray and Dickens disagreed. Dickens deplored Thackeray's literary scenes in *Pendennis*, while Thackeray loathed the Guild's benefit performances and objected to their co-operative scheme as a 'literary soup kitchen', protesting against 'a set of men who will be martyrs, who are painting their faces and asking for your money, who want to make literature a chronic beggary under the name of the

---

[30] [Charles Dickens],'Old Lamps for New Ones', *Household Words*, 12 (15 June 1850), 265–7, 266. For an interesting argument about the treatment of time in Dickens's version of artistic labour in this period, see Jennifer Ruth, 'Mental Capital, Industrial Time: The Professional in *David Copperfield*', *Novel*, 32/3 (Summer 1999), 303–30.

[31] Martha Woodmansee, *The Author, Art, and the Market* (1994), 1 [unpaginated]. She credits Paul Oskar Kristeller with this observation.

[32] Mary Poovey, *Uneven Developments* (1988), 105.

Guild . . . that humbug the booth of Literature and Art'.[33] But the charge was the same in both cases: vulgarity and indignity. Under the surface of the 'Dignity of Literature' exchange was a series of complex reactions that, when uncovered, exposed the precarious and frightening relationship of literature to display, and of writing to ephemeral performance, at a time when the Exhibition in Hyde Park was demonstrating worrying new disparities between display and worth. The Exhibition had spawned a brief efflorescence of Exhibition merchandizing—'It was "exhibition" hat, "exhibition" razor strop, "exhibition" watch; nay, even "exhibition" weather, "exhibition" spirits, sweethearts, babies, wives—for the time.'[34] The 'sense of novelty' was necessarily short-lived, though.[35] If writing was also perceived as a spectacle or a performance—Dickens and Thackeray 'daring death' by writing up to the copy-deadlines in the periodicals each month—it threatened to incorporate an obsolescence that made it difficult to argue for its endurance as property after its first evanescent appearance on the bookstalls.

Despite the perceived disagreement between Dickens and Thackeray over the representation of literature, Thackeray, like Dickens, insisted on the 'useful work' of writing. He had struggled for much longer than Dickens as a hack writer, before he, like Goldsmith, had 'the lucky hit, which trebles his usual gains' with *Vanity Fair* in 1848.[36] But even after his success, he continued to insist on the craft and effort of writing: 'The last effort at Potry [*sic*] I made was for the 1 of May Exhibition—The verses flow easily enough, but they took 5 days of the hardest labour I ever endured in my life—clearing a primaeval forest is nothing to it.'[37] Thackeray deliberately characterized writing as 'labour' in order to attack what he saw as Forster's and Dickens's sentimentalization of the profession. For example, in his 1851 lectures on humorists of the eighteenth century, he spoke explicitly and deliberately of Goldsmith as a 'skilful workman'.[38]

---

[33] W. M. Thackeray, *The Critic* (15 March 1852). Thackeray, MSS 9? July 1851 (National Library of Scotland), quoted in Gordon Ray, *Thackeray: The Age of Wisdom* (1958), 152–3.

[34] Thomas Hardy, 'The Fiddler of the Reels', in *Outside the Gates of the World: Selected Short Stories* (1996), 334–50, 334.

[35] Ibid.

[36] W. M. Thackeray, *The English Humorists of the Eighteenth Century. A Series of Lectures Delivered in England, Scotland, and the United States of America* (1853), 309.

[37] W. M. Thackeray to Mr Hawkins (7 July 1851), *LWMT* ii. 787.

[38] Thackeray, *English Humorists*, 309.

This was partly a hit at Forster's melodramatic portrayal of Goldsmith as a starving genius in his 1848 biography, which pictures the eighteenth-century writer '[i]n a garret, writing for bread, and expecting to be dunned for a milk-score'. Forster used the Goldsmith biography to promote 'the duties and responsibilities assumed by the public writer; and of the social consideration and respect that their effectual discharge should have undisputed right to claim'.[39] Thackeray refused such high-flown rhetoric, and his description of the repetitive and dull labour of the hired writer in *Pendennis* provoked protest: 'we know how the life of any hack, legal or literary, in a curacy, or in a marching regiment, or at a merchant's desk, is dull of routine, and tedious of description. One day's labour resembles another much too closely.'[40] He had already made the same point in his 1846 article on the writer Blanchard, in which he had objected to Bulwer Lytton's suggestion that Blanchard could have produced work of genius if he had not been obliged to struggle for a living, 'Let us be content with our *status* as literary craftsmen, telling the truth as far as may be.'[41]

While he was careful to compliment Dickens in his 1851 lectures, he also hit at the melodramatic tendencies of the Guild and drew the same comparison between writing and other occupations, including inventing, that had already caused so much offence in *Pendennis*: 'Don't we see daily ruined inventors, grey-haired midshipmen, balked heroes, blighted curates, barristers pining a hungry life out in chambers, the attorneys never mounting to their garrets, whilst scores of them are rapping at the door of the successful quack below? If these suffer, who is the author, that he should be exempt?'[42] Dickens and Forster were shocked by this view because it seemed to reserve no 'supplementary' value for literature beyond that of the

---

[39] John Forster, *The Life and Adventures of Oliver Goldsmith, A Biography in Four Books* (1848), 120 and 697.

[40] W. M. Thackeray, *The History of Pendennis His Fortunes and Misfortunes His Friends and His Greatest Enemy* (1994), 449–50.

[41] 'A Brother of the Press on the History of a Literary Man, Laman Blanchard, And the Chances of the Literary Profession in a Letter to the Reverend Francis Sylvester at Rome, from Michael Angelo Titmarsh, Esquire', in *The Works of William Makepeace Thackeray*, xxv (1886), 84–97, 87.

[42] Thackeray, *English Humorists*, 319. W. J. Reader records that there was a glut of attorneys between 1841 and 1851, and that '[s]hocking stories were told of young barristers slowly starving to death, from want of employment, in their chambers in the Temple', *Professional Men* (1966), 154.

point of sale in the marketplace.[43] Thackeray even made the extreme assertion that intellectual property was impossible of retention, '[t]he picture or article once done and handed over to the public, is the latter's property, not the author's, and to be estimated according to its honest value,' suggesting that the market was adequate to fix such an 'honest value'.[44] But Thackeray was perhaps more worried than he seemed about the propriety and dignity of literature, and more active in establishing the 'status' of the literary craft than Dickens or Forster gave him credit for. He, too, saw literature as a serious matter of public utility: 'we may never forget truth & Justice and kindness as the great ends of our profession . . . our profession seems to me to be as serious as the Parson's own', and far from being opposed to state pensions, he quietly used his influence to ensure that writers were represented on the lists.[45]

But if Thackeray was largely in agreement on the claims of the 'profession', then what was the 'Dignity of Literature' exchange and

[43] For Thackeray, slavery is an image that brings together his worries about his identity being violated by the exposure of writing 'in his own person', the publicity of the marketplace, and, by a curious muddling of the book with the author, the shame of being sold into alienated labour, of the loss of self-possession, and, ultimately, of abjection. '[W]e'll take him to market and sell him', exclaims Warrington, speaking of Pen's autobiographical novel, *Walter Lorriane*, so, by an uncomfortably clear association, of Pen himself (523). *Pendennis* itself, is, of course, a broadly autobiographical work, too, so the trail leads ultimately back to Thackeray himself. And the identification of Pen with a slave is consolidated in the last words of the novel, a dusty answer to the opening words of *David Copperfield*, in which we are asked to 'give a hand of charity' to Pen 'who does not claim to be a hero, but only a man and a brother' (977). The allusion to the Abolitionist motto, 'Am I not a Man and a Brother?' is too startling to ignore. Clearly Thackeray shares with Dickens the worry about just what it was they were both selling in the literary marketplace, and what they would be able to retain. See Deborah A. Thomas, 'Bondage and Freedom in *Pendennis*', in *Thackeray and Slavery* (1993), 76–95 and John Sutherland, 'Thackeray as Victorian Racialist', *Essays in Criticism*, 20 (1970), 441–5. See also Brantlinger's discussion of Thackeray and slavery in *Rule of Darkness: British Literature and Imperialism, 1830–1914* (1988).

[44] Thackeray, 'A Brother of the Press on the History of a Literary Man', 89. Andrew H. Miller, 'Longing for Sleeve Buttons', in *Novels Behind Glass: Commodity Culture and Victorian Narrative* (1995), 14–49, is interesting on Thackeray and value. See also Joseph Litvak, ' "Kiss me, stupid": Sophistication, Sexuality and *Vanity Fair*', *Novel: A Forum on Fiction*, Winter, 29/2 (1996), 223–42.

[45] Meeting Lord Stanley at the Great Exhibition, Thackeray mentioned the case of the elderly Anna Jameson to him, and she was duly awarded a pension of a hundred pounds a year (*LWMT* ii. 282). He was supportive of Leigh Hunt's state pension, too, and wrote to congratulate him upon it, and upon the Guild's performance for his benefit. Thackeray to Mark Lemon (24 February 1847), *LWMT* ii. 281–2, 282. Lord Stanley to Thackeray (3? July 1851) and Thackeray to Lord Stanley of Alderley (4 July 1851), both *LWMT* ii. 786. Thackeray to Leigh Hunt (June ? 1847), *LWMT* ii. 307.

the animosity that followed really all about? In his letter to the *Morning Chronicle*, Thackeray indirectly attacked Dickens's Guild for 'rais[ing] piteous controversies, upon a question which all people of sense must take to be settled' and he complained elsewhere about the 'absurd outcry' on behalf of authors.[46] He seems to suggest that all the fuss is excessive and vulgarly disproportionate to a grievance that he sees as exaggerated in its claims, especially when the claims of the authors were compared to the similar predicaments of other professionals.

The title of Dickens's Guild carried with it a deliberate suggestion of craftsmanship and trade, and one of its problems was its need to reconcile its argument for the utility and instrumentality of literature with Dickens's own need to prove that while writers were hard-working, they were not, as Thackeray had suggested, 'just like any other daily toiler', and that, in particular, they were not at all like the daily toilers at Warren's Blacking Warehouse.[47] Without a codified set of entrance qualifications, it proved difficult to elevate writing fully into a profession, and the choice of 'Guild' may reflect the need to reinstate a model of craftsmanship and a level of exclusivity, so that the 'class' of writers could be recognized by a shared and sharable body of technical knowledge. One reviewer of Thackeray's *Pendennis* pointed to this difficulty:

It in reality only differs from other professions by being open to the whole world. There are no lets and hindrances to introition—no articles to be subscribed—no probationary dinners to be undergone—no qualifications to be tested—no degrees to be taken—no diplomas to be granted, before the man of letters begins his practice and gathers his constituents around him.[48]

Mechanical engineering, still reliant on apprenticeships at mid-century and resistant to scientific theory or educational qualifications, was experiencing similar difficulties. The Institute of Mechanical Engineers was founded in 1857, and Dickens's and

---

[46] W. M. Thackeray, 'The Dignity of Literature', *Morning Chronicle* (12 January 1850), 4. Thackeray to Paul Émile Daurand Forgues (16 September 1854), *LWMT* iii. 390.

[47] W. M. Thackeray, *Pendennis* (1994), 450. The term 'Guild' is perhaps suggestive less of free trade than of a more archaic, feudal system of trade organization.

[48] [J. W. Kaye], '*Pendennis*—The Literary Profession', *North British Review*, 13 (August 1850), 335–72, 369–70.

Bulwer's Guild was an earlier attempt, among others, to achieve a similar professional body for literature.[49]

While it was all very well that '[j]ournalism has made literature a business . . . [and] [t]he literary man is now a workman, in the best sense of the word,' Dickens and others searched for another, supplementary index of value that could mark the writer's superiority to the marketplace.[50] Looking forwards, into the technologically-led future of the publishing trade, this must have seemed a difficult task. Instead, these writers looked backwards. The Guild's play was set in a pantomime world of heroic writers and villainous publishers, which lent a lurid and melodramatic certainty to the rights and wrongs of the case. Presumably, the representation of dead and securely famous writers (the lines David Fallen quotes from his master work are taken from John Dryden's *Indian Emperor* (I. i. 27–8)) was dramatically a more straightforward proposition than putting contemporary writers upon the stage.[51] But, in fact, by casting prominent contemporary literary writers as actors in a play about the eighteenth-century literary scene, the Guild achieved a kind of double temporal perspective that allowed it to suggest both progress and stasis in the development of the role of the writer over the intervening century. The need to hold in reserve some less public quality than marketability—a quality that endowed literary writing with an intrinsic value beyond a market value—underlay the Guild's campaign. Even public funding, through pensions and grants, would never be commensurate with the value of literature. As John Forster insisted in the *Morning*

---

[49] Others included the Society of British Authors, which was born and buried in 1843 (to rise again under Walter Besant in 1884 as the Society of Authors); the Association for the Protection of Literature, with which Dickens was involved, 1843–9; and the Royal Literary Fund. Dickens was elected to the Committee of the RLF in 1839 and contributed to an attack on the administration of the Society in 1858. However, the Society outlasted his Guild, which, although it built three houses at Stevenage to accommodate needy artists, could find no tenants. Its failure was apparent by the mid-1860s, but it was finally wound up in 1897, and the balance of its accounts split between the Royal Literary Fund and the Artists' General Benevolent Institution. Information from Bonham-Carter, *Authors by Profession*, 83–7, and Nigel Cross, *The Common Writer* (1985).

[50] Anon., 'Literary Adventurers', *All the Year Round* (10 October 1863), 152–6, 156.

[51] Daniel Hack has argued that it was the taint of charity, rather than the taint of trade, that Dickens was anxious to avoid when setting up the Guild, 'Literary Paupers and Professional Authors: The Guild of Literature and Art', *Studies in English Literature 1500–1900*, 39/4 (Autumn 1999), 691–713.

Chronicle, 'Literature and literary men can give, and do give, much more to the State than the State can ever repay.'[52] Literature had to be priceless, as well as a commodity.

Thackeray scorned Bulwer Lytton's Guild play for its historical setting, because 'the times are altered, the people don't exist'.[53] But when he in turn found himself accused of moral levity in *Vanity Fair* and *Pendennis*, he also turned back to the last century, in his 1851 lectures on humorists of the eighteenth century and in *The History of Henry Esmond*, which he started writing in September 1851. The first edition of the novel was issued using old typeface, with running heads in Latin, and an epistle dedicatory to his patron, Lord Ashburton, indispensable to 'a book which copies the manners and language of Queen Anne's time'.[54] Anxious to establish his own literary posterity, Thackeray drew upon an eighteenth-century model of authorship to create the impression of substance, while Dickens publicly reviled 'that one disgraceful leaf of dedication which formed the blot upon the literature of past ages' and '[t]hat huckstering, peddling, pandering to patronage for the sale of a book, the offspring of intellect and genius'.[55] Yet Dickens's indignant insistence on 'genius' is as much a return to the terms of the eighteenth century as Thackeray's franker 'copying' of them. Thackeray's work ironically acknowledges the tactic, whereas terms such as 'genius' and 'inspiration' stand unquestioned beside 'hard work' and 'labour' in Dickens's rhetoric.[56] Hillis Miller has read *Henry Esmond* as a text

---

[52] Quoted by Hack from the *Morning Chronicle*.

[53] W. M. Thackeray, Speech at the Annual Dinner of the Literary Fund (14 May 1851). See Cross, *The Common Writer*, 72. Bulwer Lytton was the aristocratic heir to Knebworth House, and his considerable income from his novel-writing helped him to maintain an extravagant lifestyle. Thackeray's dislike of and scorn for Bulwer may have been connected with his general dislike of aristocratic display, which he saw as anachronistic.

[54] W. M. Thackeray, 'To the Right Honourable William Bigham, Lord Ashburton', *The History of Henry Esmond, Esq. A Colonel in the Service of Her Majesty Q. Anne Written by Himself* (1852), i.

[55] K. J. Fielding (ed.), *The Speeches of Charles Dickens* (1960), 5. See also p. 213 for the speech to the Royal Literary Fund Annual General Meeting (12 March 1856).

[56] Helen Small has pointed out that *Not So Bad As We Seem* was performed at Devonshire House to an audience that included the Queen, the Duke of Wellington, and numerous aristocrats, and that the printed version of Bulwer Lytton's play includes a fulsome dedication to the Duke of Devonshire. She argues that this does not detract from Dickens's genuine desire to free the literary profession from patronage, however. Helen Small, 'The Debt to Society' (forthcoming).

that constantly and ironically undermines all kinds of 'legitimate authority', including, finally, its own narrative integrity.[57] But Thackeray does insist on the integrity of the writer, Addison, in this novel, whom, we are told, entertains Esmond graciously in his 'shabby' room—'the greatest courtier in the land could not have a more splendid politeness, or greater dignity of manner'.[58] Addison's 'dignity of manner' owes much to Macaulay's account of the writer, in which he claimed that Addison had, 'without inflicting a wound, effected a great social reform, and . . . reconciled wit and virtue, after a long and disastrous separation, during which wit had been led astray by profligacy, and virtue by fanaticism'.[59] In his portrait of Addison's 'dignity of manner' and his moral influence, Thackeray creates his own model of a literary writer who quietly and unobtrusively manages to effect a 'great social reform'. In *Esmond*, Addison maintains his independence and integrity despite the circumstances and contingencies of the market in which he finds himself, without recourse to extravagant claims of 'genius' and the 'pricelessness' of art.

One of the problems for both engineers and writers was the need to unify occupations that embraced practitioners from very diverse class backgrounds. This was critical to the 'Dignity of Literature' issue. For Dickens, the question of intellectual property and professionalization was tied up closely with the problem of his own class identity: a vexed one for a man 'not high bred but excellent company' such as himself.[60] Intellectual property represented the vital differential between the hack writer and the man of letters, and between the operative and the inventor. It also represented the differential between alienated labour and unalienated labour, and, even more fundamentally for Dickens, between shameful trade and professional pride. Perhaps it stung Dickens that Thackeray remarked in his 'Dignity of Literature' letter to the *Morning Chronicle*, that 'the pen gives a place in the world to men who had none before', as Dickens

---

[57] J. Hillis Miller, '*Henry Esmond*: Repetition and Irony', in *Fiction and Repetition: Seven English Novels* (1982), 73–115, 115.

[58] W. M. Thackeray, *The History of Henry Esmond* (1970), 233.

[59] [T. B. Macaulay],'The Life of Joseph Addison, by Lucy Aikin, in 2 vols', *Edinburgh Review*, 157 (July 1843), 193–260, 260. Ray tells us that Thackeray read this article and that both his account of Addison in his lecture and his portrait in *Esmond* were 'substantially coloured by the Macaulayan view of the English eighteenth century'. Gordon N. Ray, *Thackeray, The Age of Wisdom 1847–1863* (1958), 145.

[60] Charles Kingsley to his wife, quoted in Susan Chitty, *The Beast and the Monk: A Life of Charles Kingsley* (1974), 174.

himself was just such an *arriviste*, always the 'newer' man, even though he and Thackeray were born within a year of each other.[61] Even the reviewers picked up on the class difference between the two writers. David Masson detects 'the effect of . . . classical studies' on Thackeray's prose style, while in Dickens he sees a 'keen and feminine sensibility . . . we do not see in him that habitual knowingness, that close-grained solidity of view, that impressive strong sense, which we find in what Thackeray writes'.[62] And another reviewer of *Pendennis* calls Thackeray's an 'honest and manly nature': Thackeray's virility is a measure of his pedigree, while Dickens's 'femininity' denotes his indeterminate class position.[63] Some reviewers were positively cruel in their snobbery:

> But in Mr. Dickens's voluminous works, we do not remember to have found many traces of these solid acquirements [of Thackeray, Bulwer Lytton, and Scott]; and we must be permitted to say, for it is no reflection on any man out of the legal profession, that his notions of law, which occupy so large a space in his books, are precisely those of an attorney's clerk. He knows what arrest for debt is, he knows how affadavits are sworn.[64]

Dickens, of course, knew only too well, and not just in his capacity as a former attorney's clerk, 'what arrest for debt is'.[65] His ungentlemanliness and his lack of a classical education made Dickens's fiction vulnerable to accusations of effeminacy, so that the analogy of invention provided him with a means of representing his work as belonging to another kind of masculine 'public' world. Dickens was excluded from the culture of the university-educated (idle) gentleman, but he styled himself instead as an example of the 'new' man: a hard-working, Smilesian man-of-action.

'I do not like to think of our confrères painting their faces and grinning in farces,' wrote Thackeray, explaining why he thought the Guild's plays 'unworthy and derogatory to our calling'.[66] Dickens disliked Thackeray's satires of modern writers, 'Novels by Eminent

---

[61] Thackeray, 'Dignity of Literature', 4.

[62] [David Masson], 'Thackeray and Dickens', *North British Review*, 15 (May–August 1851), 57–89, 62, 63, and 64.

[63] [Kaye] '*Pendennis*—The Literary Profession', 372.

[64] Anon., 'The License of Modern Novelists', *Edinburgh Review*, 106 (July 1857), 124–56, 128.

[65] For an account of his father's imprisonment for debt and his own miserable stint as a worker at Warren's Blacking Warehouse, see Dickens's 'Autobiographical Fragment', John Forster, *Life of Charles Dickens* (1911), i. 22.

[66] Thackeray to Daurand Forgues (16 September 1854), *LWMT* iii. 390.

Hands', because, for writers, 'depreciating or vulgarizing each other' was too easy.[67] And Dickens and Forster felt that Thackeray's portrayal of a drunken 'literary supper' in *Pendennis*, which the writer, Shandon, leaves 'reel[ing] in his walk . . . the cabman on his box jeering at him', denigrated the profession.[68] The charge of vulgarity flew backwards and forwards between them. Thackeray could be casually snobbish about Dickens, as when he bumped into the writer and his family on their holidays in 1849, and reported that they were 'all looking abominably coarse vulgar and happy', but his worry about Dickens's vulgarity went much deeper than this.[69] He objected to Dickens's *David Copperfield* because of its 'exaggeration', famously protesting that, 'in a drawing-room drama a coat is a coat and a poker a poker; and must be nothing else according to my ethics, not an embroidered tunic, nor a great red-hot instrument like the Pantomime weapon'.[70] Connecting Dickens to the theatricality and immoderate display of the Pantomime, Thackeray's charge of vulgarity reveals a worry about ephemeral and trivial self-display through writing, and the self-caricature in circus-dress that Thackeray drew in a letter to the Carlyles in May 1851, as he commenced his first lecture series, revealed his own uncomfortable self-consciousness about performing. Under the drawing he wrote, 'Equilibrist and Tightrope dance[r] in ordinary to the nobility & the Literati' (see Fig. 5).[71]

Janice Carlisle and Garrett Stewart have argued that Victorian novelists at mid-century cultivated an intimacy of address to their readers: 'The novelist's basically theatrical stance as a performer or entertainer, combined with his ability to take over the function of traditional religion, creates an almost inconceivably literal sense of intimacy.'[72] Indeed, copyright legislation relied upon a notion of the investment of the author's personality in the text to support the case for individual ownership. Mark Rose reminds us that, 'literary property was underwritten by the personality of the author'.[73] In 1851,

---

[67] Dickens to Thackeray (9 January 1848), *LWMT* ii. 336–7.
[68] Thackeray, 'A Dinner in the Row', *Pendennis* (1994), 439.
[69] Thackeray to Mrs Brookfield (24 July 1849), *LWMT* ii. 569.
[70] Thackeray to David Masson (6? May 1851), *LWMT* ii. 772 and 773.
[71] Thackeray to Mr And Mrs Carlyle (23? May 1851), *LWMT* ii. 775.
[72] Janice Carlisle, *The Sense of an Audience: Dickens, Thackeray, and George Eliot at Mid-Century* (1982), 34. Garrett Stewart, *Dear Reader: The Conscripted Audience in Nineteenth-Century British Fiction* (1996).
[73] Mark Rose, *Authors and Owners* (1993), 129.

FIG. 5. Self-caricature by Thackeray.

David Masson shows how closely readers identified writers with their work when he remarked that, '[w]hen we say "Pendennis" and "Copperfield," . . . it is really the same as if we said Thackeray and Dickens.'[74] Thackeray himself participated in such an approach when he announced at the beginning of his first lecture on Swift, 'it is of the men and their lives, rather than of their books, that I ask permission to speak to you'.[75] Even at the time, reviewers noticed this, 'Mr. Thackeray is the very reverse of a *myth*. His identity does not recede from us, but comes out boldly to meet us.'[76] But such intimacy is in fact part of an illusion created by both Dickens and Thackeray, whose frequent apostrophe to the 'dear reader' is part of a deliberate attempt to create themselves as personalities, and therefore to establish themselves in their readers' minds as the originators of the text.[77] At the same time both Dickens and Thackeray do 'recede from us' in

[74] [David Masson], 'Thackeray and Dickens', *North British Review* (August 1851), 57–89, 58.
[75] Thackeray, *English Humorists*, 1.
[76] [Kaye] '*Pendennis*—The Literary Profession', 335.
[77] See Garrett Stewart, *Dear Reader* (1996).

that they were keen to avoid an over-identification with their work that would rob it of its 'public' value. In Bulwer Lytton's *Not So Bad As We Seem*, the destitute hero, David Fallen, keeps to his principles and refuses to sell Lord Henry de Mowbray's private memoirs, saying, '[b]egone I will not sell a man's hearth to the public,' drawing a boundary around the private domestic space, and hiding it from public view.[78] Both *David Copperfield* and *Pendennis* are disguised autobiographies that defy straightforward attempts to identify their protagonists with their authors. Dickens and Thackeray were keen to defend the boundary between 'a man's hearth' and its exposure to the 'public view', at the same time as they realized the market value of personal experience.

In his lectures on the English humorists of the nineteenth century, Thackeray dwelt affectionately on the personalities of the authors he discussed. It is through speaking of the men and their private lives that Thackeray is able to convert them into public property. Ironically, by the very emphasis on their individualities and eccentricities, they are written into the hearts and minds of the nation and they become national treasures. The lectures were highly influential on the development of the literary profession, as was recognized at the time, 'Mr. Thackeray has made clear to all—what was previously acknowledged only by a few—that a study of these authors is an indispensable part of an Englishman's education.'[79] Thackeray helped to create an identity and a context for Addison, Steele, Swift, Sterne, and Goldsmith, and was thus directly involved in the formation of the canon that would be taken up by the universities later in the century. In creating a literary genealogy for the contemporary Victorian novelist in these lectures, Thackeray was as crucially engaged as Dickens in imagining literary writing as a profession with an independent history and lineage. Yet Thackeray always avoided over-identifying himself with any kind of campaign.

The 'Dignity of Literature' exchange is helpful in providing a moment, at the precise mid-point of the nineteenth century, for close examination of the question of professional authorship. But the exchange only begins to come into clear focus if it is projected back on to the debates around intellectual property that were current at this time, and to the forthcoming Exhibition, with which Dickens,

---

[78] Sir Edward Bulwer Lytton, *Not So Bad As We Seem*, 86.
[79] Anon., *Morning Chronicle* (27 June 1853).

Forster, and Thackeray were all involved.[80] All three actively participated in the construction of authorship as personality, both in their
campaigns for intellectual property rights, and in their own writing—Thackeray chose, in his lectures on the eighteenth-century
humorists, to speak about the imprint of the personalities of the men
on the books, and Dickens was quick to understand the power of the
named brand: 'Conducted by Charles Dickens' appeared on every
single page of his new journal, *Household Words*, and he famously
liked to refer to himself as the 'Inimitable'. Yet both writers were also
very worried about making an exhibition of themselves, and investing too much of their private selves in their literary property which
was always, finally, on display and destined to become the property
of the public. Their hold on their own work was fleeting, and its
rapid consumption threw them back upon their inventiveness again
and again, 'ever trying after something that is never reached', as
Dickens put it.[81] Thackeray was probably right to caricature himself
as a trapeze artist: the balance enshrined in the copyright law between private property and public exposure was, in practice, extremely difficult to maintain.

Act 4, Scene 2 of Bulwer Lytton's play takes place in David Fallen's
garret, '[t]he scene resembling that of Hogarth's "Distrest Poet" ', yet
while Dickens had no problem with the representation of the scene
of writing on stage, he had almost entirely concealed it in the novel
he had just completed.[82] David Copperfield, although he claims to
'have come out in another way', in taking to authorship, alluding to
the exposure of publication, describes his occupation thus: 'I wrote a
little something, in secret, and sent it to a magazine, and it was published in the magazine. Since then I have taken heart to write a good
many trifling pieces. Now, I am regularly paid for them. Altogether, I
am well off; when I tell my income on the fingers of my left hand, I
pass the third finger and take in the fourth to the middle joint.'[83] The
secrecy, self-deprecation, and curious theatre of the fingers that

---

[80] Thackeray's friendship with the Coles ensured that he followed developments
closely at this time, and he was a patriotic fan of the Exhibition, which he described as
'a noble awful great love inspiring goose flesh bringing sight'. Thackeray to Mrs
Brookfield (1 May 1851), *LWMT* ii. 768. He was present at the opening ceremony,
and wrote, 'I think the English compartment do beat the rest entirely,' Thackeray to
Mrs Brookfield (29 April 1851), *LWMT* ii. 767.

[81] Forster, *Life of Charles Dickens*, ii. 219.

[82] Ibid. 83.   [83] Charles Dickens, *David Copperfield* (1983), 512.

stands for David's income in this passage give an impression that he has not, in fact, 'come out' at all. Indeed, the rest of the chapter is given over to David's recollections of his marriage to Dora and the next chapter, 'Our Housekeeping', is very much about staying in ('I was engaged in writing at home') while Dora lovingly holds his pens.[84] While Dickens does insist upon David's hard work—representing him as 'industrious', and 'labour[ing] hard at [his] book', the process of writing is hidden from view in the private space of the home.[85] Dickens creates a private space for his public work that exonerates him from the potential alienation of a more public workplace. Dickens's novels of the 1850s discussed in this chapter are curiously both full of writing and devoid of writers. The result is that writing in these texts often lacks authority, is misdirected, misleading, severed from its source, or lost.[86] David and Dora's disappointing servant, Paragon, for example, has 'a written character, as large as a proclamation' which inflates her value preposterously.[87] And that writing is treacherous and ultimately unaccountable becomes even clearer in Dickens's next novel, the sombre *Bleak House*, which was written alongside the glittering Guild performances of *Not So Bad As We Seem*.[88] Plot similarities between the two have been noticed before, and the novel is dedicated to 'My Companions in the Guild of Literature and Art', but little critical attention has been paid to the ways in which questions about the literary profession and the performance of authorship migrate across from play to novel.[89]

[84] Charles Dickens, *David Copperfield* (1983), 528, 529.

[85] Ibid. 529 and 562. See Mary Poovey, *Uneven Developments* (1988), ch. 4, for a discussion of the ways in which writing and housekeeping are both figured as unalienated labour in *David Copperfield*. Richard Salmon has recently argued that 'labour is the endlessly-acknowledged source of David's triumphant achievements as a professional writer—it is revealed . . . as the ultimate foundation of literary value' concluding that 'Dickens's text follows Thackeray's [*Pendennis*] in disavowing a "Romantic" model of spontaneous poetic self-expression in favour of disciplined literary labour.' 'The Disenchantment of the Author: Labour Theories of Writing in Dickens and Thackeray' (unpublished MS).

[86] Murray Baumgarten points out that *David Copperfield* is full of writing, but only notices in passing that much of this writing is ineffective, 'Writing and *David Copperfield*', *Dickens Studies Annual*, 14 (1985), 39–59.

[87] Dickens, *David Copperfield*, 518.

[88] The year 1851 included his father's death on 31 March 1851 and his baby daughter Dora's death on 14 April 1851.

[89] See Stanley Friedman, '*Bleak House* and Bulwer's *Not So Bad As We Seem*', *Dickens Quarterly*, 9/1 (March 1992), 25–9. I am struck by the similarities of the plots of both Dickens's novel and Bulwer's play to August von Kotzebue's *The Stranger*. Both Pen and David go and see this play, as did Thackeray and Dickens.

BLEAK HOUSE AND THE ACCOUNTABILITY OF WRITING

It has often been noticed that Dickens's almost schematically topical novel, which he started in November 1851, contains not one reference to the Great Exhibition.[90] Philip Landon suggests that Dickens is actively competing for popularity with Paxton and his Palace, and he draws a close parallel between realistic fiction and the Exhibition: 'Both the [Crystal] Palace and the novel evince a nostalgic impulse to extract a coherent narrative from the potentially overwhelming vistas of the secular universe.'[91] Like many recent critics, he reads *Bleak House* as a Foucauldian 'disciplinary text', which 'steer[s its readers] towards the normative enclosures where health and safety are maximised'.[92] But *Bleak House* seems somewhat limited in its disciplinary effectiveness. Inspector Bucket, after all, fails to catch up with Lady Dedlock, and the 'detective' trail goes, quite literally, 'cold and dead', rather than achieving the completion and the full recuperation of meaning to be expected from the 'classic realist' text.[93] Similarly, the many documents in the text remain 'litter', like the contents of Miss Flite's reticule, and never achieve authority (51). Jarndyce *vs.* Jarndyce ends in a giant dumping of scrap paper, 'great bundles of paper began to be carried out—bundles in bags, bundles too large to be got into any bags, immense masses of papers . . . which the bearers staggered under, and threw down . . . anyhow, on the Hall pavement' (922). The 'labyrinthine urban novel' remains just that, labyrinthine, and bewildering: the London that Esther experiences as 'such a labyrinth of streets, that I soon lost all idea of where we were' (827), is emphatically not the newly signposted, leg-

[90] See John Butt and Kathleen Tillotson, *Dickens at Work* (1957), 183–93; Richard D. Altick, *The Presence of the Present: Topics of the Day in the Victorian Novel* (1991), 421–2; Philip Landon, 'Great Exhibitions: Representations of the Crystal Palace in Mayhew, Dickens and Dostoevsky', *Nineteenth-Century Contexts*, 20/1 (1997), 27–59, 36. In 'The Last Words of the Old Year', *Household Words*, 41 (4 January 1851), 337–9, Dickens suggests that, instead of the Great Exhibition, a 'dark Exhibition of the bad results of our doings!' should be mounted, p. 338.

[91] Philip Landon, 'Great Exhibitions: Representations of the Crystal Palace in Mayhew, Dickens and Dostoevsky', *Nineteenth-Century Contexts*, 20/1 (1997), 27–59, 30. Landon reminds us that Dickens briefly and unsuccessfully edited Paxton's *Daily News*—a paper that both started and failed in 1846, and that both Paxton and Dickens were protégés of the Duke of Devonshire.

[92] Ibid. 48. See also readings by Catherine Belsey, Jeremy Tambling, D. A. Miller, and Bruce Robbins.

[93] Charles Dickens, *Bleak House*, ed. Norman Page and J. Hillis Miller (1985), 869. All subsequent references appear in the text in parentheses.

ible, disciplined London of the Great Exhibition. Street-signs had been put up for the first time for the Great Exhibition, as *Chambers's* reported, '[y]ou may now know whereabouts you are when walking our streets, for the names of the thoroughfares are newly and universally painted at their extremities and intersections.'[94] The Commissioners were proud of the innovation of public toilets at the Exhibition, too, whereas sanitary conditions in *Bleak House* are famously appalling.

For the novel to be truly disciplinary, Dickens would have had to reform Jo, but, staring up at the cross on top of St Paul's, 'the crowning confusion of the great, confused city' (326), Jo does maintain some subject position in the text, however tentative, and the novel just about manages to resist the urge to clean him up. Jo and Gridley remain human wastage to the end, despite their partial retrievals by the deathbed scenes at the shooting gallery. Neither of them would, after all, have been able to afford to see the Exhibition, and Dickens's reinstatement of wastage in his text, when it was rendered invisible by the paradigm of productive order and industrious efficiency on display at the Crystal Palace, makes it clear that his project is at least attempting a challenge to this paradigm, and not merely reproducing it.

It is worth remembering that Dickens confidently predicted that the Exhibition would fail as a disciplinary exercise:

I have always had an instinctive feeling against the Exhibition, of a faint, inexplicable sort. I have a great confidence in its being a correct one somehow or other—perhaps it was a foreshadowing of the bewilderment of the public. My apprehension—and prediction—is, that they will come out of it at last, with that feeling of boredom and lassitude (to say nothing of having spent their money) that the reaction will not be as wholesome and vigorous and quick, as folks expect.[95]

Evidence given in the last chapter confirmed that the public was not always entirely taken in by what another Foucauldian critic, Tony

---

[94] Anon., 'Things Talked of in London', *Chambers's Edinburgh Journal* (31 May 1851), 350–2, 350. In 1850 *Household Words* had complained about the lack of street-signing in the city. 'Chips' column: 'Streetography', *Household Words*, 38 (14 December 1850), 275–6.

[95] Charles Dickens to Wills (27 July 1851) *LCD* vi. 448–9. The letter discusses *Punch's* 'falling' (p. 448) for the Great Exhibition after its initial mockery of the scheme. Thackeray's view was just the opposite and he gave *Punch's* mockery of the Exhibition as one of his reasons for resigning from the journal.

Bennett, describes as the 'exhibitionary complex' which, he says, functions by 'simultaneously ordering objects for public inspection and ordering the public that inspected'.[96] Dickens seems to be saying that the Exhibition, which he himself found so overwhelming, ran the risk of producing the same nausea and alienation in other spectators. And that for Jo, who will not even get the chance to see the Exhibition, London will continue to be an 'unintelligible mess' anyway (275).[97] In his text then, unlike the 'well-arranged book' of the Crystal Palace, loss and waste are not repressed, recuperated, or recycled.[98] Indeed, loss and waste inform *Bleak House*, and one of the reasons for this is that, in this novel, Dickens continues with the perilous attempt to represent writing and the writer that he had begun in its predecessor, *David Copperfield*. In his significant move away from the first-person narrator to the curious bifocality of his two narrators in the new novel, he was attempting to investigate, and, indeed, to display, the perils of writing, while continuing to absent his own person from the narrative. Part of what is bleak about *Bleak House* is Dickens's own piercing sense of the unavoidable loss and cost involved in the personal investment necessary for human creativity. And this led to a recognition of the difficulties of constructing writing as a calm and equable 'profession': could he, after all, be both the Inimitable *and* a professional? The conflict, between intense, even excessive, personal investment and professional withdrawal is always legible in a text that asks both how to give an account, and how to stand accountable. Dickens's fierce appropriation of the text, and his simultaneous distancing of it, achieved partly, but not solely, through his double narration, makes for a powerful assessment of writerly responsibility.

Bleak House launches an uncompromising investigation of what happens to writing once it is severed from its source, once it loses its

[96] Tony Bennett, 'The Exhibitionary Complex', in *The Birth of the Museum: History, Theory, Politics* (1995), 59–88, 61.

[97] A poem published in *Household Words* just before the Exhibition opened made a similar point. 'But what to me are these inspiring changes, That gorgeous show, | that spectacle sublime? | My labour, leagued with poverty, estranges | Me from this mental marvel of our time. | I cannot share the triumph and the pageant, | I, a poor toiler at the whirling wheel, | The slave, not servant, of a ponderous agent, | With bounding steam-pulse, and with arms of steel.' Anon., 'A Voice from the Factory', *Household Words*, 54 (5 April 1851), 35–6, 36.

[98] Description of the Great Exhibition from Samuel Phillips, *Guide to the Crystal Palace and Park* (1857). David Trotter has written interestingly on mess in the novel in *Cooking with Mud* (2000).

original authority and is left floating unanchored, circulating, open to misinterpretation, diversion, theft, and piracy. Dickens explores the dangerous vulnerability of the unparented text. And this is, of course, exactly what happens to Esther, too, severed from her source and original—her mother. Esther's vulnerability and her attempt to establish her own authority and value make up half the narrative of the book. She is the unlicensed copy, the pirate edition, of Lady Dedlock, whose 'picture has never been engraved', (138) but whose image has been reproduced, and is circulating, dangerously, both in Mr Weevle's (presumably unauthorized) cheap reproductions in the Galaxy Gallery of British Beauty (340), and in the person of Esther. Esther's shame centres on her sense of criminality in her own survival as a copy of her mother. In fact the novel is full of copies and copying: it even opens with an emphasis on copying in chapter 1, 'the copying clerk in the Six Clerks' Office . . . has copied his tens of thousands of Chancery-folio-pages' (50) because the cause demands that 'everybody must have copies, over and over again, of everything that has accumulated about it in the way of cartloads of papers'; Nemo is a law-writer who lives by copying (185); Krook has 'a turn for copying from memory' (107); Mr Badger rejoices that he 'possess[es] the original [Mrs Badger] and ha[s] no copy' (227); a lithographic artist shares the premises with Turveydrop's Dancing Academy; Charley's little sister becomes 'exactly what Charley used to be' (933); George recognizes his nephew because he looks 'very like me before I was set up' (902); and, of course, Bleak House itself spawns a diminutive copy in the 'pretty tiny weeny cottage' (912) that Jarndyce gives to Esther. Copies can blur distinctions and make both origin and ownership disputable. The novel's interest in reproduction and legitimacy is both genealogical and literary: after all, Guppy recognizes Esther in Lady Dedlock's portrait, but Lady Dedlock recognizes Hawdon in his handwriting.

Identity is legible in words, just as it is in flesh, but this does not necessarily make writing accountable. Hawdon only authors the legal documents he copies in the most literal sense, and he is as absent from them as he is present in them. Dickens speculates that for Jo, when the day begins, 'all that unaccountable reading and writing, which has been suspended for a few hours, recommences' (275). Three times at the inquests the two gentlemen write with 'ravenous little pens on tissue paper' (512, 524, 614)—their writing seeming rather to consume itself than to communicate meaning. Similarly, Gridley writes on desperately up to his death, '[a] table and some shelves were covered with manuscript papers, and with worn pens, and a medley of such tokens', the instruments of literacy have become 'tokens'—signs emptied of power (406). There may be a nostalgia for coherent order in realist writing, as Landon suggests, but the written order is never responsible or effective in this text. Neither the narration, nor the documents that appear within it, command any final authority. The two narratives add to the confusion. Jeremy Tambling has stated that *'Bleak House* gives a broadly public narrative alongside a private one and suggests they cannot meet'.[99] He does not develop the suggestion that the two narratives may be in active competition for ownership of the text, yet they surely are, and in this sense they do meet.

Esther's intense personal identity is pitted against the other dispersed and apparently sourceless narration. Dickens's possessiveness and self-identification with everything he produced, exacerbated by his bitter experience of piracy and unauthorized copying, competes in *Bleak House* with his generosity and need to be instrumental in his writing. The sense of a possibility of coherence and community clashes with, but also disguises, his own possessive individualism. And, once again, the division echoes that of the copyright debate. The inimitable and autonomous author, whose intellectual ownership is absolute, faces the 'intellectual patriot' who serves the community by surrendering his property to the state at the end of its copyright term or at his death.[100] Dickens figures this hiatus metonymically by opposing Esther's intense self-consciousness and instinctive retentiveness, to the images of dispersal and connection that characterize the other narration.[101]

Esther, like David Copperfield before her, is a diligent worker, escaping a sense of shame and achieving authority through efficient paperwork, but she becomes burningly self-conscious whenever she is observed at her work, as when Mr Guppy arrives: 'Well I was full of business, examining tradesmen's books, adding up columns, paying money, filing receipts, and I dare say making a great bustle about it' (173). But while David Copperfield was disturbingly secretive about

---

[99] Jeremy Tambling, 'Introduction', in id. (ed.), *New Casebooks. Bleak House. Charles Dickens* (1998), 1–28, 19.

[100] [David Brewster], 'Mr. Babbage on the Exposition of 1851', *North British Review*, 15 (August 1851), 529–68, 561.

[101] Jonathan Arac has written about Dickens's use of 'overview' in *Commissioned Spirits* (1979).

being a writer and his texts were 'unaccounted for', Esther is bodily present to account for her text, indeed, she is even scarred in the course of her narrative by the events that happen in it. By making her female and self-deprecating, Dickens distances her emphatically from himself, and finds a way of 'naturalizing' any anxiety he may feel in establishing his own written authority by performing his own presence. In his memoir of the Warren's Blacking days, Dickens famously recalls how he and his friend, Bob Fagin, sat in the light of the window at Warren's tying labels on to the bottles with 'great dexterity', so that often people in the street would stop and watch: 'Sometimes there would be quite a little crowd there. I saw my father coming in at the door one day when we were busy, and I wondered how he could bear it.'[102] Steven Marcus has written that this scene 'seems at once flat and over-intense; it is characterized by extreme, if unarticulated, ambivalence: pride in dexterity and shame over the work; pleasure in skilful performance before a crowd or "audience", yet anxiety and humiliation at being observed or seen; and of course an utter mélange of feelings about being seen by his father'.[103] This double desire, to be seen but not be conscious of being seen, animates both Esther's and the novel's ambivalence about the display of authority.

Like her face, Esther's narrative is scarred by her unaccountable shame and the repressions it produces. 'I cannot tell in words' (564), she writes when describing her conversation with her mother, and she is occasionally wilfully secretive, 'I have omitted to mention in its place . . .' (233). Yet Esther is authoritative, knowing, and articulate, despite excusing herself for using elaborate language, 'I had alleviated (if I may use such a term)' (680) and her initial declaration, 'I know I am not clever' (62). Harold Skimpole insists three times in the novel that 'Miss Summerson has such a knowledge of detail, and such a capacity for the administration of detail, that she knows all about it' (489, 491, 654). Hers is the authority we learn to trust precisely because it is embodied as a first-person voice. But this is also what makes it untrustworthy and allows Esther to break off in mid-sentence at the end of the novel. By contrast, the other narrative is ungendered, uninflected, unembodied, written rather than spoken,

---

[102] Forster, *Life of Charles Dickens*, i. 34.

[103] Steven Marcus, *Dickens: from Pickwick to Dombey* (1975), 369–70. My attention was drawn to Marcus's reading by Robert Newsom, 'The Hero's Shame', *Dickens Studies Annual*, 11 (1983), 1–24.

and has often been described by critics as 'the omniscient narrator', although Audrey Jaffe has rightly questioned such a description.[104] This narrative uses images of dispersal, from the famous opening in which mud spreads and fog seeps, through the crow's flight across London (182), to the repetitive refrain of the rain blurring the view at Chesney Wold and the images of drifting miasmic disease. It has the perspective of a grand narrative that runs directly counter to the detail of Esther's account by generalizing and personifying: 'even the Fine Arts . . . must array themselves in the milliners' and tailors' patterns of past generations, and be particularly careful not to be in earnest' (211). While Esther's narrative is insistently and deliberately authored, and Esther as its point of origin is embodied in the text, the other narrative seems unauthored, a disembodied, unowned voice. The contrast of the two raises questions about origins: Where does the text come from? Who owns it? And, for that matter, Where does Esther come from? Who owns her?

As 'public surveillance' the unowned narrative fails because of the obvious obtrusion of Esther's private and detailed knowledge, and her precise control of it. Much of the perplexity of Esther's narrative is born of her attempt to preserve modesty and privacy while realizing that, to achieve authentic authority, she must stand accountable for every detail of her own behaviour, 'I want to be quite candid about all I thought and did' (280), and that she must also account for the behaviour of others. She is a spy, as Skimpole suggests, but she is not professionally disinterested like Tulkinghorn. The struggles she has with disclosure are precisely the struggles Dickens had with the conflict between professional withdrawal and writerly involvement, and this conflict is legible within Esther's narrative, as well as between Esther's narrative and the other more generalized one.[105]

Tambling is right to suggest the proximity of the two narratives in *Bleak House* to public and private, but they do not represent such separate or evenly balanced categories as this suggests. In fact, the problem Dickens seems to be dramatizing is the one at the heart of both copyright and patent law. Where is the perfect compromise

---

[104] Audrey Jaffe, '*David Copperfield* and *Bleak House*: On Dividing the Responsibility of Knowing', in Tambling (ed.), *New Casebooks. Bleak House Charles Dickens*, 163–82.

[105] Bruce Robbins has also taken 'the example of professionalism [as] . . . a context for Dickens's social analysis, a site of his personal ambivalence', in 'Telescopic Philanthropy: Professionalism and Responsibility in *Bleak House*', in Tambling (ed.), *New Casebooks. Bleak House. Charles Dickens*, 139–62, 140.

between private ownership and public display that will guarantee both the national utility of invention and its profitability to its author? At a time when the Great Exhibition was calling public attention to the dangers inherent in the display of intellectual property, copyright was becoming more and more identified with privacy. Mark Rose has argued that copyright continues to be 'associated with our sense of privacy and our conviction, at least in theory, that it is essential to limit the power of the state'.[106] But the privacy afforded by copyright law is always partial—the right to own one's ideas for a limited period before they become public property. And for those ideas to achieve a market value, they must be published and on display, thus always running the risk of piracy and copying. Display, therefore, both creates and threatens the value of intellectual property. In *Bleak House* Dickens asks just how exposed a writer needs to be in order to acquire value. Esther exposes herself to dirt, to germs, to desire, and to risk in the course of her quest for a valuable and 'legitimate' life. That publicity and exposure, however painful, do ultimately create value is one of the messages of a novel that moves forcefully, even violently, from the old order to the new.

For Esther's privacy is not the same as Tulkinghorn's secrecy. The lawyer sits in his room in which 'everything that can have a lock has got one; no key is visible' (182). Esther's privacy creates a sense of the sovereignty and self-possession of the private subject, 'the tendency of the inward forces which make [her] a living thing', in J. S. Mill's words, whereas Tulkinghorn 'is indifferent to everything but his calling. His calling is the acquisition of secrets, and the holding possession of such power as they give him, with no sharer or opponent in it' (567).[107] Tulkinghorn's dead collection of secrets represents power without responsibility, and Dickens rejects the complacent professionalism that sanctions such a withdrawal from personal accountability. Tulkinghorn also wants to 'hold possession . . . with no sharer' while Dickens is seeking a way, in this novel, to hold possession, and to share. He also makes the point that Tulkinghorn, rich and professional, is 'able to afford' (182) this kind of withdrawal, while Esther, poor, dependent, and unprofessional as she is, cannot. He too, as a writer, could not afford to withdraw from exposure, publication, and competition. Despite his claim to 'Inimitability', he

---

[106] Mark Rose, *Authors and Owners* (1993), 142.
[107] J. S. Mill, 'On Liberty', *Utilitarianism, On Liberty, Considerations of Representative Government* (1993), 127.

worried about his 'opponents' and he worked hard to 'sustain my place in the minds of thinking men though fifty writers started up to-morrow'.[108] Esther navigates a position between shameful exposure and shameful secrecy that proves a fairly uncomfortable compromise, but at least allows her to maintain some opacity and to 'limit the power of the state' in Rose's sense. Through the double dramatization of the writing, Dickens is not so much setting public discipline against private 'discourse', and thus creating the illusion of the free subject in Esther, as interrogating the difficult compromises involved in the ownership and sharing of knowledge in a society in which boundaries between public and private were shifting fast. In other words, the subject is Dickens himself and his ownership—or not—of the writing he shares with all his 'unknown friend[s]' (932).

The problematic figure of Harold Skimpole bridges the two narratives in the novel. Critics have become increasingly interested by Skimpole in recent years, a character famously based on Dickens's friend Leigh Hunt, for whom Dickens's amateur theatrical troupe had given several benefit performances in 1847.[109] But reading the novel *à clef* obscures the ways in which Skimpole resonates with the central conflict in the text between accountability and unaccountability. Despite his fine tastes, Skimpole is not an artist, but 'a perfectly idle man' (659), and his dependency and laziness, particularly in the latter part of the novel, betray something of Dickens's anxiety about the stereotype of the idle gentleman artist. Skimpole's idleness may also suggest Dickens's worries about charitable relief of the kind given by the Royal Literary Fund, and that proposed by the Guild.[110] Dickens described the Guild project in jest to Thackeray as 'a wild and egotistical fancy', acknowledging his own will to power behind the artistic 'community' that he envisaged at Knebworth.[111] Skimpole similarly hides his possessive individualism behind a fan-

---

[108] A remark he made congratulating himself upon the quality of his *Martin Chuzzlewit*. Forster, *Life of Charles Dickens*, i. 289.

[109] Dickens had given benefit performances for Leigh Hunt and John Poole in Manchester and Liverpool in 1847, whereas Skimpole seems the very embodiment of all the arguments against the Guild—encouraging, as it might, dependency and lack of accountability in its beneficiaries. Perhaps Skimpole includes elements of the character of Leigh Hunt's son, John Horatio Leigh Hunt, who was a persistent begging-letter writer, often signing his father's name.

[110] Although the prospectus claimed there would be no charity involved, in fact the Guild was to function the same way as the RLF, with a list of subscribers, and a Committee making grants to artists and writers in need.

[111] Dickens to Thackeray (9 January 1848), *LWMT* ii. 336.

tasy of community, claiming that '[p]ossession is nothing to me. Here is my friend Jarndyce's excellent house. I feel obliged to him for possessing it. I can sketch it, and alter it. I can set it to music. When I am here, I have sufficient possession of it, and have neither trouble, cost, or responsibility' (120). It is significant, of course, that he never does sketch it, or set it to music. Trouble, cost, and responsibility are just what Dickens implies must be invested in the creation of intellectual property. But Skimpole's creativity is unaccountable, and costs him nothing, culminating in his elaborate self-extenuation for accepting a bribe from Inspector Bucket and betraying Jo because '[t]he State expressly asks him to trust to Bucket. And he does. And that's all he does!' (886). It is a radical and deliberate irony that Skimpole's lazy unscrupulousness in obeying Bucket gives him a claim to be a model citizen. *Bleak House* portrays a mobile society in which a growing bureaucracy and ever-improving technologies for cultural dissemination made for a diminishing sense of personal responsibility. The promiscuous circulation of text severed from its meaning in the novel, like the illiterate Krook's blind copies of letters on the wall, makes it all the more urgent that literature, like Esther herself, achieves 'true legitimacy' (914) through accountability. Bruce Robbins, discussing Dickens's ambivalence about the growth of an impersonal state, has argued that 'professions, as in *Bleak House*, might belong both to the problem and to the solution'. Dickens certainly seems to suggest that an engaged and accountable professionalism is crucial for literary writers who need to balance their private ownership of their literary property, with its publication and instrumentality.[112]

The word 'property' occurs no less than fifty times in *Bleak House*. Property is central to almost every plot in the novel: there is a property dispute between Boythorn and Lord Dedlock (298); Smallweed's chair 'is reported to contain property to a fabulous amount' (343); and, arriving at the dead Krook's house to scavenge through its filthy contents, we are told that the grotesque Smallweed 'still repeats like an echo, "the—the property! The property!—property!"' (522). Even George Rouncewell worries about inheriting from his mother and diverting property from his brother's children.

---

[112] Robbins, 'Telescopic Philanthropy', in Tambling (ed.), *New Casebooks. Bleak House. Charles Dickens*, 139–62, 157. See also my own 'Monstrous Displacements: Anxieties of Exchange in *Great Expectations*', *Dickens Studies Annual*, 30 (2001), 243–62.

The novel, of course, revolves around the rotten centre of the Courts of Chancery, the Court that historically determined the inheritance of property, and the complex inheritance plot of the Jarndyce and Jarndyce case. We are told in chapter 1 that, 'Scores of persons have deliriously found themselves made parties in Jarndyce and Jarndyce, without knowing how or why; whole families have inherited legendary hatreds with the suit' (52). The novel, then, is centrally interested in property and possession, and seems to be built around a conventional 'inheritance' plot. But, in fact, in its movement from Lady Dedlock to Esther—from the lady of the manor to the doctor's wife, and from Chesney Wold to the 'pretty house' (934) that Mr Jarndyce gives to Esther at the end, the novel dramatizes a hegemonic shift from the aristocratic ruling class to the newly enfranchised professional middle class. The old order of patriarchal inheritance is dwindling and making way for a new model of fungible property as earned by hard work and as exchangeable and circulating. Yet the transition from the one paradigm to the other is not as simple as such a traditional reading of the mid-Victorian novel would have us believe.

Dickens was stalked by death in the year of 1851. His father died on 31 March and his baby daughter, Dora, died two weeks later on 14 April. Death and loss creep into the novel in many ways, but not least through Dickens's identification of property with death. All forms of property—inherited and commodified—seem oddly dependent on death in the novel. This is, of course, particularly true of the vague and ghostly property that seems to haunt the absent centre of the Jarndyce and Jarndyce case. As Ada says of Richard in chapter 60, so many of the characters are 'ruined by a fatal inheritance', the inheritance, of course, not of the property, but of its ghost in the trial itself, which generates, not wealth or possessions, but 'dead suitors, broken, heart and soul, upon the wheel of Chancery' (547). The inheritance which can ruin—the legacy that is death—becomes curiously pertinent to Esther's plot, 'the bastard daughter's quest for her legacy' as Hilary Schor has described it, in which Esther seeks to escape what she calls 'my inheritance of shame' (667).[113] It seems that finally all her mother can bequeath to her is the 'crushed and torn piece of paper blotted with wet', delivered to Guster, that both prefigures and memorializes the crushed and torn body with its

---

[113] Hilary Schor, '*Bleak House* and the Dead Mother's Property', *Dickens and the Daughter of the House* (1999), ch. 4, 101–23, 101.

'dank hair' 'cold and dead' that Esther finds in the paupers' grave-
yard in chapter 59. Lady Dedlock's death is, finally, her bequest to
Esther. And, indeed, so much of the literal property that we see in the
novel draws attention to the deathliness of the commodity form:
human hair, bones, old clothes, old paper, and so on. In *Bleak House*
the speculation of property becomes the speculation of death, perhaps reflecting Dickens's anxiety that literary property (his own
property in his novel) was ultimately dependent upon posterity, and,
therefore, upon his own death.[114]

Publication is a horror to Lady Dedlock, 'So! All is broken down.
Her name is in these many mouths, her husband knows his wrongs,
her shame will be published—may be spreading while she thinks
about it' (815), but in truth, as Dickens has already pointed out, hers
is only a 'little world' (447). The name of Dedlock at the end of the
book is, in fact, not 'published' but muffled and faint in 'dull repose'
(932), whereas the name that is becoming a household name 'in
many mouths' is Rouncewell (902). Publicity, no longer shameful,
is a phenomenon of the new age that Dickens inhabits. The
housekeeper at Chesney Wold has a son who is a 'Wat Tyler' to Sir
Leicester. Her grandson is called Watt, after the inventor (135). The
move from Wat to Watt neatly summarizes the progress of workers
from political radicalism to commercial respectability. Dickens's
support of the ascendancy of the Rouncewell name means that at its
close, the book silently draws closer to the Exhibition of 1851. Up
until then, exhibitions have come off rather badly in the novel. The
shabby exhibitions and freak shows around Leicester Square (356)
are mentioned with contempt, and it is tempting to imagine the Crystal Palace when the Court of Chancery is described as 'all that full
dress and ceremony, and to think of the waste, and want, and beg-
gared misery it represented; to consider that . . . this polite show
went on calmly from day to day' (399). Yet among the few truly instrumental documents that appear in *Bleak House* are those in
Rouncewell's office, 'account books . . . and some sheets of paper,

---

[114] While the market gives value, Dickens also expresses an anxiety in the novel
about objects losing another kind of value through their involvement with the commerce—perhaps their artistic or moral value. At the very end of the novel, we are told
that Mrs Jellaby's work in Borrioboola-Gha 'turned out to be a failure in consequence
of the King's wanting to sell everybody—who survived the climate—for Rum' (987).
This is Dickens's joke, of course, but it also reveals a horror that underlies the novel as
a whole—the fear that commodities could become more powerful than individuals—
and that values could be distorted and inverted by the marketplace.

blotted with hosts of figures and drawings of cunning shapes' (903). As Dickens knew, Paxton's original idea for the 'cunning shape' of the Crystal Palace was scribbled on blotting paper during a meeting of the Midland Railway Company Board in June 1850.[115] It is this kind of instrumental literacy—writing that gets things done—that seems to suggest an alternative at the end of the novel to the ravenous lawyers' pens. The novel looks forward to a future when self-made men such as Joseph Paxton and Charles Dickens alongside Rouncewell, would come into their inheritance. Dickens does not share Mr Turveydrop's theory of degeneration, 'I see nothing to succeed us, but a race of weavers' (246), and although his enthusiasm for the Exhibition as disciplinary was limited, the novel he started two years later, *Little Dorrit*, shows how closely the writer associated his model of literary accountability with the model of scientific and mechanical progress and national utility that had been on display at the Crystal Palace.

'A POOR MAN'S TALE OF A PATENT' AND *LITTLE DORRIT*: INVENTING A FUTURE

Dickens was involved with the Society of Arts, which he joined in 1849, and its Committee for the Legislative Recognition of Inventors, at the same time as he was setting up the Guild. The aims of the two organizations were similar, and an identification of the one issue with the other may help explain some of the oddities of Dickens's portrayal of inventors in his work. Intellectual property was a subject that occupied him throughout his career, and it was certainly this aspect of the question, and not the economic argument of innovation incentive that attracted him to the patent question. It was not unusual at this time to write about inventors. In fact, more and more popular 'industrial' biographies were appearing: Mary Strickland's *A Memoir of the Life, Writings, and Mechanical Inventions, of Edmund Cartwright* came out in 1843; James Muirhead's *The Origin and Progress of the Mechanical Inventions of James Watt* was published by John Murray in 1854; Samuel Smiles's *The Life of George Stephenson, Railway Engineer* in 1857; and his *Self-Help*, written in 1854, was lying in a drawer, waiting to be pulled out and

---

[115] Anon., 'The Private History of the Palace of Glass', *Household Words*, 43 (18 January 1851), 385–91, refers to 'the blotting-paper plan', 387.

published at the end of the decade.[116] Novels were also appearing in the early 1850s that made use of the stereotype of the inventor, often in a sentimental or moral context. Elizabeth Gaskell's *Mary Barton* (1848) makes the upright Jem Wilson an inventor and a patentee. Geraldine Jewsbury's *Marian Withers* and Margaret Oliphant's *John Drayton: Being the History and Early Life of a Liverpool Engineer* were both published in 1851; Dinah Mulock published her *John Halifax Gentleman* in 1856, and Dickens's friend John Saunders wrote the absurdly melodramatic *Abel Drake's Wife*, published in 1862, which was turned into a play. This was the golden age of what Patrick Brantlinger has called 'industrial success literature'.[117] But Dickens's direct involvement in the patent reforms and his interest in intellectual property, coupled with an imagination that often worked by analogy, make his literary appropriation of the stereotype of the inventor more subtle and more revealing than most.

Dickens wrote 'A Poor Man's Tale of a Patent' in October 1850 to support Cole's campaign for wider access to patent protection. As a piece of journalism, its concision and impact are impressive. In what purports to be a monologue by the artisanal inventor, Old John, Dickens also reports the remarks of William Butcher, a Chartist friend, and Thomas Joy, a London carpenter with whom Old John stays while pursuing his patent application, thus animating and deepening the debate without prejudicing Old John's political innocence. Dickens also ventriloquizes the official language of the Patent Office: 'At the Patent Office in Lincoln's Inn, they made "a draft of the Queen's bill," of my invention and a "docket of the Bill." I paid five pound, ten, and six, for this. They "engrossed two copies of the bill; one for the Signet Office, and one for the Privy-Seal Office." I paid one pound, seven, and six, for this.'[118] Despite the terms of the

---

[116] Mary Strickland, *A Memoir of the Life, Writings, and Mechanical Inventions, of Edmund Cartwright D.D., F.R.S., Inventor of the Power-Loom* (1843); James Patrick Muirhead, *The Origin and Progress of the Mechanical Inventions of James Watt, Illustrated by his Correspondence with his Friends and the Specifications of his Patents* (1854); Samuel Smiles, *The Life of George Stephenson, Railway Engineer* (1857). Samuel Smiles recalled that his *Self-Help* started as a lecture to working men in 1845, the original manuscript was rejected during the Crimean War by Routledge, and the book 'was not published for many years after the date of its first delivery as a lecture'. Samuel Smiles, *Autobiography* (1905), 134.

[117] Patrick Brantlinger, 'The Entrepreneurial Ideal', *The Spirit of Reform* (1977), 109–27, 120.

[118] [Charles Dickens], 'A Poor Man's Tale of a Patent', *Household Words* (19 October 1850), repr. in Michael Slater (ed.), *Dickens's Journalism: The Amusements*

actual debate in the 1850s, Dickens, like Cole, chooses to represent the poor, artisanal inventor of the 1830s. 'Old John' is a 'working-man', 'a smith by trade', who is semi-literate, 'not used to writing for print', and relies on friends, including the dangerously literate and articulate Chartist, William Butcher, to write letters and declarations on his behalf.[119] His inventive labour is solitary and long, and takes place not at the Birmingham Manufactory in which he works, but at home, 'I have been twenty year, off and on, completing an invention and perfecting it' (287). We are never told the nature of the 'Inven-tion' although Dickens's description of Old John 'perfect[ing] of it on Christmas Eve' (287) and he and his wife 'let[ting] some tears fall over the model' (287) hints at its messianic power. Old John is family man, 'a good workman. Not a Teetotaller; but never drunk' (288) and, expressly, 'not a Chartist' (285). Old John is, in effect, quite the virtuous working-class man: innocent, faithful, and power-less.

The representation of the inventor in 'A Poor Man's Tale of a Patent' is recognizably that of the 1830s. Old John inhabits the Birm-ingham that Dickens had visited as a Parliamentary reporter back in 1834, and described then as 'the town of dirt, ironworks; radicals, and hardware'.[120] The presence of William Butcher, a Chartist, in the story also locates it in the 1830s, as by 1850 the threat of Chartism was already much diminished. Similarly, the representation of Old John as a solitary artisanal inventor harks back to an earlier stereo-type, whereas, as we have seen, most inventions in the 1850s were acknowledged as happening in the workplace. The representation of the Invention itself, which takes twenty years to perfect, ignores the reality of the competitive capitalist marketplace in which speed of in-novation was as important as innovation itself. More broadly, the class terms of the discussion, 'it falls heaviest on the working man' (287), and the appeal to morality, 'redress of wrong, or furtherance of right' (287), make the article read like an intervention in the Reform debate of the 1830s. William Butcher, who, despite his threatening name, is a 'Moderate' Chartist (287), uses familiar

---

of the People and Other Papers: Reports, Essays and Reviews 1834–51 (1996), 284–90, 288. Dickens took these details either from Cole's pamphlet, or from his own reports of the patent debate in the 1830s.

[119] [Dickens], 'A Poor Man's Tale of a Patent', 285. All subsequent references are given parenthetically in the text.

[120] Charles Dickens to Thomas Beard (29 November 1834), *LCD* i. 47.

arguments, 'anyone may rob you of the fruits of your hard work' (287): the stress throughout is on Old John's ownership of his labour. Although we are told that 'my invention is took up now, I am thankful to say, and doing well' (290), there is little emphasis on the social utility argument—we are briefly reminded '[h]ow hard on me, and how hard on the country if there's any merit in me' (290), but the principal emphasis is on Old John 'being tired of my life, while I was Patenting my invention' and the unfairness of the present system of fees. Such emphasis on the working man, as we have seen, is a feature of the earlier debate. Certainly, Butcher's threat, that the present system is 'a Patent way of making Chartists' would have packed a heftier punch in the turbulent 1830s. Dickens's reporting of the patent debates in Parliament back in the 1830s was probably in his mind as he wrote.

There were other reasons for his choice of focus, too. Dickens was himself, as Forster reminds us, a self-made man, and was attracted by the patent debate because it seemed to him to be primarily a debate about fairness and class.[121] That he chose to represent it as such in *Household Words* is unsurprising, given his already strong investment in the defence of intellectual property for writers. He clearly sees the two issues as parallel, and this link becomes manifest in the novel he started to write in 1855, *Little Dorrit*. The connection between 'A Poor Man's Tale of a Patent' and *Little Dorrit* has, of course, been noticed before.[122] For Dickens, journalism and fiction were always closely allied, and Daniel Doyce shares many of Old John's characteristics, as we shall see.[123] But Doyce also performs other symbolic work in this multiplot novel which is much concerned with finding the way forward and creating a future.

It is impossible to include a discussion here of the novel that Dickens wrote between *Bleak House* and *Little Dorrit*: *Hard Times* (1854), but it is important to note that he continued to explore the pressures of industrialization on cultural production, and that he

[121] John Forster quotes a letter from Dickens's old schoolfriend, Dr Henry Danson, who says, '[d]epend upon it, he was quite a self-made man, and his wonderful knowledge and command of the English language must have been acquired by long and patient study after leaving his last school,' Forster, *Life of Charles Dickens*, i. 44.

[122] See Jeremy Phillips, *Charles Dickens and 'A Poor Man's Tale of a Patent'* (1984).

[123] For more on Dickens's journalism, see Kathryn Chittick, *Dickens and the 1830s* (1990) and Michael Slater (ed.), *Dickens' Journalism: Sketches by Boz and Other Early Papers, 1833–39* (1994).

connected this with an incidental examination of the aesthetics of realism in *Hard Times*.[124] In the episode of a Commissioner's visit to
the school in chapter 2, he satirizes the Department of Practical Art
that grew out of the Exhibition, and seems to suggest rather unfairly
that Henry Cole's Department was opposed to imagination and creativity. In fact, the Commissioner's objections to realistic representations of flowers and animals on carpets and furnishings are more
reminiscent of Ralph Wornum's essay on taste or Owen Jones's lecture on the results of the Exhibition than of Cole's position, and
Dickens's satire is probably aimed against what he perceived to be
the excessively disciplinary tendencies of the Exhibition Commissioners rather than at Cole directly.[125] In a letter to Cole he says, 'I
often say to Mr. Gradgrind that there is reason and good intention in
much that he does—in fact, in all that he does—but that he over-does
it.'[126] Ruskin maintained that Dickens was a 'pure modernist' and
that '[h]is hero is essentially the ironmaster; in spite of *Hard
Times*'.[127] Certainly the northern firm of Rouncewell returns in
Little Dorrit as the firm of Doyce and Clennam, in the heart of
London. Dickens may not have been very well acquainted with
northern industrial towns, as *Hard Times* reveals, but he was well acquainted with engineers, among them, Brunel, Paxton, and indeed
his own brother, Alfred. In the same week that he wrote to Cole,
Dickens also wrote to John Scott Russell, another of the Exhibition's
Commissioners, to recommend his brother, a 'practical and perse-
vering fellow' in the hope that 'I may possibly help him to some engineering employment'.[128]

As Dickens had foreseen in *Bleak House*, the brief period of national complacency engendered by the Crystal Palace soon fell away
to reveal enduring class antagonisms. The autumn of 1854 saw a
serious cholera outbreak in London, the first for five years, drawing
attention back to inadequate public sanitation after all the

[124] See Katherine Kearns, *Nineteenth-Century Literary Realism: Through the
Looking Glass* (1996).
[125] See K. J. Fielding, 'Charles Dickens and the Department of Practical Art',
Modern Language Review, 48 (1953), 270–7.
[126] Dickens to Henry Cole (17 June 1854), *LCD* vii. 354.
[127] John Ruskin to Charles Eliot Norton (19 June 1870), *Letters of John Ruskin
Volume II, 1870–1889*, in *The Library Edition of the Works of John Ruskin on CD
Rom* (1996), xxxvii. 7.
[128] Dickens to J. Scott Russell (12 June 1854), *LCD* vii. 351. Alfred had trained as
a civil engineer and had recently been building railways in Yorkshire.

trumpet-blowing about national progress that had accompanied the Great Exhibition in 1851. Within a month the Crimean War had also started. Ironically, it was new telegraphic technology that made this war the first to be fully and rapidly reported, and by late autumn daily reports were coming in describing the appalling conditions at Sebastopol. Dickens was horrified by the administrative incompetence that the war reports revealed.[129] The link between technological advancement and moral improvement no longer seemed so certain. In April 1855, just as he was restlessly preparing to start a new book, then called 'Nobody's Fault', he wrote to the MP Austen Layard in support of his proposed resolutions about the state of the nation. As Dickens saw it, 'the disgusted millions with this unnatural gloom and calm upon them, are confirmed and hardened in the very worst of moods. Finally, round all this is an atmosphere of poverty, hunger, and ignorant desperation.'[130] Later the same month, he complained to Forster of 'a non-working aristocracy, and a silent parliament, and everybody for himself and nobody for the rest'.[131] His prediction of renewed working-class unrest was proved just: in June and July there were disturbances in Hyde Park over Lord Robert Grosvenor's Sunday Trading Bill. Police responded to the disturbance on 1 July with excessive brutality, and several letters of protest appeared in *The Times*, including one from John Leech, written at Dickens's urging.[132] Layard did raise the matter of administrative reform, and that of 'jobbing' or nepotism in the civil service, in Parliament in June. Unsurprisingly, his resolutions were overwhelmingly defeated. As a result, a non-Parliamentary body, the Administrative Reform Society, was formed and Dickens made a twenty pound subscription.[133] '[T]he time for

[129] At the suggestion of Angela Burdett Coutts, Dickens commissioned a mechanical engineer, William Jeakes, a 'man ingenious in his trade' to design and construct a drying machine for Miss Nightingale's use to be sent to the hospital at Scutari. Charles Dickens to Miss Burdett Coutts (21 January 1855), *LCD* vii. 507.

[130] Dickens to A. H. Layard (10 April 1855), *LCD* vii. 587. See Trey Philpotts, ' "To Working Men" and "The People": Dickens's View of Class Relations in the Months Preceding *Little Dorrit*', *Dickens Quarterly*, 7/2 (June 1990), 262–75.

[131] Dickens to John Forster (27 April 1855), *LCD* vii. 599.

[132] Dickens to John Leech (4 July 1855), *LCD* vii. 666.

[133] Dickens made the subscription on 7 May 1855. See *LCD* vii. 611. The objectives of the Society were, however, vague and it later collapsed. Carlyle told Duffy that all the talk about administrative reform at this time was 'very idle and worthless'. Sir Charles Gavan Duffy, *Conversations with Carlyle* (1892), 196. See Olive Anderson, 'The Janus Face of Mid-Nineteenth-Century English Radicalism: The Administrative Reform Association of 1855', *Victorian Studies*, 8 (1965), 231–42.

Dandy insolence is gone forever', he exclaimed passionately to his friend Macready on 30 June 1855.[134] Writing from France at the end of the year, he expressed 'my fear that our national glory is on the decline'.[135]

This, then, was the uneasy background against which Dickens started restlessly to cast about for the opening to his new story.[136] He wrote frequently to friends at this time of 'the wandering-unsettled-restless uncontrollable [*sic*] state of being about to begin a new book . . . I sit down to work, do nothing, get up and walk a dozen miles, come back and sit down again next day, again do nothing and get up.'[137] *Little Dorrit* is even more divided than *Bleak House*. One division figures another, and every thesis seems to carry its antithesis with it. At a structural level, a melodramatic and overdetermined plot conflicts with the imagery of shadows and indeterminacy throughout; the past conflicts with the present, both poignantly, as for Arthur Clennam with his aching sense of belatedness, and sometimes comically, as through Flora Finching's reappearance. Amy's understanding is painfully opposed to Clennam's, and property and labour are set apart throughout the book, with Casby and Pancks as the exemplary case: 'Pancks is only the Works; but here's the Winder!'[138] It is no great surprise, then, to find that the character of Daniel Doyce, the inventor in the novel, is similarly divided and reflects the deep uncertainties of Dickens's own thinking about creativity and intellectual ownership.

---

[134] Dickens to Macready (30 June 1855), *LCD* vii. 664. Dickens spoke at a meeting of the Administrative Reform Society on 27 June 1855, his first and only foray into politics. His speech was afterwards published as a pamphlet. See K. Fielding (ed.), *The Speeches of Charles Dickens* (1960), 200.

[135] Forster, *Life of Charles Dickens*, ii. 191.

[136] William Myers notices the influence on the novel of Dickens's anger at the maladministration of the Crimean War. Trey Philpotts takes this point further by defending the Doyce plot from the charge made by Sucksmith and others that Dickens's exposure of the inefficient and expensive patent system was already out of date in 1855, as the Patent Law Amendment Act had been passed in 1852. Discussing Dickens's disgust at obstructive British bureaucracy which prevented the fast production of improved weaponry during the Crimean, Philpotts suggests that 'Doyce's troubles were not only not "out of date" in 1855, they constitute the very substance of the political and social dialogue.' William Myers, 'The Radicalism of *Little Dorrit*', and Trey Philpotts, 'Dickens, Patent Reform, and the Inventor', 168.

[137] Charles Dickens to Leigh Hunt (4 May 1855), *LCD* vii. 608–9.

[138] Charles Dickens, *Little Dorrit* (1979), 778. All references to *Little Dorrit* hereafter appear in the text. Jeff Nunokawa has drawn attention to the Casby-Pancks plot, *The Afterlife of Property* (1994), 19–39.

In many ways Daniel Doyce closely resembles Dickens's portrait of Old John of 'A Poor Man's Tale of a Patent'.[139] Described as an 'honest, self-helpful, indefatigable old man, who has worked his way all through his life' (692), he is the son of 'a north-country black-smith' (184), apprenticed to a locksmith, then bound to an engineer, later working on the banks of the Clyde, presumably in shipbuilding, then in Lyons, Germany, and St Petersburg, where he 'had done very well indeed—never better' (185).[140] Like Old John he is modest and self-effacing, and believes in '[t]hrift and perseverance': 'If I have a prejudice connected with money and money-figures' . . . 'it is against speculating' (653).[141] At his first appearance in *Little Dorrit*, Doyce is described as 'of unoffending appearance' (112) and 'a quiet, plain, steady man' (113), before Mr Meagles declares, '[h]e is the most ex-asperating man in the world; he never complains!' (114). As it is William Butcher's role to complain for Old John, so it is Mr Meagles's role to complain on Doyce's behalf: 'He is a man to be shirked, put off, brow-beaten, sneered at, handed over by this highly-connected young or old gentleman to that highly-connected young or old gentleman . . . he is a man with no rights in his own time or his own property' (114). As in 'A Poor Man's Tale of a Patent', Dickens deflects class antagonism from Doyce himself, who remains un-tainted by self-interest or radicalism.[142] In fact, Dickens's portrayal of Daniel Doyce conforms very closely to the model of the stereo-typed inventor that developed in the Reform press of the 1830s.

[139] Some marginal critical attention has been given to Doyce's role in *Little Dorrit*. George Levine comments that Daniel Doyce has something 'oddly other-worldly about him'. '*Little Dorrit* and Three Kinds of Science', *Darwin and the Novelists: Patterns of Science in Victorian Fiction* (1988), 153–76, 172. William Myers similarly draws attention to Doyce's 'intellectual repose'. William Myers, 'The Radicalism of *Little Dorrit*', in John Lucas (ed.), *Literature and Politics in the Nineteenth Century: Essays*, (1971), 77–104, 96.

[140] Like Old John's sons, the eldest of whom 'was a good workman' (285) and is now an engineer in Italy, and two others who are 'doing well at Sydney' (285), Doyce's mechanical talents are better appreciated abroad. Returning from abroad at the end of the book, he is 'no public offender, bless you, now! He's medalled and ribboned, and starred and crossed, and I don't-know-what all'd, like a born nobleman' (796).

[141] G. R. Searle has suggested that *Little Dorrit* draws on the heated debate that had preceded and accompanied the legalization of limited liability in the acts of 1855 and 1856. Certainly, Dickens is careful to emphasize the mutual knowledge and trust upon which the Doyce–Clennam partnership is based. See G. R. Searle, *Morality and the Market in Victorian Britain* (1998).

[142] In fact, Doyce's transformation into a 'nobleman' happens during his absence abroad, and so is occluded from the text. Jeff Nunokawa has pointed to a similar eva-sion on Dickens's part, when Clennam and Amy burn the piece of paper that docu-

Doyce's patient suffering over his invention, 'it was evident that he had grown the older, the sterner, and the poorer for his long endeavour' (117), his innate gentlemanliness, his self-sufficiency, and the implication of the mysterious power of his invention: all these attributes belong to the earlier period.

This representation of the inventor also reflects Dickens's model of his own creativity.[143] Peter Garrett in *The Victorian Multiplot Novel* has explained Doyce's self-effacement in the novel as an inventor as representing '[t]he anxious need to ground the novel's own fictions . . . representing an author who does not create but only discovers an objective truth'.[144] This is true, but Garrett does not go on to investigate this anxiety in relation to Dickens's own troubled self-perception as an artist. Like Old John's mysterious 'Invention', Doyce has taken many years to perfect his autotelic and miraculous machine, '(involving a very curious secret process)' (113). Daniel Doyce 'consol[es] himself by muttering with a sigh . . . that the thing was as true as it ever was' (500). Doyce's invention is not contingent and obsolescent like the real thing, but is transcendent and eternal. In his own account, Doyce effaces his own labour, and presents his invention as predetermined:

He had the power, often to be found in union with such a character, of explaining what he himself perceived, and meant, with the direct force and distinctness with which it struck his own mind . . . His dismissal of himself from his description, was hardly less remarkable. He never said, I discovered this adaptation or invented that combination; but showed the whole thing as if the Divine artificer had made it, and he had happened to find it . . . so calmly convinced he was that it was established on irrefragable laws. (501)

Certainly, this mysterious description of Doyce's inventive process seems to reflect Dickens's visionary accounts of his own. In a letter to

---

ments the fact that his fortune has been stolen from her, 'the act of appropriation that makes her his fortune is carefully obscured by the narrative'. In *The Afterlife of Property* (1994), 29.

[143] Harvey Peter Sucksmith has suggested that Dickens is less concerned with patent law in the Doyce plot, than with 'the stifling of creativity'. 'Introduction', *Little Dorrit* (1991), p. ix. Trey Philpotts also draws attention to the fact that Dickens does not once use the word 'patent' in *Little Dorrit*, and argues that Dickens changed his mind about patent law between the publication of 'A Poor Man's Tale of a Patent' in October 1850 in *Household Words* and *Little Dorrit*, 1855–7. I argue that Dickens's omission of the word 'patent' from *Little Dorrit* has more to do with his desire to make Doyce represent a more general creativity than that of the mechanical inventor. Philpotts, 'Dickens, Patent Reform, and the Inventor', 158–69.

[144] Peter K. Garrett, *The Victorian Multiplot Novel: Studies in Dialogical Form* (1980), 84.

G. H. Lewes in 1838, he discussed the inception of a scene in *Oliver Twist*, 'how it came I can't tell. It came like all my other ideas, such as they are, ready made to the point of the pen—and down it went'.[145] In a memoir of Dickens, Lewes likened the novelist's genius to hallucination, 'in no other perfectly sane mind . . . have I observed vividness of imagination approaching so closely to hallucination'.[146] Similarly in a letter to Forster in 1841, Dickens cast himself as a visionary creator, divinely inspired:

May I not be forgiven for thinking it a wonderful testimony to my being made for my art, that when, in the midst of this trouble and pain, I sit down to my book, some beneficent power shows it all to me, and tempts me to be interested, and I don't invent it—really do not—*but see it*, and write it down.[147]

Steven Marcus has suggested that Dickens's early 'self-surprised style' was reinforced if not created by his time as a stenographer, which taught him to subordinate his conscious thought to the speeches he was reporting, and thus encouraged a kind of automatic writing.[148] Even in 1850, David Masson can still trace 'a dangerous resemblance to common talk' in Dickens's prose.[149] The 'danger', presumably, is in the immediacy, contingency, and redundancy of conversation. Andrew Miller has described Dickens's 'hurling himself into his texts, willing them, daring death'.[150] He borrows Lukàcs's Marxist terms to define Dickens as a 'capitalist' who does not perceive his own self-division, whereas he argues that Thackeray is closer to the 'worker' who 'denied the scope for such illusory activity, perceives the split in his [own] being'.[151] On the contrary, Dickens, like Thackeray, was painfully aware of this split, but went to elaborate lengths to deny it, and to heal it imaginatively in his texts.

---

[145] Dickens to G. H. Lewes (?9 June 1838), *LCD* i. 403. The editors speculate that the scene in question is probably the one in chapter 34 in which Oliver dreams of Fagin and Monks, and wakes to find them looking in at the window.

[146] [G. H. Lewes], 'Dickens in Relation to Criticism', *Fortnightly Review*, 11 (February 1872), 141–54, 144.

[147] Dickens to Forster in 1841, quoted in Rosemary Ashton, *Dickens, George Eliot, and George Henry Lewes: The Hilda Hulme Lecture, 1991* (1992), 17.

[148] Steven Marcus is careful to describe only Dickens's early writing in this way. Steven Marcus, 'Language into Structure: *Pickwick* Revisited', *Daedalus*, 101/1 (Winter 1972), 183–202, 193.

[149] [David Masson], 'Thackeray and Dickens', *North British Review*, 15 (May–August 1851), 57–89, 65.

[150] Andrew H. Miller, *Novels Behind Glass* (1995), 146.   [151] Ibid. 146.

Certainly the 'split' was gaping for Dickens as he consolidated his early success in the 1850s. His son, Charley, reported that Dickens started *Little Dorrit* 'in a panic lest his powers of imagination should fail him'.[152] And Forster reports that, '[i]t was during the composition of *Little Dorrit* that I think he first felt a certain strain upon his invention', and the strain was noticed by the *Edinburgh Review*, which describes the plot of Little Dorrit as 'cumbrous' and 'strained to excess'.[153] Indeed, Dickens was feeling the pressure of his labour more than ever at this time, driven by the remorseless demands of a hungry market:

However strange it is to be never at rest, and never satisfied, and ever trying after something that is never reached, and to be always laden with plot and plan and care and worry, how clear it is that it must be, and that one is driven by an irresistible might until the journey is worked out! It is much better to go on and fret, than to stop and fret.[154]

Dickens's struggle to create an imagined space for creativity which was free from the exigencies of the market and self-sustained, leads us back to Daniel Doyce.

Yet the parallel between Dickens, the literary creator, and the inventor, Doyce, is not straightforward in *Little Dorrit*. For a start, Doyce is not consistently presented as a visionary. He himself refuses to dramatize his own predicament, '[m]ine is not a particular case. I am not worse used than a hundred others' (115–16). By making him representative of the many others frustrated by the Circumlocution Office and the Barnacles, Dickens directs attention away from Doyce the individual, and towards the systemic problem instead. Every so often, Dickens tries to make this more general point clear, '[t]here was something almost ludicrous in the complete irreconcileability of a vague conventional notion that he must be a visionary man, with the precise, sagacious travelling of his eye and thumb over the plans' (501). Doyce has to represent both legal constructions of the inventor at once; the autonomous genius, and the servant of the state. Trey Philpotts has suggested that the inventor is based on Dickens's

---

[152] Henry Dickens, *Recollections* (1934), quoted in Peter Ackroyd, *Dickens* (1991), 784.
[153] Forster, *Life of Charles Dickens*, ii. 216. Anon., 'The License of Modern Novelists', 124–56, 126.
[154] Forster, *Life of Charles Dickens*, ii. 219.

acquaintance, Isambard Kingdom Brunel.[155] But Brunel entirely rejected the representation of 'the solitary inventor' and considered patents 'productive of almost unmixed evil'.[156] Doyce is not based on a person, but on a debate—the patent and copyright debates, to be precise. The fragile division between the private and public spheres that Dickens figured through his narration of *Bleak House*, is internalized in Doyce in *Little Dorrit*, who holds a private property in his skill, but offers a public property in his invented machine. And, as in *Bleak House*, this is one of the many divisions that remains unhealed at the end of the narrative.

Even in his descriptions of Doyce as a 'precise, sagacious' craftsman, Dickens stops short of displaying his commercial labour. Labour is effaced in all descriptions of Doyce. The workers in Doyce and Clennam's factory are scarcely visible, only 'the clink of metal upon metal' can be heard (129). Doyce's lack of interest in speculation and commercial activity conflicts with his role as the owner of a 'concern' which 'prospered' (500).[157] So what exactly is the problem with labour in this novel? Both Mary Poovey and Andrew Miller have suggested that writing and housekeeping are figured as unalienated labour in Dickens's work.[158] In *Little Dorrit*, though, no labour is unalienated, with the unique and significant exception of Doyce's. We hear little of Clennam's former occupation in the 'East', and when he becomes a partner in Doyce's business, the work is figured as pure pleasure, 'a welcome change' (260). But his disastrous mismanagement of the firm's funds serves to warn of the dangers of treating work in this way. The person who is most often figured as working is, of course, Little Dorrit herself who is introduced thus,

[155] He points out that Doyce is not presented as a 'speculator type' but rather as 'the solitary inventor apart from systems of any sort and immune from class prejudices'. Trey Philpotts, 'Dickens, Patent Reform, and the Inventor', 158–69, 165.

[156] Isambard Kingdom Brunel, Witness, 'Report and Minutes of Evidence Taken Before the Select Committee of the House of Lords appointed to consider of the Bill intituled, 'An Act further to amend the Law touching LETTERS PATENT FOR INVENTIONS;' etc.', 482 (MS pagination).

[157] Patrick Brantlinger has said that Doyce maintains 'good industrial relations' with his workers in a factory that is figured as the 'heart' of Bleeding Heart Yard, but this is perhaps going too far. In fact, Doyce has no relations with his workers, because the workers are largely written out of the text. Patrick Brantlinger, *The Spirit of Reform* (1977), 113. When Doyce leaves for his contract abroad, the workers do briefly appear, '[t]he workmen were at the gate to see him off, and were mightily proud of him' (654). They then disappear from the text for good.

[158] Mary Poovey specifically of *David Copperfield* in *Uneven Developments* (1988); and Andrew Miller of *Our Mutual Friend* in *Novels Behind Glass* (1995).

'Little Dorrit let herself out to do needlework. At so much a day—or at so little—from eight to eight, Little Dorrit was to be hired' (45). Little Dorrit's labour is emphatically alienated, she is 'so conscious of being out of place' (44). Yet her involvement with labour seems to make her invisible both to her family who are 'lazily habituated to her' (77), and to Clennam, who is distracted by Pet Meagles. Little Dorrit, meanwhile, literally collapses into her work, '[a] delicately bent head, a tiny form, a quick little pair of busy hands, a shabby dress . . . were Little Dorrit as she sat at work' (45). Work seems to threaten the basis of identity, unless it can be represented, as is Doyce's invention, as unalienated.

Mr Gowan the painter in *Little Dorrit*, supposed by some critics to represent Thackeray, was always connected to the Doyce plot in Dickens's mind.[159] He told Forster that 'Society, the Circumlocution Office, and Mr. Gowan, are of course, three parts of one idea and design'.[160] Henry Gowan, the dilettante artist, stands for all the 'Dandy insolence' that Dickens despised, and, perhaps, envied just a little. He insists on Doyce's hard work, as he continues with his invention and 'soberly work[s] on for the work's sake' (500), while Gowan describes his creative work thus: 'But what I do in my trade, I do to sell. What all we fellows do, we do to sell. If we didn't want to sell it, for the most we can get for it, we shouldn't do it. Being work, it has to be done; but it's easily enough done. All the rest is hocus-pocus' (393). Gowan brings shame upon the profession of art not by his casual exposure of it as a 'trade', but by his claiming that it is 'easily enough done'. He makes it clear that writers are included in this description, '[p]ainters, writers, patriots, all the rest who have stands in the market' (302). Gowan suggests that the 'hocus-pocus' is necessary to create value. He feels that he must act the part of the artist, '[t]o keep up the pretence as to labor [*sic*], and study, and patience, and being devoted to my art, and giving up many solitary days to it, and abandoning my pleasures for it, and living in it, and all the rest of it' (393). The market's insistence on vulgar display is seen as a threat to authentic and painful creativity, as the Guild's play had warned, 'genius

---

[159] Although he is more like Warrington than Thackeray. See K. J. Fielding, 'Thackeray and the Dignity of Literature', *Times Literary Supplement* (19 September 1958), 536, and (26 September 1958), 552. Also Mark Cronin, 'Henry Gowan, William Makepeace Thackeray and the Dignity of Literature Controversy', *Dickens Quarterly*, 16/2 (June 1999), 104–45.

[160] Forster, *Life of Charles Dickens*, ii. 203.

less shaped to the taste of the many, can win not the ear of the day'.[161] The conflict is dramatized by the contrast of the venal Gowan, with his 'slight, careless, amateur way', with Doyce, working on his invention, 'with pleasure in it and love of it' (501). Doyce is embodied in his labour, while Gowan is detached from his. When read together, as part of 'one idea and design', Gowan's counterpointing to Doyce in the novel brings the debate about professionalism and its occlusion of the stain of trade into sharp focus. All of Gowan's skill is invested in an empty display of value, and he forms no attachment to his work. Once it is sold, it is no longer his property in any sense. Whereas Doyce is identified with his work in a way that Dickens suggests lends it a supplementary value immune to market economics. Dickens himself was a great exponent of hard work and made it known what hard work his writing was, emphasizing his own painful investment in his labour. Even when sold, Doyce's machine remains Doyce's machine, just as Dickens's novels remain Dickens's novels, even after publication and distribution.

Yet, Doyce is not finally entirely effective as the avatar of the author in the novel. Throughout the book, Dickens appropriates narrative conventions and repositions them to produce a self-reflexive commentary on the social experiences that they formulate. So, Dickens both deploys the stereotype of the inventor and exposes the limitations of that stereotype, participating in conventional constructions of experience while simultaneously challenging them. This is, in fact, the way Dickens always worked, both in his books and in his life. His work with the Administrative Reform Society, and his anger at the government's mismanagement of the Crimean War, stand witness to his commitment to the growth of an efficient state bureaucracy, and to the development of an accountable professionalism. The explicit political intention of the Doyce plot and the satire on the Circumlocution Office is to show the national disadvantage of an inefficient bureaucracy that fails to capitalize on native talent. Yet there is an underlying fear in the novel of the encroaching power of modern bureaucracy, and Dickens was certainly disturbed by any development which appeared anti-individualist.[162] He continued to insist on the importance of individual effort as his anxiety about an interventionist bureaucracy grew more general and the British state

[161] Sir Edward Bulwer Lytton, *Not So Bad As They Seem* (1853), 57.
[162] See Robbins, 'Telescopic Philanthropy' 139–62.

grew in both complexity and function through the latter half of the century. Dickens's view was promulgated in *Household Words*, which proclaimed in 1851 that '[w]e must all be free agents, and never feel that the law has a bit in our mouths, except when we offend the principle of justice'.[163]

Alongside the explicit political message to reform the state apparatus, there is a less explicit desire in *Little Dorrit*, also encoded within the representation of Daniel Doyce himself, for the triumph of the individual over the state, '[y]ou won't have occasion to trouble the Circumlocution Office any more. Let me tell you, Dan has done without 'em' (796) cries the triumphant Meagles in the final chapter of the novel. Dickens allows Doyce to dodge his symbolic role as national martyr when he achieves great success 'directing works' (796) abroad by his own independent efforts. Although Doyce must 'hide' his works and labours 'under lock and key' (796) once he returns to England, Dickens's warning that Britain's inventive talent will be better exploited abroad by competing states, such as Germany, is somewhat undermined by the lasting impression at the end of the book of Doyce's extravagant personal success. But *Little Dorrit* is, of course, much more than a novel about Daniel Doyce. An examination of the wider narratological structure of the book reveals the deep conflict between its deterministic, melodramatic elements, and the indeterminate shadowy metaphor that tangles around them. Dickens is attracted to the conservative closure and essentialist individualism of melodrama, but a political insight into systemic and environmental determinants obliges him to critique such an ideological position, even as he assumes it. Thus, at the end of the book, the heroic Daniel Doyce has succeeded in all he attempted, even though the Circumlocution Office has failed him and made a victim of him. Similarly, *Little Dorrit* ends with Amy Dorrit and Arthur Clennam's marriage and intimations of the happiness of their personal future developing in 'the fulness [*sic*] of time' (801); *Little Dorrit* also ends with the uncertain dread of an unresolved social and political future threatened by class division and systemic iniquity.

The novel's irresolution owes much to the imagery with which Dickens renders the future obscure. In part one, chapter XXVI, Arthur Clennam ruminates over his relations with Henry Gowan and

---

[163] Anon., 'The Good Side of Combination [*sic*]', *Household Words*, 81 (11 October 1851), 56–60, 57. It seems that there is a mistake in the titling of this article, which is advertised on the cover of the issue as 'The Good Side of Competition'.

Minnie Meagles: 'Where are we driving, he and I, I wonder, on the darker road of life? How will it be with us, and with her, in the obscure distance?' (310). Throughout *Little Dorrit*, Dickens mixes metaphors of time and shadow, producing a dense fabric of imagery that denotes the uncertainty and invisibility of the future, and challenges the apparent determinism of the conventional melodramatic plots in the novel. 'Time shall show us' (173), 'should a wrong come to light', 'the shadow of a supposed act of injustice' (311): shadows and foreshadowings play across the narrative. Descriptions of 'barred light' recur throughout the text, in reiteration of the much-discussed prison imagery of the novel.[164] The Circumlocution Office is, significantly, 'shady' (525), Minnie Gowan, once married, lives under 'the touch of shadow' (495), 'the shadow of the wall' (537) appears frequently, and there is a 'shadow thickening and thickening' as Arthur walks towards his familial home with a growing dread of the dark secrets it harbours (526). '[S]ome tinge of dark shadow' (526) and 'the shadow still darkening' (526): the shadows dance around the narrative as a constant but unobtrusive reminder of the difficulty of seeing ahead along 'the darker road of life' and, of course, of the relentless passing of time itself as shadows lengthen towards evening. Dickens's dislike of speculation is imaginatively rendered in *Little Dorrit* by his insistence on the shadiness and unreliability of the future. As in *Bleak House*, it seems that speculating on the future leads only to an apprehension of death, and that for Dickens, speculating on the future life of his own intellectual property brought with it uncomfortable intimations of mortality.

Little Dorrit is a novel obsessed with seeing and knowing, but this is a more sophisticated and self-conscious pantomime than Thackeray allowed when he accused Dickens of excessive and vulgar theatricality in his work. George Orwell noticed that Doyce's 'physical appearance is hit off with the typical Dickens touch; he has a peculiar way of moving his thumb, a way characteristic of engineers'.[165] He was quite right to notice that all of the descriptions of Doyce in

---

[164] For instance, Amy Dorrit: 'looking up at the sky through the barred window, until bars of light would arise, when she turned her eyes away, between her and her friend, and she would see him through a grating, too' (68). For a classic discussion of critical attention to the prison images in the novel, see Philip Collins, '*Little Dorrit*: the Prison and the Critics', *Times Literary Supplement* (18 April 1980), 445–6.

[165] George Orwell, 'Charles Dickens' (1940), in *George Orwell: The Collected Essays, Journalism and Letters*, i. ed. Sonia Orwell and Ian Angus (1970), 454–504, 487.

Little Dorrit are visual and 'external'. The inventor is first described as 'a short, square, practical *looking* man . . . [who] had the *appearance* of a sagacious master in some handicraft' (112–13).[166] Clennam's first view of Henry Gowan is of the young man: 'idly tossing stones into the water with his foot. There was something in his way of spurning them out of their places with his heel, and getting them into the required position, that Clennam thought had an air of cruelty in it' (197). While writing *Little Dorrit*, Dickens was also immersed in writing, producing, and acting in the melodrama he wrote with Wilkie Collins, *The Frozen Deep*.[167] In the novel, as in the play, exaggeration and overdetermination threaten to undermine any coherent sense of the individual, as Doyce's stereotyping into repeated gesture does occasionally threaten to undermine his moral superiority in *Little Dorrit*.[168] But the novel differs from the play in refusing to clear up all its own messes. Whereas Richard Wardour identifies and delivers Frank Aldersley to Clara Burnham in *The Frozen Deep*, and then tidily dies, Clennam makes many mistakes in attempting to puzzle out the truth, and is then left to create an uncertain future. He is puzzled not only by the central mystery of Mrs Clennam's history, or of Amy's love for him, but also in his everyday observations. Surprised by Mr Meagles's social aspirations, for example, 'Clennam looked at Doyce; but Doyce knew all about it beforehand, and looked at his plate, and made no sign, and said no word' (200). These dumbshows express the complexities and illegibilities of human social experience. In the remorseless 'externality' of *Little Dorrit*, Dickens suggests that such minute manifestations of inner life are all that remain in a society that increasingly insists on external display. Furthermore, he suggests that seeing and knowing are fatally disjunct in a society that too often identifies and values by appearance. This was a worry that the display at the Crystal Palace had triggered, too. For *Little Dorrit* is an even bleaker book than *Bleak House*. In

---

[166] Emphases added.

[167] Christina Crosby, in 'History and the Melodramatic Fix', illuminatingly discusses the links between *The Frozen Deep*, the melodrama written and performed by Dickens and Wilkie Collins in 1857, and *Little Dorrit*, which Dickens was writing at the time. Christina Crosby, *The Ends of History: Victorians and 'The Woman Question'* (1991), 69–109. See also Paul Schlicke, *Dickens and Popular Entertainment* (1985); and Claire Tomalin, *The Invisible Woman: The Story of Nelly Ternan and Charles Dickens* (1990).

[168] William Myers has said that Dickens's prose at times is 'almost violent in its simplifications'. 'The Radicalism of *Little Dorrit*', in John Lucas (ed.), *Literature and Politics in the Nineteenth-Century: Essays* (1971), 77–104, 81.

it, Dickens is much less sure of the role of writing in a display culture, and his faith in the instrumentality of literature seems, temporarily at least, to have abandoned him. 'I have no present political faith or hope—not a grain', he wrote to Macready in October 1855.[169]

Christina Crosby has argued that Dickens's use of melodrama in *Little Dorrit* 'saves us from thinking of the openness and hazards of history', and that 'melodrama provides Dickens with a mode that is "historical" in its insistence on a past that is lost but not forgotten, that figures history as home'.[170] But 'history' is emphatically *not* figured as home in *Little Dorrit*. The guiding idea of *Little Dorrit*, rather than the past, is the future. Contemporary readers were not enthusiastic about the novel, complaining that it contained 'no central interest' and that 'it neither begins nor ends'.[171] Dickens, while drawing upon melodramatic conventions, deliberately disturbs the closure of melodrama in order to challenge such narrative determinism with a new model of causal complexity. He allows considerable determining power in the plot to failures, mistakes, and misunderstandings, for example. As contemporary reviews implied, the wedding fails to achieve the ethical totality of the happy ending in melodrama, nor does it silence history—history continues in 'the noisy and the eager, and the arrogant and the froward and the vain, fretted, and chafed' (802) with which the novel ends—or refuses to end. In *Little Dorrit*, Dickens may, as Crosby suggests, attempt to use sentiment to manage history, but equally he also uses actual, historical time to undermine sentiment.[172]

Dickens begins to move away in *Little Dorrit* from the painful project of representing writing which had seemed so urgent in the early 1850s, but, through the counterpointing of the painter, Gowan, and the inventor, Doyce, he instead creates a fantasy of unalienated creative labour which stands for '[p]ainters, writers, patriots, all the rest' (302). Finally, though, the device of Doyce fails to achieve a consolatory value for creative work. The virtuous inventor is exposed as a static stereotype by the very text that he inhabits, a text that is 'driven by an irresistible might', refusing to tidy up behind itself,

---

[169] Dickens to W. C. Macready (4 October 1855), *LCD* vii. 716.

[170] Christina Crosby, *The Ends of History* (1991), 109 and 70.

[171] *Saturday Review* (4 July 1857), 15; *Examiner* (13 June 1857), 372; *Leader* (27 June 1857), 616–17.

[172] Iain Crawford, ' "Machinery in Motion": Time in *Little Dorrit*', *Dickensian*, 84/414 (Spring 1988), 30–41, 39.

insisting on the difficulties of seeing and knowing, and of inventing a future. Dickens, chasing his own copy deadlines in an unequivocally capitalist marketplace, 'hammering away in [a] strenuous manner at my book', was only too aware of the difficulty and labour of inventing a future.[173] The space he tries to clear for unalienated creative labour in *Little Dorrit* cannot finally resist the onrush of time and the fretting and chafing of the marketplace.

In the spring of 1858, Charles Dickens found himself, like Clennam and Amy on the final page of *Little Dorrit*, stepping from inside to outside, as he stepped out of an art gallery on to a London street. The outside had a

barbarous tendency to reality, to change and movement, and to the knowledge of the Present as a something of interest sprung out of the Past and melting into the Future . . . I understand now, what I had never understood before, why there were two sentries at the exhibition door. These are . . . allegorical personages, stationed there . . . to keep out Purpose, and to mount guard over the lassitude of the Fine Arts, laid up in the lavender of other ages.[174]

Stepping out into reality, exposing oneself to the 'barbarous' risk of the present moment, melting into the future: this was how it felt to be modern at the dawn of 1860. Art could either submit to being laid up in lavender, mounting guard over a fragile patrimony, or it would have to speed up a bit. Caught between the heritage of the past and the riskiness of the future, Dickens's sense was that the only way to posthumous survival was through embracing that hazardous present. Even back in 1850, he had written of 'the solemn hopes . . . awaken[ed] in the labourer's breast . . . that his name may be remembered in his race in time to come'.[175] Just as the Rouncewell name breaks the 'Deadlock' of *Bleak House*, by the end of the 1850s what had looked like vulgarity at the beginning of the decade had become—for better or for worse—'modernity'.[176]

---

[173] Dickens to Macready (4 October 1855), *LCD* vii. 714. He is referring to chapter 10 in which the Circumlocution Office and Daniel Doyce are first introduced. In the same letter he announces, 'I have no present political faith or hope—not a grain', 716.

[174] [Dickens], 'An Idea of Mine', *Household Words* (13 March 1858), 289–91, 289.

[175] [Dickens], 'A Preliminary Word', *Household Words*, 1 (30 March 1850), 1.

[176] This concept of modernity is, I am arguing, very specific to the 1850s. By the mid-1860s, Dickens was once again worried by 'vulgarity' as he makes clear in his portrait of the Veneerings in *Our Mutual Friend* (1864–5).

5

Women, Risk, and Intellectual Property: Elizabeth Gaskell and George Eliot in the 1860s

'I, too, have my vocation,—work to do'[1]

ON 14 March 1856, 'the petition of Elizabeth Barrett Browning, Anna Jameson, Mrs Howitt, Mrs Gaskell, etc.' was presented in Parliament, by Lord Brougham in the Upper House and by Sir Erskine Perry in the Commons.[2] Marian Evans, very shortly to 'become' George Eliot, had also signed. The petition called for property rights for married women: 'it is time that legal protection be thrown over the produce of their labour, and that in entering the state of marriage, they no longer pass from freedom into the condition of a slave, all whose earnings belong to his master and not to himself'.[3] In the event, it was not until 1 January 1883 that married women ceased to share the condition of slaves under British law. Until then, all of a married woman's income belonged to her husband; she could not bind herself to a contract; and she could only make a will, or make any fiscal arrangement, with the consent of her husband.

The 1856 petition asked MPs to consider the plight of all married women, and particularly working women, 'women [employed in] the processes of trade . . . sempstresses, laundresses, charwomen, and other multifarious occupations', but it is striking that the petition was submitted by, and rapidly became associated very closely

---

[1] Elizabeth Barrett Browning, *Aurora Leigh* (1856), ii. 454. I quote from *Elizabeth Barrett Browning: Aurora Leigh and Other Poems*, ed. John Robert Glorney Bolton and Julia Bolton Holloway (1995), 45.

[2] Lee Holcombe, *Wives and Property* (1983), 85–6.

[3] Ibid. 237. The full text of the petition is given by Holcombe as 'Appendix One—Petition for Reform of the Married Women's Property Law, Presented to Parliament 14 March 1854', 237–8.

with, literary writers.[4] The popular poet Caroline Norton's energetic pamphleteering about the injustice of the abuse of her property by her estranged husband had already brought the issue some celebrity. She ends her *Letter to the Queen* of 1855: 'Meanwhile, my husband has a legal lien (as he has publicly proved) on the copyright of my works. Let him claim the copyright of THIS!'[5] More than the issue of married women's property, the campaign and the 1856 petition served to highlight the issue of *intellectual* property for women. In presenting the petition to the Commons, Sir Erskine Perry reminded the House that the signatories included many women 'who had made the present epoch remarkable in the annals of literature'.[6] The *Westminster Review*, in a supportive article, reminded its readers of the exemplary state of the intellectual property law across the Atlantic: 'The laws of New York further provide that deposits made in any savings bank, or other institution of the kind, made by the wife, shall be payable to her only. A wife may also take out a patent for her own invention, and enjoy the profit of it independently of her husband.'[7] The wives of New York could become inventors and writers in their own right, while the wives of England were bonded to their masters.

Lord Brougham's Law Amendment Society, which had campaigned for the 1852 Patent Law reform, took up the cause and sponsored a public meeting in London on 31 May 1856. Mrs Jameson, Mrs Howitt, and 'many other lady authors' were reported as present.[8] Serjeant Talfourd, a friend of Caroline Norton's, and the champion of the 1842 Copyright Act, was a supporter, too. The petitioners claimed that 'married women of education are entering on every side the fields of literature and art, in order to increase the family income by such exertions'.[9] The reactionary *Saturday Review*

---

[4] [Caroline Frances Cornwallis], 'The Property of Married Women: Report of the Personal Laws Committee (of the Law Amendment Society) on the Laws Relating to the Property of Married Women, London 1856', *Westminster Review*, NS 10 (October 1856), 331–60, 337.

[5] Caroline Norton, *A Letter to the Queen on Lord Chancellor Cranworth's Marriage & Divorce Bill* (1855).

[6] *Hansard*, Parl. Debs. (series 3), vol. 142 (1856), cols. 1273–6.

[7] [Cornwallis], 'The Property of Married Women' (1856), 353. George Eliot was still involved with the *Review* at this time, although she was already writing *Amos Barton* and was withdrawing from the day-to-day running of the periodical.

[8] Anon., '"The History of the Law Amendment Society from its Institution in 1844, till the Present Time", *Law Review*, 21, 1854/5', in *North British Review* (August 1855), 326–37. For a report of the meeting, see *The Times*, 2 June 1856, 5.

[9] Holcombe, *Wives and Property* (1983), 237.

dismissed the 'petticoat rebellion' as 'a few literary ladies whose peculiar talents had helped to place them in a rather anomalous position'.[10] Like their male counterparts, in their campaign to raise
awareness of their plight, female authors needed to deny the charge
of 'peculiarity' and 'anomalousness', and so they aligned themselves
with other women working in 'the processes of trade'. They also
needed to draw public attention to the financial returns of the trade
of writing in order to show the unfairness of the property laws. But,
here the analogy between male and female authors and inventors
ends, because women, both married and unmarried, held a very different relation from men to both property and art in this period.

According to the influential eighteenth-century codifier of British
law, Sir William Blackstone, the common law's treatment of married
women constituted a form of protection, '[b]y marriage the very
being or legal existence of a woman is suspended, or at least it is incorporated or consolidated into that of the husband, under whose
wing, protection and cover she performs everything, and she is therefore called in our law a *feme covert*,' and '[e]ven the disabilities
which the wife lies under, are for the most part, intended for her protection and benefit. So great a favourite is the female sex of the laws
of England.'[11] A married woman then was seen as 'covered' by her
husband, and the married women's property debate raised fears
about the incapacity of womankind to withstand exposure to the
marketplace if this cover should be removed. Faced with a Married
Women's Property Bill in 1857, the Attorney General, Sir Richard
Bethell, objected 'to the placing of the women of England in a
"strong-minded and independent position," which so few [choose]
for themselves, and which position . . . consist[s] in the rendering of
them accountable for everything which they might say or do', and
was not one 'which the best and most amiable of the women of
England were anxious to occupy'.[12] Exposing a woman to the

[10] Anon., 'Law for Ladies', *Saturday Review* (24 May 1856), 77–8, 77. Despite its
dismissive tone, the *Saturday Review* is alarmed to see that the Law Amendment
Society is becoming involved.

[11] Sir William Blackstone, quoted in Ray Strachey, *'The Cause': A Short History of
the Women's Movement in Great Britain* (1928), 15. Blackstone quoted in Albert
Venn Dicey, *Lectures on the Relation between Law and Public Opinion in England
During the Nineteenth Century* (1905), 373. See Mary Poovey, 'Covered but not
Bound: Caroline Norton and the 1857 Matrimonial Causes Act', *Uneven Develop-
ments* (1988), 51–88, 71.

[12] Sir Richard Bethell (1857), *Hansard*, Parl. Debs. (series 3), vol. 145, col. 275.

contingencies and risks of the marketplace, and holding her accountable for the results worried many, who, as Bethell here does by implication, made a tacit link between female independence and moral failure, and even prostitution.

Indeed, the wider problem revealed by this debate was that of the significant hiatus or fault-line in the mid-nineteenth-century fantasy of the 'public' sphere. Dickens and Thackeray both took a broadly liberal-economic view of the public sphere as that of state administration while the private was represented by the market economy. In this way, they were able to reconcile their private ownership of their literary property with their obvious 'publicity' as writers. Dickens also worked notably hard in representing and critiquing the notion of the public sphere, which helped him shore up the territory of the marketplace as private. But an equally powerful definition of the public sphere, and the one that Bethell invokes in his raising of the spectre of prostitution in the debate about the female ownership of property, rested upon the division between the economy of wage-earners and the private sphere as the domestic or familial.[13] A woman straying from the domestic into the market economy, then, exposed the fragilities and contradictions of these simultaneously available models of the 'public.' The free-thinking *Westminster Review* challenged the boundaries in its discussion of married women's property, which took up the idea of the 'protection' of women and turned it deftly around into an argument for free-trade: 'We are only just beginning to discover that trade and commerce, in order to flourish, must be free; and the first attempts to release them from restraint were met by such pertinacious opposition, that the very measures which are now generally acknowledged to have been salutary were long delayed by it.'[14] The implication is that a national economic advantage rests in freeing women from the unnecessary protection of their husbands. It concluded by contesting that it was not necessary for women to be 'bound by no less a penalty than the loss of all personal identity' in order for them to behave responsibly and reasonably, even in the marketplace.[15]

Catherine MacKinnon has written that 'the private is everything women have been acquainted with and defined in terms of *men*'s

---

[13] See Bruce Robbins, 'Introduction: The Public as Phantom', in id. (ed.), *The Phantom Public Sphere* (1993), pp. vii–xxvi.

[14] [Cornwallis], 'The Property of Married Women', 358.

[15] Ibid. 359.

ability to have', with the result that feminists—and Caroline Norton fits the bill here as well as any of her twentieth-century counterparts—have wanted to make the private into something public open to discussion and change. But MacKinnon adds that it is also true that 'privacy is everything women as women have never been allowed to be or to have'.[16] This contradiction seems startlingly clear in the case of the long battle to make Parliament acknowledge married women's property rights. Paradoxically, women, forced to open up their private affairs to public scrutiny in order to make the case for reform, succeeded in setting off a moral panic among the more conservative members of Parliament about their imminent storming of the 'public' sphere, when in fact, they were suing primarily for the right to own *private* property, and to be granted a degree of privacy from their husbands. The paradox rests upon the fact that the idea of a fully private (in the autonomous and independent sense) woman was interpreted by many as the figure of a dangerously public female subject in the 'strong-minded and independent position' that so alarmed Bethell.

This was, of course, a particularly vexed question in relation to female authorship, as the process of writing necessarily made women 'accountable', and allowed them, by a kind of voice-throwing exercise, to participate in the public sphere of print culture without any disabling display of the body. Nevertheless, just as Esther Summerson's does in *Bleak House*, women's narratives did expose them and made their private lives public. Like Esther Summerson, too, their talent, albeit recast as virtue, could also raise them socially and legitimate what would otherwise be perceived as illegitimate. No better example here than the socially disreputable Marian Lewes, who, self-authored as the successful novelist, George Eliot, found fashionable doors thrown open to her at last. J. S. Mill, a stalwart campaigner for women's property rights and the reform of the divorce laws, asked in his *The Subjection of Women* of 1869, 'what is the peculiar character of the modern world? . . . It is, that human beings are no longer born to their place in life, and chained down by an inexorable bond to the place they are born to, but are free to employ their faculties, and such favourable chances as offer, to achieve the

<hr>

[16] Catherine MacKinnon, 'Feminism, Marxism, Method and the State: Toward a Feminist Jurisprudence', *Signs*, 8 (1983), 635–58.

lot which may appear to them most desirable.'[17] The female author, exposing herself to the risks of the literary marketplace in her efforts to 'wrest a precarious income from the publisher', was an opportunist, employing her faculties and 'favourable chances' in order to determine her own identity.[18] In that sense, she was quintessentially a modern subject.

For writers such as George Eliot, then, the will to create a personal identity through writing conflicted with the will to disavow such exposure, in ways that were more urgent than for male writers such as Dickens. For her level of visibility was also a reflection of her unmarried, and therefore uncovered state in a way that was positively perilous to the success of her work. The issue of *coverture* was an important one for all women writers, married and unmarried, in the period. Catherine Judd has remarked that '[t]here is an element of happenstance in the fact that the four most canonical nineteenth-century female novelists—Jane Austen, Charlotte Brontë, Emily Brontë, and Mary Ann Evans—published under pseudonyms, and that three of these writers used a masculine or a masculinized name.'[19] She does not comment upon the fact that all her examples were publishing as unmarried women. Married authors such as Gaskell or Oliphant were already writing under masculine names: those of their husbands.[20] After her elopement, George Eliot insisted on her married state and the protection or *coverture* of Lewes, signing herself as 'Mrs. Lewes' and correcting her friends sharply if they called her 'Evans'.[21] Standing publicly accountable for her own intellectual property would have drawn attention to her compromised position as a *femme sole*, and would have undermined her authority. Susan Snaider Lanser has noticed the widespread use of male pseudonyms

[17] J. S. Mill, *The Subjection of Women* (1869), in *On Liberty and Other Essays* (1991), 471–582, 488.

[18] Anon., 'Man's Might and Woman's Right', *Saturday Review*, 27/2 (3 May 1856), 5–6, 6.

[19] Catherine A. Judd, 'Male Pseudonyms and Female Authority in Victorian England', 252. The exception is Jane Austen, who published as 'A Lady'.

[20] Judd's argument comes closer to my own when she says that 'Evans's and the Brontës' use of the male pseudonym is not a usurpation of the patronym, rather it is a creative appropriation of the possibilities inscribed in the nineteenth-century myth of subjectivity's division into distinct private and public realms,' 259. However, she does not consider the effect of married status on the construction of the author as public or private.

[21] GE to Bessie Rayner Parkes (22 March 1856), *GEL* ii. 231–2, 232.

after 1860 for women writers—I would suggest that this may represent a response to the rise of a more professionalized, and more 'masculine', public culture of letters in this period.[22] Clearly, women writers often used male pseudonyms as a way of avoiding being judged on grounds of gender in this public culture of letters.

Dickens and Thackeray, as we have seen, were part of this development, and gender was central to the 'Dignity of Literature' debate. The 'manly' Thackeray stood against the effeminate sentimentality of Dickens, and suggested that 'men of letters stand for themselves. Every day enlarges their market, and multiplies their clients.'[23] In his essay on Laman Blanchard, Thackeray quotes disdainfully from an obituary by Bulwer Lytton that cast the writer as an impoverished genius displaying, 'the rarest kind of strength, depending less upon a power purely intellectual, than upon the higher and more beautiful heroism which women, and such men alone as have the best feelings of a woman's nature, take from instinctive enthusiasm for what is great, and uncalculating faith in what is good'.[24] Thackeray particularly disliked the feminizing of literary work and worked hard, as we saw in the last chapter, to construct writing as manly labour.[25] In his 1841 essay, 'A Fashionable Authoress', he had called for an end to womanly writing: 'No more fiddle-faddle novels! no more namby-pamby poetry! no more fribble "Blossoms of Loveliness"!'[26] He adds that '[l]iterature and politics have this privilege in common, that any ignoramus may excel in both. No apprenticeship is required, that is certain; and if any gentleman doubts, let us refer him to the popular works of the present day.'[27] Similarly, in asking, 'whether Literature shall continue to be an exception from all other professions and pursuits', Dickens and Bulwer Lytton's Guild was arguing for literature as a more rigorous, specialized, and—finally—masculinized profession, and Dickens's use of the analogy of mechanical invention supported such an argument. When Mrs Gaskell showed some

---

[22] Susan Sniader Lanser, 'Woman of Maxims: George Eliot and the Realist Imperative', *Fictions of Authority: Women Writers and Narrative Voice* (1992), 81–101.

[23] [William Makepeace Thackeray], 'A Brother of the Press', 96.

[24] Quoted from Bulwer Lytton, ibid. 91.

[25] For an alternative and suggestive view of Thackeray's own construction of 'manliness', see Joseph Litvak, 'Kiss Me, Stupid: Sophistication, Sexuality, and *Vanity Fair*', *Novel*, 29/2 (Winter 1996), 223–42.

[26] William Makepeace Thackeray, 'The Fashionable Authoress' (1841). Reprinted in *A Shabby Genteel Story and Other Writings* (1993), 299–311, 311.

[27] Ibid. 306.

sensitivity about Dickens's cutting of her novel, *North and South*, for *Household Words*, he saw her, significantly, not as an author with an active sense of her own intellectual property, but as an insubordinate wife, famously joking, 'If I were Mr G. O Heaven how I would beat her!'[28]

As Mary Poovey has put it, women in this period held a 'passive or metonymic relation to property'.[29] They were more often figured *as* property than as the holders of such. They bore a similarly tangential and difficult relationship to art: 'Representing creativity as masculine and Woman as the beautiful image for the desiring male gaze, High Culture systematically denies knowledge of women as producers of culture and meanings.'[30] Excluded, like Mary Shelley, from the myth of Romantic creativity, throughout the nineteenth century women were largely represented as modern muses: the private means to public artistic expression. One writer in 1883 explained that women would always be inferior writers to men because 'children are the best poems Providence means women to produce'.[31] So how did female writers in this period negotiate the inheritance of a highly gendered model of creativity? I have deliberately chosen two female writers for this investigation of the 1860s: Elizabeth Gaskell and George Eliot.[32] In this, I am concurring with Rita Felski in positing women's central importance to the analysis of modernity.[33] Felski has argued that women have been neglected in analyses of the modern because the woman is '[s]een to be less specialized and differentiated than man, located within the household and an intimate web of familial relations, more closely linked to nature through her reproductive capacity, women embodied a sphere of atemporal authenticity seemingly untouched by the alienation and fragmentation of modern life.'[34] Her partial concealment or 'cover' under this construction meant that the risks attached to writing were

---

[28] Charles Dickens to W. H. Wills (25 November 1851), *LCD* vi. 545.

[29] Poovey, *Uneven Developments*, 75.

[30] Griselda Pollack, *Vision and Difference: Femininity, Feminism and Histories of Art* (1988), 17.

[31] Eric S. Robertson, *English Poetesses: A Series of Critical Biographies, with Illustrative Extracts* (1883). See Christine Battersby, *Gender and Genius. Towards a Feminist Aesthetic* (1989), and Alan Richardson, 'Romanticism and the Colonization of the Feminine', in Anne K. Mellor (ed.), *Romanticism and Feminism* (1988).

[32] I would hate to give the impression that women started writing only in the 1860s, however.

[33] Rita Felski, *The Gender of Modernity* (1995).   [34] Ibid. 16.

simultaneously greater and fewer for a woman writer in the mid-nineteenth century than for her male counterpart. Indeed, women writers sometimes seem less encumbered by worries about the trade of writing than their male counterparts, perhaps because of the paradox at the heart of the mid-century configuration of the 'private' which we have already identified. Much has been said about the difficulties of the woman writer, and the risk posed to her virtue by publication, with its connotations of sexual display for economic gain.[35] Even at the time, Caroline Norton directly acknowledged this problem to Mary Shelley, 'I think there is too much fear of publicity about women; it is reckoned such a crime to be accused, and such a disgrace, that they wish nothing better than to hide themselves and say no more about it.'[36] But less has been said about the ways in which middle-class women were perhaps better equipped to understand and to comment upon the risks of an emerging marketplace at mid-century than middle-class men. Anthony Giddens has described the modern experience of powerlessness, as 'a tacit acceptance of circumstances in which other alternatives are largely foreclosed'.[37] Women were already better accustomed to living with such foreclosure, and had always lived with greater levels of dependency than men. The 1856 petition drew attention to the appalling risks to which a woman exposed herself in marriage. For many women, life was already a lottery over which they had little, if any, control. Mrs Glover, for example, a celebrated actress, abandoned by her husband, had all her assets stripped from her by a court that ruled 'the husband had the right to his wife's earnings'.[38] Such blatantly unfair discrimination had kept women out of the intellectual property de-

---

[35] For examples, see Sandra Gilbert and Susan Gubar, *The Madwoman in the Attic* (1979); Mary Poovey, *The Proper Lady and the Woman Writer* (1984); Catherine Gallagher, 'George Eliot and *Daniel Deronda*: The Prostitute and the Jewish Question', in Ruth Bernard Yeazell (ed.), *Sex, Politics and Science in the Nineteenth-Century Novel* (1986); and Barbara Leah Harman, 'In Promiscuous Company: Female Public Appearance in Elizabeth Gaskell's *North and South*', *Victorian Studies*, 31/3 (Spring 1988), 351–74.

[36] Quoted in Karen Chase and Michael Levenson, *The Spectacle of Intimacy: A Public Life for the Victorian Family* (2000), 41.

[37] Anthony Giddens, *The Consequences of Modernity* (1991), 90. Giddens makes no comment on gender and modernity. Ulrich Beck briefly discusses gender in *Risk Society: Towards a New Modernity* (1992) (first published in Germany in 1986 as *Risikogesellschaft*). I am risking generalizations here, and, of course, there is much to be said about the dependence of working-class men in this period, too.

[38] [Cornwallis], 'The Property of Married Women', 343.

bates at law, but it also marginalized them in ways that could potentially make them less anxious about professional status and self-
exposure, having their private identities only too securely defined by
a culture that simply could not conceive of a fully 'public' woman.

Unlike Thackeray and Dickens, Gaskell and Eliot were not publicly involved with the debate about authorship in the 1850s, or with
the campaign to improve copyright protection. Gaskell seems rather
an onlooker than a participant, writing scathingly about Bulwer
Lytton's Guild play which she saw in Manchester in February 1852,
'[Forster] said the play was *very* heavy, and so it was. . . . The play is
very long too—3 hours & a half . . . And very [altered word] stupid
indeed.'[39] Her friend Charlotte Brontë agreed that the group's campaign for improved intellectual property rights for authors was ineffective, 'I cannot see that Sir E. Bulwer and the rest *did* anything; nor
can I well see what it is in their power to do.'[40] By contrast, Gaskell
thought Thackeray's lectures on the 'English Humorists of the
Eighteenth Century', which she heard in Manchester in the autumn
of 1852, were 'delightful'. The Gaskells were socially involved with
Dickens's group: in September 1852, William Gaskell went to a ban-
quet held by the Guild of Literature and Art, and when Dickens
called the next day they were both invited behind the scenes of another of the Guild's plays, *Used Up*.[41] Despite her distance from any
public campaign, Gaskell did write to the Royal Literary Fund in
support of individual cases, petitioning in 1852 for a grant for 'a
poor authoress'.[42] As her writing career flourished, she also took increasing responsibility for the management of her own intellectual
property. In 1857 she explained to the publisher George Smith that
she had sold all her copyrights 'out & out' as she put it, except those
for her *Household Words* stories.[43] In 1861, she wrote to John

[39] ECG to Agnes Sandars (née Paterson) (11 February 1852), *FLG* 61–4, 64.
[40] CB to George Smith (8 July 1851). *The Letters of Charlotte Brontë, with a Selection of Letters by Family and Friends 1848–1851*, ed. Margaret Smith (2000), ii.
662–5, 662. CB is referring here specifically to the 'barren result' of the International
Copyright Meeting, but her remarks follow on from her commendation of
Thackeray's views about the 'social observations and individual duties' of literary
men, thus implying a more general comparison of the positions of the two 'sides' in the
'Dignity of Literature' debate. ECG quoted this letter in her *Life of Charlotte Brontë*.
[41] ECG to Marianne Gaskell (4 September 1852), *LG* 197–8, 197.
[42] Selina Davenport, a novelist who had achieved a moderate popularity earlier in
the century. ECG to Octavian Blewitt (30 June [1850]); (17 March 1852); (22 March
1852), *FLG* 49–50, 67–8.
[43] ECG to George Smith (26 November 1857), *LG* 483–4, 484.

Chapman asking for clarification on the state of her account with his firm.[44] It is clear that the publishers dealt directly with her, despite her married status as legally invisible. The cheques were made out to William, but the business was conducted by Gaskell herself.

Nevertheless, it is perhaps significant that while Dickens was fretting over his Guild, Gaskell was writing *Ruth*. In fact, Gaskell agreed with Charlotte Brontë that one should not earn one's living by writing, but that 'one should only write out of the fullness of one's heart, spontaneously'.[45] Eliot's situation in the early 1850s was different. Far less financially or socially secure than Gaskell, she was working hard as co-editor with Chapman, writing the prospectus for the *Westminster Review*, and arranging contributions for the first issues. Chapman was already in trouble with the Booksellers' Association for discounting books imported from North America, and so Eliot was more knowledgeable than most about the economics of the booktrade at mid-century. It is possible that she contributed to the article 'The Commerce of Literature' which appeared in the April 1852 issue of the *Westminster*, and she attended a meeting in May called by Chapman and chaired by Dickens which drew up resolutions against price-fixing. Yet, although she was well apprised of the issues, her account of this meeting is still that of an observer, rather than a participant, and once she herself joined the circle of famous authors at the end of the decade, she lost no time in disengaging herself from the economic world of publishing, choosing rather to represent her own fiction as a moral form of 'good work'.[46] As authors, both she and Gaskell were more concerned to develop the sympathy of the reading public through their work, than to worry over the status of the profession of writing. Both constructed their literary works as gifts to the public. In a sense, both women writers embraced a model of philanthropy and charity that Dickens and his followers were so energetically rejecting in their bid to create a masculine literary profession.

George Steiner has defined creativity as the 'enactment of freedom. It is integrally at liberty. Its existence comports implicitly and explicitly the alternative of non-existence. It could not have been.'[47] This

[44] ECG to ?Frederick Chapman (27 April ?1861), *LG* 651–2.

[45] ECG to Maria James (29 October 1851), *LG* 166–8, 168.

[46] See GE to the Brays (5 May 1852), *GEL* ii. 23–5, 23.

[47] George Steiner, *Grammars of Creation Originating in the Gifford Lectures for 1990* (2001), 107.

runs counter to the Romantic, deterministic idea of literature as inspiration, which Caroline Norton herself fell back upon in her attempt to argue for her ownership of her work. She described her literary earnings as 'the grant of heaven, not the legacy of earth'.[48] But it was perhaps particularly easy for a female author in the nineteenth century to imagine that her work could 'not have been', and was something deliberately grabbed and 'made' out of an extraordinary effort. On Gaskell's part the effort was to find time away from the duties of a middle-class mother and minister's wife in order to write. Securely married, she exploited her private status in order to construct her own ordinariness and to deflect the image of the woman writer as anomalous. Yet there is nothing ordinary about her work, which is quietly concerned to examine the pervasive effects of mechanization on both established social values and the conventions of writing itself. Gaskell realized very early that the limits of technology are falsely imposed, and that, in truth, it knows no boundaries and has become the fabric and medium of modern living. Her work challenges conventional legal definitions of intellectual property in profound and radical ways. In Eliot's case, a sense of the contingency of her work, and of the ambition that pushed steadily through the exigencies and conventionalities of a female existence, haunted her in ways that mark her earlier fiction in particular. Despite her avowed belief in Comtean determinism, Eliot's writing returns almost obsessively to scenes of chance and risk—to events that might not have happened. To defend herself against this sense of the accidental, over her writing career she developed a model of an embattled and fragile culture reliant upon exceptional individuals to preserve its traditions against the onslaughts of aggressive technology, constructing her own model of Coleridgean heroic determinism, and—simultaneously—positing a public sphere as far removed from the state, and the economy, as possible. In this model, 'public'

---

[48] Caroline Norton quoted by J. W. Kaye. [J. W. Kaye], 'The "Non-Existence" of Women', *North British Review* (August 1855), 536–62, 538. Mary Poovey has drawn attention to the way in which Norton's arguments often entrap themselves in their appropriation of 'male' or melodramatic rhetoric. Margot Finn challenges Poovey's reading of the Norton affair, arguing that Norton, in fact, enjoyed considerable financial credit under *coverture* even after her separation from her husband. See Margot Finn, 'Women, Consumption and Coverture in England, *c*.1760–1860', *The Historical Journal*, 39/3 (1996), 703–22. Maxine Berg has argued that women exercised more power over property in the eighteenth century than is generally supposed. Maxine Berg, 'Women's Property and the Industrial Revolution', *Warwick Economic Research Papers*, 382 (October 1991).

denotes community and citizenship as distinct from both state sovereignty and the economy. It is, however, a model that is challenged by
the evidence of the writing itself. In a complicated manœuvre, Eliot
insists on her works as the property of an enlightened public in order
to establish her own claim not as their 'polluted source', but as a public benefactor. Like Gaskell, Eliot seems less interested in establishing
her intellectual property in her writing than in establishing its public
usefulness. Gaskell and Eliot are very different examples of 'the
woman writer' in the 1860s, both in their work, and in their attitudes
to their work, and, as such, prove the fatuity of making too many
broad generalizations about such a species. Nevertheless, together
they do both pose new questions about intellectual property, and
about the boundaries between the private and the public throughout
the 1860s.

ELIZABETH GASKELL'S *COUSIN PHILLIS*: INVENTORS IN
THE KITCHEN

On New Year's Day, 1856, Elizabeth Gaskell wrote to her friend,
Tottie Fox, in reply to her request for a signature on the petition for
married women's property rights:

I don't think it is very definite, and *pointed*; or that it will do much good . . .
a husband can coax, wheedle, beat, or tyrannize his wife out of something
and no law whatever will help this that I see. (Mr Gaskell begs Mr Fox to
draw up a bill for the protection of *husbands* against wives who will spend
all their earnings.) However our sex is badly enough used and legislated
against, there's no doubt of *that*—so though I don't see the definite end proposed by these petitions I'll sign.[49]

In the spring of 1850, she had told Tottie that she had received £20
from *Household Words* for 'Lizzie Leigh' and that 'Wm [William,
her husband] has composedly buttoned it up in his pocket. He has
promised I may have some for the Refuge [for women].'[50] Yet, although Holcombe has characterized Gaskell as cheerfully assenting
to her husband's appropriation of her literary income throughout
her career, there is evidence that she, like other middle-class wives,
retained more control of her earned income than this account sug-

[49] ECG to Eliza Fox (*c.*1 January 1856), *LG* 379.
[50] ECG to Eliza Fox (26 April 1850), *LG* 110–14, 113.

gests. Indeed, as Margot Finn has pointed out, the increasing concern over female consumption in this period does not support the thesis that all women were economically inactive.[51] In 1865, Gaskell had the financial independence to enter into the secret purchase of a house to surprise her husband, while worrying that 'writing will be the only way to pay off the debt' and 'I shall never write up the money for the house I'm afraid.'[52] *Coverture* gave Gaskell the freedom to assume the voice of the provincial, irreproachable wife, which itself 'covered' a sophisticated and tenacious understanding of the encroachments of modernity into the processes and meanings of ordinary life. In her letters she constructs her art as a protective cover or 'shelter', rather than as a medium of publicity, 'I am sure it is healthy for [women] to have the refuge of the hidden world of Art to shelter themselves in when too much pressed upon by daily small Lilliputian arrows of peddling cares . . . I have felt this in writing.'[53] Gaskell's construction of the masculine, public world of letters as a 'refuge' from the private, domestic world that was generally itself figured as 'sheltered' is typical of her quiet and tenacious radicalism. While Gaskell sometimes gives vent in her letters to a longing to go back to the old days of wifely obedience, 'I am sometimes coward enough to wish that we were back in the times of darkness where obedience was the only seen duty of women,' she is well aware of the undesirability of such an answer, and her support of initiatives to improve the lot of women was always of a highly practical and immediate kind. Hence her dislike of the lack of 'definite point' to the petition, and her direct support from her earnings of the women's refuge.[54] For Gaskell, the challenge was to change the culture rather than just the law.

David Trotter sees Gaskell as one of the 'less likely candidates' to write about contingency and modernity, although he acknowledges that she does just this, particularly in her late work: 'To think about the immanence of the future in the present, in the way she does in "Cousin Phillis" and *Wives and Daughters*, is to think about contingency, about something which may or may not happen.'[55] In my

---

[51] See Finn, 'Women, Consumption and Coverture'. See also Berg, 'Women's Property and the Industrial Revolution'.
[52] ECG to Marianne Gaskell (22 August 1865), *LG* 936–8, 938.
[53] ECG to Eliza Fox (*c*.February 1850), *LG* 106–7, 106.
[54] ECG to Eliza Fox (?April 1850), *LG* 107–10, 109.
[55] David Trotter, *Cooking with Mud: The Idea of Mess in Nineteenth-Century Art and Fiction* (2000), 121 and 122–3.

view, Gaskell is clearer than any other novelist of the period about the social effects of technology and invention, and about the pain involved in moving blindly forward into a pathless future without concomitant cultural change. Gaskell's 1863/4 novella, *Cousin Phillis*, reveals the quiet radicalism that underlies her ostensibly 'domestic' fiction. Trotter finds it a 'wonder' that Gaskell was able to write about chance at all, 'respectful as she unfailingly was of generic convention', but if we look hard enough beyond Gaskell's own conventional disavowals and the small domestic detail of her fiction, it becomes clear that she was not, in fact, entirely respectful of generic convention after all, nor, indeed—and the point is related—of gender conventions.[56]

'[N]ot scientific nor mechanical' was Gaskell's own emphatic assessment of herself in a letter to her friend Anne Robson in September 1851, in which she describes a recent trip to the Great Exhibition: 'Of course, we did the Exhibition. I went 3 times, & should never care to go again; but then I'm *not* scientific nor mechanical. Meta and Wm went often, but not enough they say. That's difference of opinion.'[57] She does not dilate upon the Exhibition in her letters, and the only other mention of it in a letter to her daughter Marianne serves to confirm her lack of enthusiasm. She compares it unfavourably with the Duke of Wellington's funeral: 'As far as I can hear it, it [the funeral] was a far better way of expressing a nation's feeling than spending money on that great humbug of an Exhibition.'[58] And in an irritable letter written in August 1861, Gaskell reports that the British Association of Science is meeting in Manchester in September, and consequently her house will be full of scientific guests, about which she sighs: 'I half wish the whole affair was over, not being scientific.'[59] Such remarks suggest that she viewed science and technology as a monolithic and impenetrable body of knowledge alien to her and her everyday experience.

[56] David Trotter, *Cooking with Mud: The Idea of Mess in Nineteenth-Century Art and Fiction* (2000), 125.
[57] ECG to Anne Robson (1 September 1851), *LG* 159–61, 159. 'Meta and Wm' are Gaskell's daughter and husband, William.
[58] ECG to Marianne Gaskell (22 November 1852), *LG* 211–13, 211.
[59] ECG to Charles Eliot Norton (28 August 1861), *LG* 664–7, 667. In April 1861 she had written, 'We must come home however against the British Association in full health; for we are going to have our house full,—Mr and Mrs Brodie, Mr and Mrs Wedgwood and one or two others.' ECG to Charles Eliot Norton (16 April 1861), *LG* 645–51, 646.

But it would be misleading to read this hostility to science and invention in terms of a conventional female aversion to the technical, based on ignorance or impatience. There is plenty of evidence to contradict such a view. As a young woman, Gaskell had stayed with her relation, William Turner, in Newcastle; a Minister, a friend of George Stephenson, and enthusiastic secretary of the Newcastle Literary and Philosophical Society; a 'pioneering figure' in the history of science.[60] After she was married, and living in Manchester, the Gaskells numbered many of the most prominent inventors and engineers of the day among their friends, including James Nasmyth, the inventor of the steam hammer; Joseph Paxton, the designer of the Crystal Palace; and William Fairbairn, inventor of the riveting machine, and witness to the 1851 Select Committee on Patents.[61] Gaskell visited Manchester's manufactories, and knew the Kay-Shuttleworths, and many other manufactory owners, and wrote knowledgeably in her letters and her fiction about the effects of industrialization on the city's various communities.[62] She was so well connected in industrial Manchester that she could instantly rustle up an entire itinerary of factory tourism for her visitors:

I enclose some of my cards. If you have time, they will enable you to see some of the things best worth in Manchester [including] ... '*Murray's* FINE spinning-mills,' in Union St ... '*Hoyle's*' print-works ... '*Whitworth's*' Machine{ry} Works ... these works are very interesting, if you do not get a stupid *fine* young man to show you over—try rather for one of the *working* men. *Sharp & Roberts, Bridgewater Foundry.* Good to see in the Railway-Engine line. LOCKETTS. *Very* clever *small* machinery. For instance, they engrave the copper rollers used in calico printing.[63]

[60] Jenny Uglow, *Elizabeth Gaskell: A Habit of Stories* (1993), 59. Gaskell stayed in Newcastle in the winters of 1829 and 1830.

[61] Ibid. 560. Other scientists of the Gaskells' acquaintance included George Allman, Professor of Zoology at Edinburgh University; Lord Francis Egerton, patron of Manchester science; Benjamin Brodie, Professor of Chemistry at Oxford; the physicist, James Joule; and the chemists, James Allan, Edward Schunk, and Henry Roscoe.

[62] Sir James Kay-Shuttleworth was the author of *The Moral and Physical Condition of the Working Classes Employed in the Cotton Manufacture in Manchester* (1832). Gaskell also read industrial fiction and biography. For example, she was enthusiastically reading Henry Morley's *Palissy the Potter* (1852) when it had to be returned to the library. See ECG to Elizabeth Holland (after 8 December 1852), GL 217–18, 218.

[63] ECG to Unknown (9 March [1864]), LG 729–30. The date and addressee of this letter are unclear.

Gaskell's Unitarianism also predisposed her to applaud scientific endeavour, as a positive manifestation of man's perfectibility, or self-redemption, through the effort of reason. As R. K. Webb remarks, 'Unitarians [. . .] had repeatedly stressed the importance of pursuing truth . . . Here was an anchor of Unitarian commitment to toleration and religious liberty; here, too, was a key to Unitarian responsiveness to science.'[64] Theologically, Gaskell's immediate circle focused less on the threat of science to scripture, and more on the potential practical value of scientific progress to society. While Gaskell was highly sceptical of the simplistic attempts of political economists to rationalize technological change by denying its social costs, she herself is exercised throughout her work by the problem of how to palliate the pain of industrialization and the consequent social transformation. In *Mary Barton* (1848) and *North and South* (1854), she had examined the effects of industrialization on the working-class population of Manchester, and in both she had used female characters as a means of symbolically resolving class iniquities.[65] After *North and South*, she did not return to a directly industrial subject in her longer fiction until 1863, when she wrote the novella, *Cousin Phillis*.

Gaskell started *Cousin Phillis* directly after finishing her bleak novel, *Sylvia's Lovers*, and continued writing throughout the autumn and winter of 1863: the novella appeared in parts in the *Cornhill* between November 1863 and February 1864.[66] At first reading, the work seems to mark a complete departure from *Sylvia's Lovers*. It has been described as a 'simple tale' of 'homely charm', and indeed, Gaskell seems initially to have restored the control of nature to man; there is nothing of the wild landscape or treacherous sea

[64] R. K. Webb, 'The Gaskells as Unitarians', in Joanne Shattock (ed.), *Dickens and Other Victorians: Essays in Honour of Philip Collins* (1988), 144–71, 148.

[65] See Deirdre David, *Fictions of Resolution in Three Victorian Novels: North and South, Our Mutual Friend, Daniel Deronda* (1981); Catherine Gallagher, *The Industrial Reformation of English Fiction: Social Discourse and Narrative Form, 1832–1867* (1985); Rosemarie Bodenheimer, *The Politics of Story in Victorian Fiction* (1988), and Ruth Bernard Yeazell, 'Why Political Novels Have Heroines: *Sybil*, *Mary Barton*, and *Felix Holt*', *Novel: A Forum on Fiction*, 18/2 (Winter 1985), 126–44.

[66] Jenny Uglow has suggested that Gaskell's portrayal of Minister Holman's shock at his daughter's confession of her love for Holdsworth owes something to her own state of mind at the time of writing *Cousin Phillis*, as news reached her in March 1863 of the sudden engagement of her daughter, Florence, to a young barrister, and 'scientific' young man, Charles Crompton. Uglow, *Elizabeth Gaskell*, 538.

of *Sylvia's Lovers* in the cultivated garden and farm where most of the action of *Cousin Phillis* takes place.[67] Even the surrounding countryside is described as 'very wild and pretty' (3). Gaskell has changed the scale, and the brevity and intimacy of the novella form support the theme of her story. For *Cousin Phillis* is precisely about looking closely, about attention to detail. The initial impression is that the wide created universe has been circumscribed and shrunk into the garden of Hope Farm: 'there was a low wall round it, with an iron railing on top of the wall, and two great gates, between pillars crowned with stone balls, for a state entrance' (8). This is a place where order and privacy prevail, superficially at least. Yet there are four mechanics and engineers in *Cousin Phillis*. In fact, every male character in the story, with the exception of the farm-labourer, Timothy Cooper, and the ministers, is to some degree involved in mechanics or engineering.

Cousin Phillis is Gaskell's most focused consideration of the impact of invention and innovation on seemingly traditional lifestyles, and in it she deploys very similar inventor stereotypes to those that we encountered in Dickens's work. In fact, in Mr Manning, the artisan-inventor of the 1830s, and Holdsworth, the new commercial man, we find another Doyce and Gowan. But, unlike Dickens, Gaskell does not identify herself with the inventors in her tale. This may be part of a feminine strategy of disavowal, obscuring her own act of literary creativity. But, for a married woman writer, an analogy between writers and inventors based upon a shared anxiety about intellectual property would be tenuous to say the least in the face of a law that does not admit her to hold any property. Although both Gaskell and Eliot drew deeply upon Romantic aesthetics, it remained difficult for them to identify with the masculine stereotype of the artist-creator. Through Phillis, Gaskell examines a similar dynamic of exclusion through male science, and the dangers presented by a culture growing ever more divisive and opaque. The inventor in Gaskell's work comes to represent a modernity that encroaches into domestic spaces only to reinforce traditional boundaries between the private and the public sphere.

Gaskell's friend, Catherine Winkworth, gives the following account in a letter to Emily Shaen of a visit to Mr Nasmyth's Patricroft

---

[67] A. W. Ward, 'Introduction', Gaskell, *The Works of Mrs. Gaskell*, vii. *Cousin Phillis and Other Tales*, ed. A. W. Ward (1906), pp. xii, xvi. All further references to *Cousin Phillis* appear in parentheses in the text.

works made by a party comprising herself, Selina Winkworth, Gaskell, and her eldest daughter Marianne. Leaping up to explain the workings of some piece of machinery, Nasmyth 'illustrated with impromptu diagrams on the wall alternately with a piece of white chalk and a sooty fore-finger'.[68] Jenny Uglow notices the transposition of this incident into Gaskell's *Cousin Phillis* when the irrepressible Mr Manning, an inventor and the narrator's father, uses the same method of illustration:

I saw my father taking a straight burning stick out of the fire, and, after waiting for a minute, and examining the charred end to see if it was fitted for his purpose, he went to the hard-wood dresser, scoured to the last pitch of whiteness and cleanliness, and began drawing with the stick; the best substitute for chalk or charcoal within his reach, for his pocket-book pencil was not strong or bold enough for his purpose. When he had done, he began to explain his new model of a turnip-cutting machine to the minister, who had been watching him in silence all the time. Cousin Holman had, in the meantime, taken a duster out of a drawer, and, under pretence of being as much interested as her husband in the drawing, was secretly trying on an outside mark how easily it would come off, and whether it would leave her dresser as white as before. (34)

The similarity of the accounts is undeniable, but Gaskell transposes the inscription from a factory wall to a hardwood dresser in the kitchen of the Holmans' farmhouse. The comfortable small 'business' of Cousin Holman's surreptitious attempts to assess the damage to her dresser, frames the scene with the recognizable referents of domestic comedy. But, in fact, Cousin Holman's dresser *will* never be as white as before.

Gaskell chooses to represent the nineteenth-century 'march of progress' in terms of intimate material changes that penetrate the most traditional of homes, and when inventors break into the female domain of the kitchen, they leave an indelible mark. Technological innovation crosses classes and creeds and threatens traditional boundaries, just like the railway lines that Holdsworth is laying over 'the shaking, uncertain ground' (5). And, while acknowledging the potential of technological change, Gaskell also struggles to include its direct effects on individual lives. Mr Manning's improvised drawing on the dresser does not represent only the turnip-cutting ma-

---

[68] Catherine Winkworth to Emily Shaen (18 March 1856). Quoted in Uglow, *Elizabeth Gaskell*, 667–8.

chine, it also stands for the principle of improvisation itself. For, as Phillis will discover, when the future is no longer predicated on the past, improvisation is the only recourse. Excluded, though, from any formal education or training, Phillis is stranded in the modern world without the apparatus she needs in order to participate fully in her own culture.

Niklas Luhmann has complained about '[t]hose who enter the lists against the risk of technology [and who] see themselves as defenders of nature (ignoring its icy temperatures, radioactivity, wilderness and infertility).'[69] But in *Cousin Phillis* it transpires that nature, too, is not without its own risks—it is while working in an unhealthy 'dark overshadowed dale' (40), for example, that Holdsworth contracts the 'low fever'. Similarly, Ulrich Beck has claimed that 'the concept of the classical industrial society is based on the antithesis between nature and society (in the nineteenth century sense), [whereas] the concept of the (industrial) risk society proceeds from "nature" as integrated by culture'.[70] As we shall see, Gaskell makes no such distinction between (safe) nature and (risky) technology, and her work throws such a broad-brush characterization of nineteenth-century thinking into question. Indeed, *Cousin Phillis* articulates a sharp warning about the risks involved in attempting to maintain such a conservative position in the face of oncoming modernity. Gaskell understands with a clarity that is remarkable so early in the process of modernization, that technology *is* the new nature, and she foresees the catastrophe that will ensue if traditional ideas of what is 'natural' are not urgently reconsidered.[71] Despite critics' descriptions of the opening chapters as describing 'an organic, pre-industrial idyll', in fact, the entry of new technology in the form of Holdsworth and his railway lines on Hope Farm merely reveals the pre-existent cracks in that idyll.[72] Gaskell's hostility is not directed at the new technologies, but rather at the increased specialization that excludes 'ordinary' people and renders them powerless in an increasingly illegible world. Much less concerned than Dickens or Thackeray with the preservation of individual intellectual property, including her own, she

---

[69] Niklas Luhmann, *Risk: A Sociological Theory*, trans. Rhodes Barrett (1993), 86.
[70] Beck, *Risk Society*, 81.
[71] Emerson was also early to see new technology as the 'organised nature' within which modern lives were increasingly embedded. R. W. Emerson, 'The Uses of Great Men', *Essays, Lectures and Orations* (1851), 327. George Eliot owned this edition.
[72] Linda Ruth Williams, 'The Story as Case History: *Cousin Phillis*', in *Critical Desire: Psychoanalysis and the Literary Subject* (1995), 25–37, 27.

stresses instead the importance of the wider public dissemination of knowledge in all her work.

Mr Manning, like Daniel Doyce, is a discourse rather than a character. He is introduced leaving Paul at his new lodgings in Eltham, where he is reported to have delivered 'a few plain precepts' (1) to his son. Gaskell's emphasis, in all the sporadic glimpses of Mr Manning in the story, is on his rejection of superfluity, verbal or economic:

> He was a mechanic by trade; but he had some inventive genius, and a great deal of perseverance, and had devised several valuable improvements in railway machinery. He did not do this for profit, though, as was reasonable, what came in the natural course of things was acceptable; he worked out his ideas, because, as he said, 'until he could put them into shape, they plagued him by night and by day'. (1)

The scattered clues about Mr Manning in a narrative from which he is largely absent can be gathered up into the hero-victim inventor, a stereotype that, as we have seen, was originally created during the debate about patent rights in the 1830s. Unlike Jem Wilson's 'crank, or somewhat', though, Mr Manning's inventions are not only in the form of 'devised . . . improvements' to machinery already in existence.[73] He is also the creator of Manning's Patent Winch, ' "It was in the *Gazette*" ', boasts Paul, ' "It was patented. I thought every one had heard of Manning's patent winch" ' (20). During the narrative, too, Mr Manning is busy designing 'Manning's driving-wheel' (32). But Gaskell privileges perseverance over genius, of which Manning only possesses 'some', and she insists on the Holmans' ignorance of his great innovation in shunting. At the start of the novel it is noted, carefully, that Paul's situation as a clerk to a railway engineer is 'rather above his own [his father's] in life' (1), which is that of a mechanic, so that Mr Manning's partnership with Ellison represents a significant social leap. Yet Gaskell stresses that profit is ' "a long way off, anyhow" ' (35), and, indeed, when Paul subsequently makes a visit home to Birmingham he finds no evidence of sudden social transformation, '[t]here was no display of increased wealth in our modest household' (53). Manning's intellectual property represents moral rather than material wealth.

---

[73] Gaskell, *The Works of Mrs. Gaskell*, i. *Mary Barton and Other Tales*, ed. A. W. Ward (1906), 162.

Nevertheless, while Gaskell plays down Mr Manning's growing fame and fortune, she allows other, contradictory evidence to accrue. For instance, Holdsworth, in paying homage to the older man, shows Paul his 'ungrudging admiration of his *great mechanical genius*' (39), and is reported to have spoken of Mr Manning 'often . . . as having the same kind of genius for mechanical invention as that of George Stephenson' (32).[74] While Holdsworth seems to see a greatness of genius in Mr Manning that makes him a powerful figure, he also gives an account of Mr Manning's life that fits it perfectly for the pages of George Lillie Craik's *Pursuit of Knowledge Under Difficulties*:

Here's a Birmingham workman, self-educated, one may say—having never associated with stimulating minds, or had what advantages travel and contact with the world may be supposed to afford—working out his own thoughts into steel and iron, making a scientific name for himself—a fortune, if it pleases him to work for money—and keeping his singleness of heart, his perfect simplicity of manner.   (40)

'Through Mr. Manning Gaskell shows that the older, simpler order can co-exist with industrial progress,' claims Jenny Uglow.[75] I argue that Gaskell knows that the 'older, simpler order' of artisans is as much of a myth as the 'natural' sexual innocence of women. Yet she only engages explicitly with the latter in *Cousin Phillis*. The implication that 'older' and 'simpler' are adjectives that sit logically together is an assumption founded on the very myth of progressive development that Gaskell attacks elsewhere in her work. Yet Uglow's is precisely the reading that the representation of Manning is constructed to produce. By using the old Reform stereotype of Mr Manning, Gaskell creates an 'older, simpler order' that separates the 'Birmingham workman' from the processes of 'industrial progress', and furthermore separates 'industrial progress' from its inevitable corollary, social change.[76] But in other elements of her story, she seems to be criticizing exactly such a separation. Deirdre David has argued that the female is often victimised as a symbolic solution to such divisions

---

[74] Emphasis added.   [75] Uglow, *Elizabeth Gaskell*, 544.
[76] The intentionality of this representation is perhaps not entirely clear from my reading. I am not suggesting that Gaskell intended to write the working classes out of any share in industrial progress, and therefore, social change. I am rather attempting to argue that Gaskell, once she decides to deploy the good and worthy stereotype of Mr Manning, is locked into a discourse that inevitably produces this outcome.

in Gaskell's work, but I would argue that in the later fiction, this is not quite what happens.[77] The openness at the end of the novella, which finishes with Phillis's words 'I will,' is less an evasion than a deliberate refusal to resolve. Gaskell leaves Phillis poised on the edge of a risky future. The rupture between past and future dramatized by the ending is both painful, and liberating: suggesting that openness and flexibility are always exposing, always risky, but remain the only alternatives in a society which was becoming terminally unpredictable.[78]

In contrast to Mr Manning, Holdsworth is an educated and well-read engineer, a southerner and a 'gentleman'. Gaskell evades the fact that Holdsworth is a civil engineer, the long-established and respectable branch of engineering, unlike mechanical engineering, which is Manning's trade. Significantly, he is not reported as holding any patents of his own, being rather the hireling of large and powerful corporations. As they are created in different genres, the two men cannot communicate and it is, perhaps, significant that their conversation is not represented, but reported by Paul. Indeed, between them, Mr Manning and Holdsworth create a kind of palimpsest of the development of engineering over the previous seventy-five years. Holdsworth's letters bring 'a whiff of foreign atmosphere into . . . [Minister Holman's] circumscribed life' (76). Holdsworth, unlike Mr Manning, represents industrial progress as change: old stories

[77] Deirdre David, *Fictions of Resolution in Three Victorian Novels: North and South, Our Mutual Friend, Daniel Deronda* (1981). This reading revises my previous published account of Gaskell's tale in Clare Pettitt, ' "Cousin Holman's Dresser": Science, Social Change, and the Pathologization of the Female in Gaskell's *Cousin Phillis*', *Nineteenth-Century Literature*, 52/4 (March 1998), 471–89. I now argue that in the 1860s Gaskell is suggesting that women are peculiarly well adapted to deal with contingency and risk, and that in Phillis Holman and Molly Gibson we see more cautiously positive accounts of women and modernity. See also my review article, 'An Everyday Story: Wives, Daughters and Nineteenth-Century Natural Science', *Studies in History and Philosophy of Biological and Biomedical Sciences*, 33 (2002), 325–35.

[78] Uglow argues convincingly that Mr Manning is based on Gaskell's acquaintance, James Nasmyth, giving as evidence the Patricroft works visit and an anecdote apparently told by Nasmyth about gentlemen-apprentices wearing gloves, which appears as a shared joke between Holdsworth and Mr Manning in *Cousin Phillis*. See Uglow, *Elizabeth Gaskell*, ch. 25. If this is the case, I think it is only important in so far as it exacerbates Gaskell's problems with the representation of Mr Manning. Maxine Berg writes, 'By the 1820s and 1830s James Nasmyth, James Fox, Matthew Murray, Sharp, Roberts & Co., Hicks, Hargreaves & Co., Fairbairn and Lillie, and Joseph Whitworth were directing large-scale machine shops, foundries and engine factories in the Midlands and the North,' *The Machinery Question*, 153–4. Nasmyth was clearly a rich industrialist, while Manning is represented as simultaneously successful and poor.

will necessarily be interrupted: the romantic hero will suddenly leave for Canada, never to return.

The scene in which Mr Manning draws the turnip-cutting machine on the dresser, and another, when Paul espies Holdsworth, Phillis, and Minister Holman, 'I counted their heads, joined together in an eager group over Holdsworth's theodolite' (56), both use physical science as the focus of an unorthodox grouping. The heads 'joined together' are temporarily united by shared enthusiasm. Yet there is a jarring note in these fantasies of class reconciliation over the theodolite, the turnip-cutter, or in Mr Manning's friendship with Holdsworth. All the risk of damage that invention also threatens erupts elsewhere. Looking at Mr Manning's drawing of the turnip-cutting machine, Phillis is 'leaning over and listening greedily . . . sucking in information' (34), and although her head is one of the three 'joined together' over the theodolite, 'she had hardly time to greet me, so desirous was she to hear some answer to *her father's question*' (56).[79] Engineering science is male and exclusively so in this narrative, and Phillis can only gratify her appetite for technical knowledge by eavesdropping on male conversations. Unlike Sylvia in *Sylvia's Lovers*, she is hungry for 'masculine news' (41), but like Sylvia she has no control over her own 'feminine' story. She is dangerously exposed, and it is through Phillis, and not through Holdsworth, that Gaskell explores contingency in the story. Gaskell is engaging more explicitly than she has ever done before in the debate surrounding the social position of women, the education of women, and the property of women, which was being exhaustively conducted in the periodical press in the late 1850s and the 1860s. She uses that debate through her representation of Phillis to open up some of the ideological problems produced in the text by her portrayal of technological change. In addition, I suggest that it is Phillis, rather than any of the male inventors in the text, who stands for Gaskell's sense of her own creativity. Just as Caroline Norton had made the reality of female alienation 'distressingly visible' through her public exposure of her private life, through Phillis, Gaskell reveals the private suffering of a woman alienated and denied any cultural capital or intellectual property of her own.[80] Phillis's marginalization, her exclusion from the ownership of knowledge,

---

[79] Emphasis added.
[80] Poovey, *Uneven Developments*, 78.

surely reflects Gaskell's own sense of her precarious guest-status as a woman writer in the male world of letters, yet equally important is the sense of risk that accrues around her female character. The tone of mingled hope and fear with which Phillis ends the novella foreshadows that of the utopian writing that was to become popular at the end of the century. It reflects the risks that Gaskell herself was taking in publishing—hoping for personal recognition, but fearing too public an exposure—and it reflects her political hope for a broader public life for women, underwritten by better property rights, along with her fear that such justice would never be done.

An article in the *Englishwoman's Journal* in 1858 pleaded for more educational opportunities and jobs for women: 'Let woman put her shoulder to the slowly revolving wheel of progression, and she need not fear to be left behind, nor to be refused the countenance of her fellow-worker, man.'[81] Phillis keeps trying to put her shoulder to the wheel, but is constantly repelled by the centrifugal force of male exclusivity. The debate over female education extended into discussions of married women's property, too. J. W. Kaye argued that '[t]here would be more good wives and good mothers, if women were better trained to take a part in the active business of life—if they were educated as though they might be neither wives nor mothers, but independent members of society, with work of their own to do seriously, earnestly, and with all their might.'[82] Although Gaskell was careful to preserve some public distance from the 'strong-minded women' campaigning for women's rights in the 1860s, she was privately acquainted with many of them, and supported their work.[83] However quietly she engaged with the organized radical opposition to 'the established opinions of the world', she was well aware of what those opinions consisted. Here, for instance, is W. R. Greg discussing womankind in his well-known article in the *Westminster Review*, entitled 'Prostitution':

[81] Anon., 'Female Education in the Middle Classes', *English Woman's Journal*, 1/4 (June 1858), 217–27. 227. See also Gaskell's friend Harriet Martineau's article, 'Female Industry', *Edinburgh Review* (April 1859), 293–336.

[82] [J. W. Kaye], 'The "Non-Existence" of Women', 558.

[83] The most prominent was the 'Langham Place' group of campaigners for women's rights. In 1857 Barbara Leigh Smith Bodichon and Bessie Rayner Parkes, who were both Unitarians, established what became the *English Woman's Review*. The *Review* shared its Langham Place offices with The Society for Promoting the Employment of Women, founded in 1859 and run by Jessie Boucherett. Barbara Bodichon went on to become one of the founders of Girton College, Cambridge in the 1870s. See Pam Hirsch, *Barbara Leigh Smith Bodichon, 1827–1891: Feminist, Artist and Rebel* (1998).

the desire scarcely exists in a definite and conscious form, till they *have* fallen. In this point there is a radical and essential difference between the sexes . . . In men, in general, the sexual desire is inherent and spontaneous, and belongs to the condition of puberty. In the other sex, the desire is dormant, if not non-existent, till excited; always till excited by undue familiarities.[84]

This is precisely the view of feminine passivity—here sexual, in Gaskell both sexual and intellectual—that she attacks in *Cousin Phillis*. It seems, too, to be Minister Holman's view: when he accuses Paul of 'put[ting] such thoughts into the child's mind . . . spoil[ing] her peaceful maidenhood' (98), he assumes that Phillis is 'dormant' in Greg's phrase, just as Holdsworth likens her to the sleeping beauty, 'I shall come back like a prince from Canada, and waken her to my love' (64). It is only Paul and Phillis who 'kn[o]w that the truth was different' (98).

Cousin Phillis is a detective novel, but it is a pathologized detective novel in which the detective is also the criminal. Paul certainly transgresses when he tells Phillis that Holdsworth loves her, but he is also the anxious detector of signs by which he, and the reader, attempt to piece together the possible state of Phillis's invisible inner life. The signs are almost entirely somatic, rather than psychological or verbal. Phillis's body becomes a theatre where all the activity and emotion that is denied free expression displays itself. Phillis's 'large, quiet eyes' and 'white skin' (9) are disturbed by Holdsworth's arrival, at their introduction, she is 'blushing a little', 'flushed' (45), and 'in a blushing hurry' (46), later her eyes are 'glad and bright' and a word from Holdsworth 'call[s] out her blushes' (57), when Holdsworth draws her portrait 'her colour came and went, her breath quickened' (59). After Holdsworth's departure, Paul notices 'her face white and set, her dry eyes', 'as pale as could be' (66), looking 'so pale and weary' (67), and hearing him read out a letter from Holdsworth, Paul notices 'two spots of brilliant colour on the cheeks that had been so pale before' (69). At chapel on Christmas day, the gossips talk about the possibility of Phillis dying of 'a decline', 'her grey eyes looked hollow and sad; her complexion was of a dead white' (70), in the kitchen Paul hears 'a noise which made me pause and listen—a sob, an unmistakable, irrepressible sob' (71). The pause, indicated here by a dash on the page, dramatizes Paul's detective activity, and

---

[84] [W. R. Greg], 'Prostitution', *Westminster Review*, 53 (July 1850), 448–506, 456–7. Greg adds, 'We do not mean to say that uneasiness may not be felt—that health may not sometimes suffer; but there is no consciousness of the cause,' 457.

implicates the reader as witness. This is the climax of the mystery for
Paul, the detective, although not, of course, for the reader who has
been patiently assembling not only the clues about Phillis's state
of mind, but also those that indicate that Paul's own inexperience
makes him an unreliable narrator. The vital clue for Paul is the book
containing Holdsworth's margin notes: 'Could that be it? Could that
be the cause of her white looks, her weary eyes, her wasted figure, her
struggling sobs?' (71). This is a clue that reveals Phillis's inner life
to Paul 'like a flash of lightning on a dark night' (71), yet Phillis continues to express nothing verbally, and it is only through somatic
symptoms that Paul reads her happiness when he tells her that
Holdsworth loves her, '[h]er eyes, glittering with tears as they were,
expressed an almost heavenly happiness' (74). Part Four opens with
the chapel gossips complimenting Cousin Holman on 'her daughter's
blooming looks' (75) and Paul notes that '[h]er state of vivid happiness this summer was markedly different to the peaceful serenity of
former days' (80). After Paul tells her of Holdsworth's marriage to
Lucille Ventadour, her parents continue to read Phillis's symptoms as
purely physical, her mother interprets her show of temper as a reaction to the stormy weather. It is the servant, Betty, who reads the truth
of the symptoms: ' "you've likely never heared of a fever-flush . . .
What makes her come in panting ready and ready to drop into that
chair" ' (87–8). When Holdsworth's letter arrives with the public
announcement of his marriage, 'her face was brilliantly flushed; her
eyes were dry and glittering' (91); and Paul reports the pathological
signs of Phillis's reaction in minute detail: 'But once my eyes fell upon
her hands, concealed under the table, and I could see the passionate,
convulsive manner in which she laced and interlaced her fingers perpetually, wringing them together from time to time, wringing till the
compressed flesh became perfectly white . . . I wondered that others
did not read these signs as clearly as I did' (94–5). After Phillis con-
fesses her love for Holdsworth to her father, Paul remarks Minister
Holman's failure to notice Phillis's symptoms: 'her beautiful eyes dilated with a painful, tortured expression. He went on, without notic-
ing the look on her face; he did not see it, I am sure' (100). Then comes
the collapse, which throws both Minister Holman and Paul into silence ('I pointed to the quivering of the muscles round her mouth'
(100)), and the subsequent brain fever.

Gaskell's portrayal of Phillis almost exclusively through somatic
symptoms is extraordinary. She demonstrates to shocking effect the

pressure under which women are placed by the lack of any expressive outlet. As Susan Gubar has said 'within the life of domesticity assigned [to the woman] . . . from birth, the body is the only accessible medium for self expression'.[85] Phillis says very little in the novella, and less and less as it proceeds. Gaskell powerfully dramatizes the pathologization of women by a society that, literally, makes them ill. Linda Ruth Williams reads Phillis simply as 'the figure of the hysteric', but such a basic Freudian reading is hardly adequate.[86] Phillis's silence and pain fulfil a wider function than that of a 'case study' in the novella, through the way that Gaskell relates her to the male community of engineers and inventors. All of them, despite their remarkable inventive and mechanical gifts, fail Phillis in their various ways. Holdsworth fails her by underestimating her and by allowing himself to ignore the pain that he knows he has caused her by lazily relying on the 'established opinions' that characterize women as passive sleeping beauties. Minister Holman fails repeatedly and obstinately to read his daughter's symptoms as signs of an independent subjectivity. Mr Manning reads Phillis only in terms of another woman, 'poor Molly', who pined away for love of him many years before, or as a potential wife for Paul. He reinforces the established opinions that militate against female subjectivity when he assures Paul that marriage and children would cure Phillis of Latin and Greek (37). Paul himself, although he reads Phillis almost obsessively closely, does not always read her correctly. And he fails her most disastrously when, albeit in an effort to comfort her, he misjudges the effect and miscalculates the risk of telling her about Holdsworth's 'love' for her. Their mechanical knowledge has failed all of them in interpreting Phillis as a subject. The mechanisms of turnip-cutters, drive wheels, winches, and railway tracks the men examine and understand in minute detail, but the hidden mechanisms of the woman who sits beside them receive no attention, even when she begins to malfunction seriously. Paul is, of course, the exception, but his attempted reading of Phillis leads him to an act that ultimately causes more pain. He knows the facts, and he sees the symptoms, but he fails adequately to infer Phillis's inner life from them. His naive assumption is that Phillis can be 'mended' by the information he gives her.

[85] Susan Gubar, 'The Blank Page: Issues of Creativity', in Elaine Showalter (ed.), *The New Feminist Criticism: Essays on Women, Literature, and Theory* (1986), 292–33, 296.
[86] Linda Ruth Williams, *Critical Desire* (1995), 37.

Catherine Belsey has remarked that illness in nineteenth-century fiction is often used as a strategy to express 'the problem of change it symbolises'.[87] Certainly, Gaskell is obedient to the convention in so far as Phillis's body becomes the site of radical transformations which are hinted at but not represented as connected to the invention and technology in the text. Yet the ending is less orthodox. At last, Phillis speaks, and makes a demand: 'She blushed a little, as she faltered out her wish for change of thought and scene' (109). It is true that she also blushes, but only 'a little'. 'Her wish for change' carries the ideological burden of the text, and that she chooses to go to Mr Manning for her change is perhaps less significant than that she chooses to go to urban, industrial Birmingham. Gaskell wrote to the publisher George Smith that Phillis 'in a town, among utterly different people & scenery, cures herself'.[88] Phillis's final paradoxical remark: 'Then—we will go back to the peace of the old days. I know we shall; I can, and I will!' (109) demonstrates the irreversible change that has taken place in her, 'the peace of the old days' rested upon her dependency and trust. Now she has spoken, and taken a new responsibility for herself, the peace of the old days will never return. The conventional rupture of her illness is repeated, much less conventionally, by the abrupt ending of the story that offers no clues as to Phillis's future, and leaves her only with a lack. Esther Summerson received restitution for her smallpox by her marriage to Alan Woodcourt, but Phillis's loss is not redeemed, and she faces the future still scarred by the broken promises and accidents of the past. Ian Hacking has dated a new reflexive awareness of chance to the 1860s, as a result of the growth of statistical science, which proved that 'the past does not determine exactly what happens next': certainly, at the end of *Cousin Phillis*, Gaskell simply abandons her heroine to the unknown future.[89]

In fact, the published ending was not the one originally intended by Gaskell, as is revealed in a letter to George Smith, in which she sketches out her plans for an extra two numbers of the story, which were never to be written. Years later, Paul, married, returns to find

---

[87] Catherine Belsey, *Critical Practice* (1980), 74. See also Miriam Bailin, *The Sickroom in Victorian Fiction: The Art of Being Ill* (1994) and Athena Vrettos, 'From Neurosis to Narrative: The Private Life of the Nerves in *Villette* and *Daniel Deronda*', *Victorian Studies*, 33 (1990), 551–79. Also Athena Vrettos, *Somatic Fictions: Imagining Illness in Victorian Culture* (1995).

[88] ECG to George Smith (10 December [1863]), *FLG* 259–60, 259.

[89] Ian Hacking, *The Taming of Chance* (1990), 1.

Heathbridge struck by typhus, and 'find[s] [Phillis] making practical use of the knowledge she had learnt from Holdsworth and . . . levelling & draining the undrained village'.[90] She is running her father's farm, and has adopted two orphaned children, but has never married.[91] This putative ending could be read conventionally as a fable of loyalty to the memory of true love, or it could be read more radically as a male-less fantasy of female reproductive and productive self-sufficiency, and—importantly—the ownership and management of property.

But even by the end of the published story, it is not victimized womanhood, or not only that, that Phillis has come to represent. She has come to stand for every woman denied any intellectual property, and—more generally—every individual in the 1860s who was becoming unconsciously embedded in a modern society increasingly dependent upon technologies and bureaucracy. Phillis's lack of control of the future is no longer merely female—it is modern, and it is the reader's too. Gaskell sanctions Phillis's need to hold on to the past, and not merely to move restlessly around, like Holdsworth, but she also exposes its difficulty. Phillis may be victimized as a woman, but Gaskell suggests that her 'female' awareness of dependency and risk at the end of the tale equips her better for that future than Paul Manning ever could.[92] For Gaskell, the inventor can no longer stand for the creator, in the way that Daniel Doyce could for Dickens. It is Phillis who is the most modern character in the text: beside her, Mr Manning crumbles into the dusty pile of out-of-date texts from which he is composed, while Holdsworth's disappearance from the story enacts his absorption into corporate employment. That Phillis is female is crucial: her dependency on, and exclusion from, the world of the male engineers in the tale allows her femininity to stand for a peculiarly *modern* state of subjection to a technological culture. Because there is nowhere obvious for a female character to go, once

[90] ECG to George Smith (10 December [1863]), *FLG* 259–60.

[91] J. A. V. Chapple discusses two unpublished letters from Gaskell to George Smith written in December 1863. These are reprinted in J. A. V. Chapple, 'Cousin Phillis: Two Unpublished Letters from Elizabeth Gaskell to George Smith', *Études anglaises*, 23 (1980), 183–7.

[92] Andrew Miller has suggested that female subjectivity is portrayed as positive, open, and flexible in the earlier *Cranford* (1851). I agree with his reading, but suggest that the threats that assail Phillis in *Cousin Phillis* a full decade later reveal Gaskell's apprehension of increasing dependency on technology. Andrew H. Miller, *Novels Behind Glass* (1995), 91–118.

the conventional endings of marriage or death are denied her, she is forced to take responsibility for her own future. In the planned ending, she uses the 'knowledge she had learnt' to take on the role of an engineer, managing a group of 'common labourers' herself.[93] So, despite the strong presence of engineers and inventors in the book, it is Phillis who ends the story by enunciating the future tense. It is through Phillis, too, that Gaskell expresses the pain of loss that is unavoidable in a society that is so rapidly effacing its past, while failing to create adequate opportunities for cultural change. For Gaskell, reforming the intellectual property laws was a far less important social goal than extending the reach of education and enfranchising those groups who were excluded from 'owning' their own culture. Through her work and through the example of her own life, she advocated nothing less than a redrawing of the boundaries between private and public, so that women could enter the public arena without threatening their domestic status.

FORWARD-LOOKING THOUGHTS: GEORGE ELIOT'S
SILAS MARNER, *BROTHER JACOB*, AND *THE*
LIFTED VEIL

Marian Evans was far more enthusiastic about the petition for married women's property rights than was Gaskell, signing it herself and recommending it to other friends, saying that this was a proposal for reform 'which would help to raise the position and character of women' even if it was but 'one round of a long ladder stretching far beyond our lives'.[94] Ironically enough, though, her name did not appear among the leading signatories. Mary Howitt, who was the leader of the petition campaign in London felt that it was 'most needful to have an eye to the moral status of the persons supporting this

---

[93] ECG to George Smith (10 December [1863]), *FLG* 259–60, 260.

[94] Lee Holcombe, *Wives and Property* (1983), 70. Holcombe suggests that it may also have been Eliot and Lewes who put forward a revision of the wording of the original petition to suggest that the law bore unfairly on men too, citing the husband's legal responsibility for her debts contracted before marriage, and the wife's 'too unlimited power' of contracting debts in the name of her husband. Eliot wrote to Sara Hennell, 'I suppose you have received the revised edition [of the Petition] with the clause about the husband being responsible for the wife's debts.' GE to Sara Sophia Hennell (19 February [1856]), 227–9, 227. Lewes, was, of course, responsible for his own wife's Agnes's debts, despite their separation.

movement,' and this might explain why Marian Evans's name was buried in the small print.[95] She had, after all, only recently become the lover of the married Lewes. Her own ambivalence about her identity in the late 1850s and early 1860s animates her writing over the period when her fiction propelled her suddenly to fame, at the same time that her private life condemned her to social exile. It is no coincidence that the issue of intellectual property became a very complicated and significant one for her at this time.

While Eliot does not engage as directly with inventions as Gaskell does in *Cousin Phillis*, her work during 1859 and 1860 seems to return repeatedly to the broader issues of intellectual property. While jealous of her property in her works, she was also, by her own admission, 'much in need of the warmly expressed sympathy which only popularity can win'.[96] Like Gaskell, she was far more exercised by her readers' responses to her work, than by her own construction as an author. Like Gaskell, Eliot described her work as a contribution to society, rather than a way of earning a living, '[a]n author who would keep a pure and noble conscience, and with that of developing instead of degenerating intellect and taste, must cast out of his aims the aim to be rich.'[97] Nevertheless, she cannily declined to sell copyrights of *Scenes of Clerical Life, Adam Bede, The Mill on the Floss*, and *Silas Marner* for £3,000 to the publisher, Blackwood, in 1861, preferring to hold on to her literary property in the hope of seeing its value increase.

'[T]he story is not what the author originally intended it to be, but is huddled up at the end,' mused Eneas Sweetland Dallas in a review of *Silas Marner* in *The Times* in 1861.[98] Dallas is puzzled because:

a hero whose mind is nearly a blank and whose life is represented as the sport of chance, is at variance with the spirit of her books . . . As in one fit of unconsciousness he lost his all, so in another he obtained a recompense. In either case he was helpless, had nothing to do with his own fate, and was a mere feather in the wind of chance. From this point forward in the tale,

[95] Mary Howitt, *An Autobiography* (1889), ii. 115. A Committee run by Barbara Leigh Smith circulated petitions throughout the country—more than seventy petitions with over 26,000 signatures were gathered for presentation to Parliament. The London petition had more than 3,000 signatures.

[96] GE to John Blackwood (31 January 1859), *GEL* iii. 6–7, 6.

[97] George Eliot, *Essays of George Eliot*, ed. Thomas Pinney (London: Routledge & Kegan Paul, 1963), 439, 440–1.

[98] [Eneas Sweetland Dallas], 'Silas Marner', *The Times*, 29 April 1861. Repr. in Gordon S. Haight (ed.), *A Century of George Eliot Criticism* (1966), 17–20, 19.

however, there is no more chance—all is work and reward, cause and effect, the intelligent mind shaping its own destiny.[99]

He can only conclude that Eliot was temporarily diverted in writing the story of perseverance and reward that she had planned. In this section I want to examine this diversion by 'the wind of chance' in three of her oddest works. The shaping function of chance and contingency in Eliot's late work has been noticed before, but little attention has been given to its eruption into her earlier fiction.[100] I am particularly interested in the three short texts she wrote between 1859 and 1860, in the year in which the 'Liggins Affair' unfolded. Under the pressure of persistent rumours of Joseph Liggins's authorship of *Adam Bede*, Eliot was forced to reveal herself as the writer in June 1859, only to suffer the claims of another Coventry connection, Charles Holt Bracebridge, who began to identify and name the characters in her books as real people. *The Lifted Veil* was finished on 26 April 1859, just a week or so after a letter had appeared in *The Times* declaring that Liggins was 'George Eliot'.[101] Throughout the summer and autumn of 1859, Eliot was troubled by the threatened appearance of *Adam Bede Jnr.*: a novel capitalizing on the huge success of her *Adam Bede*. *Brother Jacob* was written in August 1860, and *Silas Marner: The Weaver of Raveloe* was written over the autumn and winter of 1860.[102] These three shorter works were later collected together in one volume in the Cabinet Edition of 1878. Space will not permit similar attention to be given to the two major novels of this period, *Adam Bede* (1859) and *The Mill on the Floss* (1860), but my contention is that the outburst of chance in her shorter, more experimental works at this time is directly related to her consciousness of the chanciness of her own position as the writer of the 'big' novels, her rupture from her own past, and her need to find a value for her literary work beyond that of the economic. Thus, while we can wit-

---

[99] [Eneas Sweetland Dallas], 'Silas Marner', *The Times*, 29 April 1861. Repr. in Gordon S. Haight (ed.), *A Century of George Eliot Criticism* (1966), 18–19.

[100] See Trotter, *Cooking with Mud*.

[101] See Henry Smith Anders to the Editor of *The Times* (13 April 1859), *GEL* iii. 48. *Adam Bede* was published in three vols., 1 February 1859. *The Lifted Veil* was published in *Blackwood's*, 1 July 1859. *The Mill on the Floss* was published in three vols. 4 April 1860. Leah Price, *The Anthology and the Rise of the Novel from Richardson to George Eliot* (2000), 135, records that two sequels did appear to *Adam Bede*, one falsely claiming to be by George Eliot.

[102] *Brother Jacob* was not published until 1864, in the *Cornhill*, 10 (July 1864). *Silas Marner* was published on 2 April 1860.

ness Eliot's affront at the Liggins fraud, and her frustrated need to claim her literary property as her own, in the fiction she writes directly after *Adam Bede* she is engaged in a complex discussion of the issues of intellectual property and invention, which finally places more emphasis on the public sphere than on the personal ownership of inventions.

Throughout 1859, Eliot's anxiety about the endurance of her own literary reputation had led her to dwell often on the idea of her own death, as is manifested in her odd 'jeu de mélancholie', *The Lifted Veil*, written in the spring of that year, under the increasing pressure of her anonymity.[103] Despite the success of *Adam Bede*, the whole of 1859 had been overshadowed first by Liggins and then by the threat of an unauthorized sequel to the novel, which she discussed with Dickens when he came to visit her and Lewes. To her old Coventry friend, Charles Bray, she wrote, 'Dickens has given me a frightful idea of the trouble and expense that belongs to a resistance of these piratical proceedings . . . What an Autumn! There never was such a dead robbery committed on one's [two words deleted] gold—one's autumnal gold.'[104] These associations of both robbery and gold with literary ownership and piracy, present themselves obliquely again in the two short texts she went on to write the following year: *Brother Jacob* and *Silas Marner*. In the autumn of 1860 the strain of the previous year began to show. She complained of feeling 'even more autumnal than my years', she was dosing herself with an alarming mixture of 'bluepill and hydrochloric acid', and '[q]uinine and steel', and her work on *Silas Marner* was punctuated with worries about her own mortality, both in physical and in literary terms.[105] Worrying about the reception of *The Mill on the Floss*, she remarked, 'I am always in a state of fear, more or less rational,' and this was indeed a period of her career in which she was peculiarly anxious about the future.[106]

Eliot had been supporting herself as a journalist before turning to fiction in the mid-1850s, and so her knowledge of the contingencies of the literary marketplace was more immediate than Gaskell's. Of

[103] GE to John Blackwood (31 March [1859]), *GEL* iii. 40–1, 41.
[104] GE to Charles Bray (21? November 1859), *GEL* iii. 210–11.
[105] GE to Charles Bray (14 July [1860]), *GEL* iii. 323–4, 324. GE to Sara Sophia Hennell (13 November [1860]), *GEL* iii. 358–9, 359. GE to Mrs Richard Congreve (7 December 1860), *GEL* iii. 363–4, 363.
[106] GE to John Blackwood (3 April 1860), *GEL* iii. 284–286, 285.

the three works I am discussing in this section, *Silas Marner* contains the most complex examination of that marketplace and the status of intellectual property, and represents her attempt to make sense of her new role as best-selling author. It is a text constructed around ideas of money and theft—first the theft of the money of which Silas is wrongly accused in Lantern Yard, and then the theft of his 'guineas'. She spoke of *Silas Marner* as a very personal piece: to Blackwood she confided, 'I should not have believed that anyone would have been interested in it but myself (since William Wordsworth is dead),' and she described it as 'a sort of legendary tale'.[107] I suggest that it was so personal to Eliot because in it she encoded so many of the anxieties of the previous year. In *The Lifted Veil* and *Brother Jacob* she examines similar themes, articulating her fears about her own posterity as an artist, and about the consumption of her texts. All three of these 'odd' texts show her struggling to shape a role for herself as a serious literary writer in an increasingly masculinized marketplace. Ruby Redinger, in her 1975 book *George Eliot: The Emergent Self*, was the first critic to consider these 'minor' writings seriously and to place them in the context of Eliot's launch into fiction writing, and I build upon her valuable work here.[108] While Redinger is keenly aware of the economics of this phase of Eliot's career, her direct concern is not with Eliot's attitudes to questions of intellectual property, which is my own primary interest here.

THE LIFTED VEIL: DEATH AND POSTERITY

Both the narrative and the protagonist of this novella, the sickly Latimer, are obsessed with death: 'continually recurring, was the vision of my death—the pangs, the suffocation, the last struggle, when life would be grasped at in vain'.[109] Why should Eliot have written so gloomy and bitter a first-person narrative, while she was in the middle of writing *The Mill on the Floss*, and just at the time that *Adam Bede* was enjoying its great success? Gillian Beer has cited *The*

---

[107] GE to John Blackwood (24 February 1861), *GEL* iii. 382–3, both quotations 382.

[108] See Ruby V. Redinger, *George Eliot: The Emergent Self* (1975), ch. 6, entitled 'My Present Past', which contains Redinger's valuable discussion of these texts.

[109] George Eliot, *The Lifted Veil*, in *George Eliot: The Lifted Veil and Brother Jacob*, ed. Helen Small (1999), 36. All references will hereafter be given in parentheses in the text.

Lifted Veil as an instance of Eliot's 'alternative imagination', and it certainly reveals something of the strain that she was under in the months leading up to her disclosure of her identity, as John Black-wood noticed, in his polite, but clearly horrified reception of the story, 'you must have been worrying and disturbing yourself about something when you wrote'.[110] In a later letter, he 'wish[es] the author in a happier frame of mind and not thinking of unsympathising untrustworthy keepers of secrets', connecting the story with Eliot's own worries about secrecy and exposure at this time.[111] The climactic transfusion scene in the novella centres upon 'the locking-up of something in Bertha's cabinet' (35) and in subtler ways, too, the chief organizing theme of the tale is dread of exposure.[112] The story starts as '[t]he time of my end approaches' (3) and continues 'always with a sense of moving onward' (3), ending with 'death . . . at hand' (39) and 'death . . . hovering' (40), finally closing upon 'the scene of my dying struggle' (43). From the first page, death is the known ending, and three deaths occur in the story before Latimer's own. Eliot's sister, Chrissey, died of tuberculosis in March 1859, just as the two were trepidatiously commencing a reconciliation after long years of coldness. Meanwhile, her long separation from her brother Isaac continued as if death had come between them. She was, therefore, intensely conscious of death as the interruption of any attempt to establish meaning, and the dread of the fate of her own reputation as a writer is perhaps figured by the failure of posthumous recuperation in the transfusion scene, in which 'the moment of death [is] the sealing of her secret' (41). Eliot's ambivalent desire for self-revelation and her simultaneous dread of its reception perhaps explains the curious tonal vacillation between hope and despair in this novella.

On 23 April 1859 the *Critic* had directed an attack on anonymous publishing at 'George Eliot' declaring that, 'anonymous authorship is really opposed, not only to the letter of the law, but to the moral good of society'.[113] On the same day, a writer in the *Leader* agreed: 'the critical law has always regarded such concealments as a species

---

[110] Gillian Beer, 'Putting on Man's Apparel: The Early Fiction', in *George Eliot* (1986), 52–81, 79. John Blackwood to GE (18 May 1859), *GEL* iii. 67–8, 67.

[111] John Blackwood to GE (8 July 1859), *GEL* iii. 112–13, 112.

[112] Kate Flint has suggested that the intravenous transfusion from male to female is important as an analogue of Eliot's sense of her own 'borrowed' creativity, 'Blood, Bodies, and *The Lifted Veil*', *Nineteenth-Century Literature*, 51/4 (March 1997), 455–73.

[113] Anon., 'Sayings and Doings', *Critic* (23 April 1859), 387.

of literary fraud'.[114] The *Critic*'s main contention was that the author's name underwrote the work in a way that encouraged—or discouraged—public confidence and trust in the product; the emphasis in the article was squarely on fairness to the consumer:

A name upon a title-page is some guarantee for the value of the book; for it enables you to test the author by his book, and the book by its author. Art is so long and life so short, that the question of whether a certain train of speculation is worth following or not, should be abbreviated as much as possible; and this the confession of the author's name tends very much to do.[115]

The sensation caused by the anonymous publication of Chambers's *Vestiges of Creation* in 1847 provided a point of reference: indeed, the *Critic* makes the comparison directly.[116] In principle, Eliot shared this view, at least as far as periodical publishing and reviewing were concerned.[117] Three days after these attacks appeared in print, Eliot completed *The Lifted Veil*. At this stage, she was still reading her critics, although a couple of months later Lewes was to put a stop to this, insisting that she be protected from harsh criticism.[118] The charge of fraudulence lodged deep in her, and all three of the short works she produced in the following year represent attempts to wrestle with her ambivalence about the provenance of her work, and the degree to which her credibility as a writer depended upon her publicly owning her own fiction. In some of its most embittered passages, *The Lifted Veil* seems directly to articulate her reaction to the kind of criticism expressed by the *Critic* and the *Leader*:

while the creative brain can still throb with the sense of injustice, with the yearning for brotherly recognition—make haste—oppress it with your ill-considered judgements, your trivial comparisons, your careless misrepresentations. The heart will by-and-by be still . . . Then your charitable speeches may find vent; then you may remember and pity the toil and the struggles and

---

[114] Anon., *Leader* (23 April 1859), 524. See *GEL* iii. 62 n.

[115] Anon., 'Sayings and Doings', *Critic* (23 April 1859), 387.

[116] See James A. Secord, *Victorian Sensation: The Extraordinary Publication, Reception, and Secret Authorship of Vestiges of the Natural History of Creation* (2000).

[117] George Eliot had, for example, a hand in drafting the prospectus for the *Fortnightly Review*, when Lewes became the editor in 1865, and the published prospectus made signed articles one of its most prominent policies. See Gordon S. Haight, *George Eliot: A Biography* (1968), 380.

[118] In fact, Eliot did not read these particular articles until a least a week after publication, but Blackwood reported their content to the couple on 27 April. See John Blackwood to George Eliot (27 April 1859); George Eliot to John Blackwood (29 April 1859) and GHL to John Blackwood (30 April 1859); *GEL* iii. 57–9, 60–1, 61–2.

the failure; then you may give due honour to the work achieved; then you may find extenuation for errors, and may consent to bury them.   (4)

Death seems to hold out the promise of recompense, or—in Andrew Bennett's phrase—a 'redemptive supplement': 'But we all have a chance of meeting with some pity, some tenderness, some charity, when we are dead: it is the living only who cannot be forgiven—the living only from whom men's indulgence and reverence are held off, like the rain by the hard east wind' (4).[119] If Eliot seems to stake some grim hope on a posthumous reputation, it is only through the bitterly ironic acknowledgement that to become immortal, one has first to die: 'the triumph comes suddenly, and we shudder at it, because it is held out by the chill hand of death' (22). Aware that her self-exposure must come soon as the author of *Adam Bede*, she is rehearsing the unforgivable visibility of the female body that such exposure will mean. She suggests that her literary reputation will finally depend upon her own bodily disappearance in death, but even this seems a precarious hope at times. Through Latimer she articulates her own anxiety about the future of her work, and therefore about its intrinsic value. Despite insisting upon Latimer's failure as a poet, it is to the analogy of literary writing that she turns to express his predicament, and, perhaps, her dread of her own ambition: 'the idea of future evil robbed the present of its joy, and for whom the idea of future good did not still the uneasiness of a present yearning or a present dread. I went dumbly through . . . the poet's suffering' (25). Her anxiety also circles around the Coleridgean distinction between fame and reputation. Latimer's bitter remark about his servants serves equally well for Eliot's anonymous critics and readers, '[t]hey judge of persons as they judge of coins, and value those who pass current at a high rate' (33). Even as she rides the wave of *Adam Bede*'s success, Eliot cannot trust that such an over-inflation will not lead to as sharp a devaluation of her literary 'currency'.

Latimer is a failed poet whose father has 'slight esteem' (281) for literature, and that '[t]o this negative view he added a positive one, derived from a recent connection with mining speculations; namely, that a scientific education was the really useful training for a younger son' (282). Eliot makes it explicit that Latimer's father's positive view of science is bound up with its money-making potential. This marks the start of what becomes, throughout *The Lifted Veil*, a concerted

---

[119] Andrew Bennett, *Romantic Poets and the Culture of Posterity* (1999), 75.

attempt on Latimer's part to distance the scientific, money-making
world from his own sensitive, artistic self. In the same scene Latimer
is subjected to a phrenological examination by Mr Letherall, whom
he describes as having 'pulled my head about as if he wanted to buy
and cheapen it' (282). Capitalist activity is figured by Latimer
throughout the story as violent and repugnant, unreflective and
grossly material. Latimer is a 'fragile, nervous, ineffectual' (14) narrator who often rebounds into a sense of his own fraudulence and the
meaninglessness of his existence, declaring that 'I shall leave no
works behind me for men to honour', and 'I have no near relatives
who will make up, by weeping over my grave, for the wounds they
inflicted on me when I was among them' (4). Latimer's misery—and
perhaps Eliot's too—seems peculiarly focused on the sense of estrangement that his 'unhappy gift of insight' (15) brings him and
upon his longing to escape the 'fatal solitude of soul in the society of
one's fellow-men' (7). He imagines a communicative exchange in
which he could '*believe* . . . in the listening ear and answering soul, to
which his song will be floated sooner or later'—in an emphatic passage that reflects Eliot's own deep and enduring concern with finding
a readership, and particularly a future readership ('sooner *or later*')
able to appreciate the moral value of her work. Lucy Newlyn has
suggested that for Romantic writers, the spectre of 'future readers
threaten[s] the sanctity and security of the author' and Eliot certainly
seems to have inherited what Newlyn terms 'the anxiety of reception'
in her anxiety to control the future reception of her work.[120] Latimer
insists that '[w]e learn *words* by rote, but not their meaning; *that*
must be paid for with our life-blood, and printed in the subtle fibres
of our nerves' (34), suggesting an active, even physical, model of
reading that eschews passivity and demands instead an arduous
commitment. Over her career, Eliot was to construct a model of a
morally strenuous readership that satisfied her need for a 'public'
sphere not defined economically, but rather as a sphere of moral
virtue and high culture. Such a model allowed her to fantasize something approaching an *exchange* between the writer and the actively
responsive reader.

G. H. Lewes, already acting as Eliot's husband and agent, asked
Blackwood in June 1859 if Eliot's signing *The Lifted Veil* in her own

---

[120] Lucy Newlyn, 'Coleridge and the Anxiety of Reception', *Romanticism*, 1/2
(1995), 206–38, 215. Newlyn extends some of the ideas in Harold Bloom's celebrated
The Anxiety of Influence: A Theory of Poetry (1973).

name might put a stop to the Liggins imposture. Blackwood, always the better tactician, dismissed the idea, which led to some coldness between him and the couple.[121] 'I did not care to use her name,' Blackwood explained later to a friend.[122] More directly, Eliot's friend Barbara Bodichon wrote with characteristic candour at around this time to warn her of a conversation with Owen Jones and his wife about the possible public reaction to the disclosure of the authorship of *Adam Bede*, 'they thought you would do the book more harm than the book would do you good in public opinion'.[123] She was right: after the disclosure Joseph Munt Langford recorded a friend's surprise after reading *Adam Bede*, that 'such a book can come from a polluted source'.[124] In the spring and early summer of 1859, Eliot was made morbidly aware of her own dubious social position and the possible damage this could cause to her literary reputation. In *The Lifted Veil* Latimer differentiates his readers into two groups, 'those who readily understand, and . . . those who will never understand' (34). Eliot's dislike of her own 'fraud' of anonymity and her desire to reveal her true identity conflict with her fear that the group of readers who do not understand, or the 'mass', may then come to predominate in their rejection of the transgressive female writer. Her anonymity becomes a hated necessity—a kind of *coverture*, which imprisons her while also protecting her. She writes bitterly about the alienation of her state through Latimer, 'the relation between me and my fellow men was more and more deadened' (36).

In *The Lifted Veil* Eliot is also worrying at the limits of her own intellectual property, and finally at the limits of her own selfhood, when she creates the 'torment' of Latimer's 'diseased participation in other people's consciousnesses' (17). Here she may be reflecting upon Charles Bracebridge's exposure of her appropriation of the life stories of local Nuneaton people in *Scenes of Clerical Life*, as she certainly felt a belated compunction about her own transgression into the private spaces of others.[125] But, more generally, she seems to be

---

[121]   GHL to John Blackwood (13 June 1859), *GEL* iii. 83.

[122]   John Blackwood to Joseph Munt Langford (18 November 1859), *GEL* iii. 206–7, 206.

[123]   Mme Eugène Bodichon to GE (28 June 1859), *GEL* iii. 102–3, 103. Lewes responded in a private 'P.P.S.' to this letter, asking Barbara not to send any such '*unpleasant*' information in future. GE and GHL to Mme Eugène Bodichon (30 June 1859), *GEL* iii. 105–6, 106.

[124]   Joseph Munt Langford to John Blackwood (23 August 1859), *GEL* iii. 209 n. 2.

[125]   Eliot wrote to John Gwyther, who claimed to be the original of Amos Barton, not denying his claim, but insisting on the 'large amount of arbitrary, imaginative

preoccupied by the difficulty of defining a line between mental privacy and public intellectuality. In September of 1859, writing of her own 'morbid sensibility', and of the 'pain . . . [which is a] clog on my mental activity', she clearly feels that her own privacy has been violated by the Liggins affair: 'I only wish I could write something that would contribute to heighten men's reverence before the secrets of each other's souls, that there might be less assumption of entire knowingness.'[126] Although her work relied more and more upon an appeal to 'other people's consciousnesses', she remained curiously aloof from close contact with those 'other people' who were her readers. Mrs Oliphant famously described her as 'kept . . . in a mental greenhouse' by Lewes, but the greenhouse was more of Eliot's own making than this suggests.[127] Lewes became her 'cover', but the woman behind was always ambivalent about the public and took her own prophylactic measures, too.

The Lifted Veil reveals Eliot's growing understanding of risk and self-exposure as crucial to the creative endeavour, and her acknowledgement that 'the maintenance of that doubt and hope and effort are the breath of its life' (29). In a hymn to 'the honey of probability' (29) she seems to accept the impossibility of 'lifting the veil' upon her future status as a writer, and that, instead, she must move blindly forward, through 'the thorny wilderness which must be still trodden in solitude, with bleeding feet' (21). Yet death, in the literal and literary sense, still haunts the tale. 'Our impulses, our spiritual activities, no more adjust themselves to the idea of their future nullity, than the beating of our heart, or the irritability of our muscles' (29): the concept of future nullity, dramatized by Latimer's silencing on the last page of the book by death, reveals Eliot's dread of the insecure posterity of her work. She is occasionally able, like Latimer, to imagine herself briefly in the role of the Romantic writer in the grip of determinism, 'I was too completely swayed by the sense that I was in the grasp of unknown forces, to believe in my power of self-release' (33).

addition' included in her version of the clergyman's story. GE to John Gwyther (15 June 1859), *GEL* iii. 85–6, 86. See also GE to John Blackwood (28 May 1858), *GEL* iii. 459–60. She writes about a letter received by Blackwood from Newdegate, claiming that Gilfil was his grandfather. She responds by claiming that her stories are made from 'a combination of subtle shadowy suggestions with certain actual objects and events', 459.

[126] GE to Charles Bray (26 September 1859), *GEL* iii. 162–4, 164.
[127] Margaret Oliphant, *The Autobiography of Margaret Oliphant: The Complete Text*, ed. Elisabeth Jay (1990), 15.

But she is equally aware of her writing as deliberate, and willed, even wilful—something which could not have been, 'I was only suffering the consequences of a deed which had been the act of my intensest will' (33). Finally, Latimer's narrative fails to offer any sure hope of posthumous recuperation, paralysed as it is by his sense of his own obliteration: 'And beyond all these, and continually recurring, was the vision of my death—the pangs, the suffocation, the last struggle, when life would be grasped at in vain' (36). This early tale drama-tizes, with a painful immediacy, 'the stress of creative energy' upon which Eliot was still brooding at the end of her writing career.[128]

BROTHER JACOB: THE CONSUMING READER AND CAVEAT EMPTOR

'[I]t was always my *fears* that painted my future for me,' claimed Eliot in the summer of 1860, and her habit of secrecy, underpinned by a fear of disclosure or theft, also animates the two short novellas that she wrote before she started *Silas Marner*.[129] In *Brother Jacob*, the first fiction Eliot wrote after her disclosure of her true identity, David Faux changes his name and invents a new genealogy for him-self, after stealing some guineas from his mother. In *The Lifted Veil*, Latimer's 'gift' of foresight robs him of the pleasure of speculation and, similarly, the proleptic narrative robs the reader of the suspense of an imagined future. Eliot's own identification with David and Latimer in these tales has been noticed before, but little has been said specifically about their connections with Eliot's own worries about her intellectual property.

Anthony Trollope agreed entirely with the *Critic*'s dislike of anonymous publishing in his *Autobiography*: 'It is as natural that a novel reader wanting novels should send to a library for those by George Eliot or Wilkie Collins, as that a lady when she wants a pie for a picnic should go to Fortnum & Mason.'[130] The female shopper, be it for books or pies, was much in Eliot's mind as she wrote *Brother Jacob* with her true identity—and sex—just exposed. Ease of

---

[128] George Eliot, 'How We Come to Give Ourselves False Testimonials, and Believe in Them', *The Impressions of Theophrastus Such* (1995), 97–104, 104. First pub-lished 1879.

[129] GE to Mme François d'Albert-Durade (3 July 1860), *GEL* iii. 313–14, 313.

[130] Anthony Trollope, *Autobiography* (1946), 187.

consumption, the principle of consumer selection, and the commodification and 'branding' of literature worried Eliot in ways that she explored tangentially in this curious short tale. With an appropriately culinary double entendre, she described it as 'only a trifle': a phrase that links the work not only with 'the abundant lozenges, candies, sweet biscuits and icings' sold by the story's 'calculating confectioner' anti-hero, but also with money in the tale—as David uses precisely the same expression to describe his father's legacy.[131] In this fable, which trembles on the brink of fairy tale and the truly fabulous, food and money are not only interchangeable, but seem to blur disturbingly into one another. The dancing master cannot give up his lessons, 'because he made his bread by them' (49); on a visit home, David 'partak[es] of the family beans' (51) by stealing his mother's savings; we are told that 'metaphysics would not have found him so much as salt to his bread' (49), and, in the most elaborately detailed scene of the story, he beguiles his brother Jacob by affecting to transform his mother's stolen guineas into yellow lozenges and back again. 'If he could only be kept so occupied with the lozenges as not to see the guineas before David could manage to cover them!' (54). The joint preoccupation in this anxious and highly worked scene with the fungibility of commodities, and with concealment and the threat of exposure, seems to relate very obviously to the Liggins affair, to the way in which Eliot's novels seem suddenly to have transmuted into money, and to her worries about their consumption, alongside her sense of her own fungibility, and her own magical change from anonymous journalist to brand-name novelist.[132] There is perhaps something disingenuous in Eliot's later claim that 'when a *name* is precisely the highest-priced thing in literature, any one who has a name will not, except when there is some strong motive for mystification, throw away the advantages of that name. I wrote anonymously while I was an unknown author, but I shall never, I believe, write anonymously again.'[133] The high-priced 'name' to which

---

[131] GE to Sara Sophie Hennell (25 June 1864), *GEL* iv. 155–7, 157. Under the title 'The Idiot Boy' the story was rejected by the publishers Sampson Low. Eventually Eliot gave it to George Smith at the *Cornhill* in recompense for the loss he had suffered over *Romola*: an act that was all the more generous because by then Chapman had made her a substantial offer for it. The stock of her name was rising.

[132] Alexander Welsh remarked that '[g]old literally makes an appearance at this time in Eliot's fiction,' and Ruby Redinger has suggested this relates to George Eliot's own influx of income as a result of the success of the 'big' novels. Alexander Welsh, *Eliot and Blackmail* (1985), 168. Redinger, *The Emergent Self*, 435.

[133] GE to Sara Sophia Hennell (23 April [1862]), *GEL* iv. 25–6, 25.

she now laid such proud claim was, however, still the pseudonym of 'George Eliot', and the writer constructed as George Eliot still partially 'covered' the woman, Marian Evans.

While the theme of theft must recall the Liggins affair, Eliot, like David Faux, has also been trading under an assumed name, 'Edward Freely was the name that shone in gilt letters on a mazarine ground over the doorplace of the new shop' (63), while 'George Eliot' shone in gilt letters on the cover of the first edition of *Adam Bede*. In the summer of 1859, the *Athenaeum*, one of the periodicals to which Eliot and Lewes subscribed, had attacked Eliot for her 'attempt to mystify the reading public', sneering that '[n]o woman of genius ever descended to such a *ruse*—no book was ever permanently helped by such a trick.' The article left Eliot 'very poorly and trembling' after reading it.[134] Eliot's story reflects both her own uneasy sense of fraudulence and trickery, and her retreat from such a construction into a reinstatement of a model of inherited tradition for artistic endeavour—when culinary skill is finally returned to the matrons and daughters of Grimworth.

The description of Freely's window display is revealingly conducted in highly artistic terms that link back to Eliot's discussion of realism and Dutch painting in chapter 17 of *Adam Bede*—it is variously 'a sight to bring tears into the eyes of a Dutch painter' and 'a faëry landscape in Turner's latest style'. Freely, who could 'invent delightful things in the way of drop-cakes' (50), and whose 'soul swelled with an impatient sense that he ought to become something very remarkable' (50), is linked to Eliot herself, albeit in terms that Helen Small has aptly described as 'robustly comic'.[135] Indeed, Eliot almost over-eggs the pudding when she adds, 'If he had fallen on the present times, and enjoyed the advantages of a Mechanics' Institute, he would certainly have taken to literature and have written reviews' (50). The story does, however, reveal anxieties and vulnerabilities that make it, or its author, seem rather less than robust at times. It is, after all, significant that David Faux is the male 'professional' exponent of a traditionally female amateur art-form—fancy cooking. Part of the comedy derives from his anomalous position as usurper

---

[134] 'The only papers we see are the Athenaeum and Saturday Review,' GHL to John Blackwood (30 April 1859), *GEL* iii. 61–2, 61. Anon., 'The Weekly Gossip', *Athenaeum* (2 July 1859), 20. GE to Mme Eugène Bodichon (2 July 1859), *GEL* iii. 108–9, 109.

[135] Helen Small, 'Introduction', *George Eliot: The Lifted Veil and Brother Jacob*, p. xxx.

of the domestic culinary skills of Mrs Mole and Mrs Chaloner, but his anomalous gender-position, like that of Latimer in *The Lifted Veil*, seems to reflect in mirror-image Eliot's sense of her own ambition to usurp the male world of serious professional literature, and to eschew the amateurish female literary marketplace of light confections and 'silly novels', in her own phrase. Yet, what makes the novella confusing, despite its presentation as a fable, with an obligingly obvious epigraph from La Fontaine, is Eliot's own slippage in the text—under the cover of a somewhat inscrutable irony, she moves her own subject-position from the producer to the consumer, and then transforms the consumers back to producers. It is never quite clear whose side she is really on.

For, while Eliot seems to identify herself up to a point with David, the most engaged focus in this story is not on artistic production, but on consumption: it is full of eating, from Jacob's 'gustative content' (54) as he munches David's yellow lozenges, to Penny Palfrey's looking 'like a fresh white-heart cherry going to be bitten off the stem by [David's] lipless mouth' (79).[136] Eliot's real ambivalence in this tale is less about her own role as artist, anonymous or otherwise, than about the effects of her work and her name on her consumers—her new reading public. She describes a display culture that makes value difficult to calculate, and which demands wariness from shoppers:

if new-comers were to bring in the system of neck-and-neck trading, and solicit feminine eyes by gown-pieces laid in fan-like folds, and surmounted by artificial flowers, giving them a factitious charm (for on what human figure would a gown sit like a fan, or what female head was like a bunch of China-astars?), or, if new grocers were to fill their windows with mountains of currants and sugar made seductive by contrast and tickets,—what security was there for Grimworth, that a vagrant spirit in shopping, once introduced, would not in the end carry the most important families to the larger market town of Cattleton, where, business being done on a system of small profits and quick returns, the fashions were of the freshest, and the goods of all kinds might be bought at an advantage?   (61–2)

---

[136] Susan de Sola Rodstein has noticed this too, remarking, 'Indeed, cooking and eating, her most private metaphors of literary creation (usually confined to her correspondence), structure *Brother Jacob*.' She goes on to argue that the story recommends hoarding over spending, whereas I would contest that it merely recommends spending wisely. Susan de Sola Rodstein, 'Sweetness and Dark: George Eliot's "Brother Jacob"', *Modern Language Quarterly*, 52/3 (1991), 295–317, 295.

While this passage seems ironically to imply that competitive commercialism—'a vagrant spirit in shopping'—is a social good in guaranteeing fresher, cheaper goods, the idea is immediately countered by the fear of the Grimworth consumer that cheapness does not guarantee quality. Mimicking the argument used by the Reform periodicals at an earlier period against the introduction of cheap publications, the Grimworth conservatives worry that strangers could trade in 'showy and inferior articles—printed cottons and muslins which would leave their dye in the wash-tub, jobbed linen full of knots, and flannel that would soon look like gauze' (62). The Lewes's friend, Herbert Spencer, had just completed an essay on 'The Morals of Trade' in which he had declared that 'trade is essentially corrupt . . . It has been said that the law of the animal creation is— "Eat and be eaten;" and of our trading community it may similarly be said that its law is—Cheat and be cheated.'[137] Indeed, 1857 and 1858 had been ignominious years for commerce, with over-speculation and fraudulent trading leading to a series of bank collapses. One commentator estimated that '[f]*ifty millions sterling* are computed as the liabilities of the mercantile houses who have succumbed to the pressure of the last few months and the losses which will result from their suspension, are but a small part of those of the whole community,' and goes on to call for the more effective criminalization of 'the fraud and dishonesty with which our commercial honour is so deeply stained'.[138] The old principle of caveat emptor was becoming much more difficult for the consumer, in a market that was no longer local. That Eliot saw this as extending to the literary profession is clear in her late essay 'Moral Swindlers' in which she compares 'a man who uses either official or literary power as an instrument of his private partiality or hatred, or a manufacturer who devises the falsification of wares, or a trader who deals in virtueless seed-grains', but it is also implicit in the much earlier *Brother Jacob*.[139]

In Eliot's passage, though, it is specifically 'feminine eyes' that are 'solicit[ed]' by people such as Eliot herself, who come from 'nobody knew where', and Eliot seems primarily troubled here by the idea of

[137] Herbert Spencer, 'The Morals of Trade' (1859), in *Essays, Scientific, Political, and Speculative* (1996), iii. 113–51, 138. The essay was originally published in the *Westminster Review* in April 1859.

[138] William Romaine Callender, *The Commercial Crisis of 1857: Its Causes and Results. Being the Substance of a Paper Read Before the Manchester Statistical Society* (1858), 5 and 37.

[139] George Eliot, 'Moral Swindlers', *Theophrastus Such* (1995), 121–8, 126.

her female readership. Perhaps she is responding to Barbara
Bodichon's delight at her novels' anonymous successes, '*that you*
whom they spit at should do it!'—it may be Eliot's fear that she will
not only be spat at, but spat out by her genteel female readers, now
that her identity is known, that animates the energetic disgust which
accompanies many of the descriptions of eating in the tale.[140] The
guineas, even as they are transformed into lozenges by Faux, 'vomit
forth' (53) from their leather bag, and the tale often tips into nausea,
framing its descriptions of sugary excess through 'the eyes of a bil-
ious person' (63). Much of the disgust coagulates around Faux himself, with his 'pasty visage, lipless mouth, and stumpy hair' (51), as
he perpetrates 'the gradual corruption' (64), 'perversion', and 'the
growing demoralization' (65) of Grimworth's females. Eliot's own
sense of sexual transgression projected on to Faux certainly seems
less than robustly comic, as she articulates, albeit 'from a great distance', her worries about her own perceived corruption and contam-
ination of her female readership.[141] But then the focus changes, and
the agency becomes confused: 'In short, the business of manufacturing the more fanciful viands was fast passing out of the hands of
maids and matrons in private families, and was becoming the work
of a special commercial organ . . . I am not ignorant that this sort of
thing is called the inevitable course of civilization, division of labour'
(66). In one generalizing stride, Eliot moves to a discussion of professionalization and specialization, which problematizes a straightforward reading of Faux's confectionary as analogous to Eliot's
creativity. Nevertheless, in the fantasy that follows of the halting
of the 'inevitable course' of competitive capitalism, Eliot reveals her
own uneasiness with the 'cheapening' of the commercial literary
marketplace, and articulates her wistful desire to relocate her own
creativity in the private sphere, becoming a Mrs Palfrey, who 'like
other geniuses, wrought by instinct rather than by rule, and possessed no receipts' (72) and whose '[k]nowledge . . . is like Titian's
colouring, difficult to communicate' (72). As in *Cousin Phillis*, invention finds its way into the kitchen in this story—but while
Gaskell's novella suggested that even the kitchen—especially the
kitchen—would be changed by the onward march of technological

[140] Mme Eugène Bodichon to GE (26 April [1859]), 56–7, 56.
[141] Alexander Welsh, *George Eliot and Blackmail* (1985), 163, noticed that Eliot's
portrayal of Freely 'treat[s] from a great distance themes of particular interest to the
author', but he does not go on to explore these themes.

change, *Brother Jacob* shows female invention in retreat to the kitchen, as progress is halted and we are returned to the past by 'a fine peripateia or downfall by which the progress of the corruption was ultimately checked' (64). Eliot, both having and eating her cake, fantasizes a return to amateur production for private consumption, while ruefully recognizing her own kinship with the 'professional' and financially greedy capitalist, Faux. Her uncomfortable shift from producer to consumer and back again in the tale demonstrates her anxiety at the moment of her 'unveiling' about the subsequent re-evaluation of her own confections, and her desire to please the palate of the novel-reading public—a public which she knew to be predominantly female. And underlying all of this is the wistful desire of the exile to settle herself into Mrs Palfrey's comfortable, conventional, female kitchen, and not to feel out of place there. The story seems to reflect Eliot's confusion about her own literary output: her fantasy of private, affectionate, amateur production for a known community, and her painful and slightly queasy recognition of the realities of the book trade in the mid-nineteenth century.

As Peter Allan Dale notes, David Faux is a young man greatly given to calculating consequences, although he is unable to second-guess his simple brother, Jacob, 'I doubt whether [Jacob] would not have puzzled the astute heroes of M. de Balzac, whose foresight is so remarkably at home in the future' (56).[142] George Eliot had first read Balzac's tale of the miser, *Le Père Goriot*, in October 1855, and described it as 'a hateful book'. She was again reading Balzac in spring and summer of 1859, throughout the period of most intense strain as Liggins and Bracebridge both made her anonymity difficult to preserve, and the future of her own writerly identity was in question. Despite her revulsion from Balzac's novel, she was clearly fascinated by his view of chance and futurity.[143] David's gambling calculations ultimately fail him, his credit collapses: 'how is he to foresee the day of sad wisdom' (144) and *Brother Jacob*, as we have seen, ends by restoring the pre-commercial past, where value is predicated upon the inheritance of the 'secrets of the finer cookery' into which

---

[142] Peter Allan Dale, 'George Eliot's "Brother Jacob": Fables and the Physiology of Common Life', *Philological Quarterly*, 64/1 (1985), 17–35, 27.

[143] George Eliot, *Essays* (1966), 146. Elizabeth Gaskell was also influenced by Balzac in the 1860s, as a mention of 'Eugenie Grandet' (1833) in one of her letters confirms. *FLG* 146, n. 3. Philip Yarrow suggests that *Cousin Phillis* resembles Balzac's novel in its main outline. Philip Yarrow, 'Mrs. Gaskell and France', *Gaskell Society Journal*, 7 (1993), 16–36, 31.

'daughters [a]re again anxious to be initiated' (87): the 'growing heritage' is protected from the chanciness and disruption of commercial competition.[144] Finally, a Burkean ideal of inheritance surplants a flexible and contractual model of property in the tale.

The dénouement of *Silas Marner*, like that of *Cousin Phillis*, is brought about by the incursion of new technology into the backward landscape of Raveloe. Godfrey Cass 'had gone into the draining', Mr Osgood's fields are being drained (148), and it is this that leads to the discovery of Dunstan's drowned skeleton. It is the change that Silas has learnt to accept, 'Eppie, things *will* change, whether we like it or no; things won't go on for a long while just as they are and no difference' (149). But there is also a significant difference between Gaskell's novella and *Silas Marner*. While Gaskell ends *Cousin Phillis* with Phillis on the brink of leaving for Birmingham, Silas's trip back to 'the streets of a great manufacturing town' (177) happens before the end of Eliot's story. A factory stands on the site of the old Lantern Yard, and Silas leaves 'bewildered by the changes thirty years had brought' (177), unable to find anyone with any memory of his former Chapel. Gaskell's story ends with a young woman moving outwards towards the risks and contingencies of modern urban life, but *Silas Marner* ends with Marner in retreat from the city, and with Eppie's dismissal of it as 'a dark, ugly place' (178). That Eliot returns them to Raveloe betrays less of a conservatism, perhaps, than a doubleness—Marner is both returned and uprooted. He is, in fact, forced to realize with brutal clarity the discontinuities of his existence and the annihilation of the past, 'The old home's gone; I've no home but this now' (179). Alexander Welsh noticed that '[a]ll [Eliot's] later novels contain within the action a marked discontinuity between the present and some experience of the past that has been deliberately or otherwise forgotten,' but I would suggest that such discontinuities and forced forgettings are just as clearly, and just as painfully, a part of her earlier fiction, too.[145]

---

[144] Eliot used this phrase in the epigraph that she added to *The Lifted Veil* in 1873, and it appeared in print for the first time in the Cabinet Edition of 1878.

[145] Welsh, *George Eliot and Blackmail*, 159.

From 'the little bag of church money' (12), to the 'desirable tithes' (7) of Raveloe, to the fireside chat in the Rainbow where time is measured 'since afore the Queen's heads went out on the shillings' (52), money or references to money appear on almost every page of *Silas Marner*.[146] Yet Eliot is at pains to emphasize, too, that Raveloe represents an economy at an early stage of development, which stands 'aloof from the currents of industrial energy and Puritan earnestness' of the commercial towns. Her story starts in the late eighteenth century, when Silas is already one of 'the remnants of a disinherited race' (5), and by the end of the tale his trade is moribund: 'he had nothing but what he worked for week by week, and when the weaving was going down too—for there was less and less flax spun' (141). In fact, even at mid-century, hand-loom weavers continued to ply their trade, as is clear from Mayhew's description of the dismal trip to Manchester in *Mr. Sandboys*, and as the *Edinburgh Review* of 1849 had noticed before him:

the weaving machines did not at first appear so hopelessly superior. The hand-loom weavers found themselves able to 'live in the race' with the steam engine, although at a terrible sacrifice. The competition has been persevered in, with melancholy pertinacity, to the present day;—until Society has the burden and the scandal of a numerous class of individuals, industrious but ill-judging, who have, even in good times, to battle for a bare subsistence against fearful odds; and who, in the frequently recurring periods of depression, present the most afflicting spectacles.[147]

By the 1850s and 1860s, then, hand-loom weavers had come to represent precisely the painful 'uneven development' of modern manufacturing techniques that left a 'disinherited race' still clinging to outmoded technologies. Indeed, in 1860 Eliot was much taken up with the collapse of the ribbon industry in Coventry, and the consequent suffering among the weavers that she observed through her friend Charles Bray's letters.[148] This perhaps contributed to her portrait of Silas as obsolescent if not yet obsolete, accompanied by a sense of belatedness, and representing a rupture with the past, which contemporary readers would have recognized as sharply topical. The

---

[146] *Silas Marner: The Weaver of Raveloe* (1996). All references will hereafter appear in parenthesis in the text.

[147] Anon., '*The Patent Journal*', *Edinburgh Review* (1849), 47–83, 79.

[148] Charles Bray was a ribbon manufacturer who attempted to help the ribbon weavers at this crisis. See Efraim Sicher, 'George Eliot's "Glue Test": Language, Law, and Legitimacy, in *Silas Marner*', *Modern Language Review*, 94/1 (1999), 11–21.

atmosphere of loss and disinheritance emanating from Silas, and the intense wish-fulfilment of his release from his solitary occupation by the arrival of Eppie, all surely point to a connection with George Eliot herself. The double perspective of the text that both insists on the economic realities of circulation and exchange, but also holds Silas separate from this reality, looking back on an imagined past, is tied up with Eliot's fear that literary property achieves value only through exchange and circulation, and the conflict of this with her wish for an innate and stable value for her work.

Alexander Welsh has noticed that 'Marner . . . is like an intellectual without book-learning,' and Rosemarie Bodenheimer has compared him directly to George Eliot, both 'living internal lives completely at odds with the prevailing opinions about them'.[149] Silas Marner is not an inventor, but he is an 'artisan' (9) who 'work[s] at his vocation' (6) and is regarded with distrust by the people of Raveloe who view strangers as 'aliens' (6), and are suspicious of his 'reputation for knowledge' and his 'skill in handicraft' (5). The sound of his loom is 'questionable', not 'natural' like the 'winnowing-machine' or the flail (6). His perceived 'unnaturalness' may well link to Eliot's worry about her own skilled craft of novel-making, and her perilous status as the unmarried companion of Lewes. Marner's solitude as he 'worked at his vocation' in a 'state of loneliness' (6) reflects the stereotype of the male heroic creator, but it also articulates Eliot's own female experience of writing at this time. After her return from Germany with Lewes in 1857, 'ladies' no longer visited her, and she speaks of her new pug dog, who arrived in Wandsworth at the end of July 1859 (a gift from her publisher, John Blackwood), as coming 'in compensation for lost friends'.[150] The connections of loss and recompense are much in her thoughts at this time, and her losses had been great. She was doubly outcast by her relationship with Lewes, and by her creativity. As Mill had sadly observed in his 'On Liberty', 'the man, and still more the woman, who can be accused either of doing "what nobody does," or of not doing "what everybody does", is the subject of as much depreciatory remark as if he or she had committed some grave moral delinquency'.[151] In writing novels, Eliot was already not doing 'what everybody does': and on

---

[149] Welsh, *George Eliot and Blackmail*, 161, and Rosemarie Bodenheimer, *The Real Life of Mary Ann Evans: George Eliot, Her Letters and Fiction* (1994), 205.

[150] GE to Mme Eugène Bodichon (27 July [1859]), *GEL* iii. 123–4, 123.

[151] J. S. Mill, 'On Liberty', *On Liberty and Other Essays* (1991), 76.

top of this she really had committed, in the eyes of Victorian society, and indeed, in her own eyes to a certain extent, a 'grave moral delinquency'. Rather than cultivating the male stereotype of the autonomous solitary creator, she actively constructed a different model of herself as literary artist, and some of the negotiations she is in the process of making at this time with traditional notions of authorship and literary property are projected in *Silas Marner*.

What Marner is creating at his loom is money, not cloth. The cloth is merely fungible. At first, Marner seems to 'weave, like the spider, from pure impulse' (16), but when he accumulates a surplus, he starts to hoard. The analogy between Marner's hoarding of his guineas and intellectual hoarding is made explicit, '[h]is life had reduced itself to the functions of weaving and hoarding, without any contemplation of an end towards which the functions tended'—Eliot is careful to point out that this hoarding impulse can be also be observed in those working on 'erudite research, some ingenious project, or some well-knit theory' (20). Marner's gold at one level stands for intellectual property, and this is a familiar association for Eliot, who had reversed the analogy in a letter to Blackwood discussing her writerly identity in 1858, '[o]ne ought to say "No" to an impertinent querist as one would decline to open one's iron chest to a burglar.'[152] If we follow the clue and read Marner as analogous to other kinds of intellectual labourers, we find that the first impulse underlying the hoarding is proprietorial: 'it was pleasant to feel them in his palm, and look at their bright faces, *which were all his own*' (17).[153] But in order to preserve this enjoyable sense of ownership, and even of perfect identity with the money, Marner, who has 'no relation to any other being' (20) cannot exchange his coins, 'he would on no account have exchanged those coins, which had become his familiars, for other coins with unknown faces' (19).[154] This describes an artistic problem for Eliot that links her to Dickens and Thackeray in the last chapter: the problem of establishing property in intellectual labour. In Eliot's case this problem was rendered even more urgent as she had recently been forced to disclose her own name, and was only just 'owning up' to her work. Marner's worry is that in 'spending' his

---

[152] GE to John Blackwood (1 December 1858), *GEL* ii. 505.
[153] Emphasis added.
[154] Jeff Nunokawa has read Marner's hoarding of the gold as a sexual metaphor for a masturbatory refusal of contact or circulation. Jeff Nunokawa, *The Afterlife of Property: Domestic Security and the Victorian Novel* (1994).

gold, and sending it into circulation, he will lose it and encounter instead only 'unknown faces'. For Eliot, the worry was to do with publication, which threatened her already precarious identity in forcing her to encounter the 'unknown faces' of the novel-reading public, which she envisaged as either hostile, ignorant, undeserving—or frequently, all three.

Spending in the tale is generally questionable—the 'swopping and betting' (24) of the unregenerate Cass brothers, who both overspend to excess, ends in disaster for both of them. Yet the alternative offered by Marner, to continue to hoard, is also clearly and strongly figured as morally wrong. Warnings of the harmfulness of intellectual hoarding had often been issued in the course of the patent debate, '[t]here are many secret inventions of value, which it is not the interest of inventors to disclose under the present system; but they are practised in secret, to a very limited extent by one individual, so that the public derive only a very small benefit from them.'[155] Eliot seems to display a similar worry about holding back from circulation. Her tale implies that art that is not 'spent' can be neither instrumental, nor of benefit to the public. She warns that the solitariness of the inventor can become like Silas's self-absorption in his hoarded gold, 'a hard isolation' (43). That true value only accrues through use is clear in the discussion over the 'ownership' of Eppie when Godfrey Cass tries to claim her back: 'I've a natural claim on her that must stand before any other' (169), he says, but Eliot makes it clear that by failing to disclose his paternity he has forfeited any 'right' to his daughter. Property resides in use, not in statutes alone, and Eppie is now Marner's daughter. Godfrey is forced to realize that 'there's debts we can't pay like money debts, by paying extra for the years that have slipped by' (174). Eliot seems to suggest through Godfrey's hoarding of his secret, that disavowal undermines ownership, and thus she links the text once more to her own confusion over her disclosure of authorship. She had written to Blackwood in April 1859 that 'while I would willingly, if it were possible—which it clearly is not—retain my incognito as long as I live, I can suffer no one to bear my arms on his shield'.[156] Through Godfrey, she shows the justice of Marner's claim on Eppie, while resisting Liggins's claim upon her work, thus

[155] 'Patents for Inventions; Report from Select Committee on the Law Relative to Patents for Inventions. Ordered by House of Commons to be Printed 12 June 1829', *Reports from Committees 1829*, i. 415–676, 134 (548).
[156] GE to John Blackwood (Wandsworth, 29 April 1859), *GEL* iii. 60–1, 60.

proving to herself that her art (and, indeed, her remuneration for her art), belong to her not because it bears, or doesn't bear, her name, but rather because it represents her labour. At the same time, she is able to reassure herself that she has done the right thing in publicly laying claim to her work.

So, if both hoarding and spending are wrong, Eliot searches for a role for property that is wholesome. With Eppie's arrival, Marner finds a reason for his work. While his gold had been 'hidden away from the daylight' (125), Eppie is a child 'seeking and loving sunshine' (125), and Marner slowly begins to come out of hiding and to expose himself to the bright light of the future: 'The gold had kept his thoughts in an ever-repeated circle, leading to nothing beyond itself; but Eppie was an object compacted of changes and hopes that forced his thoughts onward, and carried them far from their old eager pacing towards the same blank limit—carried them away to new things that would come with the coming years' (125). Eppie becomes the means of a meaningful circulation and exchange: it is because of her that the women of Raveloe start to visit and take Marner into their confidence. Marner no longer hoards once there is an object and purpose in Eppie. Eliot described her self-disclosure to Elizabeth Gaskell in similar terms of exposure to the light, 'now that I am ceased to be a mystery and am known as a mere daylight fact'.[157] She wrote to Blackwood that she wanted *Adam Bede* to be 'a real instrument of culture', and she shows Eppie becoming exactly this for Marner.[158] For writing to be instrumental, it must be put into circulation, exchanged, and used: it cannot be hoarded. In *Silas Marner*, she rejects the stereotype of the original solitary genius in favour of a more dynamic model of literary agency, which places as much emphasis on the transmission of culture to her readers, as on its production. Eppie 'force[d] [Marner's] thoughts onward . . . carried them away to new things', just as Barbara Bodichon early recognized in Eliot's writing 'a power to sway the people', and Eliot was to place more and more emphasis on the moral influence of her writing on its readers throughout her career.[159] In his grief and isolation, after Dunstan's theft and before Eppie arrives, Marner thinks '[f]ormerly his heart had been as a locked casket with its treasure

---

[157] GE to Mrs William Gaskell (Wandsworth, 11 November 1859), *GEL* iii. 198–9.
[158] GE to John Blackwood (Wandsworth, 10 April 1859), *GEL* iii. 43–4, 44.
[159] Mme Eugène Bodichon to GE (30 June–1 July 1859), *GEL* iii. 107–8, 107.

inside; but now the casket was empty, and the lock was broken. Left groping in darkness, with his prop utterly gone, Silas had inevitably a sense, though a dull and half-despairing one, that if any help came to him it must come from without' (81). Eliot, too, seems to feel that, after the violation of her property by Liggins and Bracebridge, and her forced exposure, the help must come from 'without'. Even though she was morbidly sensitive to criticism, 'I *do* feel more than I ought about outside sayings and doings,' she also realized that her books would be worthless if unread.[160] Rejecting the conventional masculine model of the writer, with its focus on inspiration and production, she reaches towards a more feminized (but not exactly female) model of literary ownership and value instead. As Silas recovers his connections to his community, he is increasingly feminized in the text, although it remains critical that he was not conceived as a female character. While Eliot wants to feminize the model, she equally rejects a directly female example. Silas becomes, after all, both 'father and mother' (141) to Eppie.[161]

In *Silas Marner*—'quite a sudden inspiration' that came just at the time that Eliot adopted Lewes's three sons—the child becomes strangely confused with literary labour.[162] It is, in fact, as Rosemarie Bodenheimer notices, around this time that Eliot starts to refer to her books as 'children'.[163] The motto of the tale is taken from Wordsworth, 'A child, more than all other gifts | That earth can offer to declining man, | Brings hope with it, and forward-looking thoughts'. If the child in *Silas Marner* is representative of Eliot's work, it reveals her fantasy of linking herself back into the world (130), and, importantly, of linking herself, through her literary work and her relationship with Lewes, to the future and 'forward-looking thoughts'. Lewes himself employs the analogy when he writes to Blackwood that, 'Mrs. Lewes . . . will rock the cradle of the new "little stranger" with fresh maternal vigour,' and Eliot calls *The Mill on the Floss* 'my youngest child' in a letter of 1860.[164] In *Silas Marner* children repeatedly figure futurity: the childless Nancy, for example,

[160]   GE to John Blackwood (Wandsworth, 16 October 1859), *GEL* iii. 184–5, 184.

[161]   Nancy Paxton has briefly discussed Eliot's use of 'maternal' feelings as descriptive of her relationship to her work. See Nancy Paxton, *George Eliot and Herbert Spencer: Feminism, Evolutionism, and the Reconstruction of Gender* (1991), 24–5.

[162]   GE to Charles Bray (Hastings, 19 March 1861), *GEL* iii. 391–2, 392.

[163]   Bodenheimer, *The Real Life of Mary Ann Evans*, 230.

[164]   GHL to John Blackwood (22 July 1859), *GEL* iii. 117. GE to William Blackwood (24 August 1860), *GEL* iii. 334–5, 335.

laments that 'a man wants something that will make him look forward more' (155). The traditional trope of the work of art as child appears often, of course, in the copyright and patent debates, and, indeed, Wordsworth himself used it. As Rosemary Coombe reminds us, the comparison is useful to those who seek to extend copyright protection because '[t]he child is the means by which the father's immortality is to be realized.'[165] The arguments to improve copyright and patent protection, as we have seen, placed their emphasis on the moral importance of providing for posterity, and on delivering inheritable property. Marner looks forward to a developing understanding and exchange 'with the coming years, when Eppie would have learned to understand how her father Silas cared for her' (125), just as Eliot looked forward hopefully to a growing understanding with her readers. But, while Eliot is taking up a well-rehearsed trope when she uses Eppie to stand for value and posterity, the trope traditionally refers to paternity. Indeed, female reproductivity was more often used to explain women's supposed lack of investment in the public field of artistic creativity. It is, then, unsurprising that in all three of these texts Eliot identifies herself with a male character, which allows her to figure her creativity without exposing herself to difficult questions about her own womanhood and reproductive status.[166]

In *Silas Marner*, Eliot feminizes a male character, mirror-imaging her own masculinization through her pseudonym, but also—and more positively—suggesting a different model of the relationship to labour. A neighbour compliments Marner, 'you're partly as handy as a woman, for weaving comes next to spinning' (130), and in his

---

[165] The trope was common in the Renaissance period. Shakespeare compares writing to 'Those children nurst, delivered from thy braine, | To take a new acquaintance of thy minde,' Sonnet 77, *Shakespeare's Sonnets*, ed. Katherine Duncan-Jones (1998), 265. The Renaissance trope of the child as textual copy is recalled by George Eliot in *Middlemarch*, ch. 29, when she writes that from Casaubon's point of view, an important result of marriage would be that he would be able to 'leave behind him that copy of himself which seemed so urgently required of a man—to the sonneteers of the sixteenth century'. For Casaubon, human and literary posterity are confused, and—of course—he ends up leaving neither behind him. See also Rosemary J. Coombe, 'Challenging Paternity: Histories of Copyright', Review Article, *Yale Journal of Law and the Humanities*, 6 (1994), 397–422, 404.

[166] In later work, such as her poem, *Armgart*, and the later novel, *Daniel Deronda*, Eliot does grapple more directly with the problem of the female artist. See Kathleen Blake, '*Armgart*—George Eliot on the Woman Artist', *Victorian Poetry*, 18 (1980), 75–80.

'mothering', Silas finds himself absorbed in a new kind of feminized work that seems less alienated than the other, '[t]he weaving must stand still a long while this morning, for now Eppie must be washed and have clean clothes on' (111). This work is absorbing and forward-looking, rather than circular, '[h]e had plenty to do through the next hour' (111). When Eppie tells Godfrey Cass that if he asked her to leave Marner, '[y]ou'd cut us i' two' (170), she reminds us again of the unalienated labour that Marner has invested in her. The feminized Marner comes to stand for the masculinized Eliot in her search for a value for her literary labour which exists both beyond the marketplace and beyond traditional constructions of the (male) artist. Gillian Beer, among others, has noticed that Eliot's work is full of adopted children, and I suggest that this allows her to metaphorize children, while avoiding the over-identification that is assumed to be involved in the biological maternal relationship.[167] A child that comes, in Wordsworth's phrase, as 'a gift', like Eppie, can represent the contingency and chanciness of creativity or 'production' while remaining distinct and separate, with none of the complications of biological reproduction. She is both 'owned' by Marner, and belongs only to herself, just as '[m]y books don't seem to belong to me after I have once written them,' as Eliot remarked while writing *Silas Marner*.[168] Thus, she is able to negotiate the traditional trope of paternity for literary creativity in a way that both contains and effaces her female identity. Just as Marner is reorientated to the future by the child, Eppie, the value that Eliot locates is in the future, in the gift that she can make to posterity through her writing—the way in which she can, herself, become 'an instrument of culture'.

In the same letter in which she hopes *Adam Bede* will become 'a real instrument of culture', she jokes with Blackwood about the rumour that Liggins has given 'his' manuscript to Blackwoods 'freely' (44). 'Conceive the real George Eliot's feelings, conscious of being a base worldling—not washing his own slop-basin, and *not* giving away his M.S.!' (44). Eliot's sense of herself as a 'base worldling' and her need to see herself as the creator of 'instruments of culture' are not as opposed as they at first seem. Anxieties about the marketplace do surface in *Silas Marner*. Doctor Kimble, we are told by the narrator, was 'not one of those miserable apothecaries

---

[167] Gillian Beer, *George Eliot* (1986).
[168] GE to François d'Albert-Durade (London, 29 January 1861), *GEL* iii. 373–4, 374.

who canvas for practice in strange neighbourhoods' (98), for example. But Eliot, by her own admission, enjoyed earning money, and Lewes acted so energetically as her agent, that he was described by George Simpson as 'an avaricious soul'.[169] When Blackwood offered her a bonus payment of £400 in recognition of the huge success of *Adam Bede*, she wrote back to him, 'I certainly care a great deal for the money, as I suppose all anxious minds do that love independence and have been brought up to think debt and begging the two deepest dishonours short of crime.'[170] While at first she was playful with the idea of Liggins, as soon as she heard that he was receiving financial donations as a result of his false claim, she felt the situation was 'getting serious' (53) and she and Lewes were soon attempting publicly to name him a 'swindler' and an 'imposter'.[171] Similarly, the disclaimer that appeared in the *Daily News* on 31 October 1859, against the publisher Newby's sequel to *Adam Bede*, dwelt on the financial implications of the deception, '[t]he unauthorised use of a popular author's title *for purely commercial purposes* is scarcely fair dealing towards the public.'[172] Clearly, it was not in her role as artist that she felt most threatened by Liggins and Newby, but rather in that of proprietor and stockholder. Nevertheless, the appeal is couched in terms that emphasize not so much the wronged producer as the wronged consumer: it is, she implies, her readers that she wishes to protect, as well as her profits.

I started my discussion of Eliot's work in this period by quoting E. S. Dallas's bewilderment with the incursion of chance into the narrative of *Silas Marner*. Reading the novel against Eliot's own troubles over her intellectual property and her worries about the future of her writing career, it becomes clear that she is more interested in chance than perhaps even she wants to admit. Chance in *Silas Marner* is emphatically double-edged. It brings great luck and great misfortune, and it makes, as we are reminded in ch. 9, a very bad mistress. In fact, this passage is so homiletic in tone that it was selected by Alexander

---

[169] George Simpson to Joseph Munt Langford (Edinburgh, 16 November 1859), *GEL* iii. 204–5.

[170] GE to John Blackwood (Wandsworth, 21 May 1859), *GEL* iii. 69–70, 69.

[171] Eliot and Lewes sent a letter to *The Times* calling Liggins an imposter and a swindler on 25 June 1859. GE to the Editor of *The Times* (Wandsworth, 25 June 1859), *GEL* iii. 92–3. Later, on the advice of John Blackwood, she suppressed the letter and it was never published. GE to John Blackwood (Wandsworth, 29 June 1859), 105.

[172] *Daily News* (31 October 1859), 3. *GEL* iii. 208 n. Emphasis added.

Main for his *Wise, Witty and Tender Sayings in Prose and Verse Selected from the Works of George Eliot*:[173]

Favourable Chance is the god of all men who follow their own devices instead of obeying a law they believe in. Let even a polished man of these days get into a position which he is ashamed to avow, and his mind will be bent on all the possible issues that may deliver him from the calculable results of that position. Let him live outside his income, or shirk the resolute honest work that brings wages, and he will presently find himself dreaming of a possible benefactor . . . not yet forthcoming . . . Let him forsake a decent craft that he may pursue the gentilities of a profession to which nature never called him, and his religion will infallibly be the worship of blessed Chance, which he will believe in as the mighty creator of success. The evil principle deprecated in that religion, is the orderly sequence by which the seed brings forth a crop after its kind.   (73–4)

Despite this manifesto, though, chance defiantly erupts in a novel that is informed by Eliot's sense of the chanciness of her own position, both her own great luck and the huge risk she is running. To some degree, after all, she herself had recently been found in a position that she was 'ashamed to avow', and had forsaken the 'decent craft' of journalism for the 'profession' of novel-writing, and had met with great success. Both Silas's losses, first of his reputation when he is framed for the theft in Lantern Yard, and then of his gold when Dunstan robs his house, happen while he is caught in a cataleptic trance and is 'powerless to resist' (110). They are, to that extent, accidents.[174] But Eppie arrives at just such another 'chancy' moment, so that Marner's redemption also comes by chance while he is unconscious. While Dallas quoted the Wordsworth motto to the novel as proof that Eliot's true interest in the story was not with chance, I would argue that, on the contrary, Eppie represents the 'happy accident' of inspiration, courted by genius 'placing itself in an attitude of receptivity towards all sublime chances', as Eliot puts it in another

[173] Alexander Main, *Wise, Witty and Tender Sayings in Prose and Verse Selected from the Works of George Eliot*, 4th *Edition With Supplementary Sayings from 'Daniel Deronda' and 'Theophrastus Such'* (1880), 156–7. The protracted warning against the underestimation of risk quoted below was also selected by Main, 158–9.

[174] Eliot had been fascinated by a trip to Pompeii 'suddenly arrested by the fiery deluge', on her visit to Italy in the summer of 1860, before she wrote *Silas Marner*. The sudden accidents or catastrophes in *Silas Marner*, during which Marner is caught motionless, may owe something to her impressions of the site. GE to Mrs Richard Congreve (Naples, 5 May 1860), *GEL* iii. 292–3, 293.

novel.[175] Certainly, she describes *Silas Marner* itself as just such a chance inspiration, 'I am writing a story which came across all my other plans by a sudden inspiration,' she told Blackwood.[176]

After all, in ch. 5, Eliot had deliberately reinforced the presence of chance in the novel by referring directly to the new theories of probability:

[Marner was] free from the presentiment of change. The sense of security more frequently springs from habit than from conviction, and for this reason it often subsists after such a change in the conditions as might have been expected to suggest alarm. The lapse of time in which a given event has not happened, is, in this logic of habit, constantly alleged as a reason why the event should never happen, even when the lapse of time is precisely the added condition which makes the event imminent. A man will tell you that he has worked in a mine for forty years unhurt by an accident as a reason why he should apprehend no danger, though the roof is beginning to sink; and it is often observable, that the older a man gets, the more difficult it is to him to retain a believing conception in his own death. This influence of habit was necessarily strong in a man whose life was as monotonous as Marner's—who saw no new people and heard of no new events to keep alive in him the idea of the unexpected and the changeful.   (41)

Like Gaskell, Eliot seems to insist on the inadequacy of the past to predict future events, and to give as sibylline a warning against neglecting the possibilities of accident as she does against courting chance. Main reprinted both these long admonitory passages as belonging to George Eliot '*In Propria Persona*', and they do seem to speak out of the text, and represent the two extremities between which Eliot herself is negotiating. Once again, hiding and hoarding, or the retreat from chance, are opposed to spending and gambling, or the reliance on chance. The opposition is not resolved: chance in Eliot's earlier fiction seems to signify both hope and fear—the fear of getting robbed and the hope of getting read.

George Levine has argued for George Eliot as a 'consistent determinist', but I would argue that her position, despite her enthusiastic

[175] Of Will Ladislaw in George Eliot's *Middlemarch*, ch. 10.

[176] GE to John Blackwood (London, 12 January 1861), *GEL* iii. 371–2, 371. Sally Shuttleworth is very suggestive on the rupture that these incursions of chance make upon George Eliot's concept of psychology. Sally Shuttleworth, '*Silas Marner*: A Divided Eden', in Nahem Yousaf and Andrew Maunder (eds.), *New Casebooks: The Mill on the Floss and Silas Marner* (2002), 204–24. See also Sally Shuttleworth, *George Eliot and Nineteenth-Century Science: The Make-believe of a Beginning* (1984).

engagement with Comte's ideas at this time, was much more flexible.[177] Comte was antagonistic to Quetelet's thinking about probability, which he misread, deploring the 'entire absence of Law' implied by the 'so-called Calculus of Chances'. Nevertheless, he recognized its importance.[178] Eliot was intensely conscious of the rupture in her own life, and aware that it was only by a series of accidents that she had arrived in the odd position of being a famous novelist. Yet admitting to the determining power of chance was risky for her, as it would mean exposing the contingency and precariousness of her own social and moral position, and facing up to the discontinuities of her own personal history and the rifts with her family. According to Comte's system, as Lewes characterized it, 'the past rules the present, lives in it, and that we are but the growth and outcome of the past', and Eliot strove to make sense of her own life in such a way.[179] She reaches for deterministic explanations, even as chance forces its way into her story. Even though Dunstan's theft is figured, as we have seen, as an unexpected accident, Eliot still gives a painstaking explanation of how the accident came about: because Marner had a piece of pork to roast for his supper, because he forgot the thread for his weaving and went out to get it, because he could not lock his door, because he was using the key to hang the pork over the fire to roast— this trail of detail leads with as sure a mechanism as that of Oedipus's demise, to Dunstan's robbery and Marner's despair. While it is inescapable that all narrative, once written, is determined, so that representing the openness of the future is invariably problematic, Eliot seems particularly self-conscious in the way in which she anxiously embeds chance events in her texts in the context of a greater determinism. In this, she seems to be following the very newest formulation of probability theory, which was only just emerging at this time. Hacking tells us that the idea of determinism as everything that happens forming a chain of causality came into play only in the period from the 1850s to 1870s.[180] But Eliot's anxious deterministic logic is also an attempt to resuscitate the Comtean ideal of fixed laws of de-

---

[177] George Levine, 'Determinism and Responsibility', *PMLA* 77 (June 1962), 268–79, repr. in Gordon S. Haight (ed.), *A Century of GE Criticism* (1965), 349–60, 349.

[178] Auguste Comte, *Système de politique positive* (1851–3), I. 381, quoted in Ian Hacking, *The Taming of Chance* (1990), 143.

[179] GHL and GE to Sara Sophia Hennell (Wandsworth, 9–10 July 1860), 318–20, 320.

[180] See Hacking, *The Taming of Chance*, 142–9, 148.

velopment in a tale which, as Dallas was right in observing, is somewhat hijacked by accidents. Eliot's discomfort with the idea of chance makes her find contexts for it. It is perhaps because Dolly Winthrop finds a way to bring together chance and determinism in *Silas Marner* that she carries so much of the moral weight of the tale, and Dolly's sayings were also enthusiastically quoted by Main, 'We may strive and scrat and fend, but it's little we can do arter all—the big things come and go wi' no striving o' our'n—they do, that they do' (121). The 'useful' (144) Dolly puts her blind trust in 'Them', 'because there's things I don't know on, for it's little as I know—that it is' (145). Dolly's comfortable sense of what Luhmann has called 'second-order observation' again allows Eliot to feminize the achieved wisdom in the text, and to show that such a feminine sense of dependency and powerlessness in the face of contingency ultimately constitutes a powerful and dignified acceptance of the proliferating risk of modernity.[181] Silas himself is brought to agree with Dolly that he is powerless in the face of some higher power, 'there's dealings with us—there's dealings' (145), he concurs.

Eliot's distrust of chance was also related to her worry about the open market. As she jotted down on the flyleaf of a book about property law, 'Ce n'est pas avec des mots qui ne significent rien, comme *laissez faire, laissez passer*; qu'on peut aujourd'hui donner satisfaire à des hommes qui demandent: Que faut-il faire, et par où faut-il passer?'[182] The unregulated lottery of the market does not establish categories of value that endure for the future. Her ventriloquized question, 'Que faut-il faire?' remains explicitly blocked by free-market economics. She tries to grasp at an idea of ultimate determinism to escape the worrying openness of chance. To believe oneself to be born a great artist is more comfortable than to admit to striving to write and trying one's luck with the publishers. Deirdre David has

---

[181] By 'second-order observation' Luhmann means the ways in which ordinary people are obliged to assess risks not from their knowledge of the factors involved, but rather from their assessment of the expert's knowledge of the factors involved, and of the quality of information that they are receiving from them. Niklas Luhmann, *Risk: A Sociological Theory*, trans. Rhodes Barrett (1993). Eliot mentions God or Providence rarely in the text, and Dolly's use of 'Them' allows her to leave the text open to a Comtean interpretation of humanist determinism.

[182] Joshua Williams, *Principles of the Law of Real Property, Intended as a First Book for the Use of Students in Conveyancing* (1865). This volume is among the collection of George Eliot's books in Dr Williams's Library. The translation is: You cannot satisfy the man who asks 'What should we do?' or 'Where should we go?' with words that mean nothing, such as *laissez-faire* and *laissez-passer*.

pointed to Eliot's invention of herself as a 'majestically sybilline moral voice', as an attempt to make her talent seem inevitable and her position beyond question.[183] Yet Eliot was also honest about her first attempts to write fiction, which she took up to see if she could make some much-needed money from the 'experiment' and, early in her career, she still unselfconsciously described her writing as a craft: 'There are *two* portraits in the clerical scenes; but that was my first bit of art, and my hand was not well in—I did not know so well how to manipulate my materials.'[184] Throughout her career there are also signs of the effort that the construction of a 'moral voice' has cost her—early, in *Silas Marner*, in which she reverses hastily away from chance, allowing Silas to recover 'a consciousness of a unity between his past and present' (143), and fantasizing a healing of the rupture from her own past. Much later, at the other end of her novel-writing career, she opens up the question once more, with her dramatization of the female artist in the Princess Alcharisi in *Daniel Deronda* (1876), around whom there hovers a moral ambivalence, which centres on the question of whether she had a choice to give up everything (including the infant Daniel) for her art or not. Eliot's need to find a value beyond that of the risky market led her to construct herself as a born artist, but there was always a sense that she might have been otherwise. That sense was part guilt, and part wistfulness, a longing to have stayed, like Priscilla Lammeter, whom Blackwood regretted he didn't see more of in *Silas Marner*, cheerfully unexceptional and single, caring for her ageing father.

Once her identity was public, by the middle of 1859, Eliot became acutely aware of the riskiness of her own success: 'But now it seems impossible I shall ever write anything so good and true again. I have arrived at faith in the past, but not at faith in the future,' she worries after *Adam Bede*.[185] Thinking of starting *Silas Marner* and planning *Romola*, she writes 'just now I am quite without confidence in my future doings'.[186] The longing for a 'faith in the future' is the 'lack'

[183] 'Eliot transforms herself from an industriously intelligent provincial girl to a majestically sybilline moral voice,' Deidre David, *Intellectual Women and Victorian Patriarchy: Harriet Martineau, Elizabeth Barrett Browning, George Eliot* (1987), 164. Sarah Wah has discussed Eliot's relationship to her reading public in ' "No Amount of Wishing will turn a Plum into an Orange": Popularity and the Popular Novel in George Eliot's *Romola*', unpublished MS.

[184] GE to Mr and Mrs Charles Bray and Sara Sophia Hennell (Wandsworth, 27 June 1859), *GEL* iii. 99. See also 'How I Came to Write Fiction', *GEL* ii. 406–10.

[185] GE to William Blackwood (Wandsworth, 6 May 1859), *GEL* iii. 66.

[186] GE to John Blackwood (Wandsworth, 28 August 1860), *GEL* iii. 339–40, 339.

which animates *Silas Marner*, and it is difficult not to read the novel in terms of Eliot's own anxieties about the future of her writing career and the nature of her contribution to posterity. She was also worried about the hands into which her published work might fall by accident. She was peculiarly resistant to mass publishing, despite her desire, and need, to make money for the upkeep of Lewes's wife, Agnes, and his three sons, and the fact that the commencement of her novel-writing career happened to coincide exactly with a sudden boom in periodicals publishing. Lewes remarked in the winter of 1859, 'What days these are for furious speculation in the periodical world!' (208).[187] David Masson launched *Macmillan's* on 1 November 1859; Thackeray was the first editor of the *Cornhill* which appeared in January 1860; and Dickens set up *All the Year Round* in April 1859.[188] Dickens tried to tempt Lewes into persuading Eliot to write for him, suggesting that '[a]n immense new public would probably be opened to her' (203), but this was the worst inducement he could have offered.[189] Eliot disliked the idea of an 'immense public', and feared compromising her standards for such a market: 'If I could be seduced by such offers, I might have written three poor novels and made my fortune in one year . . . Satan, in the form of bad writing and good pay is not seductive to me.'[190] She was also frightened by the 'death-defying' risks that Thackeray and Dickens took with their serial publications, confiding in John Blackwood that 'I think I should worry myself even more if I began to print before the thing is essentially complete.'[191] In this, she resembled Gaskell, who declared of periodicals that 'I dislike & disapprove of such writing \ for myself \ as a general thing,' giving as the reason her own need to retain the control and ownership of her writing, 'I choose my own subjects when I write, and treat them in the style that I myself prefer.'[192] After *Scenes of Clerical Life*, which appeared in numbers in *Blackwood's Magazine* in 1857, Eliot stuck to the traditional three-volume novel form for *Adam Bede* and *The Mill on the Floss*,

---

[187] GHL to John Blackwood (Wandsworth, 18 November 1859), *GEL* iii. 208.
[188] T. W. Heyck supplies figures for 'New Magazines Begun in London, 1800–1900'. The peak comes between 1861 and 1870, when 170 new magazines were launched. Between 1891 and 1900, only thirty appeared: *The Transformation of Intellectual Life in Victorian England* (1982), 201.
[189] Charles Dickens to GHL (London, 14 November 1859), *GEL* iii. 203–4.
[190] GE to Charles Bray (Wandsworth, 25 November [1859]), *GEL* iii. 213–14, 214.
[191] GE to John Blackwood (Wandsworth, 16 October 1859), *GEL* iii. 184–5, 185.
[192] Gaskell to Unknown (11 December 1862), *LG* 699.

perhaps adhering to an older model of a polite reading community based upon library-borrowing, rather than the new cheaply available form of fiction in the periodicals.[193] Working on the first volume of *The Mill on the Floss* in the autumn of 1859, she writes to Blackwood that '[t]he great success of "Adam" makes my writing a matter of more anxiety than ever: I suppose there is a little sense of responsibility mixed up with a great deal of pride.'[194]

This 'sense of responsibility' made her particularly receptive to readers who she felt appreciated her writing. Replying to Elizabeth Gaskell's complimentary letter in which she had described 'plodging [*sic*] through our Manchester streets to get every number' of *Amos Barton*, Eliot thanked her for 'the only sort of help I care to have— an assurance of fellow-feeling, of thorough truthful recognition from one of the minds which are capable of judging as well as being moved', adding 'we all need to know as much as we can of the good our life has been to others'.[195] If, in *Silas Marner*, she was expressing worries about spending and entering into circulation, here she reveals her belief that spending becomes a good if her readers take the right things from her books. It has been suggested that Eliot was primarily concerned with the consumption of her fiction, but it seems that it was the more dynamic model of exchange that was her ideal of creative value.[196] Unmediated or uncontrolled consumption was a horror to her, as *Brother Jacob* showed. As Aaron Winthrop remarks in *Silas Marner*, 'there need nobody run short o' victuals if the land was made the most on, and there was never a morsel but what could find its way to a mouth' (140). For Eliot, in order for her writing not to be wasted or squandered, it was important, not that it reached readers, but that it reached the right readers. She was affronted by a French review that compared her work to Dinah Mulock's, 'the most ignorant journalist in England would hardly think of calling me a rival of Miss Mulock—a writer who is read only by novel readers, pure and simple, never by people of high culture . . . we belong to an entirely different order of writers'.[197] Her elevation of the novel form

[193] *Scenes of Clerical Life* was completed before it was sent to Blackwood to be published in *Blackwood's Magazine*. *Romola* was Eliot's first serialized piece in the *Cornhill*.
[194] GE to John Blackwood (Wandsworth, 16 October 1859), *GEL* iii. 184–5, 185.
[195] Elizabeth Gaskell to George Eliot (10 November [1859]), *LG* 592. GE to Mrs William Gaskell (Wandsworth, 11 November 1859), *GEL* iii. 198–9.
[196] See e.g. Leah Price, 'George Eliot and the Production of Consumers', *The Anthology and the Rise of the Novel* (2000), 105–56.
[197] GE to François d'Albert-Durade (Venice, 7 June 1860), *GEL* iii. 300–3, 302.

to address 'people of high culture', and her insistence on 'the high responsibilities of literature that undertakes to represent life', allowed her to affect to be turning her back on the 'low' literary marketplace that was fuelled by the reviews she refused to read and the gossip she refused to acknowledge.[198] She begs Sara Hennell '*not* to re-open the subject of people's sayings and doings about me, which I wish to be closed forever', and significantly characterizes herself as on display as if on a stage, '[a]nd now let the curtain drop, or at least let me go out of the theatre and hear no further report of what goes on there.'[199] In fact, she was well aware of the value of literary gossip, as her advice to Sara herself, on the publication of her own book, demonstrates, '[l]et half a dozen competent people read her book, and an opinion of it will spread quite apart from either praise or blame in reviews and newspapers.'[200] Eliot may have desired to remain outside the theatre of her own fame, but she had no intention of letting the curtain drop. She knew as well as did Dickens and Thackeray, the importance of display as the creator of value in the modern literary marketplace.

Elizabeth Gaskell and George Eliot were writing in very different circumstances. But they both placed an emphasis on the reception of their work, rather than on its production, and on their readers, rather than on their own status as authors, reflecting their distinctive and complex relationships with their intellectual property as women in the nineteenth century. I have argued that their lack of emphasis on their own roles as producers was partly owing to a need to disavow their own anomalous status as women producers in a male marketplace, but also, and importantly, as a result of their necessarily less direct relationship with that marketplace because of the way in which they were perceived to be covered by husbands and male agents. Because that marketplace seemed more remote to them than to their male contemporaries, it was easier for them to characterize their work less as a profession than as a 'voluntary service' to the community, which enabled the fantasy of an affective relationship with individual readers. Such a construction of female labour was firmly underwritten by the culture in which they were living.[201]

---

[198]   GE to John Blackwood (London, 30 March 1861), *GEL* iii. 394.

[199]   GE to Sara Sophia Hennell (Wandsworth, 14 November [1859]), *GEL* iii. 200–1.

[200]   GE to Mrs Charles Bray (Wandsworth, 10 July 1860), *GEL* iii. 321–2, 322. Sara Hennell's book was *Thoughts in Aid of Faith*.

[201]   See Dorice Williams Elliott, 'The Female Visitor and the Marriage of Classes in Gaskell's *North and South*', *Nineteenth-Century Literature*, 49/1 (June 1994), 21–49.

Denied access to the public sphere, other than as consumers, they were able to steal in without having explicitly to confront the problems of their own 'public' status, as Thackeray and Dickens felt that they had to do. The sense of risk and contingency that pervades the work of Gaskell and Eliot, then, must be related to their own sense of the precariousness and anomalousness of their careers as intellectual women.

By the end of the century, though, a more widespread discomfort about the public sphere and about the control of literary reception across time and distance became less distinctively 'feminine' and more identifiably 'modern'. The next and final chapter looks at the impact of the electric age, starting in the 1880s, on the concept of intellectual ownership. Thomas Hardy provides a case study of the late-Victorian writer facing a modern marketplace that threatens to sweep his works away from 'this side of the Atlantic' to the other, out of his control.[202] The chapter suggests that the issue of international copyright that became newly pressing at the end of the century reflected new constructions of time and space that challenged afresh traditional notions of authorial identification with the work, and, indeed, with its consumers.

[202] Thomas Hardy to G. H. Thring (4 March 1902), *Collected Letters*, iii. 7–8, 8 and 7.

6

'The singing of the wire':
Hardy, International Copyright,
and the Ether

IN her dystopic essay of 1878, 'Shadows of the Coming Race', George Eliot went so far as to imagine the disappearance, not only of intellectual property, but of its necessary corollary—the individual consciousness:

> When, in the Bank of England, I see a wondrously delicate machine for test-ing sovereigns . . . when I am told of micrometers and thermopiles and tasimeters which deal physically with the invisible, the impalpable, and the unimaginable; of cunning wires and wheels and pointing needles which will register your and my quickness so as to exclude flattering opinion; of a machine for drawing the right conclusion, which will doubtless by-and-by be improved into an automaton for finding true premises; of a microphone which detects the cadence of a fly's foot on the ceiling, and may be expected presently to discriminate the noises of our various follies as they soliloquise or converse in our brains—my mind seeming too small for these things . . . I exclaim—'Am I already in the shadow of the Coming Race?'[1]

The vision of a world taken over by machines makes the writer fear that the boundaries between human consciousnesses will soon be in-vaded and that consequently individuality itself will be made obso-lete, and human art and invention will 'subside like the flame of a candle in the sunlight'.[2] Despite the admission at the end of the essay, that '[n]obody really holds' such ideas of the future, the writer's long-ing for 'an occasional famine of invention' articulates a real fear, at the dawn of the 1880s, that technology no longer threatened just the

---

The quotation in the title is from Thomas Hardy, *A Laodicean: A Story of To-day* (1995), 22.

[1] George Eliot, 'Shadows of the Coming Race', *Impressions of Theophrastus Such* (1995), 129–30.   [2] Ibid. 133.

boundaries of property, but of individual human consciousness itself.[3]

Just as improved printing technologies had affected the debate on intellectual property in the 1830s, so new electrical applications posed a renewed threat to the notion of the single author in the last decades of the century. The threat of the 'cunning wires and wheels and pointing needles' suggested by Eliot was particularly focused on the diffusion of electric networks, the key technology in what would come to be termed the 'second industrial revolution'. Electricity, of course, was not an invention. It had been around for a long time. Alexander's Needle Electric Telegraph and Charles Shepherd's electric clocks had been on display in 1851 in the Crystal Palace, but it was to be another thirty years before electricity began materially to alter the urban landscape.[4] It took the invention of the dynamo to turn electricity into a commercially viable energy source. When it did, though, the change was striking—even alarming—as Robert Louis Stevenson recorded in 1881 in his elegiac 'A Plea for Gas Lamps': 'A sedate electrician in a back office touches a spring—and behold! From one end to another of the city, from east to west, from the Alexandra to the Crystal Palace, there is light,' and furthermore, a light which is 'horrible, unearthly, obnoxious to the human eye'.[5]

Experiments with electricity can be traced back to the seventeenth and eighteenth centuries, and, indeed, Mary Shelley's 1818 novel, *Frankenstein*, discussed in the Introduction, includes reference to Franklin's famous experiments with electric power. From the seventeenth century, the word 'ether' had been used by both poets and scientists to explain the inexplicable. Poets used it to describe the mysterious imaginary space from whence their inspiration came, and scientists used it to describe the galvanic fluid that they believed gave life.[6] In both cases the ether stood for the life-force, or for the pre-

[3] George Eliot, 'Shadows of the Coming Race', *Impressions of Theophrastus Such* (1995), 134, 129.

[4] K. G. Beauchamp, *Exhibiting Electricity* (1997), 87–8. The parent clock mechanism was mounted in the Great Transept, and was linked electronically to two other clocks elsewhere in the Exhibition hall.

[5] R. L. Stevenson, 'A Plea for Gas Lamps', in *Virginibus Puerisque and Other Papers* (1915), 189–93, 191–2. The impact of electricity on London and in Britain in general, though, was less rapid or complete than its diffusion in the United States, partly as a result of the constraints introduced in the 1880s by the public gas companies in an attempt to protect their monopolies on lighting in the cities. I am, nevertheless, concentrating on the British example in this chapter.

[6] See the *Oxford English Dictionary*, 'ether', definitions 1a and 2. 'By some it was supposed to be the constituent substance, or one of the constituents, of the soul.' And 5a, b, and c, 'Hence *colloq.*, wireless, "the radio".'

existent material of life and art. In the nineteenth century the ether was thought to be the medium through which radio waves and electromagnetic radiations were propagated. And the word gained a new force in the popular writing of the late century, as electric and creative power once more became associated with one another in the psychic or 'weird' sciences. In the last year of the nineteenth century, the *Daily News* hailed the 'age of ether-wave telegraphy and the Röntgen rays'.[7]

Electricity is an energy that can act at a distance.[8] With electricity came the possibility of remote control, a means of attenuated influence, so that a technician 'in a back office' could illuminate London at the touch of a switch. The separation of agent from agency suggested a new model of power that provoked excitement and dread in equal measure. Eliot's paranoid dread of an unregulated power that would soon be able 'to discriminate the noises of our various follies as they soliloquise or converse in our brains', is typical of the 1880s and 1890s, when discussion of how the new electrical technologies should be installed and regulated for domestic use provoked similar fears about the invasion of private spaces.[9] Concerns about the newly powerful electrical companies ran alongside fashionable discussions of psychological phenomena such as telepathy and hypnosis, which often mobilized electricity as a metaphor, and as an explanation, for the process of transmission across space and time. As Pamela Thurschwell has written, 'At the end of the nineteenth century, science is severing the links between materiality, visibility and transmission, allowing for a sort of telepathic imaginary.'[10] In

---

[7] *Daily News* (26 May 1899), 5/1. Quoted in the *Oxford English Dictionary* under 'ether'. Critics have noticed the links between the advent of the wireless and modernist writing (see e.g. Gillian Beer, *Open Fields: Science in Cultural Encounter* (1996) and Steven Connor, *Dumbstruck: A Cultural History of Ventriloquism* (2000), but I would argue that the disembodied voice became a suggestive possibility much earlier in the history of electric technology. Jay Clayton has argued similarly in 'The Voice in the Machine: Hazlitt, Hardy, James', in Jeffrey Masten, Peter Stallybrass, and Nancy Vickers (eds.), *Language of Machines: Technologies of Literary and Cultural Production* (1997), 209–32.

[8] Iwan Rhys Morris, *Frankenstein's Children: Electricity, Exhibition, and Experiment in Early-Nineteenth-Century London* (1998), 260.

[9] Carolyn Marvin, writing of the cultural effects of electricity, has noticed that, '[a]lthough an express mission of science was to kill magic and myth, electrical experts were deeply implicated in the production of both,' *When Old Technologies Were New: Thinking About Electric Communication in the Late Nineteenth Century* (1988), 56.

[10] Pamela Thurschwell, *Literature, Technology and Magical Thinking, 1880–1920* (2001), 29. See also Steven Connor, 'The Machine in the Ghost: Spiritualism,

the last two decades of the nineteenth century, a writing of 'the electrical sublime' emerges, in which the electric current comes to stand either positively for the power of creativity itself, or negatively, for the power of undue influence and the invasion and disruption of the category of individual identity.[11]

In her 1889 novel, *Ardath: The Story of a Dead Self*, Marie Corelli draws an explicit parallel between electricity and the creative 'Spirit':

If the hands on the telegraph dial will not respond to the electric battery, the telegram cannot be deciphered. But it would be foolish to deny the existence of the electric battery because the dial is unsatisfactory! In like manner, when, by physical incapacity, or invented disease, the brain can no longer receive the impressions or electric messages of the Spirit, it is practically useless.[12]

But when the protagonist of the story, Mr Alwyn, a poet suffering writer's block, is cured by 'a strong mesmeric or magnetic influence' during an electric storm, and produces 'the best poem since Keats's St. Agnes Eve', worries about intellectual property immediately surface. ' "But the question is—considering how it was written—can I, dare I, call this poem *mine*?" '[13] Emerging theories of the unconscious in this period raised worries about the very possibility of thinking original thoughts. If creative ideas were available to everybody through the ether, then it became difficult to claim individual ownership of them. With the threat to the construction of the rational self-governing individual came an equal threat to the construction of intellectual property.

This transgression of the boundaries of selfhood is made even more explicit in Kipling's curious story, 'Wireless', in which the painful creative process of Keats's composition of 'The Eve of St Agnes' travels not only through space, but through time, in its transmission to the consumptive young pharmacist, Shaynor, who writes out the poem in full without previously knowing a word of Keats. At the same time a young electrician, Mr Cashell, is conducting an

Technology, and the "Direct Voice" ', in Peter Buse and Andrew Stott (eds.), *Ghosts: Deconstruction, Psychoanalysis, History* (1999), 203–25, and Nicholas Royle, *Telepathy and Literature* (1990).

[11] James W. Carey, 'The Mythos of the Electronic Revolution', with John J. Quirk in *Communication as Culture: Essays on Media and Society* (1989), 113–41, 123. Carey's phrase follows Leo Marx's coinage, 'the technological sublime' in *The Machine in the Garden: Technology and the Pastoral Ideal in America* (1964).

[12] Marie Corelli, *Ardath: The Story of a Dead Self* (1889), 44.

[13] Ibid. 127 and 87.

experiment in the transmission of radio waves over 'a long-range installation'.[14] Showing the narrator an instrument called a 'coherer', he explains, ' "That is the thing that will reveal to us the Powers— whatever the Powers may be—at work—through space—a long distance away." '[15] The story seems to suggest some concordance between the transmission 'through space' from 'a long distance away' of electric currents, and of brain waves. In both cases, the point of origin is obscure and difficult to track, the point of reception is where our attention is focused. The narrator concludes that 'like causes *must* beget like effects' so that the ' "Hertzian wave of tuberculosis . . . in conjunction with the main-stream of subconscious thought common to all mankind, has thrown up temporarily an induced Keats." '[16] Just as Darwin's theories turned scientific attention from the individual to the species, the idea of the 'main-stream of subconscious thought common to all mankind' underlay a new model of consciousness that was invested in shared psychological characteristics, rather than in the notion of the special individual.

While both Corelli and Kipling reach for Keats as the obvious paradigm of inspiration and originality in these stories, they also throw such a Romantic model of inspiration into question by suggesting that similar artistic effects can be produced or simulated scientifically, or even coincidentally. If Keats stands for the distinctive individual ownership of creative talent, electricity, by its crossing of the boundaries of time and space, seems to threaten that distinction, and thus to throw traditional categories of individuality and property into renewed question. Fears about the transmission of information across vast distances, untethered from origins, and no longer 'belonging' to individuals or places, caused Thomas Hardy to reflect upon the dangers of new technologies and media, ' "I feel a great sense of unreality around me—hear voices which have no real owners," ' he reflected and asked, ' "Why do we believe what we only half believe . . . what is only in the air round us, & is in no true sense a part of ourselves?" '[17] As we shall see, Hardy himself was anxious

[14] Rudyard Kipling, 'Wireless', in *Traffics and Discoveries* (1904), 211–39, 216.
[15] Ibid. 219.
[16] Ibid. 230, 231.
[17] Thomas Hardy, *The Literary Notebooks of Thomas Hardy*, ed. Lennart A. Björk (1985), i. 180, Entry 1421, and 156, Entry 1316. Hardy is commenting upon a serialization of Auberon Herbert's *A Politician in Trouble about his Soul* in the *Fortnightly Review*, 1883–4. See Tim Armstrong, *Haunted Hardy: Poetry, History, Memory* (2000), 36–7.

about owning his own voice, and went to elaborate lengths to ensure that his intellectual property remained intact even as it travelled through time and space.

In Kipling's 'Wireless', the electrician remains shut in 'the inner office', unaware of the remarkable transmission of Keats's poem which is taking place simultaneously in the more public space of the pharmacist's shop.[18] By the 1880s, a paradigm shift from the inventor to the invention was well underway: the electrician was now 'sedate' in a 'back office', no longer the heroic agent of change, but the obedient servant of the machine, and a loyal company man. Indeed, rather than controlling events, Kipling's electrician not only fails to notice the paranormal transmission in the room next door, but also fails to connect his own machinery, receiving only ' "odds and ends of messages coming out of nowhere—a word here and there—no good at all" ' (239): all the agency in the tale is lodged—significantly—off the premises. Rhys Morris has suggested that, with the emergence of electricity, '[t]he powers of nature, rather than artisans or labourers, were increasingly regarded as the ultimate producers of a whole new range of commodities.'[19] The model of origin was clearly shifting—messages arrive 'coming out of nowhere'.

As early as 1862, Bulwer Lytton in his novel, *A Strange Story*, has a 'weird and wizard-like' scientist ask, ' "Why, after all, should there not be in Nature one primary essence, one master substance, in which is stored the specific nutrient of life?" '[20] In 1871 he uses the idea of electricity as that elemental energy in *The Coming Race*, this time famously characterized as '*vril*':

I should call it electricity, except that it comprehends in its manifold branches other forces of nature, to which, in our scientific nomenclature, differing names are assigned, such as magnetism, galvanism, &c. These people consider that in vril they have arrived at the unity in natural energetic agencies, which has been conjectured by many philosophers above ground, and which Faraday thus intimates under the more cautious term of correlation:—'I have long held the opinion,' says that illustrious experimentalist, ' . . . that the various forms under which the forces of matter are made manifest . . . are so directly related and mutually dependent, that they are convertible, as it were, into one another, and possess equivalents of power in their action.'[21]

[18] Rudyard Kipling, 'Wireless' (1904), 229.
[19] Iwan Rhys Morris, *Frankenstein's Children* (1998), p. xii.
[20] [Edward Bulwer Lytton], *A Strange Story* (1862), 353, 271.
[21] Edward Bulwer Lytton, *The Coming Race* (1995), 20.

This is a motive power that not only drives the many ingenious machines invented by the Vril-ya, and perpetually lights their subterranean world, it also allows them to exercise remote control, so that Zee 'by a certain play of her vril staff, she herself standing at a distance . . . put into movement large and weighty substances' (54). Even more mysteriously, vril provides the means by which 'the thoughts of one brain could be transmitted to another,' and by which the narrator is hypnotized, '[a]ll power of volition left me' (73-4).[22] The idea of electricity as a 'natural' power, very different from the popular perception of gas, supported its use as a transposable term from positivist science to spiritualism and parapsychology—from the materialist world to a less literal, ghostly one. H. G. Wells took the idea of obedience to a vast natural power to a characteristic extreme in his 1895 story 'The Lord of the Dynamos', in which the black assistant to a chief electrician Holroyd secretly fetishizes and worships the powerful dynamo it is his job to tend, finally sacrificing his brutal master to it by electrocution, followed by himself, 'Azuma-zi caught the naked terminals in his hands, gave one horrible convulsion, and then hung motionless from the machine, his face violently distorted.'[23] Wells's story pivots on the irony that, while he asks the reader to smile at the naivety of Azuma-zi, technology does indeed demand the sacrifice of the individual. Arriving after the first death, and hurriedly removing 'the distorted remains of Holroyd . . . [t]he expert was chiefly anxious to get the machine at work again, for seven or eight trains had stopped mid-way in the stuffy tunnels of the electric railway.'[24] The distorting and dehumanizing effects of corporate capitalism are made to seem as 'savage' as Azuma-zi's worship of the dynamo.

'[T]he word *electricity* now sounds the note of danger,' declared Stevenson, and as inventors were increasingly absorbed into professional science and corporate commerce, processes and technologies grew ever more opaque to the lay public, and themselves became the focus of dread.[25] George Eliot had foreseen the threat of 'unowned

---

[22] Ibid. 21.

[23] H. G. Wells, 'The Lord of the Dynamos', in *The Stolen Bacillus and Other Stories* (1895), 192–213, 212.

[24] Ibid. 206, 207.

[25] R. L. Stevenson, 'A Plea For Gas Lamps' (1915), 192. I. C. R. Byatt agrees that 'the role of the individual inventor became relatively less important and that of the existing electrical engineering firms more important', *The British Electrical Industry 1875–1914: The Economic Returns to a New Technology* (1979), 2.

technology' in 'Shadows of the Coming Race' in which '[n]o fame is asked by the inventor, and none is given to him.'[26] Indeed, it became less and less easy to see who did own electrical technology and invention, and the scientific inventor, in popular science fiction of the early twentieth century, is no longer in a position of control—instead, he (and it is generally 'he') is cast as ineffectual or psychotic. The distinguished physicist Lord Kelvin opened the new Neptune Bank power station on Tyneside with the words, 'I don't know what electricity is, and cannot define it—I have spent my life on it—I do not know the limits of electricity but it will go beyond anything we conceive of today.'[27] In the last two decades of the nineteenth century, electrical power seemed potentially unlimited in its applications, and—therefore—potentially uncontrollable in its dispersal. The electrician was its servant, rather than its master.

THE ELECTRICAL INDUSTRY AND THE PUBLISHING INDUSTRY

By 1886 W. T. Stead felt that '[t]he telegraph and the printing press have converted Great Britain into a vast agora, or assembly of the whole community.'[28] Certainly the growth of the electricity industry and the explosion of the publishing market are not such separable phenomena as they first seem. Both the technology of printing and the new electrical communications technologies allowed for a kind of dissociated presence, for the transmission of thoughts and ideas across time and space. And as the transmission times shortened, the distances involved lengthened—the 'vast agora' now extended well beyond Britain.[29] Both industries were confronted with the unignor-

[26] Eliot, 'Shadows of the Coming Race', 66.

[27] Lord Kelvin, speech on the opening of Neptune Bank Power Station on Tyneside in 1901, in North Eastern Electricity Board Archives. Quoted in Leslie Hannah, *Electricity before Nationalisation* (1979), 2.

[28] W. T. Stead, 'Government by Journalism', *Contemporary Review*, 49 (May 1886), 653–74, 654. Quoted in Richard Salmon, ' "A Simulacrum of Power": Intimacy and Abstraction in the Rhetoric of the New Journalism', in Laurel Brake, Bill Bell, and David Finkelstein (eds.), *Nineteenth-Century Media and the Construction of Identities* (2000), 27–39, 30–1.

[29] Although the 1842 Copyright Act had included some provision for international protection, it mainly dealt with penalties for piracies, and was largely ineffective in providing any means for the detection of violations of copyright. It also failed to cover 'the colonies', 'no doubt by an oversight in drafting'—including North America, and,

able problem of a global market, of aggressive North American commercialism encroaching upon British markets, and the need for accelerated productivity, standardization of systems, prices, and access for consumers. As David Harvey has pointed out, 'The incentive to create the world market, to reduce spatial barriers, and to annihilate space through time is omnipresent . . . Innovations dedicated to the removal of spatial barriers . . . have been of immense significance in the history of capitalism, turning that history into a very geographical affair.'[30] International copyright, like electronic communications technology, needs to be considered within a context of 'complicated interrelationships among colonial expansion, trade relations, and geopolitical influence'.[31]

The debates about the future development of both industries were largely taken up by disputes over the proper level of government regulation of trade and the protection of the consumer. Both were complicated by the loosening of the free-trade orthodoxy in the face of the growing industrial strength of Germany and, especially, the United States of America, which seemed to threaten British commercial interests in new and worrying ways. As the key emergent technology of the last decades of the century, electrical applications developed under the aegis of monopoly capitalism to a far greater extent than previous technologies, and this was one of the reasons that electricity appeared so powerful. Byatt reminds us that these were 'international companies with branches in many different countries. The main ones were based in Germany and the United States.'[32] The fierce patent disputes and aggressive company takeovers that attended the development of an internationally standardized electrical system took place at the same time as the piracy of British books by North American publishers fuelled the debate about the establishment of an international copyright law.

despite some subsequent tinkering with the law, 'the royal commission was able to demonstrate in 1878, few authors or publishers received a penny' in recompense for colonial reprinting. See Simon Nowell-Smith, *International Copyright Law and the Publisher in the Reign of Queen Victoria* (1968), 25, 26. In 1846 an agreement with Prussia was reached, in 1852 with France, in 1857 with Spain, and with the Kingdom of Sardinia in 1861. It was not until the Chace Act of 1891, that the first United States International Copyright Act was passed, and it was, of course, to the anglophone markets that British writers were losing most throughout the century.

[30] David Harvey, *The Condition of Postmodernity* (1989), 232.
[31] Rosemary J. Coombe, 'Challenging Paternity: Histories of Copyright', Review Article, *Yale Journal of Law and the Humanities*, 6 (1994), 397–422, 422.
[32] Byatt, *British Electrical Industry*, 2.

Patent law had traditionally put the emphasis on the initial stages of invention, but now the time-span of patent protection became increasingly contentious, as rival electrical companies competed to exploit new technical developments. The debate over the point at which an invention should become freely public was reignited by the municipal ownership of British electrical supply systems in the 1880s, and the vicious 'patent wars' over electrical amenities and services in the 1880s and 1890s were fought out in an international marketplace. Temporality was more important in the debates about intellectual property legislation in the late-Victorian period than it had been earlier in the century. The international copyright debate was less concerned with new publication than with what happened to the notion of intellectual property years, or even decades, after a new work had appeared. Not only that, but it was also concerned with the ways in which publication could be controlled in a global marketplace, and most particularly, in North America.[33] The emphasis had shifted from the point of production to the point of consumption, and the debate was now less about establishing ownership than about controlling reception.

Paxton's Crystal Palace, at its second location in Sydenham, hosted two specialist electrical exhibitions, one in 1882 following the larger Paris International Exposition of Electricity of the year before, and another in 1892 just after the opening of the new Sydenham Power Station, which provided mains wiring for the exhibits.[34] These exhibitions flanked the decade in which electricity emerged as a serious commercial proposition and became a significant power source for the nation.[35] An International Congress of Electricians took place alongside the 1881 Exposition of Electricity in Paris, which laid the groundwork for devising an internationally recognized system of electrical units and voltages. In 1894 this system achieved legal status after another agreement reached at another Congress which took place at the Chicago Columbian International

[33] See Stephen Kern, *The Culture of Time and Space 1880–1918* (1983), 1, and N. N. Feltes, 'International Copyright: Structuring "the Condition of Modernity" in British Publishing', in Martha Woodmansee and Peter Jaszi (eds.), *The Construction of Authorship* (1994), 271–80.

[34] Beauchamp says the first Exhibition took place in 1881, but the contemporary journals describe the Exhibition in 1882. K. G. Beauchamp, *Exhibiting Electricity* (1997).

[35] Information from Beauchamp, *Exhibiting Electricity*, and Iwan Rhys Morris, *Frankenstein's Children* (1998).

World Exhibition in 1893. By no means entirely coincidentally, this was also the decade of the Berne conferences of 1884, 1885, and 1886 which led up to the Berne Convention of 1887, and—finally—an International Copyright Law agreed with the United States of America in 1891. International copyright had been discussed at length in Britain by the 1876 Royal Commission, which had reported to Parliament in 1878. Both the electrical and the publishing industry were forced to seek internationally standardized codes of practice in order to compete in an increasingly global marketplace.

In both debates, free-trade arguments were beginning to wear thin in the face of American competition. Reports from the 1882 Sydenham Exhibition that 'many minor exhibitors are, and have been for some time, endeavouring to break down the monopoly in telephones now possessed by the telephone companies holding the Bell and Edison patents' revealed the extent of the problems of patent ownership.[36] It was alleged that smaller companies had found their exhibits mysteriously vandalized.[37] Bell and Edison defended their patents energetically, and when they failed to win a case, they absorbed their competitors instead: 'In 1883 the Edison and Swan [British] interests merged after a clash over patents. They then used their strong patent position to try and eliminate competition.'[38] British anti-monopoly legislation could do nothing to prevent the activity of American companies and by the late 1890s, the market was flooded with North American products: the London underground, for example, was built and electrified with exclusively American-designed technology. Similarly, British copyright legislation was powerless when confronted by the 'piracy' of British texts in North America and more widely. Walter Besant, later to become the President of the Incorporated Society of Authors, complained in 1876 that all his works 'have been reproduced, principally by pirates, in America, Canada, India, Victoria, and South Australia . . . these reproductions of novels take place every day in Greater Britain, to the serious loss and injury of the writers'.[39] It was difficult to see how a

[36] 'The Crystal Palace Electrical Exhibition', *The Telegraphic Journal and Electrical Review* (18 February 1882), 113.

[37] Ibid.

[38] Byatt, *British Electrical Industry*, 155.

[39] [W. Besant], *This Son of Vulcan: A Novel* (1876) i. pp. iii, iv. Thomas Hardy was in the audience on 2 March 1887 when Besant gave a paper on 'The Security of Literary Property'—at the first of three 'conferences' organized in London by the Incorporated Society of Authors.

free-trade, abolitionist solution would deliver British royalties as the anglophone world was growing spatially 'Greater', in terms of the penetration of communications technologies, all the time.

Both electricity and the modern publishing industry thus also created new vocabularies of space. Speed of transmission was a major concern for both. N. N. Feltes has suggested that '[t]he pressure for a universal law of copyright . . . arose less out of a desire for juridical consistency than from the material contradictions of time and place,' suggesting that it was simply no longer feasible for British publishers to resist the demand for cheap, accessible editions of new works.[40] T. H. Farrer, a witness to the Royal Commission which discussed international copyright in 1876, drew attention to the spatial contradictions created by laws that allowed, for example, an edition of George Eliot's *Daniel Deronda* to be printed cheaply in Germany or America, but which forbade the import of cheap foreign editions into Britain: 'By our artificial laws we have in this way created a number of centres of production independent of the original centre, and we draw a hedge around each of these centres, and say that what is produced in it shall not go into the original one; and that operates against the country that makes the law.'[41] As an orthodox free-trader, Farrer saw the principle of copyright, which currently protected the production of expensive three-volume editions of novels for the British circulating libraries, as working against the interests of the consumer. The retort to such reasoning is summed up by Mr Daldy's bewildered, 'And the author is to have no control whatever?' And the writer, James Anthony Froude, who was a member of the Commission, was similarly concerned to protect the author's control of his property: 'it seems that if the author has the control in his own hands he will be able to make what guards he pleases, he must have his own publisher. If you allow a man to take any book and reprint it, whether the author likes it or not, you certainly take that power out of his hands.'[42]

[40] N. N. Feltes, 'International Copyright: Structuring "the Condition of Modernity" in British Publishing', in Woodmansee and Jaszi (eds.), *The Construction of Authorship*, 271–80, 271.

[41] T. H. Farrer, 'Minutes of the Evidence taken Before the Royal Commission on Copyright Together with an Appendix Preceded by Tables of the Witnesses and of the Contents of the Appendix' (1878), in *Reports from Commissioners, Inspectors, and Others*, vol. 6, Session 17 January–16 August 1878, xxiv. 269. Hereafter referred to as 1878 *Commission on Copyright*.

[42] Mr Daldy cross-examining Sir Charles Trevelyan, 1878 *Commission on Copyright*, 8 (266). James Anthony Froude cross-examining Sir Charles Trevelyan, ibid. 5.

A similar debate was raging over the question of who owned electricity. A Select Committee on Lighting by Electricity reported in 1879, and the resultant Electric Lighting Act of 1882 granted licences that gave rights to private companies to supply electricity for a 21-year period, after which they could be compulsorily purchased by municipal authorities and returned to public ownership. In 1888 the purchase clause was amended to 42 years. The idea was to protect the consumer from the high prices that private companies could demand if they established monopolies: like the law of patent and of copyright, this legislation aimed to encourage innovation and entrepreneurship, while protecting both the producer and the consumer from the excesses of the free-trade economy.[43] It was acknowledged as a compromise by Joseph Chamberlain at the time, 'it is difficult, and, indeed, almost impossible, satisfactorily to reconcile the rights and interests of the public with the claims of an individual, or of a company seeking, as is its natural and legitimate object, the largest attainable private gain'.[44] In this sense, the 1879 debate at Select Committee stage grappled with the same problems of principle that the 1876 Royal Commission on Copyright had also encountered: the balance of social and individual ownership, or how far books, or electrical commodities, were the property of their authors and inventors, and how far they belonged to the public. Was the power—electric or intellectual—behind these products a natural phenomenon belonging to everybody? In fact, the reality of both cases was that the markets were already too large to be controlled effectively by any *domestic* legislation.

A third Reform Act in 1884 continued the process of democratization that had begun in the 1830s by extending the franchise to all adult males.[45] Mass markets were now becoming a reality as

[43] The legislation that attempted to control the growth of the British electrical industry has been blamed for the slow take-up of electrical technologies compared to the American model, but was 'part of an attempt to regulate natural monopolies in the public interest'. Byatt, *British Electrical Industry*, 197. Also, British electricity suppliers had the problem that gas was a very well-established lighting technology in British cities and was both publicly owned and cheap.

[44] J. Chamberlain, 'Municipal Government; Past, Present and Future', *The New Review*, 61 (June 1894), 658. Quoted in Hannah, *Electricity before Nationalisation*, 23.

[45] The 1884 Act extended the 1867 concessions from the boroughs to the countryside. The vote was given to all men paying an annual rental of £10 or all those holding land valued at £10. After the Act, the British electorate numbered over 5,500,000. An act a year later redistributed constituencies, giving more representation to urban areas (especially London).

increased earnings and literacy created public demand for electric power and for literature at affordable prices. Major obstacles for both the burgeoning electricity companies, and the publishers, were the entrenched systems that it was difficult to bypass. Gas companies were mostly in municipal ownership and were reasonably efficient in distributing lighting around cities, and until the electric companies could displace them, they were blocked from developing effective systems for the distribution and delivery of electric power. For the publishing industry it was the circulating libraries which were blocking opportunities to print longer runs of cheaper editions of books. Almost every witness to the Commission agreed that the circulating libraries were exerting an undue stranglehold on the British book market.[46] Charles Trevelyan regretted that the 'library system' meant that 'the body of the people' had to wait to read new literature, 'they get it after great delay, they get it after the first interest has evaporated, and after it has become stale'.[47] In the 1880s and 1890s, then, both the electrical and the publishing industries were impatient to tap into the ever-growing market of consumers.

MAINTAINING CONTROL: HARDY AND INTERNATIONAL COPYRIGHT 1881–1897

In 1893, Thomas Hardy wrote a strange story for a special number of *Scribner's Magazine* issued to commemorate the Chicago Columbian International World Exhibition which boasted an impressive 'Electrical Pavilion'.[48] With the 'Exhibition' theme in mind, Hardy takes us back to the Great Exhibition of 1851 in 'The Fiddler of the Reels'. The tale seems to draw a division between the old order, personified in the humble Ned Hipcroft, 'a respectable mechanic',

[46] Sir Drummond Wolff's cross-examination of John Blackwood revealed their very different positions, Wolff's being an anti-copyright free-trade position, while Blackwood argued throughout for the principle of perpetual copyright. But they both agreed that the circulating libraries represented a pernicious problem, 1878 *Commission on Copyright*, 41–4. It is clear from evidence given to the Commission by publishers, though, that not only were they already producing increasing numbers of cheap editions, but that these were now appearing very rapidly after the first, expensive edition.

[47] Sir Charles Trevelyan, ibid. 2.

[48] See Thomas Hardy to Charles Scribner's Sons (20 November 1892), *Collected Letters*, i (1978), 289.

and the sinister and peripatetic Wat or 'Mop' Ollamoor, 'a man of whom so little was known', who is associated with electricity, performance, and display.[49] Ollamoor exerts 'a power which sometimes seemed to have a touch of the weird and wizardly in it' (335), exercising an 'influence' (337) over the young woman at the centre of the story, Car'line, with 'his acoustic magnetism' (347), which affects her like 'a galvanic shock' (337). While Ned is one of the artisans who builds the Crystal Palace, it is inside the Exhibition Hall, that 'a reflection of a form exactly resembling Mop Ollamoor's' (343) appears in a mirror, a substanceless shadow. The sinister Ollamoor has the power to control Car'line from a distance, making her dance 'compelled capers' (337), or making her 'start from her seat in the chimney-corner' (337) as he passes by on the road outside. For Hardy, the electrical fantasy of control from a distance was double-edged. Anxiety about the limits of individual control in a modern age crackles through his writing in the 1880s and 1890s like static interference. Hardy's ambivalence about maintaining his own position in the global marketplace, even after death, reveals the shift from the debate about the establishment of intellectual property, which had animated Dickens, Talfourd, and others at mid-century, to a debate about the preservation and control of intellectual property after publication. At what point does an invention become freely public? How much of Hardy's work already belonged to the public?

'I should dearly like to print anything I write in my own attic or cellar, & send off the copies by post,' wrote Hardy to the campaigner for author's rights, Sir Walter Besant, upon reading his article, 'Literary Property'.[50] He regrets the impossibility of controlling his own literary output through the publishers, ' . . . there being no means of controlling the supply as in the case of minerals, &c.'.[51] Hardy's retentiveness is evidenced by the fact that he never sold a copyright, except in the case of *Under the Greenwood Tree*. Throughout the 1880s and 1890s, he was keenly aware of issues of copyright, international and domestic, and even made the effort to attend the meetings of the Incorporated Society of Authors, despite his generally

---

[49] Thomas Hardy, 'The Fiddler of the Reels', in *Outside the Gates of the World: Selected Short Stories* (1996), 334–50, 338. All subsequent references appear in parentheses.

[50] [Sir Walter Besant], 'Literary Property 1: The Present Situation', *Author*, 10/6 (1 November 1899), 118–22.

[51] Thomas Hardy to Sir Walter Besant (11 November 1899), *Collected Letters*, ii. 236–7, 236.

reclusive habits.[52] Indeed, upon his death he was the President of the Society, which was one of the few institutional beneficiaries of his will.[53] Hardy's sense of the importance of maintaining control seems as much tied up with his anxieties about propriety as with property. His dread of his work being distorted, misrepresented, and vulgarized by an 'unthinking public' and by the 'eminent critics' was often justified, and he 'suffered . . . mentally' from the accusations of immorality that attended each new publication.[54] '[A] more virile type of novel is not incompatible with sound morality,' he insisted in 1891, after the critics had professed to being scandalized by *Tess of the D'Urbervilles*, and had, he felt, grossly misrepresented the novel in their periodical reviews.[55] Hardy wished to control the reception of his work. But his attitudes to its production were confusing. He was cavalier about plagiarizing passages from other writers and kept extensive and detailed notebooks full of material which often made its way whole and unacknowledged into his own work.[56] Hardy was clearly less concerned with establishing his ownership of the text at the point of production, than at its point of reception—in other words, he spent more energy in attempting to preserve than in creating the sense of his ownership of his work.

T. H. Farrer, recalcitrant free-trader, and witness to the Copyright Commission, characterized copyright as a restrictive and outmoded 'law which gives to him [the author] and his representatives absolute control over reproduction, he can secure the issue to the public of those works only which his more mature taste and opinions ap-

[52] In March 1875 Hardy joined the recently established Copyright Association, and on 10 May he waited upon the Prime Minister, Disraeli, as one of a deputation of authors seeking an improvement in domestic and international copyright laws. (See *The Times* (11 May 1875) and *The Early Life of Thomas Hardy*, 139.) In 1880 Hardy wrote to James Russell Lowell, 'I have read with great interest the outline of the proposed Copyright treaty [between England and the US] that you have communicated to me in your letter of 16th.' Hardy to James Russell Lowell (21 September 1880?), *Collected Letters*, i. 79–80. Hardy was also in the audience on 2 March 1887 when Besant gave a paper on 'The Security of Literary Property' at the first of three conferences organized in London by the Incorporated Society of Authors.

[53] See *The Times* (7 May 1920), 9.

[54] Hardy to Edmund Gosse (10 December 1882) and (19 October 1886), *Collected Letters*, i. 110, 154–5.

[55] Hardy to W. H. Massingham (31 December 1891), ibid. 250.

[56] Robert Gittings remarks upon Emma Hardy's careful copying of seventy-five of the maxims of Jesuit Balthasar Gracian from the *Fortnightly Review*, which Hardy then used extensively in *A Laodicean*. He also records Hardy's own 'silent plagiarism' of C. H. Gifford's *History of the Wars Occasioned by the French Revolution*, in the novel *The Trumpet Major*. Gittings, *The Older Hardy* (1978), 20, 42.

prove'.[57] Farrer himself was opposed to copyright as a 'monopoly', feeling that it 'not only degrades authorship by making it a matter of trade . . . it is opposed to the best interests of the public'.[58] Against such opposition, Hardy was a great supporter of the principle of the 'absolute control' of copyright, and he sought to control his literary afterlife with an anxiety and urgency that bespeaks a deep distrust of modern markets and technologies of distribution that function beyond the control of the producer. His later fiction reflects this dread in oblique but revealing ways.

Hardy fantasized control over his literary productions both through time and space. In an effort to shape and influence his posthumous reputation he ghost-wrote his own 'Biography', which was published after his death under his second wife's name. During the long and careful process of its composition, he went so far as to disguise his handwriting on the typewritten proofs, and instructed his wife that they were all ultimately to be burnt.[59] Within his own lifetime he also reissued his work in a 'standard' edition not once, but twice. The 'Wessex Novels' edition was published by the London-based firm of Osgood McIlvaine between 1895 and 1897. When the publishers were bought up by the New York house of Harper & Brothers, Hardy was uncomfortable at having been 'carried by currents, & against my intentions, into the position of having only a subsidiary branch of an American house as my English publishers' and, as he still held his copyrights, produced another 'Uniform Edition' of his work with Macmillan in London.[60] His dislike of the 'unexpected mutations' of global capital is expressed through the image of the strong and sweeping currents that he sees as carrying him bodily from 'this side of the Atlantic' to the other, and he was clearly anxious to establish his property spatially as well as temporally.[61]

Hardy's friend and fellow writer Grant Allen published a story in 1899, 'Ivan Greet's Masterpiece', about a writer who has to work for

---

[57] T. H. Farrer, 'The Principle of Copyright', *Fortnightly Review*, NS 24 (1 July–1 December 1878), 836–51, 840.

[58] Ibid. 846. During the course of his evidence to the Commission, Farrer twice invoked Lord Macaulay's use of 'monopoly' as a synonym for 'copyright' in his famous 1841 speech to Parliament.

[59] Florence Hardy disobeyed him and kept the final proof. Michael Millgate discusses Hardy's investment in his 'Biography' in *Testamentary Acts: Browning, Tennyson, James, Hardy* (1992), 110–38.

[60] Hardy to G. H. Thring (4 March 1902), *Collected Letters*, iii. 7–8, 7. See Millgate, *Testamentary Acts*, 111–15.

[61] Hardy to Thring (4 March 1902), *Collected Letters*, iii. 7–8, 8 and 7.

the aptly named *Daily Telephone* for money: 'For the most part he acquiesced, like all the rest of us, in the supreme dictatorship of Supply and Demand—those economic gods of the modern book-market.'[62] Hardy was as immersed in that modern book-market as any writer of his day, often tailoring his writing to suit the demands of specific publications, and even giving Allen himself advice on sell-ing his copyrights abroad.[63] The Society of Authors recommended the use of literary agents, and Hardy followed its advice at least once, by using a literary agent to broker North American rights for him, but on the whole he worked hard to manage and control his own lit-erary property during his lifetime.[64] Indeed, the majority of his sur-viving letters, particularly those written between 1870 and 1900, concern precise directions to publishers, and often, significantly, to American publishers, as to the terms and conditions of publication of his work.[65] He also made frequent unsolicited approaches during this period to American journals, seeking to 'place' his fiction simul-taneously with its publication in the British press and thereby to guard himself against American piracy.[66] Indeed, Hardy was on such friendly terms with Harper & Brothers that he leapt to the com-pany's defence when Rudyard Kipling accused them of piracy. Kipling subsequently lampooned Hardy in his 'Rhyme of the Three Captains', a poem that neatly literalizes the theme of literary piracy, figuring Hardy as a ship, 'Lord of the Wessex coast and all the lands thereby', which 'dips [her] flag to a slaver's rag' in tolerating the piracy of 'a lime-washed Yankee brig that rode off Finesterre'.[67] In

[62] Grant Allen, 'Ivan Greet's Masterpiece', in *Twelve Tales, With a Headpiece, a Tailpiece, and an Intermezzo* (1899), 285–324, 291–2.

[63] See Hardy to Perry Mason & Co. (5 April 1883), *Collected Letters*, i. 116: 'You may depend upon my using my best efforts to please your numerous readers; & that the story shall have a healthy tone, suitable to intelligent youth of both sexes.' The story was 'Our Exploits at West Poley'. Hardy to Grant Allen (24 April 1895), ibid. ii. 74–5.

[64] '[W]e have encouraged . . . [the author] to use the literary agent', Walter Besant, 'Literary Property 1: The Present Situation', *Author*, 10/6 (1 November 1899), 118–22, 118. A. P. Watt secured Hardy's American rights for his story 'On the Western Circuit': 'By your management the pecuniary result is bettered without mulcting any one', Hardy wrote, gratefully, to A. P. Watt (10 January 1892), *Collected Letters*, i. 251.

[65] For a discussion of Hardy's struggle to get his fiction published in the 1860s, see 'Hardy: Breaking into Fiction', ch. 10, in John Sutherland, *Victorian Novelists and Publishers* (1976), 206–25.

[66] See Hardy to W. Moy Thomas (30 December 1881), *Collected Letters*, i. 99.

[67] Rudyard Kipling, 'The Rhyme of the Three Captains' (1890), in *Rudyard Kipling: The Complete Verse* (1996), 269–72, 269, 270, 272. See Hardy to James R.

fact, Hardy was himself frustrated by the continued failure of Britain to come to copyright terms with 'incorrigible America,' and was taken by surprise by the American copyright agreement of 1891.[68]

Like Kipling, Hardy also suffered piracies of his work. An unauthorized stage version of his *Far from the Madding Crowd* irritated him in 1881, and—more seriously—when some indifferent poems were published under the name of 'Thomas Hardy' in 1882, he wrote to his friend William Moy Thomas '[a]s the safest authority I know on literary copyright' to ask 'whether an author can acquire such a right in his own name as to prevent another person who may bear it also from beginning to use it so as to convey the impression that the work is by the original writer'.[69] Both Michael Millgate and Tim Armstrong have noticed Hardy's 'claim to be both the originator of Wessex and its only legitimate exploiter', and he wrote to instruct his publishers, 'Could you, whenever advertising my books, use the words "Wessex novels" at the heads of the list? . . . I find that the name *Wessex*, wh. I was the first to use in fiction, is getting to be taken up everywhere: & it would be a pity for us to lose the right to it for want of asserting it.'[70] Hardy's appropriation of the imagined space of 'Wessex' is characteristic, not only of his skilful self-marketing, but also of his need—literally—to 'ground' his literary

Osgood (8 November 1890), *Collected Letters*, i. 218–19. Kipling had published a letter in the *Athenaeum* (8 November 1890) accusing Harper & Bros. of failing to seek permission before reprinting *The Courting of Dinah Shadd and Other Stories*. Hardy's letter defending Harper & Bros. appeared in the *Athenaeum* (22 November 1890) and provoked Kipling's verse reply in the *Athenaeum* (23 December 1882) which attacked 'Besant, Black and myself' according to Hardy (*Collected Letters*, i. 223). No great offence seems to have been taken as Hardy was dining amicably with Kipling and his father the following spring. See Hardy to Emma Lavinia Hardy (13 April 1891), 231–2, 232.

[68] Hardy to Thomas (7 August 1889), *Collected Letters*, i. 196–7. 'I am afraid, however, that we shall be almost written out before anything is done with incorrigible America,' 197. 'The passing of the Copyright Bill by the American House of Representatives is a surprise to everybody.' Hardy to Emma Lavinia Hardy (5 December 1890), ibid. 222. The American Copyright Bill was finally passed in March 1891 and came into effect in July 1891, just in time to make Hardy a considerable amount of money on the American publication of *Tess*.

[69] Hardy to Thomas (30 December 1881) and (12 August 1882), ibid. 99, 108. Arthur Copinger's *The Law of Copyright in Works of Literature and Art* (1870) was the standard reference text in this period.

[70] Millgate, *Testamentary Acts*, 112. Tim Armstrong writes, 'In the 1900s . . . Hardy regularly began to talk of Wessex as a kind of personal property', *Haunted Hardy* (2000), 27. Hardy to Edward Marston (Publisher—Samson & Low) (1888?), *Collected Letters*, i. 171.

property in a fantasy of circumscribed space that conceptually resists its universal dispersal.

Indeed, both inside and outside his fiction, the issue of controlling space seems almost to obsess Hardy in this period. He foresees perhaps better than any other writer of the period the effects of the 'growing dis-association with localities—this complete reversal of the old condition of things'.[71] The creation, or rather preservation, of 'Wessex' became part of this obsession. During the early months of 1883 he wrote an article for *Longman's Magazine*, entitled 'The Dorsetshire Labourer', which reveals his deep conflict of feeling over the changes in work patterns in the county, whose people 'have ceased to be so local in feeling or manner as formerly, and have entered into the condition of inter-social citizens, whose city stretches the whole country over'.[72] Although he could see clearly that such mobility of labour has become unavoidable when 'other communities were marching on so vigorously towards uniformity and mental equality' (262), the tone of the article is unmistakably regretful and wary of 'the power of unlimited migration', with the result that the Dorset labourers 'have lost touch with their environment' (263). The rupture of the personal from the particular space, so that agricultural labour is now hired short-term rather than 'owned' long-term, leads to a loss of 'natural' property in the land—the loss of a sense of ownership of place that cannot be redeemed by a peripatetic market that functions on a principle of speedy dispersal. This seems as much to reflect Hardy's own 'sense of the incertitude and precariousness' (257) of his hold on his own particular property in his work, as that of his fellow Dorsetshire labourers. The only remedy he can envisage is 'some system by which he [the labourer] could have a personal interest in a particular piece of land', just as Hardy himself claimed an interest in the particular piece of land that he nominated 'Wessex'.[73]

Yet, while Hardy often seems to revile the deracination and democratization of modern culture, congratulating, for example, another author-friend, George Gissing, for 'not merely striving for circulating library popularity', elsewhere he makes it clear that he is by no means opposed to popularity, mass markets, or cheap

---

[71] Hardy to Percy Bunting (5 November 1883), *Collected Letters*, i. 123.

[72] Thomas Hardy, 'The Dorsetshire Labourer', *Longman's Magazine*, 2 (July 1883), 252–69, 262.

[73] Hardy to Percy Bunting (5 November 1883), *Collected Letters*, i. 123.

editions.[74] In 1891 he wrote that 'the true evidence of being known as a writer is after all the sight of one's works scattered about book-stalls in ridiculously cheap editions', and went on to muse that without cheaply available editions of novels, 'I for one should never as a boy have wept over [Bulwer Lytton's] heroines—living as I did live in a lonely place where borrowing was impracticable'.[75] Hardy here echoes the efforts of the international copyright commission to consider 'the interests of the public, that is to say ... the diffusion of literature'.[76] And he often nudged his publishers into issuing cheap editions of his own work.[77] His own class background made him a natural enemy of elitist publishing, while his retentive dislike of publicity (he always, for example, refused to lecture or speak publicly about his work), made him nervous of mass publication. For Hardy, the enthusiasm and financial imperative for the 'scattering about' and distribution of his work necessitated a firm compensatory hold over his property in it.

The proliferation of print and the commercialization of publishing towards the end of the century opened up more opportunities for writers but had the perhaps perverse effect of making some even more tenacious of their intellectual property. As the tide of printed matter rose, the author found him or herself rudely deposed from the position of sage, or preacher.[78] By the end of the nineteenth century, the public cultural realm that Eliot, for example, had fantasized in order to legitimate her commercial activity as a writer, was already vanishing from view. The ever-growing global marketplace at the end of the nineteenth century made it difficult to imagine a public space that was not commercial. As foreign markets opened up, it became more and more difficult for any writer to imagine that he or she was addressing a known constituency of readers.[79]

Because of the loss of the construction of a public sphere based upon 'moral virtue', literary writing was less and less characterized

[74] Hardy to George Gissing (1 July 1886), ibid. 149.
[75] Hardy to Lord Lytton (15 July 1891), ibid. 239–40, 240.
[76] Sir Charles Trevelyan, 1878 *Commission on Copyright*, 2.
[77] In June 1886, Hardy was considering arranging the publication of *The Mayor of Casterbridge* in Macmillan's cheap 'Colonial Library'. Hardy to Frederick Macmillan (6 June 1886), *Collected Letters*, i. 146.
[78] See Patrick Brantlinger's discussion of George Gissing in *The Reading Lesson: The Threat of Mass Literacy in Nineteenth-Century British Fiction* (1998).
[79] M. Hansen, 'Unstable Mixtures, Dilated Spheres: Negt and Kluge's *The Public Sphere and Experience*, Twenty Years Later', *Public Culture*, 5/2 (Winter, 1993), 179–212, 200.

as instrumental, or as a public service. To establish a value in their intellectual property beyond the economic, writers were increasingly turning inwards to ideas of selfhood and self-expression. Such a change is echoed in the development, in this period, of the 'new' journalism, as anonymous periodical journalism gave way to 'signed journalism', in which, as W. T. Stead put it in 1886, 'everything depends upon the individual—the person. Impersonal journalism is effete. To influence men you must be a man, not a mock-uttering oracle.'[80] Thomas Hardy privately agreed with Stead in a letter to Edmund Gosse in the same year, written in sympathy over a kicking that Gosse had received anonymously in the pages of the *Quarterly*:

But I do seriously think that the article is a strong argument against anonymous journalism. I have suffered terribly at times from reviews—pecuniarily, & still more mentally, & the crown of my bitterness has been my sense of the unfairness of such impersonal means of attack, wh. conveys to an unthinking public the idea of an immense weight of opinion behind, to which you can only oppose your own solitary little personality: when the truth is that there is only another little solitary personality against yours all the time.[81]

Hardy's image of his 'own solitary little personality' pitted against the uncomprehending public world suggests once again his sense of the difficulty of maintaining a cohesive and defensible property in himself when confronted by an ever-growing marketplace, and an ever more opaque readership that he is only able to imagine as an 'unthinking public'.

Whereas corporatization in the electricity industry had had the effect of entirely effacing the inventor, who was now long left behind as an identifiable agency, the writer, faced with an increasingly corporatized press, emerges as more of a 'celebrity' than ever. Richard Salmon has also attended to the odd dissonance of this development: 'It is surely not coincidental that at the very moment when the material basis of the press made it harder to locate an individuated source of authorial value, the discourse of journalism should so insistently declare its personalized character.'[82] Similarly, Hardy's work in the

---

[80] W. T. Stead, 'The Future of Journalism', *Contemporary Review*, 50 (November 1886), 663–79, 663. Quoted in Salmon, ' "A Simulacrum of Power" ', 28. Laurel Brake has challenged the idea that there was a sudden change from anonymous to 'new' journalism in this period. Laurel Brake, *Subjugated Knowledges: Journalism, Gender and Literature in the Nineteenth Century* (1994).

[81] Hardy to Gosse (19 October 1886), *Collected Letters*, i. 154–5.

[82] Salmon, ' "A Simulacrum of Power" ', 29.

1880s and 1890s consciously reinforces this sense of imaginative originality, both in its concerns, but also—as Hillis Miller has noticed—in its movement away from the recognizable referents of Victorian realism. Discussing the two different endings of the *The Well-Beloved*, which were printed side by side in the New Wessex Edition, Miller remarks:

> *The Well-Beloved* is clearly something that Hardy has written, not something copied directly from real life. It is something that he might have written otherwise. In fact he has written it otherwise, changing it radically from one version to the next. The changes affirm his sovereign power as creator over a fiction which no longer needs to validate itself by its presumed correspondence to some 'reality' outside literature.[83]

I would argue, though, that this shift in the late century is perhaps less the positive affirmation of the 'sovereign power' of the writer, than a defensive reaction to the changing position of the reader. In a huge, multinational global market, the intimacy of address, albeit assumed, of Dickens and Thackeray is no longer possible. The reader can no longer be figured as part of a known constituency. The spatial attenuation of the market, particularly into North America, has made even an imaginary community impossible. The unknowable diversity of his reading public forces Hardy to fall back on his own role as producer, both in what he writes about, and how he writes it.

In June 1882, Hardy mused on the nature of creativity:

> As, in looking at a carpet, by following one colour a certain pattern is suggested, by following another colour, another, so in life the seer should watch that pattern among general things which his idiosyncracy moves him to observe, and describe that alone. This is, quite accurately, a going to Nature; yet the result is no mere photograph, but purely the product of the writer's own mind.[84]

Hardy suggests that it is 'idiosyncracy' which determines what a particular writer chooses to take from the 'general', but while he makes no great claims for the originality or creativity of the artist, he holds fast to the idea of the property in the work, significantly using a

---

[83] J. Hillis Miller, '*The Well-Beloved*: The Compulsion to Stop Repeating', in *Fiction and Repetition* (1982), 147–75, 154. *The Pursuit of the Well-Beloved* appeared as a weekly serial in the *Illustrated London News* (and simultaneously in the American *Harper's Bazaar*) from 1 October to 17 December 1892. Hardy substantially rewrote the story for volume publication in March 1897. My comments on this text are confined to the 1897 version.

[84] Journal Entry, 3 June [1882]. Quoted in F. E. Hardy, *The Life of Thomas Hardy* (1962), 153.

photograph as an example of the unmediated, and therefore un-owned work.

Yet Hardy's role as a producer who is to some degree alienated from his public is not an easy one, as he suggests in *The Well-Beloved*. Unlike his painter friend, Alfred Somers, who, in middle-age, settles into producing pictures 'addressed to the furnishing householder through the middling critic', in exchange for 'many large cheques from . . . England and America', the sculptor-hero Pierston resists such commercialism and strains towards a finer personal identity with his own work: 'He would have gone on working with his chisel with just as much zest if his creations had been doomed to meet no mortal eye but his own.'[85] Taking three generations of women in the same family as his inspiration, he creates and recreates 'the marble images of her which stood in his working-room' (125)—each Avice the 'perfect copy' (75), or 'the extraordinary reproduction' (126) of the original. Yet despite his great professional success, Pierston fails to possess any one of the original women, and is, instead 'urged on and on' (125) by 'his old trouble—his doom—his curse' (125). Pierston's artistic work seems to control him but also to evade him—the pursuit merely produces reproduction after reproduction. Finally, his attempt to grasp an ideal or an origin through his art fails, and surveying the sculptures in his studio, he murmurs, ' "I don't feel a single touch of kin with or interest in any of them whatever" ' (169). Consequently, 'he direct[s] his agent in town to disperse the whole collection', and, as an artist, Pierston dies. As the story closes, the still living Pierston 'is sometimes mentioned as "the late Mr Pierston" ' (173). If Hillis Miller is right in judging 'the *Well Beloved* [to be] one of a group of important nineteenth-century novels about art', its message is a strange one.[86] When Pierston realizes that the artist within him has died, '[a]t first he was appalled; and then he said "Thank God!" ' (166). Hardy seems to fantasize his own death, and the forced surrendering of his energetic investment in his work, and its dispersal beyond his control as a relief. Yet equally he seems appalled by even the retrospective vision of his life shorn of all intellectual property.[87] Pierston's

[85] Thomas Hardy, *The Well-Beloved: A Sketch of a Temperament* (1997), 136, 41. All subsequent references are given in parentheses in the text.

[86] Miller, *Fiction and Repetition*, 148.

[87] Such an anxiety perhaps resembles that of Wordsworth, who, as Susan Eilenberg has written, 'In seeking a way around the limitation on copyright . . . sought to

'afterlife' on the island is occupied in modernizing schemes that contribute to the obliteration of the particular character of the place and its absorption into a homogenous modern Britain as part of the march towards 'uniformity and mental equality' that Hardy spoke of in 'The Dorsetshire Labourer'. The belated and elegiac tone of the tale, with its relentless emphasis on ageing, makes it tempting to read *The Well-Beloved* as Hardy's reflection on the obsolescence of the modern artwork, and the futility of the fantasy of continued possession. It also makes it appropriate that this was the last fiction that Hardy published before picking up his career as a poet: a career that allowed him to fantasize a retreat from the mass readership of fiction, and from the public arena of the periodical press. He writes in his 'General Preface to the Wessex Edition of 1912', 'Thus much for the novels. Turning now to the verse—to myself the more individual part of my literary fruitage—I would say that, unlike some of the fiction, nothing interfered with the writer's freedom in respect of its form or content.'[88] Hardy's poetry allowed him to accommodate and preserve the particular and personal in his experience in a way that fiction had never done.

Even Pierston's home on an 'island rock in the English Channel' (41) is touched by the influence of a universalizing culture. The islander Avice Caro, for example, 'lived in a house that would have been the fortune of an artist, and learnt to draw London suburban villas from printed copies' (15). 'Printed copies' have already infiltrated the island's traditional spaces: Hardy seems to suggest that insularity is no protection against globalization. An American commentator on the international copyright question in 1879 reminded a British readership that the anglophone literary market extended well beyond 'your snug little island', and called for modernized distribution practices.[89] N. N. Feltes has suggested that

pronounce from beyond the grave a controversion [*sic*] of his own mortality. The campaign to extend the term of copyright—Wordsworth wanted it extended not to forty-two or to sixty years but forever—may have been, for him at least, an attempt to realize his intimations of immortality in legal form,' 'Mortal Pages: Wordsworth and the Reform of Copyright', *ELH* 56/2 (Summer 1989), 351–74, 369–70.

[88] Thomas Hardy, 'General Preface to the Wessex Edition of 1912', repr. in *The Mayor of Casterbridge* (1983), 413–18, 416. I say 'fantasize' advisedly, as—of course—Hardy's poetry was as much part of the literary marketplace as his fiction when he sold poems for publication.

[89] S. S. Conant, 'International Copyright I. An American View', *Macmillan's Magazine*, 40 (May 1879–October 1879), 151–61, 153.

the Commission did not finally accommodate the free-trade arguments which were so energetically presented by T. H. Farrer and Sir
Louis Mallet because 'the concrete spatial and temporal particulari-
ties of the book trade at the turn of the century' made such arguments
'insular [and] outmoded'.[90] In fact, the free-trade model had never
prevailed in any intellectual property debate during the nineteenth
century, even when free-trade thinking was at its ideologically most
dominant at mid-century.

What has shifted in the debate about intellectual property, then,
since the mid-century, is the emphasis, which is no longer on the construction of the 'original author', but on the role of the legislation to
preserve, rather than to establish, property. International copyright
was necessary to protect literary property through long-distance
transmissions and into an ever more spatially dispersed future. The
emphasis throughout the committee-stage discussion was much less
upon the right to intellectual property and more upon the means of
its control. Arthur Sullivan, one half of Gilbert and Sullivan, was by
no means the only witness to insist on such a 'legal right to control
. . . his works'.[91] The Law of International Copyright was a protectionist law in a way that previous intellectual property legislation
had never been, and offers a clear example of the revival of protectionism in British politics after 1870.[92] Hardy's work reflects such a
shift in thinking about intellectual property in this period, and
articulates anxieties about the preservation and control, rather than
the establishment of the imprimatur of ownership.

Both *A Laodicean* and *Two on a Tower*, published in 1881 and
1882 respectively, include explicit discussions of intellectual property. In *Two on a Tower*, Lady Constantine urges the astronomer,
Swithin St Cleeve, publicly to own his discovery of the secret of the
variability of the stars: ' "Publish it at once in some paper; nail your
name to it, or somebody else will seize the idea and appropriate it,—
forestall you in some way. It will be Adams and Leverrier over
again." '[93] Indeed, it transpires that '[a]nother man ha[s] forestalled

[90] Feltes, 'International Copyright', 279.

[91] Arthur Sullivan Esq., 'I am very much in favour of the composer, or the publisher
through him, having the legal right to control the performance of his works, whether
they are dramatic or whether they belong to the concert hall', 1878 *Commission on
Copyright*, 111.

[92] See G. R. Searle, 'Preface', *Morality and the Market in Victorian Britain* (1998).

[93] Thomas Hardy, *Two on a Tower: A Romance*, ed. Sally Shuttleworth (1999), 59.
All subsequent page references are given in parentheses.

his discovery by a period of about six weeks' (62). In *A Laodicean*, the architect Havill 'possesse[s] himself of Somerset's brains' by copying his rival's architectural plan, and Hardy's text stresses 'the absolute nature of the theft' (231), despite the lack of legislation at this time to protect architectural drawings.[94] Hardy himself described this curious novel as 'about art, in a mild way', and, as Gerhard Joseph has suggested of Dickens's *Martin Chuzzlewit*, it seems that Hardy may be using architectural property as an analogue for intellectual property more generally in this novel.[95]

But another incident in the plot is more significant in thinking about Hardy's understanding of the preservation of property and propriety through the treacherous process of dispersal. The architect, George Somerset, is not a wilful spender. He watches the gaming at a fashionable Monte Carlo casino, '[a]s a non-participant in its profits and losses, fevers and frenzies' (314), but others in the novel rely more on the opportunities and 'contingent intervention[s]' (320) of chance events. Already the accessory to Havill's theft of the architectural drawings, and the perpetrator of a 'telegraphic trick' (358), Dare is adept at distorting and falsifying the messages transmitted by new media. When a photograph drops accidentally out of his pocket in front of Paula Power and Charlotte de Stancy, Hardy tells us that '[i]t was neither a visiting nor a playing card, but one bearing a photographic portrait of a peculiar nature' (353). Unlike visiting or playing cards, this is a card that was not intended for circulation, but Dare chooses to publicize it, fraudulent though it is. 'It was a portrait of Somerset; but by a device known in photography the operator, though contriving to produce what seemed to be a perfect likeness, had given it the distorted features and wild attitude of a man advanced in intoxication' (334–5). To the ladies, 'that picture of Somerset had all the cogency of direct vision' (356). Hardy suggests that this is precisely the treachery of the new media that

---

[94] Thomas Hardy, *A Laodicean: A Story of To-day* (1995), 158. All subsequent page references given in parentheses. Charles Barry (President of the Royal Institute of British Architects) recorded in his evidence to the International Copyright Commission that the institute had petitioned in 1869 ' "for the protection of architects in a manner similar to that for authors and inventors" ' but without success, *1878 Commission on Copyright*, 234.

[95] Hardy to Thomas Woolner (7 December 1881), *Collected Letters*, i. 97. See Gerhard Joseph, 'Charles Dickens, International Copyright, and the Discretionary Silence of *Martin Chuzzlewit*', in Woodmansee and Jaszi (eds.), *Construction of Authorship*, 259–70, 266.

reproduce the immediacy of direct contact, fatally disjunct from actual presence. It is all too easy for Dare to write as 'G. Somerset' to 'Miss Power, Grand Hotel, Genoa' (320) by telegram, or to falsify a photograph of the architect.

Indeed, similar worries about the control of photographic images were aired during the 1876 Royal Commission on Copyright. Boydell Graves, examined by Sir Henry Holland on the subject of photographic copyright, stated that:

I think that the copyright should be vested in the person sitting for the portrait, because otherwise it might be surreptitiously reproduced, or exhibited in public windows; or being the portrait of one's wife, or near relative, it might come to be publicly exhibited with other portraits, a proceeding which might, under certain circumstances, be manifestly undesirable.[96]

The public exhibition, dispersal, or distortion of private property (here the example given is of a wife) without the control of the owner fatally disrupts the 'natural' relationship between personality and presence. It is no coincidence, for example, that Hardy sets the incident of the photograph in a foreign country, while Somerset himself is supposed to be far away.

On Paula Power's marriage, this anxiety is rewritten as comedy when one of the local dairymen comments of the de Stancy ancestral portraits in her possession: ' "Well—why can't 'em hire a travelling chap to touch up the picters into her own gaffers and gammers? Then they'd be worth something to her" ' (469). But Paula's ownership of the 'picters' does not figure her identity with them, and no amount of touching up will correct this. Paula is forced to own, albeit reluctantly, her own lineage in 'that other nobility—the nobility of talent and enterprise' (124). The 'Power' of her name is that of engineering and industry. The curious collision of the old with the new, represented by the 'telegraph-room in the tower' (232) of the de Stancy castle, seems to speak metonymically about art and property, but the messages are confused. While Hardy seems to denounce much of the contingent mobility of modernity, he sees, as he also saw in the article he wrote two years later, 'The Dorsetshire Labourer', that there is no way back. He may have buried himself in rural Dorset, but he himself was an enthusiastic sender of telegraph messages, and considered investing in the new electrical companies.[97] '[T]he little

---

[96] *1878 Commission on Copyright*, 167.
[97] See Hardy, *Collected Letters*, i. 152–3, and Hardy to Edward Clodd (20 January 1892), ibid. 254 postscript: 'I wonder if you think well of the City of London Electric Lighting Co. for an investment? It is recommended to me.'

buzzing wire' that Somerset follows across the fields leads to the telegraph, 'a machine which beyond everything may be said to symbol-
ize cosmopolitan views and the intellectual and moral kinship of all
mankind'. But then 'the modern fever and fret which consumes
people before they can grow old was also signified by the wire' (22).
The consuming of individuals by a standardized and universal culture raises the same anxieties as those expressed by J. S. Mill half a
century before, who had wondered, 'whether our "march of intellect" be not rather a march towards doing without intellect, and supplying our deficiency of giants by the united efforts of a constantly
increasing multitude of dwarfs'.[98] What place would there be for art
that was not 'rather popular than distinguished' in such a 'wired'
future?[99]

CONCLUSION

George Bernard Shaw wrote to Florence Hardy shortly after her husband's death in 1928, '[y]ou see a man like T. H. does not belong entirely to himself; and he cannot leave his widow more than he
owned.'[100] Just how much Hardy owned of himself, and how much
was legitimately public property takes us back to the crux of all discussions of intellectual property from the beginning of the century
onwards. The conflict between the social and individual ownership
of invention and information is open to endless negotiation. This
book has shown that the laws of copyright did not develop in a cultural vacuum and do not provide proof, as some historians would
have us believe, of the inevitability and authenticity of the Romantic
model of the author. Carlyle's author with his 'copy-rights and his
copy-wrongs' shared his imaginary garret with the 'poor but
ingenious artisan'.[101] By placing constructions of literary labour
in the context of other concurrent debates about the social value
of mental labour in the period, I have shown how freely literary and

---

[98] J. S. Mill, 'On Genius' (1832), in John M. Robson and Jack Stillinger (eds.),
Autobiography and Literary Essays by John Stuart Mill (1981), 329–39, 330. The
essay originally appeared in the *Monthly Repository*, NS 6 (October 1832), 649–59,
signed 'Antiquus'.
[99] Hardy, *The Well-Beloved*, 136.
[100] G. B. Shaw to Florence Hardy (27 January 1928), in Dan H. Laurence (ed.),
Bernard Shaw, Collected Letters 1926–1950 (1988), 85.
[101] 'On the Necessity and the Means of Protecting Needy Genius', *The London
Journal of Arts and Sciences*, 9 (1825), 308–19, 308–12.

mechanical inventors borrowed from one another in their defence of their rights to intellectual property, and in their construction of their own social power as professionals. If we look back to the mid-nineteenth century, we find art and technology invoked each in the service of the other. The opportunism of these analogies lays bare the constructedness of both the inventor and the author. In 1838, for example, the scientist David Brewster asked that writers should share the kind of protection abroad afforded to mechanists by patent law, warning legislators not to 'drive . . . that genius which can equally pervert as enforce the truth, into bartering its divine birthright for a mess of pottage'.[102] In 1851, art and technology came so close as to touch each other in what Carlyle termed that 'inexpressible Glass Palace with all its noisy inanity'.[103] The noisy Great Exhibition articulated more clearly, perhaps, than any other 'text' of the decade, the confrontation of the mass market and a traditional idea of 'culture'. Some, such as Carlyle and Ruskin, saw a threat; others, such as Cole and Babbage, saw an opportunity.

Any negotiation of intellectual property necessarily involves a renegotiation of the historically constructed boundary between public and private spheres, and a reformulation of the relationship between the two. The spectre of the commodity in the Crystal Palace, with its value over-invested in ephemerality and public display, sent the mid-century novelists in search of alternative sites of value. In their various ways, they created alternative public spaces in which literature could be construed as useful and instrumental, rather than ephemeral or trivial, while protecting a private space in which it remained incontrovertibly their own personal property. For Dickens and Thackeray, literature could both reflect and intervene in the public, political sphere. For Gaskell and Eliot, novels could attempt to confront some of the problems of a modernizing market culture, and could represent a personal gift to their readers, much as middle-class women offered charitable work in their local communities.[104]

---

[102] [David Brewster], 'International Law of Copyright', *Monthly Chronicle* (April 1838), 163–8, 168.

[103] Quoted Simon Heffer, *Moral Desperado: A Life of Thomas Carlyle* (1995), 291.

[104] For a discussion of this kind of 'women's work', see Dorice Williams Elliott, 'The Female Visitor and the Marriage of Classes in Gaskell's *North and South*', *Nineteenth-Century Literature*, 49/1 (June 1994), 21–49. After writing this chapter, my attention was drawn to Robert Macfarlane's 'A Small Squealing Black Pig: George Eliot, Originality and Plagiarism', in *George Eliot—George Henry Lewes Studies*, 42/43 (September 2002), 1–29. Macfarlane argues that Eliot was less interested in

When this imaginary public space was threatened by globalization at the end of the century, novelists retreated into an embattled and agonistic model of modern, private selfhood. Thomas Hardy wrote in 1887, 'The "simply natural" is interesting no longer. The much decried, mad, late-Turner rendering is now necessary to create my interest.'[105] At the end of the nineteenth century, the work-of-art is reprivatized. But rather than a return to the construction of the powerful individual Romantic genius, the artist is now discernible only in the 'rendering'. Hardy's model of the 'mad, late' style itself represents a belated snatch at a fast-receding idea of individual personality. It is no coincidence that it was in the last decades of the nineteenth century that the value accruing to 'late' works by artists and writers began to inflate, as they were newly appreciated rather than deprecated for their difficulty, and their withdrawal into 'abstract imaginings', in Hardy's phrase. 'I don't want to see the original realities—as optical effects, that is,' he wrote, 'I want to see the deeper reality underlying the scenic, the expression of what are sometimes called abstract imaginings.'[106] As technologies of reproduction—electrical communications and 'optical effects'—developed in accuracy and speed of production, the site of originality and therefore of property shifted from 'realism', now ten-a-penny, as Hardy suggests, to 'stylization'.[107] At the end of the century individuality seemed an increasingly problematic phenomenon, and could be surely glimpsed only in the private idiosyncrasies of the mature artist at the end of a long career. Originality had become less a matter of inspiration than of hard-won achievement. The patent and copyright acts of the mid-nineteenth century had defined 'originality' as subsisting in the 'rendering' or application of an idea, rather than in the idea itself, but, as this book has shown, the debating of the legislation in both cases had thrown up grandiose claims for artists and inventors as heroic originators. Only in the late-Victorian period did the legal definition begin truly to reflect the cultural consensus on the production of innovative work.

Romantic ideas of originality than she was in the new science of the 'general mind' and unconscious. I would argue that while this was certainly the case, Eliot's relationship to traditional ideas of intellectual ownership remained complex.

[105] Thomas Hardy, January 1887. Quoted in F. E. Hardy, *Life of Thomas Hardy*, 185.
[106] See Gordon McMullan, *The Invention of Late Work* (forthcoming).
[107] Thomas Hardy, January 1887. Quoted in F. E. Hardy, *Life of Thomas Hardy*, 185.

Intellectual property is, then, a culturally constructed category. Intellectual property legislation does not merely acknowledge the subject's distinctive identity, it creates it. There could be, and indeed there are, many other ways of conceptualizing property, but it is to the particular negotiations of the Victorian period that we still need to look in order to understand the endurance of a model of possessive individualism in Euro-American intellectual property law. Electronic communication today continues to put intellectual property legislation under pressures very similar to those discussed in this chapter. The 'abolitionist' resistance to Talfourd's copyright bills, for example, is especially resonant when compared to current hacker rhetoric that claims that 'information wants to be free'. The Napster controversy over music trading on the internet presents an analogous case, showing that this debate survives intact into the twenty-first century, if only because Euro-American culture still struggles and aspires to preserve a public sphere that is not wholly dominated by the capitalist marketplace, and—ultimately—because we have still not decided what exactly it means to be an individual.

Bibliography

This bibliography is limited to books and articles referred to in footnotes. Publication information for frequently cited works is provided in the note on abbreviations at the front of the book.

BOOKS AND ARTICLES, PRIMARY AND SECONDARY

A. B., A Member of the Ennis Mechanics' Institute, Letter to the Editor, 'The Patent Laws', *Mechanics' Magazine* (26 May 1827), 324–7.

ABRAMS, M. H., *The Mirror and the Lamp: Romantic Theory and Critical Tradition* (New York: Oxford University Press, 1953).

ACKROYD, P., *Dickens* (London: Minerva, 1991).

[ALISON, A.], 'The Copyright Question', *Blackwood's Edinburgh Magazine*, 51 (January 1842), 107–21.

ALLEN, G., 'Ivan Greet's Masterpiece', in *Twelve Tales, With a Headpiece, a Tailpiece, and an Intermezzo* (London: Grant Richards, 1899).

ALTICK, R. D., *The English Common Reader: A Social History of the Mass Reading Public 1800–1900* (Chicago: Chicago University Press, 1967).

——*The Presence of the Present: Topics of the Day in the Victorian Novel* (Colorado: Ohio State University Press, 1991).

ANDERSON, O., 'The Janus Face of Mid-Nineteenth-Century English Radicalism: The Administrative Reform Association of 1855', *Victorian Studies*, 8 (1965), 231–42.

ANONYMOUS, *Address of the Committee of the Society for the Diffusion of Useful Knowledge* (Charles Knight & Co., 1846).

——'Advancement in Life', *Chambers's Edinburgh Journal* (27 October 1832), 317.

——*A Letter to the Right Honourable The Earl of Derby, on the Proposed Opening of the Crystal Place on the Lord's Day* (London: Seeleys, 1853).

——'Annals of the Poor', *Chambers's Edinburgh Journal* (12 May 1832), 115–16.

——'Arago's Life of Watt', *Chambers's Edinburgh Journal* (26 October 1839), 317–18.

——'Biographic Sketches: James Watt', *Chambers's Edinburgh Journal* (24 March 1832), 61–2.

——'Biographic Sketches: Thomas Telford', *Chambers's Edinburgh Journal* (21 February 1835), 29–30.

ANONYMOUS, 'Capital and Labour', *Saturday Magazine* (8 April 1837), 133.

—— 'The Catalogue's Account of Itself', *Household Words* (23 August 1851), 519–23.

—— 'Comic Leaves From the Statute Book', *Household Words* (17 August 1850), 502–4.

—— 'The Copyright Question', *Illustrated London News*, 18 (24 May 1851), 439–40.

—— 'The Crystal Palace Electrical Exhibition', *The Telegraphic Journal and Electrical Review* (18 February 1882), 113.

—— 'Diffusion of Useful Knowledge', *Mechanics' Magazine* (Saturday, 5 May 1827), 194–200.

—— 'Disappointments of the Authors of Important Inventions', *Penny Magazine* (14 April 1832), 19.

—— 'Dissertation on First Principles of Government', *Poor Man's Guardian* (7 January 1831), 236–7.

—— 'The Eddystone Lighthouse', *Penny Magazine* (28 July 1832), 163.

—— 'Encouragement of Inventions', *Saturday Magazine* (18 June 1825), 171–3.

—— 'Evidence of Alexander Galloway', Abstracted Report of the Select Committee of he House of Commons, on the Exportation of Machinery and Artizans, *London Journal of Arts and Sciences; Containing Reports of All New Patents, with Descriptions of their Respective Principles and Properties; also Original Communications on Objects Connected with Science and Philosophy; Particularly such as embrace the most recent Inventions and Discoveries in Practical Mechanics*, 9 (1825), 101–6.

—— '*The Exposition of 1851; or, Views of the Industry, the Science, and the Government of England* by Charles Babbage, Esq. (London 1851)', *North British Review* (August 1851), 529–68.

—— 'Extraordinary Bed-ridden Mechanic', *Mechanics' Magazine* (5 June 1824), 167.

—— 'Female Education in the Middle Classes', *English Woman's Journal*, 1/4 (June 1858), 217–27.

—— 'A few Words on International Copyright—Assemblée Nationale Legislative. Projet de loi relatif à une Convention littéraire entre la France et la Grande-Bretagne, précédé de l'exposé des motifs présenté par M. TURGOT, Ministre des Affaires Etrangères. 11 Nov., 1851', *Edinburgh Review*, 95 (January 1852), 145–52.

—— 'Fluctuations of Rank Among Men', *Chambers's Edinburgh Journal* (18 January 1834), 401.

—— 'The Fourth Estate', article extracted from the *New Monthly*, *Chartist Circular* (10 July 1841), 396.

—— 'France and Free Trade', *All the Year Round* (10 March 1860), 466–72.

—— 'Galileo', *Saturday Magazine* (16 February 1833), 59.

—— 'The Good Side of Combination [*sic*]', *Household Words*, 81 (11 October 1851), 56–60.

—— ' "The History of the Law Amendment Society from its Institution in 1844, till the Present Time," *Law Review*, 21, 1854/5', in *North British Review* (August 1855), 326–37.

—— 'House-top Telegraphs', *All the Year Round* (26 November 1859), 106–9.

—— 'The Hymn of the Lancashire Cotton Spinner', *Saturday Magazine* (28 July 1832), 30.

—— 'An Idea of Mine', *Household Words* (13 March 1858), 699–704.

—— 'The Independent Potter', *Mechanics' Magazine* (30 August 1823), 12.

—— *The Industry of Nations, Part II: A Survey of the Existing State of Arts, Machines, and Manufactures* [Published under the Direction of the Committee of General Literature and Education, Appointed by the Society for Promoting Christian Knowledge] (London: SPCK, 1855).

—— 'Introduction', *Illustrated Exhibitor* (7 June 1851), 1–3.

—— 'James Watt', *Penny Magazine* (31 August 1832), 209.

—— 'James Watt from Arago's *Life of Watt*', *Saturday Magazine* (4 February 1843), 46.

—— 'Labour and Capital' (Abridged from the Economical Library), *Saturday Magazine* (26 December 1835), 246–7.

—— 'The Late Mr. Arkwright' [from the newspaper of May], *Chambers's Edinburgh Journal* (1 July 1843), 192.

—— 'Law for Ladies', *Saturday Review* (24 May 1856), 77–8.

—— 'The License of Modern Novelists', *Edinburgh Review*, 106 (July 1857), 124–56.

—— 'Literary Adventurers', *All the Year Round* (10 October 1863), 152–6.

—— 'Literary Reform', *Chartist Circular* (30 January 1841), 299.

—— 'Literary Remuneration', *Chambers's Edinburgh Journal* (27 June 1835), 169–70.

—— 'The Literary Profession', *Chambers's Edinburgh Journal* (6 August 1842), 225–6.

—— 'London Mechanics' Institution', *Mechanics' Magazine* (27 January 1827), 60–2.

—— 'Machinery and Manufactures: Review of Charles Babbage's *The Economy of Machinery and Manufactures*', *Penny Magazine* (30 June 1832), 131–2.

—— 'Man's Might and Woman's Right', *Saturday Review*, 27/2 (3 May 1856), 5–6.

—— 'The Mechanics' Almanac for 1837', *Mechanics' Magazine* (3 December 1836), 170–1.

—— 'Mechanics' Hall of Science', *Poor Man's Advocate and People's Library*, 6 (Manchester) (25 February 1832), 43–5.

ANONYMOUS, 'Memoir of James Watt, the Great Improver of the Steam Engine', *Mechanics' Magazine* (30 August 1823), 1–5.

—— 'Minutes of Evidence on the Patent Laws', *Mechanics' Magazine* (10 March 1827), 390–7.

—— 'Necessity the Mother of Invention', *Penny Magazine* (23 June 1832), 114–15.

—— 'The New Copyright Bill', *Chambers's Edinburgh Journal* (28 April 1838), 112.

—— 'Newspaper Reporting', *Metropolitan*, 5 (November 1832), 278.

—— 'Official Catalogue of the Great Exhibition of the Works of Industry of All Nations, 1851: 4th corrected edition, 15th September 1851', *Edinburgh Review*, 94 (October 1851), 557–98.

—— 'On the Evils of Individual Property', *Poor Man's Guardian* (20 August 1831), 53–4.

—— 'On the Necessity and the Means of Protecting Needy Genius', *The London Journal of Arts and Sciences; Containing Reports of All New Patents, with Descriptions of their Respective Principles and Properties; also Original Communications on Objects Connected with Science and Philosophy; Particularly such as embrace the most recent Inventions and Discoveries in Practical Mechanics*, 9 (1825), 308–19.

—— 'The Patent Journal. Nos. 1–100. London: 1846-7-8. (2). The Mechanic's Magazine. Vols XLVII. And XLVIII, London: 1846-7-8', *Edinburgh Review*, 89 (January 1849), 47–83.

—— 'The Patent Laws: A few Questions for the Consideration of those who think that Patents should be expensive', *Mechanics' Magazine* (25 April 1829), 166–7.

—— 'The Patent Laws', *Mechanics' Magazine* (10 March 1827), 149–50.

—— 'The Patent Laws', *Mechanics' Magazine* (5 May 1827), 277–8.

—— 'The Patent Laws', *Mechanics' Magazine* (26 May 1827), 324–7.

—— 'The Patent Laws', *Mechanics' Magazine* (18 April 1829), 154–6.

—— 'Patents', *Morning Chronicle* (4 June 1835), 2.

—— 'Peculiarities of Authors', *Chambers's Edinburgh Journal* (12 May 1832), 117.

—— 'Penny Magazine', *The Poor Man's Guardian. A Weekly Newspaper for the People* (4 August 1832), 486.

—— 'Popular Information on Political Economy: Patents', *Chambers's Edinburgh Journal* (13 March 1841), 59–60.

—— 'Power and Advantages of Knowledge', *Chartist Circular*, 2/109 (Glasgow), (23 October 1841), 453.

—— 'Preface to Fourth Volume', *Mechanics' Magazine* (1825), p. iii.

—— 'Preface to Volume 1', *Penny Magazine of the Society for the Diffusion of Useful Knowledge* (18 December 1832), pp. iii–iv.

—— 'The Private History of the Palace of Glass', *Household Words*, 43 (18 January 1851), 385–91.

——'Proposed New Copyright Law', *Chambers's Edinburgh Journal* (21 April 1838), 104.

——'Public Meeting for the Establishment of the London Mechanics' Institute: Report of Mr. Sheriff Laurie's Speech', *Mechanics' Magazine* (15 November 1823), 182.

——'Report of a Speech by Admiral Selwyn to the Inventors' Institute', *Inventor's Record and Industrial Guardian*, 1/1 (15 March 1879), 1.

——'Report of Meeting held to discuss Monument to the Late James Watt', *Mechanics' Magazine* (26 June 1824), 242–9.

——'Report of the Select Committee Appointed to Inquire into the Best Means of Extending a Knowledge of the Arts and of the Principles of Design Among the People (especially the manufacturing population) of the Country; also to Inquire into the Constitution, Management, and Effects of Institutions Connected with the Arts', *Mechanics' Magazine* (19 November 1836), 120–44.

——'Rich and Poor', *Saturday Magazine* (19 January 1833), 21.

——'The Rights of Property' (from Mr. Wade's 'History of the Middle and Working Classes'), *Chambers's Edinburgh Journal* (11 January 1834), 396–7.

——'Robert Boyle', *Saturday Magazine* (9 March 1833), 91.

——'Samuel Crompton, Inventor of the Spinning Mule', *Mechanics' Magazine* (14 July 1827), 446.

——'Sayings and Doings', *Critic* (23 April 1859), 387.

——'Science and Labour' (Taken from 'Rights of Industry, forming a volume of The Working Man's Companion'), *Chambers's Edinburgh Magazine* (21 December 1833), 376.

——'Sculpture and the Plastic Arts', *Illustrated Exhibitor* (18 October 1851), 383–4.

——'Sir George Head's Home-Tour in the Manufacturing Districts', *Mechanics' Magazine* (1 April 1831), 505–9.

——'Sir Humphry Davy', *Mechanics' Magazine* (13 June 1828), 279.

——'Sir Isaac Newton', *Mechanics' Magazine* (28 October 1826), 411–13.

——'Smeaton', *Saturday Magazine* (17 October 1835), 148.

——'Society: Division of Labour—Division of Property' (Extracted from Bishop Sumner's 'The Records of Creation'), *Saturday Magazine* (11 January 1834), 14–15.

——'Things of the Day: Copyright', *Blackwood's Edinburgh Magazine*, 4 (May 1842), 634–6.

——'Things Talked of in London', *Chambers's Edinburgh Journal* (31 May 1851), 350–2.

——'The Useful Education of the Unenfranchised Working Man', *Chartist Circular* (9 May 1840), 135.

——'The Value of a Penny', *Penny Magazine of the Society for the Diffusion of Useful Knowledge* (21 April 1832), 62.

ANONYMOUS, 'A Voice from the Factory', *Household Words*, 54 (5 April 1851), 35–6.

——'Walpole's Letters to the Countess of Ossory', *Edinburgh Review*, 88 (October 1848), 339–60.

——'The Weaver's Song *Not by Barry Cornwall*', *The Poor Man's Guardian. A Weekly Newspaper for the People* (3 November 1832), 587.

——'The Week—Anniversary of Death of Isaac Newton', *Penny Magazine of the Society for the Diffusion of Useful Knowledge* (22 December 1832), 375.

——'The Weekly Gossip', *Athenaeum* (2 July 1859), 20.

——'The Wisdom of Our Ancestors, or What is Property?' *Chartist Circular* (8 February 1840), 77.

——*The Young Mechanic: A Book for Boys* (London: Trübner & Co., 1871).

ARAC, J., *Commissioned Spirits: the Shaping of Social Motion in Dickens, Carlyle, Melville, and Hawthorne* (New Brunswick, NJ: Rutgers University Press, 1979).

ARAGO, M., *Life of James Watt with Memoir on Machinery Considered in Relation to the prosperity of the Working Classes. To which are subjoined, Historical Account of the Discovery of the Composition of Water by Lord Brougham and Eulogium of James Watt by Lord Jeffrey* (Edinburgh: Adam & Charles Black; London: Longman, Orme, Brown, Green & Longmans, 1839).

ARMSTRONG, T., *Haunted Hardy: Poetry, History, Memory* (Houndmills: Palgrave, 2000).

The Art Journal Illustrated Catalogue: The Industry of All Nations, 1851 (London: George Virtue, 1851; repr. in facsimile, New York: Dover, 1970).

ASHTON, R., *Dickens, George Eliot, and George Henry Lewes: The Hilda Hulme Lecture, 1991* (London: University of London, 1992).

——*The German Idea: Four English Writers and the Reception of German Thought 1800–1860* (Cambridge: Cambridge University Press, 1980).

AUERBACH, J. A., *The Great Exhibition of 1851: A Nation on Display* (New Haven: Yale University Press, 1999).

BABBAGE, C., *The Exposition of 1851; or, Views of the Industry, the Science, and the Government of England* (London: John Murray, 1851).

BAILIN, M., *The Sickroom in Victorian Fiction: The Art of Being Ill* (Cambridge: Cambridge University Press, 1994).

BAKEWELL, F. C., *Great Facts: A Popular History and Description of the Most Remarkable Inventions During the Present Century* (London: Houlston & Wright, n.d. [1859]).

BARACLOUGH, W. H., *Profit by Patents* (Birmingham: Cornish Brothers, 1897).

BARRETT BROWNING, E., *Elizabeth Barrett Browning: Aurora Leigh and Other Poems*, ed. John Robert Glorney Bolton and Julia Bolton Holloway (Harmondsworth: Penguin, 1995).

BATTERSBY, C., *Gender and Genius. Towards a Feminist Aesthetic* (London: Women's Press, 1989).

BAUDRILLARD, J., *Simulacra and Simulation*, trans. Sheila Faria Glaser (Ann Arbor: University of Michigan Press, 1994).

BAUMGARTEN, M., 'Writing and *David Copperfield*', *Dickens Studies Annual*, 14 (1985), 39–59.

BAZELEY, T., 'Cotton as an Element of Industry; its Confined Supply, and its Extending Consumption by Increasing and Improving Agencies', *Lectures on the Results of the Great Exhibition of 1851, Delivered Before the Society of Arts, Manufactures, and Commerce, at the Suggestion of H.R.H. Prince Albert, President of the Society* (London: David Bogue, 1853), ii. 107–46.

BEAUCHAMP, K. G., *Exhibiting Electricity* (London: Institution of Electrical Engineers, 1997).

BECK, U., *Risk Society: Towards a New Modernity*, trans. Mark Ritter (London: Sage, 1992).

BEER, G., *George Eliot* (Brighton: Harvester, 1986).

—— *Open Fields: Science in Cultural Encounter* (Oxford: Clarendon Press, 1996).

BELSEY, C., *Critical Practice* (London: Methuen, 1980).

BENNETT, A., *Romantic Poets and the Culture of Posterity* (Cambridge: Cambridge University Press, 1999).

BENNETT, T., *The Birth of the Museum: History, Theory, Politics* (London: Routledge, 1995).

—— 'The Exhibitionary Complex', *New Formations* 4, (Spring 1988), 73–102.

BENTHAM, J., *Jeremy Bentham's Economic Writings. Critical Edition Based on his Printed Works and Unprinted Manuscripts*, ed. W. Stark (London: George Allen & Unwin, 1952).

BERG, M., 'From Imitation to Invention: Creating Commodities in Eighteenth-Century Britain', *Economic History Review*, 55/1 (2002), 1–30.

—— *The Machinery Question and the Making of Political Economy, 1815–1848* (Cambridge: Cambridge University Press, 1980).

—— 'Women's Property and the Industrial Revolution', *Warwick Economic Research Papers*, 382 (October 1991).

[BESANT, W.], *This Son of Vulcan: A Novel*, 3 vols. (London: Sampson Low, Marston, Searle & Rivington, 1876).

BLAKE, K., '*Armgart*—George Eliot on the Woman Artist', *Victorian Poetry*, 18 (1980), 75–80.

BODENHEIMER, R., *The Politics of Story in Victorian Fiction* (Ithaca, NY: Cornell University Press, 1988).

—— *The Real Life of Mary Ann Evans: George Eliot, Her Letters and Fiction* (Ithaca, NY: Cornell University Press, 1994).

BONHAM-CARTER, V., *Authors by Profession*, 2 vols. (London: Society of Authors, 1978).

BOTTING, F., *Making Monstrous: Frankenstein, Criticism, Theory* (Manchester: Manchester University Press, 1991).

BOURDIEU, P., *Distinction: A Social Critique of the Judgement of Taste*, trans. Richard Nice (London: Routledge & Kegan Paul, 1984).

BOWLBY, R., *Just Looking, Consumer Culture in Dreiser, Gissing and Zola* (New York: Methuen, 1985).

BOYES, G., *The Imagined Village: Culture, Ideology and the English Folk Revival* (Manchester: Manchester University Press, 1993).

BRAKE, L., *Subjugated Knowledges: Journalism, Gender and Literature in the Nineteenth Century* (Basingstoke: Macmillan, 1994).

BRANTLINGER, P., *The Reading Lesson* (Bloomington: Indiana University Press, 1998).

—— *Rule of Darkness: British Literature and Imperialism, 1830–1914* (Ithaca, NY: Cornell University Press, 1988).

—— *Spirit of Reform: British Literature and Politics, 1832–1867* (Cambridge, Mass.: Harvard University Press, 1977).

[BREWSTER, D.], 'International Law of Copyright', *Monthly Chronicle* (April 1838), 163–8.

[——], 'Mr. Babbage on the Exposition of 1851', *North British Review*, 15 (August 1851), 529–68.

[——], 'Review of Babbage, *Reflexions on the Decline of Science in England, and on Some of its Causes*', *Quarterly Review*, 43 (October 1830), 305–42.

BRONTË, C., *The Letters of Charlotte Brontë, with a Selection of Letters by Family and Friends 1848–1851*, ed. Margaret Smith (Oxford: Clarendon Press, 2000), ii.

BUCK-MORSS, S., *The Dialectics of Seeing: Walter Benjamin and the Arcades Project* (Cambridge, Mass.: MIT Press, 1989).

BULWER LYTTON, E., *The Coming Race* (Stroud: Alan Sutton, 1995).

—— *Not So Bad As We Seem; or, Many Sides to a Character. A Comedy in Five Acts As First Performed at Devonshire House, in the Presence of Her Majesty and His Royal Highness The Prince Albert* (London: Chapman & Hall, 1851).

[——], *A Strange Story* (London: Sampson Low, Son & Co., 1862).

BURKE, E., *Reflections on the Revolution in France*, ed. Conor Cruise O'Brien (Harmondsworth: Penguin, 1968).

BURNLEY, J., *The Romance of Invention: Vignettes from the Annals of Industry and Science* (London: Cassell, 1886).

BUTT, J., and TILLOTSON, KATHLEEN, *Dickens at Work* (London: Methuen, 1957).

By Authority of the Royal Commission: Official Catalogue of the Great Exhibition of the Works of Industry of All Nations 1851 [Third Corrected and Improved Edition], 1 vol. (London: Spicer Brothers, 1851).

By Authority of the Royal Commission: Official Descriptive and Illustrated Catalogue of the Great Exhibition 1851, 3 vols. plus one suppl. vol. (London: Spicer Brothers, 1851).

BYATT, I. C. R., *The British Electrical Industry 1875–1914: The Economic Returns to a New Technology* (Oxford: Clarendon, 1979).

CALLENDER, W. R., *The Commercial Crisis of 1857: Its Causes and Results. Being the Substance of a Paper Read Before the Manchester Statistical Society* (London: Longman & Co., 1858).

CAREY, J. W., 'The Mythos of the Electronic Revolution', with John J. Quirk in *Communication as Culture: Essays on Media and Society* (Boston: Unwin Hyman, 1989), 113–41.

—— 'Technology and Ideology: The Case of the Telegraph', in *Communication as Culture: Essays on Media and Society* (Boston: Unwin Hyman, 1989), 217–18.

CARLISLE, J., *The Sense of an Audience: Dickens, Thackeray, and George Eliot at Mid-Century* (Brighton: Harvester, 1982).

CARLYLE, T., *The Collected Letters of Thomas and Jane Welsh Carlyle*, ed. Clyde de L. Ryals and Kenneth J. Fielding, 28 vols. (Durham, NC: Duke University Press, 1985), xi.

—— *The Collected Letters of Thomas and Jane Welsh Carlyle*, ed. Clyde de L. Ryals and Kenneth J. Fielding, 28 vols. (Durham, NC: Duke University Press, 1985), xii.

—— *Heroes, Hero-Worship and the Heroic in History* (London: James Fraser, 1851).

—— 'Signs of the Times', *Thomas Carlyle: Selected Writings*, ed. Alan Shelston (Harmondsworth: Penguin, 1971).

CHAMBERLAIN, J., 'Municipal Government; Past, Present and Future', *The New Review*, 61 (June 1894), 658.

[CHAMBERS, W.], 'The Editor's Address to his Readers', *Chambers's Edinburgh Journal* (11 February 1832), 1–2.

—— *Memoir of Robert Chambers with Autobiographic Reminiscences of William Chambers* (London: W. & R. Chambers, 1872).

CHAMBERS, W., and CHAMBERS, ROBERT, *Brief Objections to Mr. Talfourd's New Copyright Bill* (Edinburgh: Chambers, 1838).

CHAPPLE, J. A. V., '*Cousin Phillis*: Two Unpublished Letters from Elizabeth Gaskell to George Smith', *Études anglaises*, 23 (1980), 183–7.

CHASE, K. and LEVENSON, MICHAEL, *The Spectacle of Intimacy: A Public Life for the Victorian Family* (Princeton, NJ: Princeton University Press, 2000).

'CHIPS', 'Streetography', *Household Words*, 38 (14 December 1850), 275–6.

CHITTICK, K., *Dickens and the 1830s* (Cambridge: Cambridge University Press, 1990).

CHITTY, S., *The Beast and the Monk: A Life of Charles Kingsley* (London: Hodder & Stoughton, 1974).

CLAYTON, J.,'The Voice in the Machine: Hazlitt, Hardy, James', in Jeffrey Masten, Peter Stallybrass, and Nancy Vickers (eds.), *Language of Machines: Technologies of Literary and Cultural Production* (New York: Routledge, 1997), 209–32.

[COCHRANE, R.], *Heroes of Invention and Discovery: Lives of Eminent Inventors and Pioneers of Science* (Edinburgh: William P. Nimmo, 1879).

COLE, H., 'The International Results of the Exhibition of 1851', *Lectures on the Results of the Great Exhibition of 1851, Delivered Before the Society of Arts, Manufactures, and Commerce, at the Suggestion of H.R.H. Prince Albert, President of the Society* (London: David Bogue, 1853), ii. 419–51.

——*Fifty Years of Public Work of Sir Henry Cole, K. C. B.*, 2 vols. (London: George Bell & Sons, 1884).

COLLEY, L., *Britons: Forging the Nation 1707–1837* (New Haven: Yale University Press, 1992).

COLLINS, P., '*Little Dorrit*: the Prison and the Critics', *Times Literary Supplement* (18 April 1980), 445–6.

COLLINS, W., *Basil; A Story of Modern Life*, 3 vols. (London: Bentley, 1852).

——*The Frozen Deep and Mr Wray's Cash-Box* (Stroud: Alan Sutton, 1996).

——*The Letters of Wilkie Collins 1838–1865*, ed. William Baker and William M. Clarke (London: Macmillan 1999), i.

——*The Letters of Wilkie Collins 1866–1889*, ed. William Baker and William M. Clarke (London: Macmillan 1999), ii.

CONANT, S. S., 'International Copyright I. An American View', *Macmillan's Magazine*, 40 (May–October 1879), 151–61.

CONNELL, P., 'Bibliomania: Book Collecting, Cultural Politics, and the Rise of Literary Heritage in Romantic Britain', *Representations*, 71 (Summer 2000), 24–47.

CONNOR, S., *Dumbstruck: A Cultural History of Ventriloquism* (Oxford: Oxford University Press, 2000).

——'The Machine in the Ghost: Spiritualism, Technology, and the "Direct Voice"', in Peter Buse and Andrew Stott (eds.), *Ghosts: Deconstruction, Psychoanalysis, History* (Houndmills: Macmillan 1999).

COOMBE, R. J., 'Challenging Paternity: Histories of Copyright', Review Article, *Yale Journal of Law and the Humanities*, 6 (1994), 397–422.

——*The Cultural Life of Intellectual Properties: Authorship, Appropriation, and the Law* (Durham, NC: Duke University Press, 1998).

CORELLI, M., *Ardath: The Story of a Dead Self* (London: Richard Bentley & Son, 1889).

CORNER, J. and HARVEY, SYLVIA (eds.), *Enterprise and Heritage: Crosscurrents of National Culture* (London: Routledge, 1991).

CORNISH, W. R., 'The British Patent System: Historical Development', *Intellectual Property: Patents, Trade Marks and Allied Rights* (Sweet & Maxwell, 1999), pp. 110–117.

[CORNWALLIS, C. F.], 'The Property of Married Women: Report of the Personal Laws Committee (of the Law Amendment Society) on the Laws Relating to the Property of Married Women, London 1856', *Westminster Review*, NS 10 (October 1856), 331–60.

CRAWFORD, I., ' "Machinery in Motion": Time in *Little Dorrit*', *Dickensian*, 84/414 (Spring 1988), 30–41.

CRONIN, M., 'Henry Gowan, William Makepeace Thackeray, and "The Dignity of Literature" Controversy', *Dickens Quarterly*, 16/2 (June 1999), 104–45.

CROSBY, C., *The Ends of History: Victorians and 'The Woman Question'* (New York: Routledge, 1991).

CROSS, N., *The Common Writer: Life in Nineteenth-Century Grub Street* (Cambridge: Cambridge University Press, 1985).

DALE, P. A., 'George Eliot's "Brother Jacob": Fables and the Physiology of Common Life', *Philological Quarterly*, 64/1 (1985), 17–35.

DAVID, D., *Fictions of Resolution in Three Victorian Novels: North and South, Our Mutual Friend, Daniel Deronda* (London: Macmillan, 1981).

——*Intellectual Women and Victorian Patriarchy: Harriet Martineau, Elizabeth Barrett Browning, George Eliot* (Basingstoke: Macmillan, 1987).

DAVIDOFF, L., and HALL, CATHERINE, *Family Fortunes: Men and Women of the English Middle Class 1780–1850* (London: Hutchinson, 1987).

DE SOLA RODSTEIN, S., 'Sweetness and Dark: George Eliot's "Brother Jacob" ' *Modern Language Quarterly*, 52/3 (1991), 295–317.

DICKENS, C., *Bleak House*, eds. Norman Page and J. Hillis Miller (London: Penguin, 1985).

[——], 'An Idea of Mine', *Household Words* (13 March 1858), 289–91.

[——], 'The Last Words of the Old Year', *Household Words*, 41 (4 January 1851), 337–9.

[——], 'Old Lamps for New Ones', *Household Words*, 12 (15 June 1850), 265–7.

[——], 'A Poor man's Tale of a Patent', *Household Words* (19 October 1850), repr. in Michael Slater (ed.), *Dickens's Journalism: The Amuse-*

ments of the People and Other Papers: Reports, Essays and Reviews 1834–51 (London: J. M. Dent, 1996), 284–90.

DICKENS, C., The Posthumous Papers of the Pickwick Club (London: Penguin, 1986).

[——], 'A Preliminary Word', *Household Words*, 1 (30 March 1850), 1.

—— *The Speeches of Charles Dickens*, ed. K. J. Fielding (Oxford: Clarendon Press, 1960).

Dickinson's Comprehensive Pictures of the Great Exhibition of 1851. From the originals painted for HRH Prince Albert by Messrs. Nash, Haghe, and Roberts, R.A. Published under the Express Sanction of His Royal Highness Prince Albert, President of the Royal Commission, to whom the work is, by permission, dedicated, 2 vols. (London: Dickinson Brothers, 1854).

DIGBY WYATT, M., *An Address Delivered in the Crystal Palace on November 3, 1855, At the Opening of an Exhibition of Works of Art belonging to the Arundel Society, and Consisting of Tracings and Drawings from Paintings by Giotto and other early Italian Artists, with some illustrations of Greek Sculpture and of Ancient Ivory-Carving* (London: Bell & Daldy, 1855).

—— 'An Attempt to Define the Principles which should Determine Form in the Decorative Arts', *Lectures on the Results of the Great Exhibition of 1851, Delivered Before the Society of Arts, Manufactures, and Commerce, at the Suggestion of H.R.H. Prince Albert, President of the Society* (London: David Bogue, 1853), ii. 215–251.

—— *The Industrial Arts of the Nineteenth Century. A Series of Illustrations of the Choicest Specimens Produced by Every Nation at the Great Exhibition of Works of Industry, 1851 Dedicated, by permission, to his Royal Highness the Prince Albert*, 2 vols. (London: Day & Son, 1851–3).

D'ISRAELI, I., *An Essay on the Manners and Genius of the Literary Character* (London: T. Cadell, Junr., and W. Davies, 1795).

[——], *The Literary Character, Illustrated by the History of Men of Genius, Drawn from their Own Feelings and Confessions* (London: John Murray, 1818).

DUFFY, C. G., *Conversations with Carlyle* (London: Sampson Low, Marston, 1892).

DUTTON, H. I., *The Patent System and Inventive Activity During the Industrial Revolution 1750–1852* (Manchester: Manchester University Press, 1984).

EILENBERG, S., 'Mortal Pages: Wordsworth and the Reform of Copyright', *ELH*, 56/2 (Summer 1989), 351–74.

ELIOT, G., *Essays of George Eliot*, ed. Thomas Pinney (London: Routledge & Kegan Paul, 1963).

—— *The Impressions of Theophrastus Such* (London: J. M. Dent Everyman Edition, 1995).

——*The Lifted Veil and Brother Jacob*, ed. Helen Small (Oxford: Oxford University Press, 1999).

——*Silas Marner: The Weaver of Raveloe* (Harmondsworth: Penguin, 1996).

ELLIOTT, DORICE WILLIAMS, 'The Female Visitor and the Marriage of Classes in Gaskell's *North and South*', *Nineteenth-Century Literature*, 49/1 (June 1994), 21–49.

ELLIS, R., 'Preface', *Official Descriptive and Illustrated Catalogue of the Great Exhibition 1851*, 3 vols. (London: Spicer Brothers, 1851), i. pp. v–viii.

ELLISON, H., 'To Artists Who Look with Jealous Eyes on Artistical Processes, Such as Chromalithography, Etc. Etc.', in *The Poetry of Real Life. Sonnets* (London: John Lee, 1844), 66.

EMERSON, R. W., *Ralph Waldo Emerson: Selected Essays* (New York: Penguin, 1985).

——'The Uses of Great Men', *Essays, Lectures and Orations* (London: William S. Orr, 1851).

FARRER, T. H., 'The Principle of Copyright', *Fortnightly Review*, NS 24 (1 July–1 December 1878), 836–51.

FAY, C. R., *Palace of Industry, 1851: A Study of the Great Exhibition and its Exhibits* (Cambridge: Cambridge University Press, 1951).

FEATHER, J., *Publishing, Piracy and Politics: An Historical Study of Copyright in Britain* (London: Mansell, 1994).

FEINSTEIN, C., 'Pessimism Perpetuated: Real Wages and the Standard of Living in Britain during and after the Industrial Revolution', *Journal of Economic History*, 58/3 (September 1998), 625–58.

FELTES, N. N., 'International Copyright: Structuring "the Condition of Modernity" in British Publishing', in Martha Woodmansee and Peter Jaszi (eds.), *The Construction of Authorship: Textual Appropriation in Law and Literature* (Durham NC: Duke University Press, 1994), 271–80.

——*Modes of Production of Victorian Novels* (Chicago: University of Chicago Press, 1986).

FELKIN, W., *The Exhibition in 1851 of the Products and Industry of All Nations. Its Possible Influence upon Labour and Commerce* (London: Arthur Hall, Virtue, 1851).

FELSKI, R., *The Gender of Modernity* (Cambridge, Mass.: Harvard University Press, 1995).

FFRENCH, Y., *The Great Exhibition: 1851* (London: Harvill Press, n.d. [?1951]).

FIELDING, K. J., 'Charles Dickens and the Department of Practical Art', *Modern Language Review*, 48 (1953), 270–7.

FINN, M., 'Women, Consumption and Coverture in England, *c.*1760–1860', *The Historical Journal*, 39/3 (1996), 703–22.

FITZPATRICK, H. D., *Patents for Inventions* (Glasgow: n. pub., n.d. [1894]).

FLINT, K., 'Blood, Bodies, and *The Lifted Veil*', *Nineteenth-Century Literature*, 51/4 (March 1997), 455–73.

——*The Woman Reader 1837–1914* (Oxford: Clarendon Press, 1993).

[FORSTER, J.], 'The Dignity of Literature', *Examiner* (19 January 1850), 35.

[——], 'Encouragement of Literatuer [*sic*] by the State', *The Examiner* (5 January 1850), 2.

——*The Life and Adventures of Oliver Goldsmith, A Biography in Four Books* (London: Bradbury & Evans and Chapman & Hall, 1848).

——*The Life of Charles Dickens*, 2 vols. (Chapman & Hall, 1911).

FOX, R., 'Introduction', *Technological Change: Methods and Themes in the History of Technology* (Amsterdam: Harwood Academic, 1998) 1–15.

FRENCH, G. J., *The Life and Times of Samuel Crompton, Inventor of the Spinning Machine called the Mule. Being the Substance of Two Papers read to Members of the Bolton Mechanics' Institution* (London: Simpkin, Marshall; Manchester: Thomas Dinham; Bolton: J. Cunliff and Henry Bradbury; and the Committee and Librarian of Bolton Mechanics' Institution, 1859).

FRIEDMAN, S., '*Bleak House* and Bulwer's *Not So Bad as We Seem*', *Dickens Quarterly*, 9/1 (March 1992), 25–9.

GALLAGHER, C., 'George Eliot and *Daniel Deronda*: The Prostitute and the Jewish Question', in Ruth Bernard Yeazell (ed.), *Sex, Politics and Science in the Nineteenth-Century Novel: Selected Papers from the English Institute, 1983–84* (Baltimore: Johns Hopkins University Press, 1986).

——*The Industrial Reformation of English Fiction: Social Discourse and Narrative Form, 1832–1867* (Chicago: University of Chicago Press, 1985).

GARDISSAL, 'Inventors and Inventions' (translated from *La Presse*), *Mechanics' Magazine* (27 February 1847), 200–3.

GARRETT, P. K., *The Victorian Multiplot Novel: Studies in Dialogical Form* (New Haven and London: Yale University Press, 1980).

GASKELL, E. C. G., *The Works of Mrs. Gaskell*, vii. *Cousin Phillis and Other Tales*, ed. A. W. Ward (London: Smith, Elder, 1906), vii.

——*The Works of Mrs. Gaskell*, i. *Mary Barton and Other Tales*, ed. A. W. Word (London: Smith, Elder, 1906), i.

GIDDENS, A., *The Consequences of Modernity* (Cambridge: Polity Press, 1991).

GILBERT, S. and GUBAR, SUSAN, *The Madwoman in the Attic: The Woman Writer and the Nineteenth-Century Literary Imagination* (New Haven: Yale University Press, 1979).

GITTINGS, R., *The Older Hardy* (Harmondsworth: Penguin, 1978).

GODWIN, W., 'Of the Sources of Genius', *The Enquirer. Reflections on Education, Manners and Literature. In a Series of Essays* (London: G. G. and J. Robinson, 1797), 12–28.

GORDON, L. D. B.,'The Machinery of the Exhibition, As Applied to Textile Manufactures', *The Art Journal Illustrated Catalogue* (1851), pp. I**–VIII**.

GREENHALGH, P., *Ephemeral Vistas. The Expositions Universelles, Great Exhibitions and World's Fairs, 1851–1939* (Manchester: Manchester University Press, 1988).

[GREG, W. R.], 'Prostitution', *Westminster Review*, 53 (July 1850), 448–506.

GROSS, J., *The Rise and Fall of the Man of Letters: Aspects of English Literary Life since 1800* (Harmondsworth: Penguin, 1991).

GUBAR, S., 'The Blank Page: Issues of Creativity', in Elaine Showalter (ed.), *The New Feminist Criticism: Essays on Women, Literature, and Theory* (London: Virago, 1986), 292–33.

GURNEY, P., 'An Appropriated Space: The Great Exhibition, the Crystal Palace and the Working Class', in Louise Purbrick (ed.), *The Great Exhibition of 1851. New Interdisciplinary Essays* (Manchester: Manchester University Press, 2001), 114–45.

HABERMAS, JÜRGEN, *The Structural Transformation of the Public Sphere: An Inquiry into a Category of Bourgeois Society* (1962), trans. Thomas Burger (Cambridge Mass.: MIT Press, 1989).

HACK, D., 'Literary Paupers and Professional Authors: The Guild of Literature and Art', *Studies in English Literature 1500–1900*, 39/4 (Autumn 1999), 691–713.

HACKING, I., *The Taming of Chance* (Cambridge: Cambridge University Press, 1990).

HAIGHT, G. S. (ed.), *A Century of George Eliot Criticism* (London: Methuen, 1966).

——*George Eliot: A Biography* (Oxford: Oxford University Press, 1968).

HALL, C., *White, Male, and Middle-Class: Explorations in Feminism and History* (Cambridge: Polity Press, 1992).

HAMILTON FYFE, J., *The Triumphs of Invention and Discovery* (T. Nelson & Sons, 1861).

HANCHER, M., 'From Street Ballad to Penny Magazine: "March of Intellect in the Butchering Line"', in Laurel Brake, Bill Bell, and David Finkelstein (eds.), *Nineteenth-Century Media and the Construction of Identities* (Basingstoke: Palgrave, 2000), 93–103.

HANNAH, L., *Electricity before Nationalisation: A Study of the Development of the Electricity Supply Industry in Britain to 1948* (London: Macmillan, 1979).

HANSEN, M., 'Unstable Mixtures, Dilated Spheres: Negt and Kluge's *The Public Sphere and Experience*, Twenty Years Later', *Public Culture*, 5/2 (Winter, 1993), 179–212.

HARDY, F. E., *The Life of Thomas Hardy* (London: Macmillan, 1962).

HARDY, T., *Collected Letters of Thomas Hardy*, eds. Richard Little Purdy and Michael Millgate (7 vols.) (Oxford: Oxford University Press, 1978–88).

—— 'The Dorsetshire Labourer', *Longman's Magazine*, 2 (July 1883), 252–69.

—— 'The Fiddler of the Reels', in *Outside the Gates of the World: Selected Short Stories* (London: J. M. Dent, 1996), 334–50.

—— 'General Preface to the Wessex edition of 1912', repr. in Thomas Hardy, *The Mayor of Casterbridge* (Harmondsworth: Penguin, 1983), 413–18.

—— *A Laodicean: A Story of To-day* (London: Penguin, 1995).

—— *The Literary Notebooks of Thomas Hardy*, ed. Lennart A. Björk, 2 vols. (London: Macmillan, 1985).

—— *Two on a Tower: A Romance*, ed. Sally Shuttleworth (London: Penguin, 1999).

—— *The Well-Beloved: A Sketch of a Temperament* (London: J. M. Dent, 1997).

HARMAN, B. L., 'In Promiscuous Company: Female Public Appearance in Elizabeth Gaskell's *North and South*', *Victorian Studies*, 31/3 (Spring 1988), 351–74.

HARRISON, J. F. C., *Learning and Living, 1790–1960: A Study in the History of the English Adult Education Movement* (London: Routledge & Kegan Paul, 1961).

HARVEY, D., *The Condition of Postmodernity: An Enquiry into the Origins of Cultural Change* (Oxford: Basil Blackwell, 1989).

HEFFER, S., *Moral Desperado: A Life of Thomas Carlyle* (London: Weidenfeld & Nicolson, 1995).

HEIDEGGER, M., *Neitzsche*, trans. David Farrell Krell (London: Routledge & Kegan Paul, 1982).

HENSMAN, H., 'On Civil Engineering and Machinery Generally', *Lectures on the Results of the Great Exhibition of 1851, Delivered Before the Society of Arts, Manufactures, and Commerce, at the Suggestion of H.R.H. Prince Albert, President of the Society* (London: David Bogue, 1852), i. 403–40.

HEWISON, R., *The Heritage Industry: Britain in a Climate of Decline* (London: Methuen, 1987).

—— *Ruskin and Oxford: The Art of Education* (Oxford: Clarendon Press, 1996).

HEYCK, T. W., *The Transformation of Intellectual Life in Victorian England* (London: Croom Helm, 1982).

HILLIS MILLER, J., *Fiction and Repetition: Seven English Novels* (Oxford: Basil Blackwood, 1982).

HIRSCH, P., *Barbara Leigh Smith Bodichon, 1827–1891: Feminist, Artist and Rebel* (London: Chatto & Windus, 1998).

HOBHOUSE, C., *1851 and the Crystal Palace, being an account of the Great Exhibition and its contents; or Sir Joseph Paxton; and of the erection, the subsequent history and the destruction of his masterpiece* (London: John Murray, 1937).

[HODGSKIN, T.], *The Natural and Artificial Right of Property Contrasted. A Series of Letters, Addressed without Permission, to H. Brougham, Esq. MP, F.RS &c. (Now the Lord Chancellor) by the Author of 'Labour Defended Against the Claims of Capital'* (London: B. Steil, 1832).

HOLCOMBE, L., *Wives and Property: Reform of the Married Women's Property Law in Nineteenth-Century England* (Oxford: Martin Robertson, 1983).

HOMANS, M., *Bearing the Word: Language and Female Experience in Nineteenth-Century Women's Writing* (Chicago and London: University of Chicago Press, 1986).

HOOD, T., 'Copyright and Copywrong', *Athenaeum* (1837), 264.

HOWES, C., '*Pendennis* and the Controversy on "The Dignity of Literature"', *Nineteenth-Century Literature*, 41/3 (December 1986), 269–98.

HOWITT, M., *An Autobiography*, ed. Margaret Howitt, 2 vols. (London: William Isbister, 1889).

HUDSON, J. W., *The History of Adult Education* (1851) (London: Woburn Books, 1969).

The Industry of Nations, as Exemplified in the Great Exhibition of 1851. The Materials of Industry (London: SPCK, 1852).

The Industry of Nations, Part II. A Survey of the Existing State of Arts, Machines, and Manufactures (London: SPCK, 1855).

INKSTER, I., 'Introduction: The Context of Steam Intellect in Britain (to 1851)', in id. (ed.), *The Steam Intellect Societies—Essays on Culture, Education and Industry circa 1820–1914* (Nottingham: University of Nottingham, 1985), 3–19.

JACOBUS, M., *Romanticism, Writing and Sexual Difference: Essays on The Prelude* (Oxford: Clarendon Press, 1989).

JAFFE, A., 'David Copperfield and Bleak House: On Dividing the Responsibility of Knowing', in Jeremy Tambling (ed.), *New Casebooks. Bleak House. Charles Dickens* (Basingstoke: Macmillan, 1998), 163–82.

JERROLD, D., 'Christmas Thoughts of the Crystal Palace', *Illustrated London News* (20 December 1851), 738.

The Journal of the Great Exhibition of 1851 its Origin, History and Progress, 2 (23 November 1850).

JOSEPH, G., 'Charles Dickens, International Copyright, and the Discretionary Silence of *Martin Chuzzlewit*', in Martha Woodmansee and

Peter Jaszi (eds.), *The Construction of Authorship: Textual Appropriation in Law and Literature* (Durham, NC: Duke University Press, 1994), 259–70.

JUDD, C. A., 'Male Pseudonyms and Female Authority in Victorian England', in John O. Jordan And Robert L. Patten (eds.), *Literature in the Marketplace: Nineteenth-Century British Publishing and Reading Practices* (Cambridge: Cambridge University Press, 1995), 250–68.

KANT, I., *Kant's Critique of Aesthetic Judgment*, ed. James Creed Meredith (Oxford: Clarendon Press, 1911).

[KAYE, J. W.], 'The "Non-Existence" of Women', *North British Review* (August 1855), 536–62.

[——], 'Pendennis—The Literary Profession', *North British Review*, 13 (August 1850), 335–72.

KEARNS, K., *Nineteenth-Century Literary Realism: Through the Looking Glass* (Cambridge: Cambridge University Press, 1996).

KEATS, J., *The Letters of John Keats 1814–1821*, ed. Hyder Edward Rollins, 2 vols. (Cambridge: Cambridge University Press, 1958).

KELLY, T., *A History of Adult Education in Great Britain from the Middle Ages to the Twentieth Century* (Liverpool: Liverpool University Press, 1992).

KERN, S., *The Culture of Time and Space 1880–1918* (Cambridge, Mass.: Harvard University Press, 1983).

KEWES, P., *Authorship and Appropriation: Writing for the Stage in England 1660–1710* (Oxford: Clarendon Press, 1998).

KIPLING, R., 'The Rhyme of the Three Captains' (1890), in *Rudyard Kipling: The Complete Verse* (London: Kyle Cathie, 1996), 269–272.

—— 'Wireless' in *Traffics and Discoveries* (London: Macmillan, 1904), 211–39.

KITTLER, F. A., *Discourse Networks 1800/1900*, trans. Michael Metteer with Chris Cullens (Stanford: Stanford University Press, 1990).

KLINGENDER, F. D., *Art and the Industrial Revolution* (London: Winifred Klingender and Evelyn, Adams & Mackay, 1968).

KNIGHT, C., *Passages of a Working Life During Half a Century with a Prelude of Early Reminiscences*, 3 vols. (London: Bradbury & Evans, 1864).

—— *The Working-Man's Companion. The Results of Machinery, Namely, Cheap Production and Increased Employment, Exhibited: Being an Address to the Working-Men of the United Kingdom* (London: Charles Knight, 1831).

LANDON, P., 'Great Exhibitions: Representations of the Crystal Palace in Mayhew, Dickens and Dostoevsky', *Nineteenth-Century Contexts*, 20/1 (1997), 27–59.

LEVINE, G., 'Determinism and Responsibility', in Gordon S. Haight (ed.), *A Century of George Eliot Criticism* (London: Methuen, 1966), 349–60.

——'*Little Dorrit* and Three Kinds of Science', *Darwin and the Novelists: Patterns of Science in Victorian Fiction* (Cambridge, Mass.: Harvard University Press, 1988), 153–76.

LEVINE, G., and KNOEPFLMACHER, U. C. (eds.), *The Endurance of Franken-stein: Essays on Mary Shelley's Novel* (Berkeley: University of California Press, 1974).

[LEWES, G. H.], 'The Condition of Authors in England, Germany, and France', *Fraser's Magazine* (March 1847), 285–95.

[——], 'Dickens in Relation to Criticism', *Fortnightly Review*, 11 (February 1872), 141–54.

LITVAK, J., 'Kiss Me, Stupid: Sophistication, Sexuality, and *Vanity Fair*', *Novel*, 29/2 (Winter 1996), 223–42.

LUHMANN, N., *Risk: A Sociological Theory*, trans. Rhodes Barrett (New York: Aldine de Gruyter, 1993).

LUND, M., 'Novels, Writers and Readers in 1850', *Victorian Periodical Review*, 17 (1984), 15–28.

'M.', 'National Statues. No. VII. Sir Isaac Newton', *Saturday Magazine* (26 December 1835), 241–3.

[MACAULAY, T. B.], 'The Life of Joseph Addison, by Lucy Aikin, in 2 vols', *Edinburgh Review*, 157 (July 1843), 193–260.

——*Speeches, Parliamentary and Miscellaneous*, 2 vols. (London: Henry Vizetelly, 1853).

MACFARLANE, R., 'A Small Squealing Black Pig: George Eliot, Originality and Plagiarism', in *George Eliot—George Henry Lewes Studies*, 42/43 (September 2002), 1–29.

MACKINNON, C., 'Feminism, Marxism, Method and the State: Toward a Feminist Jurisprudence', *Signs*, 8 (1983), 635–58.

MACLEOD, C., 'Concepts of Invention and the Patent Controversy', in Robert Fox (ed.), *Technological Change Methods and Themes in the History of Technology* (Amsterdam: Harwood Academic, 1998), 137–53.

——'James Watt, Heroic Invention and the Idea of the Industrial Revolu-tion', in Maxine Berg and Kristine Bruland (eds.), *Technological Revolu-tions in Europe: Historical Perspectives* (Cheltenham: Edward Elgar, 1998), 96–116.

MACPHERSON, C. B. (ed.), *Property: Mainstream and Critical Positions* (Oxford: Basil Blackwell, 1978).

MAIDMENT, B., 'Entrepreneurship and the Artisans: John Cassell, the Great Exhibition and the Periodical Idea', in Louise Purbrick (ed.), *The Great Exhibition of 1851: New Interdisciplinary Essays* (Manchester: Manchester University Press, 2001), 79–113.

MAIN, A., *Wise, Witty and Tender Sayings in Prose and Verse Selected from the Works of George Eliot*, 4th Edition *With Supplementary Sayings from*

'*Daniel Deronda*' and '*Theophrastus Such*' (Edinburgh: William Blackwood, 1880).

MANDLER, P., *The Fall and Rise of the Stately Home* (New Haven: Yale University Press, 1997).

MARCUS, S., *Dickens: from Pickwick to Dombey* (New York: Basic Books, 1975).

——'Language into Structure: *Pickwick* Revisited', *Daedalus*, 101/1 (Winter 1972), 183–202.

MARTINEAU, H., 'Female Industry', *Edinburgh Review* (April 1859), 293–336.

——'Literary Lionism', *The London and Westminster Review*, 32/2 (1839), 261–81.

MARVIN, C., *When Old Technologies Were New: Thinking About Electric Communication in the Late Nineteenth Century* (New York: Oxford University Press, 1988).

MARX, L., *The Machine in the Garden: Technology and the Pastoral Ideal in America* (New York: Oxford University Press, 1964).

[MASSON, D.], 'Thackeray and Dickens', *North British Review*, 15 (May–August 1851), 57–89.

MATTHEWS, R. C. O., FEINSTEIN, CHARLES, and ODLING-SMEE, JOHN (eds.), *British Economic Growth, 1856–1973* (Oxford: Clarendon Press, 1982).

MAYHEW, H., and CRUIKSHANK, GEORGE, *1851: or, the Adventures of Mr and Mrs Sandboys and Family who came up to London to 'enjoy themselves' and to see the Great Exhibition* (London: David Bogue, n.d.).

MCFARLAND, T., *Originality and Imagination* (Baltimore: Johns Hopkins University Press, 1985).

MCGANN, J. J., *The Romantic Ideology: A Critical Investigation* (Chicago: University of Chicago Press, 1983).

MCMULLAN, G., *The Invention of Lateness* (forthcoming).

MELVILLE, L., *The Life of William Makepeace Thackeray*, 2 vols. (London: John Lane, The Bodley Head, 1910).

MICHIE, E. B., *Outside the Pale. Cultural Exclusion, Gender Difference, and the Victorian Woman Writer* (Ithaca and London: Cornell University Press, 1993).

MILL, J. S., *Collected Works of John Stuart Mill*, eds. Jean O'Grady and John M. Robson (Canada: University of Toronto Press and Routledge & Kegan Paul, 1965), 33 vols.

——'On Genius' (1832), in John M. Robson and Jack Stillinger (eds.), *Autobiography and Literary Essays by John Stuart Mill* (London: Routledge, 1981), 329–39.

——*On Liberty* (1859), in John Stuart Mill, *On Liberty and Other Essays* (Oxford: Oxford University Press, 1991), 5–128.

——*Principles of Political Economy with some of their Applications to Social Philosophy*, ed. W. J. Ashley (London: Longmans, Green & Co., 1909).

——*The Subjection of Women* (1869), in John Stuart Mill, *On Liberty and Other Essays* (Oxford: Oxford University Press, 1991), 471–582.

——*Utilitarianism, On Liberty, Considerations of Representative Government* (London: J. M. Dent, 1993).

MILLER, A. H., *Novels Behind Glass: Commodity Culture and Victorian Narrative* (Cambridge: Cambridge University Press, 1995).

MILLER, D. A., *The Novel and the Police* (Berkeley: University of California Press, 1998).

MILLGATE, M., *Testamentary Acts: Browning, Tennyson, James, Hardy* (Oxford: Clarendon Press, 1992).

MOKYR, J., 'Technological Change, 1700–1830', in Roderick Floud and Donald McCloskey (eds.), *The Economic History of Britain Since 1700*, i. *1700–1860* (Cambridge: Cambridge University Press, 1994), 12–43.

MOERS, E., 'Female Gothic', in George Levine and U. C. Knoepflmacher (eds.), *The Endurance of Frankenstein: Essays on Mary Shelley's Novel* (Berkeley: University of California Press, 1974), 77–87.

MORRIS, I. R., *Frankenstein's Children: Electricity, Exhibition, and Experiment in Early-Nineteenth-century London* (Princeton: Princeton University Press, 1998).

MUIRHEAD, J. P., *The Origin and Progress of the Mechanical Inventions of James Watt, Illustrated by his Correspondence with his Friends and the Specifications of his Patents* (London: John Murray, 1854).

MYERS, W., 'The Radicalism of *Little Dorrit*', in John Lucas (ed.), *Literature and Politics in the Nineteenth-Century: Essays* (London: Methuen, 1971), 77–104.

NEWLYN, L., 'Coleridge and the Anxiety of Reception', *Romanticism*, 1/2 (1995), 206–38.

NEWSOM, R., 'The Hero's Shame', *Dickens Studies Annual*, 11 (1983), 1–24.

NOCHLIN, L., *Realism* (Harmondsworth: Penguin, 1971).

NORTON, C., *A Letter to the Queen on Lord Chancellor Cranworth's Marriage & Divorce Bill* (London: Longman, Brown, Green, Longman, 1855).

NOWELL-SMITH, S., *International Copyright Law and the Publisher in the Reign of Queen Victoria* (Oxford: Clarendon Press, 1968).

NUNOKAWA, J., *The Afterlife of Property: Domestic Security and the Victorian Novel* (Princeton, NJ: Princeton University Press, 1994).

'Official Catalogue of the Great Exhibition of the Works of Industry of All Nations, 1851 4th corrected edition, 15th September 1851', *Edinburgh Review*, 94 (October 1851), 557–98.

OLIPHANT, M., *The Autobiography of Margaret Oliphant: The Complete Text*, ed. Elisabeth Jay (Oxford: Oxford University Press, 1990).

ORWELL, G., 'Charles Dickens' (1940), in *George Orwell: The Collected Essays, Journalism and Letters*, ed. Sonia Orwell and Ian Angus (London: Penguin, 1970), i. 454–504.

Oxford English Dictionary, at http://dictionary.oed.com/.

PARRINDER, P., *Authors and Authority: English and American Criticism 1750–1990* (London: Macmillan Education, 1991).

PATTEN, R. L., ' "The people have set Literature Free": The Professionalization of Letters in Nineteenth-Century England', *Review*, 9 (1987), 1–34.

PAXTON, N., *George Eliot and Herbert Spencer: Feminism, Evolutionism, and the Reconstruction of Gender* (Princeton, NJ: Princeton University Press, 1991).

PETERS, C., *The King of Inventors: A Life of Wilkie Collins* (London: Secker & Warburg, 1991).

PETTITT, C., ' "Cousin Holman's Dresser": Science, Social Change, and the Pathologization of the Female in Gaskell's *Cousin Phillis*', *Nineteenth-Century Literature*, 52/4 (March 1998), 471–89.

——'An Everyday Story: Wives, Daughters and Nineteenth-Century Natural Science', *Studies in History and Philosophy of Biological and Biomedical Sciences*, 33 (2002), 325–35.

——'Monstrous Displacements: Anxieties of Exchange in *Great Expectations*', *Dickens Studies Annual*, 30 (2001), 243–62.

——'Shakespeare at the Great Exhibition of 1851', in *Victorian Shakespeare*, ed., G. Marshall and A. Poole (Basingstoke: Palgrave, 2003), ii, 61–83.

PEVSNER, N., *High Victorian Design: A Study of the Exhibits of 1851* (London: Architectural Press, 1951).

PHILLIPS, J., *Charles Dickens and 'A Poor Man's Tale of a Patent'* (Oxford: ESC Publishing, 1984).

PHILLIPS, S., *Guide to the Crystal Palace and Park* (London: Bradbury & Evans, 1857).

PHILPOTTS, T., 'Dickens, Patent Reform, and the Inventor: Daniel Doyce and the Question of Topicality', *Dickens Quarterly*, 9/4 (1992), 158–69.

——' "To Working Men" and "The People": Dickens's View of Class Relations in the Months Preceding *Little Dorrit*', *Dickens Quarterly*, 7/2 (June 1990), 262–75.

POLLACK, G., *Vision and Difference: Femininity, Feminism and Histories of Art* (London: Routledge, 1988).

POLLARD, S., *The Genesis of Modern Management: A Study of the Industrial Revolution in Great Britain* (London: Edward Arnold, 1965).

POOVEY, M., *The Proper Lady and the Woman Writer. Ideology as Style in the Works of Mary Wollstonecraft, Mary Shelley and Jane Austen* (Chicago: Chicago University Press, 1984).

——*Uneven Developments: The Ideological Work of Gender in Mid-Victorian England* (Chicago: University of Chicago Press, 1988).

PRICE, L., *The Anthology and the Rise of the Novel from Richardson to George Eliot* (Cambridge: Cambridge University Press, 2000).

PROTHERO, I. J., *Artisans and Politics in Early Nineteenth-Century London: John Gast and his Times* (Folkestone: Dawson & Son, 1979).

PURBRICK, L. (ed.), *The Great Exhibition of 1851: New Interdisciplinary Essays* (Manchester: Manchester University Press, 2001).

——'Knowledge is Property: Looking at Exhibits and Patents in 1851', *Oxford Art Journal*, 20/2 (1997), 53–60.

RADIN, M. J., *Reinterpreting Property* (Chicago: University of Chicago Press, 1993).

RAY, G. N., *Thackeray: The Uses of Adversity (1811–1846)* (London: Oxford University Press, 1955).

——*Thackeray: The Age of Wisdom (1847–1863)* (London: Oxford University Press, 1958).

READER, W. J., *Professional Men: The Rise of the Professional Classes in Nineteenth-Century England* (London: Weidenfeld & Nicolson, 1966).

REDINGER, R. V., *George Eliot: The Emergent Self* (London: Bodley Head, 1975).

REDDY, W. M., 'The Structure of a Commodity Crisis: Thinking About Cloth in France Before and After the Revolution', in Arjun Appadurai (ed.), *The Social Life of Things: Commodities in Cultural Perspective* (Cambridge: Cambridge University Press, 1986), 261–84.

REYNOLDS, H., *The Law of the Land* (Camberwell, Victoria: Penguin Australia, 1992).

RICHARDS, T., *The Commodity Culture of Victorian England: Advertising and Spectacle* (London: Verso, 1990).

RICHARDSON, A., 'Romanticism and the Colonization of the Feminine', in Anne K. Mellor (ed.), *Romanticism and Feminism* (Bloomington: Indiana University Press, 1988).

ROBBINS, B. (ed.), *The Phantom Public Sphere* (for the Social Text Collective) (Minneapolis: University Press of Minnesota, 1993).

——'Telescopic Philanthropy: Professionalism and Responsibility in Jeremy Tambling (ed.), *Bleak House*', in *New Casebooks. Bleak House Charles Dickens* (Basingstoke: Macmillan, 1998), 139–62.

ROBERTSON, E. S., *English Poetesses: A Series of Critical Biographies, with Illustrative Extracts* (London: n. pub., 1883).

RODERICK, G. W. and STEPHENS, M. D., 'Mechanics' Institutes and the State', in Ian Inkster (ed.), *The Steam Intellect Societies—Essays on Culture, Education and Industry circa 1820–1914* (Nottingham: University of Nottingham, 1985), 60–72.

Rose, M., *Authors and Owners: The Invention of Copyright* (Cambridge, Mass.: London: Harvard University Press, 1993).

Ross, T., 'Copyright and the Invention of Tradition', *Eighteenth-Century Studies*, 26/1 (Fall 1992), 1–27.

—— *The Making of the English Literary Canon: From the Middle Ages to the Late Eighteenth Century* (Montreal: McGill-Queen's University Press, 1998).

Royle, N., *Telepathy and Literature* (Oxford: Basil Blackwood, 1990).

Rule, J., 'The Property of Skill in the Period of Manufacture', in Patrick Joyce (ed.), *The Historical Meanings of Work* (Cambridge: Cambridge University Press, 1987), 99–118.

Ruskin, J., *Letters of John Ruskin Volume*, ii. *1870–1889*, in *The Library Edition of the Works of John Ruskin on CD Rom* (Cambridge: Cambridge University Press, 1996), xxxvii.

—— *The Opening of the Crystal Palace Considered in Some of its Relations to the Prospects of Art* (London: Smith, Elder & Co., 1854).

—— *Ruskin's Letters from Venice 1851–1852*, ed. John Lewis Bradley (New Haven: Yale University Press, 1955).

—— *The Seven Lamps of Architecture*, ed. E. T. Cook and A. Wedderburn, *The Library Edition of the Works of John Ruskin on CD Rom* (Cambridge: Cambridge University Press, 1996), viii.

Ruth, J., 'Mental Capital, Industrial Time: The Professional in *David Copperfield*', *Novel*, 32/3 (Summer 1999), 303–30.

Salmon, R., 'The Disenchantment of the Author: Labour Theories of Writing in Dickens and Thackeray' (unpublished MS).

—— ' "A Simulacrum of Power": Intimacy and Abstraction in the Rhetoric of the New Journalism', in Laurel Brake, Bill Bell, and David Finkelstein (eds.), *Nineteenth-Century Media and the Construction of Identities* (2000), 27–39.

Samuel, R. (ed.), *Patriotism: The Making and Unmaking of British National Identity*, i. *History and Politics* (London: Routledge, 1989).

Saunders, D., *Authorship and Copyright* (London: Routledge, 1992).

Schlicke, P., *Dickens and Popular Entertainment* (London: George Allen & Unwin, 1985).

Schor, H., *Dickens and the Daughter of the House* (Cambridge: Cambridge University Press, 1999).

Searle, G. R., *Morality and the Market in Victorian Britain* (Oxford: Clarendon Press, 1998).

Secord, J. A., *Victorian Sensation: The Extraordinary Publication, Reception, and Secret Authorship of Vestiges of the Natural History of Creation* (Chicago: London: University of Chicago Press, 2000).

Seigel, J. P. (ed.), *Thomas Carlyle: The Critical Heritage* (Routledge & Kegan Paul, 1971).

SELTZER, M., *Bodies and Machines* (New York: Routledge, 1992).

SEVILLE, C., *Literary Copyright Reform in Early Victorian England: The Framing of the 1842 Copyright Act* (Cambridge: Cambridge University Press, 1999).

SHAKESPEARE, W., *Shakespeare's Sonnets*, ed. Katherine Duncan-Jones (London: Thomas Nelson & Sons, 1998).

SHAW, BERNARD, ed. D. H. Lawrence *Bernard Shaw, Collected Letters 1926–1950* (London: Max Reinhardt, 1988).

SHELLEY, M. W., *Frankenstein or The Modern Prometheus*, ed. M. K. Joseph (London: Oxford University Press, 1969).

——*The Journals of Mary Shelley, 1814–1844*, ed. Paula R. Feldman and Diana Scott-Kilvert, 2 vols. (Oxford: Clarendon Press, 1987).

——*The Letters of Mary Wollstonecraft Shelley*, ed. Betty T. Bennett (Baltimore: Johns Hopkins University Press, 1983).

SHELLEY, P. B., 'A Defence of Poetry', *The Complete Works of Percy Bysshe Shelley*, ed. Roger Ingpen and Walter E. Peck (London and New York: Ernest Benn and Charles Scribner's Sons, 1930), vii. 109–40.

SHILLINGSBURG, P. L., *Pegasus in Harness: Victorian Publishing and W. M. Thackeray* (Charlottesville: University Press of Virginia, 1992).

SHOWALTER, E. (ed.), *The New Feminist Criticism: Essays on Women, Literature, and Theory* (London: Virago, 1986).

SHUTTLEWORTH, S., *George Eliot and Nineteenth-Century Science: The Make-believe of a Beginning* (Cambridge: Cambridge University Press, 1984).

——'*Silas Marner*: A Divided Eden', in Nahem Yousaf and Andrew Maunder (eds.), *New Casebooks: The Mill on the Floss and Silas Marner* (Basingstoke: Palgrave, 2002), 204–24.

SICHER, E., 'George Eliot's "Glue Test": Language, Law, and Legitimacy in *Silas Marner*', *Modern Language Review*, 94/1 (1999), 11–21.

SISKIN, C., *The Historicity of Romantic Discourse* (New York: Oxford University Press, 1988).

——*The Work of Writing: Literature and Social Change in Britain, 1700–1830* (Baltimore: Johns Hopkins University Press, 1998).

SLATER, M. (ed.), *Dickens's Journalism: The Amusements of the People and Other Papers: Reports, Essays and Reviews 1834–51* (London: J. M. Dent, 1996).

——(ed.) *Dickens' Journalism: Sketches by Boz and Other Early Papers, 1833–39* (London: J. M. Dent, 1994).

SMALL, H., 'The Debt to Society: Dickens, Fielding, and the Genealogy of Independence', in Francis O'Gorman and Katherine Turner (eds.), *The Victorians and the Eighteenth Century: Reassessing the Tradition* (Aldershot: Ashgate, 2003).

SMALL, H., 'Introduction', *George Eliot: The Lifted Veil and Brother Jacob* (Oxford: Oxford University Press, 1999).

—— 'A Pulse of 124: Charles Dickens and a Pathology of the Mid-Victorian Reading Public', in James Raven, Helen Small, and Naomi Tadmore (eds.), *The Practice and Representation of Reading in England* (Cambridge: Cambridge University Press, 1996), 263–90.

SMILES, S., *Autobiography*, ed. Thomas Mackay (London: John Murray, 1905).

—— *The Life of George Stephenson, Railway Engineer* (London: John Murray, 1857).

—— *Self-Help; with Illustrations of Character, Conduct, and Perseverance* (London: John Murray, 1866).

—— *Self-Help: With Illustrations of Character and Perseverance* (London: John Murray, 1910).

SNIADER LANSER, S., 'Woman of Maxims: George Eliot and the Realist Imperative', *Fictions of Authority: Women Writers and Narrative Voice* (Ithaca: Cornell University Press, 1992), 81–101.

SOCIETY FOR THE ENCOURAGEMENT OF ARTS, MANUFACTURES, AND COMMERCE, *Report of the Artistic Committee to the Council* (London: Bell and Daldy, n.d. [Bodleian Library Catalogue: 1858]).

SOTHEBY, S. L., *A Few Words by Way of a Letter Addressed to the Directors of the Crystal Palace Company from Samuel Leigh Sotheby* (London: John Russell Smith, 1855).

SOUTHEY, R., *Selections from the Letters of Robert Southey*, ed. John Wood Warter, 4 vols. (London: Longman, Brown, Green, and Longmans, 1856).

SPENCER, H., *Essays, Scientific, Political, and Speculative*, 3 vols. (London: Routledge/Thoemmes Press, 1996).

SPOONER, B., 'Weavers and Dealers: The Authenticity of an Oriental Carpet', in Arjun Appadurai (ed.), *The Social Life of Things: Commodities in Cultural Perspective* (Cambridge: Cambridge University Press, 1986), 195–235.

STEAD, W. T., 'The Future of Journalism', *Contemporary Review*, 50 (November 1886), 663–79.

—— 'Government by Journalism', *Contemporary Review*, 49 (May 1886), 653–74.

STEINER, G., *Grammars of Creation Originating in the Gifford Lectures for 1990* (London: Faber & Faber, 2001).

STEPHEN, L. and LEE, SIDNEY (eds.), *The Dictionary of National Biography*, ii. *Beal–Browell* (Oxford: Oxford University Press, n.d. 'Since 1917').

STEVENSON, R. L., 'A Plea for Gas Lamps', in *Virginibus Puerisque and Other Papers* (London: Chatto & Windus, 1915), 189–93.

STEWART, G., *Dear Reader: The Conscripted Audience in Nineteenth-Century British Fiction* (Baltimore: Johns Hopkins University Press, 1996).

STRACHEY, R., *'The Cause': A Short History of the Women's Movement in Great Britain* (London: G. Bell & Sons, 1928).

STRATHERN, M., *Property, Substance and Effect: Anthropological Essays on Persons and Things* (London: Athlone Press), 1999.

STRICKLAND, M., *A Memoir of the Life, Writings, and Mechanical Inventions, of Edmund Cartwright D.D., F.R.S., Inventor of the Power-Loom* (London: Saunders & Otley, 1843).

STUART WORTLEY, E., *Honour to Labour. A Lay of 1851* (London: W. N. Wright, n.d.).

SUCKSMITH, H. P., 'Introduction', *Little Dorrit* (Oxford: Oxford University Press, 1991).

SUTHERLAND, J. A., 'Thackeray as Victorian Racialist', *Essays in Criticism*, 20 (1970), 441–5.

—— *Victorian Fiction: Writers, Publishers, Readers* (Basingstoke: Macmillan, 1995).

—— *Victorian Novelists and Publishers* (London: Athlone Press, 1976).

TAMBLING, J. (ed.), *New Casebooks. Bleak House. Charles Dickens* (Basingstoke: Macmillan, 1998).

TAYLOR, E., *Great Inventors: The Sources of Their Usefulness and the Results of Their Efforts, Profusely Illustrated* (London: Ward & Lock, n.d. [1865]).

TAYLOR, M., *The Decline of British Radicalism, 1847–1860* (Oxford: Clarendon Press, 1995).

TENNYSON, A., *The Letters of Alfred Lord Tennyson 1821–1850*, ed. Cecil Y. Lang and Edgar F. Shannon, Jr. (Oxford: Clarendon Press, 1982), i.

TENNYSON, C. and ALFRED, *Poems by Two Brothers* (Louth: W. Simpkin & R. Marshall and J. & J. Jackson, 1827).

THACKERAY, W. M., 'A Brother of the Press on the History of a Literary Man, Laman Blanchard, And the Chances of the Literary Profession in a Letter to the Reverend Francis Sylvester at Rome, from Michael Angelo Titmarsh, Esquire', *The Works of William Makepeace Thackeray*, xxv. *Miscellaneous Essays, Sketches and Reviews* (London: Smith, Elder, 1886), 84–97.

—— 'The Dignity of Literature—To the Editor of the *Morning Chronicle*', *Morning Chronicle* (12 January 1850), 4.

—— *The English Humorists of the Eighteenth Century. A Series of Lectures delivered in England, Scotland, and the United States of America* (London: Smith, Elder, 1853).

—— *The History of Henry Esmond* (London: Dent, Everyman Library, 1970).

—— *The History of Pendennis His Fortunes and Misfortunes His Friends and His Greatest Enemy* (Oxford: Oxford University Press, 1994).

THACKERAY, W. M., *The Paris Sketch Book by Mr Titmarsh* (London: George Routledge & Sons, 1885).

——*A Shabby Genteel Story and Other Writings* (London: J. M. Dent, 1993).

THEERMAN, P., 'National Images of Science: British and American Views of Scientific Heroes in the Early Nineteenth Century', in *Beyond Two Cultures: Essays on Science, Technology, and Literature*, ed. Joseph W. Slade and Judith Yaross Lee (Ames: Iowa State University Press, 1990), 259–74.

THOMAS, D. A., 'Bondage and Freedom in *Pendennis*', in *Thackeray and Slavery* (Athens, Ohio: Ohio University Press, 1993), 76–95.

THOMSON, C., *The Autobiography of an Artisan* (London: Chapman, 1847).

THURSCHWELL, P., *Literature, Technology and Magical Thinking, 1880–1920* (Cambridge: Cambridge University Press, 2001).

TIMBS, J., *Stories of Inventors and Discoverers in Science and the Useful Arts. A Book for Old and Young* (London: Kent, 1860).

TOMALIN, C., *The Invisible Woman: The Story of Nelly Ternan and Charles Dickens* (London: Viking, 1990).

TRENTMANN, F., 'Political Culture and Political Economy: Interest, Ideology and Free Trade', *Review of International Political Economy*, 5/2 (Summer 1998), 217–51.

TRITTER, D. F., 'A Strange Case of Royalty: The Singular "Copyright" Case of Prince Albert v. Strange', *Journal of Media Law and Practice*, 4 (1983), 111–29.

TROLLOPE, A., *An Autobiography* (London: Williams & Norgate, 1946).

TROTTER, D., *Cooking with Mud: The Idea of Mess in Nineteenth-Century Art and Fiction* (Oxford: Oxford University Press, 2000).

TUCHMAN, G. and FORTIN, NINA E., *Edging Women Out: Victorian Novelists, Publishers, and Social Change* (London: Routledge, 1989).

TYLECOTE, M., *Mechanics Institutes of Yorkshire and Lancashire before 1851* (Manchester: Manchester University Press, 1957).

UGLOW, J., *Elizabeth Gaskell: A Habit of Stories* (London: Faber & Faber, 1993).

VASBINDER, S. H., *Scientific Attitudes in Mary Shelley's Frankenstein* (Ann Arbor, Mich.: UMI Research Press, 1984).

VENN DICEY, A., *Lectures on the Relation between Law and Public Opinion in England During the Nineteenth Century* (London: Macmillan, 1905).

VINCENT, D., *Bread, Knowledge and Freedom: A Study of Nineteenth-Century Working-Class Autobiography* (London: Europa, 1981).

——*Literacy and Popular Culture: England 1750–1914* (Cambridge: Cambridge University Press, 1989).

VRETTOS, A., 'From Neurosis to Narrative: The Private Life of the Nerves in *Villette* and *Daniel Deronda*', *Victorian Studies*, 33 (1990), 551–79.

——*Somatic Fictions: Imagining Illness in Victorian Culture* (Stanford, Calif.: Stanford University Press, 1995).

WAH, S., '"No amount of wishing will turn a plum into an orange": Popularity and the Popular Novel in George Eliot's *Romola*' (Ph.D. thesis chapter, Cambridge University, forthcoming).

WARNER, M., 'The Mass Public and the Mass Subject', in Bruce Robbins (ed.), *The Phantom Public Sphere* (for the Social Text Collective) (Minneapolis: University Press of Minnesota, 1993), 234–56.

WARREN, S., *The Lily and the Bee: An Apologue of the Crystal Palace* (London: William Blackwood & Sons, 1851).

WEBB, R. K., 'The Gaskells as Unitarians', in Joanne Shattock (ed.), *Dickens and Other Victorians: Essays in Honour of Philip Collins* (Basingstoke: Macmillan, 1988), 144–71.

WEBSTER, AUGUSTA, 'An Inventor', in *Portraits and Other Poems*, ed. Christine Sutphin (Peterborough, Ont.: Broadview Press, 2000), 272–8.

WELLS, H. G., 'The Lord of the Dynamos', in *The Stolen Bacillus and Other Stories* (London: Methuen, 1895), 192–213.

WELSH, A., *From Copyright to Copperfield: the Identity of Dickens* (Cambridge, Mass.: Harvard University Press, 1987).

——*George Eliot and Blackmail* (Cambridge, Mass.: Harvard University Press, 1985).

WHEWELL, W., 'The General Bearing of the Great Exhibition on the Progress of Art and Science', *Lectures on the Results of the Great Exhibition of 1851, Delivered Before the Society of Arts, Manufactures, and Commerce, at the Suggestion of H.R.H. Prince Albert, President of the Society* (London: David Bogue, 1852), i. 1–34.

WIENER, M., *English Culture and the Decline of the Industrial Spirit, 1850–1980* (Cambridge: Cambridge University Press, 1981).

WILLIAMS, J., *Principles of the Law of Real Property, Intended as a First Book for the Use of Students in Conveyancing* (London: H. Sweet, 1865).

WILLIAMS, L. R., 'The Story as Case History: *Cousin Phillis*', in *Critical Desire: Psychoanalysis and the Literary Subject* (London: Edward Arnold, 1995), 25–37.

WILLIS, R., 'On Machines and Tools for Working in Metal, Wood, and Other Materials', *Lectures on the Results of the Great Exhibition of 1851, Delivered Before the Society of Arts, Manufactures, and Commerce, at the Suggestion of H.R.H. Prince Albert, President of the Society* (London: David Bogue, 1852), i. 293–320.

WILSON, JOHN, 'Agricultural Products and Implements', *Lectures on the Results of the Great Exhibition of 1851, Delivered Before the Society of Arts, Manufactures, and Commerce, at the Suggestion of H.R.H. Prince Albert, President of the Society* (London: David Bogue, 1853), ii. 3–41.

[WISE, T. J.], *An Account of the First Performance of Lytton's Comedy 'Not So Bad As We Seem' with Other Matters of Interest, by Charles Dickens* (London: Richard Clay & Sons, 1919).

WOLFF, J., *The Social Production of Art* (Basingstoke: Macmillan, 1993).

WOODMANSEE, M., *The Author, Art, and the Market: Re-reading the History of Aesthetics* (New York: Columbia University Press, 1994).

WOODMANSEE, M. and JASZI, PETER (eds.), *The Construction of Authorship: Textual Appropriation in Law and Literature* (Durham, NC: Duke University Press, 1994).

WORDSWORTH, W., *The Letters of William and Dorothy Wordsworth: The Later Years*, ii. *1831–40*, ed. Ernest de Selincourt (Oxford: Clarendon Press, 1939).

——*The Letters of William and Dorothy Wordsworth*, vi. *1835–1839*, ed. Alan G. Hill (Oxford: Clarendon Press, 1982).

WORNUM, R. N., 'The Exhibition as a Lesson in Taste: An Essay on Ornamental Art as Displayed in the Industrial Exhibition in Hyde Park, in which the Different Styles are Compared with a View to the Improvement of Taste in Home Manufactures', *Art Journal Illustrated Catalogue*, I***–XXII***.

YARROW, P., 'Mrs. Gaskell and France', *Gaskell Society Journal*, 7 (1993), 16–36.

YEAZELL, R. B., 'Why Political Novels Have Heroines: *Sybil, Mary Barton*, and *Felix Holt*', *Novel: A Forum on Fiction*, 18/2 (Winter 1985), 126–44.

YOUNG, E., *Conjectures on Original Composition*, ed. Edith J. Morley (London: Manchester University Press and Longmans, Green & Co., 1918).

OFFICIAL PUBLICATIONS

In date order.

'A Bill for the Encouragement of Philosophical and Mechanical Experiment, and for the Protection of Patentees in their Rights. 8 February 1821', *Bills Public: Session 23 January–11 July 1821* (MS pagination, 21–6), i.

'Patents for Inventions; Report from Select Committee on the Law Relative to Patents for Inventions. Ordered by House of Commons to be Printed 12 June 1829', *Reports from Committees 1829*, i. 415–676.

Hansard, Parl. Debs. (series 3), vol. 15 (1833).

Hansard, Parl. Debs. (series 3), vol. 19 (1833).

Hansard, Parl. Debs. (series 3), vol. 20 (1833).

Journal of the House of Commons, 88 (1833).

Hansard, Parl. Debs. (series 3), vol. 28 (1835).

Hansard, Parl. Debs. (series 3), vol. 30 (1835).

Journal of the House of Commons, 90 (1835).

Hansard, Parl. Debs. (series 3), vol. 42 (1838).

Hansard, Parl. Debs. (series 3), vol. 61 (1842).

Hansard, Parl. Debs. (series 3), vol. 115 (1851).

Hansard, Parl. Debs. (series 3), vol. 118 (1851).

Minutes of Evidence, Taken Before the Select Committee of the House of Lords Appointed to Consider the Bill Intituled, 'An Act to Extend the Provisions of the Designs Act, 1850, and to give protection from Piracy to Persons exhibiting New Inventions in the Exhibitions of the Works of Industry of all Nations in One thousand eight hundred and Fifty-one;' And to report thereon to the house., Brought from the Lords, 25 March 1851.

'Minutes of Evidence Taken Before the Select Committee of the House of Lords Appointed to Consider the Bill Intituled, An Act the extend the provisions of the Designs Act, 1850, and to give Protection from Piracy to Persons Exhibiting New Inventions in the Exhibition of the Works of Industry of all Nations in One thousand eight hundred and Fifty-one' (25 March 1851).

'Report and Minutes of Evidence Taken Before the Select Committee of the House of Lords appointed to consider of the Bill intituled, "An Act further to amend the Law touching LETTERS PATENT FOR INVENTIONS;" and also of the Bill, intituled, "An Act for the further Amendment of the Law touching Letters Patent for Inventions," And to Report thereon to the House'. *Reports From Committees*, 18, Session: 4 February–8 August 1851.

Report of the Commissioners Appointed to Inquire into the Cost and Applicability of the Exhibition Building in Hyde Park (London: HMSO, 1852).

First Report of the Commissioners for the Exhibition of 1851 to the Secretary of State for the Home Department (London: HMSO, 1852).

Second Report of the Commissioners for the Exhibition of 1851, to the Right Hon. Spencer Horatio Walpole (London: W. Clowes & Sons, 1852).

First Report of the Department of Practical Art (London: George Eyre & William Spottiswoode, HMSO, 1853).

Hansard, Parl. Debs. (series 3), vol. 142 (1856).

Hansard, Parl. Debs. (series 3), vols. 145 (1857).

Minutes of the Evidence taken Before the Royal Commission on Copyright together with an Appendix preceded by Tables of the Witnesses and of the Contents of the Appendix (London: George Edward Eyre & William Spottiswoode, 1878).

Index